MAJOR CONTROVERSIES
OF CONTEMPORARY HISTORY

MAJOR CONTROVERSIES

OF

CONTEMPORARY HISTORY

BY

JACQUES DE LAUNAY

Translated by

J. J. BUCKINGHAM

PERGAMON PRESS

OXFORD · LONDON · EDINBURGH · NEW YORK

PARIS · FRANKFURT

Pergamon Press Ltd., Headington Hill Hall, Oxford
4 & 5 Fitzroy Square, London W.1
Pergamon Press (Scotland) Ltd., 2 & 3 Teviot Place, Edinburgh 1
Pergamon Press Inc., 122 East 55th St., New York 22, N.Y.
Pergamon Press GmbH, Kaiserstrasse 75, Frankfurt-am-Main

First edition 1965

Library of Congress Catalog Card No. 65-13141

This is a translation from the original French
Les Grandes Controverses de l'Histoire contemporaine
published by Société Coopérative
Editions Rencontre, Lausanne in 1964

2001

CONTENTS

PART THREE — 1939–1945

PREFACE

THE CONCEPTION and preparation of the present work has been based upon an entirely new method. We have established the fact that almost eleven thousand works dealing with contemporary history (covering the period 1914 to 1945) have already been published, and the author has attempted a detailed analysis of all published sources in order to draw as near as possible to historical truth.

To begin with, a group of historians selected the thousand basic works, while the author concentrated on sixty-two essential and especially controversial points of general history. With the help of a large number of assistants the author took upon himself the task of noting the innumerable versions and interpretations given of the sixty-two controversial points. The study of all these works was carried out in the language in which they were originally written. Relevant items were transferred to 24,960 IBM punched cards. A detailed account of the method adopted is given in the bibliography published separately.

The author was thus able to sift first-hand evidence from a vast number of sources, and subject it to comparison and criticism in the traditional manner. The matter thus collected was amplified by research into unpublished documents combined with the questioning of twenty-nine witnesses who are still alive.

We should add that this work has taken five years to complete; it has cost twenty-five thousand dollars, and has necessitated numerous journeys throughout Europe, the United States and the Soviet Union. In addition to being published in the original French it is being published in the principal languages of the world, notably English, German, Spanish, Portuguese, Russian and Japanese.

This original method of approach to contemporary history has therefore cleared the experimental stage. Bearing in mind the improvements
which have been introduced there is no doubt that a large number of
historians will discover the efficiency of this method.

The work has been carried out within the framework of the publications programme of the International Commission for the Teaching
of History.★

★ The Commission is composed of:
MM. Maurice Baumont (France); B. S. Baykal (Turkey); Dr Eckert (Germany);
L.-E. Roulet (Switzerland); F. Melzi d'Eril (Italy); H. L. Mikoletzky (Austria);
Drs L. J. M. van de Laar (Netherlands); H. Vigander (Norway); D. Zaky-
thinos (Greece); E. Lousse (Belgium), President; J. de Launay, Secretary-General.

ACKNOWLEDGEMENTS

ALTHOUGH the idea and the general plan behind this work are entirely my own, together with the method of research and the system of reference to sources of information, it goes without saying that a work of this size, which has taken several years to complete, could not have been accomplished without the support of numerous persons and specialist organizations.

I am especially indebted to the I.B.M., both in Brussels and New York, who have assisted me with the technicalities connected with the perfection of the new method of bibliographical classification used in this book. That organization has enabled me to make methodical use of the tens of thousands of index cards produced for this purpose.

My personal friends, George Lovinfosse, Roger Gheysens, Robert Maxwell, M.P. and my late lamented colleague André Puttemans, General Secretary and founder of the International Commission for the Teaching of History, have all given me encouragement on several occasions, especially when the enormity of the task appeared to be beyond my strength. Mr. David Bruce, United States Ambassador in London, and Robert A. Solborg have lavished upon me the most judicious advice.

Eminent librarians, especially Mrs. Agnes F. Peterson, of the Hoover Library, Stanford University, California, and Edmond Duquenne, of the Ministry of Foreign Affairs in Belgium, have afforded me invaluable assistance in research and the opportunity to consult rare and confidential works.

Numerous colleagues have made it possible for me to study selected volumes; Jacques Willequet, of the University of Brussels, F. Gallouédec-Genuys, of the National Centre for Scientific Research, in Paris, N. von Fehleisen and Francis Leclercq have all been extraordinarily helpful in subjecting to critical examination published sources of information in their original language. They have often translated and clarified relevant texts. Without them this book would never have seen the light of day.

General E. Boltine, of the Moscow Institute of Marxism Leninism, allowed me to collect data published in Russian, a research that has proved to be of the utmost value.

Roger Gheysens, General Manager of Editions Brepols, was kind enough to read through the first draft of the whole work, making notes and suggestions which guided me in the writing of the final draft.

Emile Lousse, professor at Louvain University and Dr Georg Eckert, Director of the Brunswick Institute of School Text-books, on behalf of the International Commission for the Teaching of History, to revise the manuscript from the point of view of its impartiality and objectivity. Their scholarship served to enlighten me on many points.

Finally, I must express my gratitude to Shepard Stone and his colleagues, David Heaps and Matthew Cullen, of the Ford Foundation, to José de Azeredo Perdigao, President of the Gulbenkian Foundation, to Dr Gustav Stein, President of the Executive Committee, and G. Sluizer, Director of the European Culture Foundation. The remarkable support they have rendered has made it possible for the International Commission for the Teaching of History to realize this vast project. The work might never have been undertaken without the assistance of these institutions.

I ask all these friends and colleagues, and everyone who has in any way contributed to this work, to accept my gratitude. If, despite all the support I have received, errors and omissions do come to light, I assume entire responsibility.

JACQUES DE LAUNAY

Note

The thousand works of which the author has made use form a reference table in *The Two World Wars* Ed. Brepols, Paris and Brussels; Pergamon Press, Oxford; Macmillan, New York.

The selected bibliography connected with this work was produced by B. Schmitt, J. de Launay, E. Anchieri, M. Durica, H. Michel and J.-M. d'Hoop. All the works referred to in the footnotes of the present work are listed in the bibliography.

The work referred to above also contains an exposition of the method followed.

PART ONE

1914–1918

CHAPTER I

THE OUTRAGE AT SARAJEVO — 28TH JUNE 1914

1. Is it possible to prove the complicity of the Serbian government in the Sarajevo outrage?
2. Was Count Berchtold guilty of deliberate provocation on the 23rd July 1914?

1. The Responsibility of Serbia

On the 28th June 1914 Francis Ferdinand, Archduke of Austria and heir to the throne, paid an official visit to Sarajevo after having attended the manoeuvres at Bosnia. Dressed in the uniform of a commander-in-chief and looking resplendent in his medals, the Prince was accompanied by his wife the Duchess of Hohenberg. At their side was Marshal Potiorek, governor of Bosnia, who stated in his evidence:

The heir to the throne was seated in the rear of the carriage to the left. Her Highness the Duchess was on his right. Count Harrach was in front beside the driver, and I was facing their Highnesses. As we passed the Austro-Hungarian Bank I looked ahead, and noticed to the left of the embankment a gap in the crowd where a tall, dark young man was standing. Just as I was pointing out the splendid new Barracks of the XVth Corps I heard a small explosion, and saw a little black object pass behind the Duchess. A second later there was an explosion resembling a revolver shot. The object passed so slowly behind the Duchess that I could follow it with my eyes. Count Harrach remarked that he thought he had seen a missile. It fell in the road, and then the explosion was heard. Her Highness had the impression, as I had myself, that it was a bomb intended for the carriage, but that it had missed, causing no damage. For a moment the progress of the cortège was interrupted, but it proceeded immediately on its pre-arranged route.[1]

After a reception at the town hall the Prince continued his journey through the city packed with people. The cortège was not protected by a cordon of troops. As the official carriages turned a corner into a side street, a youth took aim and fired two revolver shots at the Duke and his wife, who were both mortally wounded. The crowd rushed

---

[1] From the evidence of Governor Potiorek — Mousset, *L'Attentat de Sarajevo*, Paris, 1930, p. 440.

3

towards the assassin, but he was led away by the police. The youth was a Bosnian student named Gavrilo Princip, and he was taken to the same prison to which the other terrorist had been taken that morning. The outrage was to have unprecedented consequences.

Had the Serbian government been a party to the plot? This was the question that immediately occupied the government at Vienna; and the purpose of the investigation opened by the Austro-Hungarian authorities was to ascertain the extent of Serbian involvement. Twenty-four youths were arraigned before the court. The trial did not begin until the 12th October 1914, when war had already begun, for Vienna did not wish that the verdict should challenge the military punitive measures undertaken against Serbia following the coup.[2] It can therefore be assumed that the magistracy did all in its power to induce the accused to denounce all their accomplices, and in particular to confess whether or not they had the backing of the Serbian authorities.

A dozen or so arguments were put forward in about 700 pamphlets and articles in the Press in an attempt to establish the real causes of the outrage. Most of them were fantastic, but four were worthy of serious consideration:

1 — The plot was conceived and organized by the government of Belgrade;

2 — It was inspired, organized and armed by a group of Serbian officers acting independently of their government;

3 — The authorities in Vienna knew that the coup would take place, but did nothing to prevent it;

4 — The attempt was the work of international Freemasonry.

The accused were scarcely more than children. Princip and Cabrinović were 19, Grabeč was 18, and their associates were aged between 16 and 19. All came from poor homes and were in a poor state of health. They had apparently been drawn towards anarchy by reading books that were more or less forbidden, and which they had in any case misunderstood. Princip and Grabeč were happy about the part they had played, but Cabrinović was inclined to regret it. The statements of the others were either confused or clumsy denials of their responsibility.

All the accused considered that the domination of the Austro-Hungarian Empire by Germans and Magyars was the sole cause of Bosnia's misfortunes.

[2] See Berchtold's letter to Ritter von Bilinski dated 1st October 1914 — Mousset, *op. cit.*, p. 16.

Cabrinović, the youth who had thrown the bomb, declared:

Our purpose was to release Bosnia from the Monarchy, an aim on which we were all agreed. A point of disagreement, however, lay in the fact that some of us were in favour of a monarchist régime under the Karageorges, while I remained to the end loyal to anarchist principles. I might have agreed merely as a compromise that the Karageorge dynasty — or, if possible, King Peter alone during his lifetime — might keep the throne, on the understanding that at Peter's death the Yugoslav Republic would be established.[3]

Princip, who had fired the shot, declared vehemently that a Yugoslav Republic was the ideal he aimed at.

It was alleged that the arms came from the Narodna Obrana, a cultural organization to which reference will be made later. This organization provided with arms anyone who wished to make things difficult for the Austro-Hungarians. The accused denied that they had been paid to carry out the coup. They had received no orders, no passwords, no plan. They themselves had conceived the coup spontaneously, having determined to kill the Governor Potiorek; the Archduke's visit was a coincidence that resulted in their selecting him as their target instead.

It was established that the assassins came from Belgrade, and had crossed the border with the connivance of Serbian custom-house officers, but there was no proof of any premeditated conspiracy controlled from Belgrade. If any of the accused admitted connexions with Freemasonry, there was no evidence that that organization had any relations whatever with the conspirators.

The attempt was really the work of Bosnian youth who refused to endure their social and economic conditions. Since 1908 revolutionary ideas had continued to develop among the young in the schools. From 1910 to 1914 five outrages had been committed in Bosnia against Austro-Hungarian officials. The Bosnian population blamed the Germano-Magyar domination for all its misfortunes, and the country's youth gave fanatical expression to those sentiments. After Sarajevo the Austro-Hungarian courts initiated proceedings against students' associations throughout the province. Four trials took place, resulting in convictions.

Narodna Obrana was the only outside link the conspirators had. This organization provided them with Serbian bombs and Belgian revolvers for the purpose of carrying out criminal attacks. Narodna Obrana was a Serbian cultural organization; it was not of a revolutionary

[3] From the verbatim report of the trial — Mousset, *L'Attentat de Serajevo*, Paris, 1930.

character, but was used as a cover by agents of a secret terrorist organization called "Union or Death" but known to the public as the Black
Hand. Its aim was to eliminate all who opposed Yugoslav expansion.
The head of "Union or Death", was Colonel Dimitrievic, Director
of Intelligence in the Serbian Army. He had been promoted colonel
for services rendered to the House of Karageorgevic. It was he who
organized the plot that resulted in the assassination on the 10th June
1903 of King Alexander Obrenovic and Queen Draga, thus allowing
Peter Karageorgevic to ascend the throne. Since then Dimitrievic had
planned repeated attempts, and rendered support to all those who
might through their terrorist activities hasten the advent of a greater
Serbia which would embrace all the southern Slavs.

In 1916 the failure of an attempt against the heir, Prince Alexander,
brought Dimitrievic's complicity into the open. The commander of
the fortress at Salonica arrested the Serbian officer, and his subsequent
trial created wide interest. He was accused of the most heinous crimes,
and some of his friends and enemies denounced him as having been
the instigator of a dozen or so attempts against the Czar, Ferdinand
of Bulgaria, King Constantine of Greece, the Emperor Francis Joseph
and Kaiser William II.[4]

Dimitrievic was condemned to death and executed. During the course
of the trial at Salonica it transpired that Major Tankosic, to whom all
requests for arms ultimately came, had warned Dimitrievic that he
was under suspicion, but that the latter had replied, "Let them do as
they like". Boghitchevic, a former Serbian minister in Berlin, declared
that the Serbian government had been informed of Dimitrievic's
activities, and had approved them. But Boghitchevic hated Pachic,
head of the Serbian government, and his evidence was extremely suspect.
Furthermore, Dimitrievic had not kept his government informed of
the details of his activities. Similarly the relations between Dimitrievic
and Artamonov, military attaché in Belgrade, produced no evidence
to suggest Russian complicity in the Sarajevo affair.

What can be deduced from all these investigations? Without a doubt
the Black Hand was aware of the plot of the Sarajevo students and did
not discourage it, though it did not foresee all the consequences. The
complicity of the Serbian government, however, was never established.
The Machiavellian design of the government at Vienna to allow the

[4] No definite proof of these allegations was produced, but King Peter of Serbia
was anxious to have done with this terrorist officer, and showed him no mercy.

Duke to be slain on account of his leaning towards the Slavs is a hypothesis without foundation, and cannot be taken seriously.

Five of the young conspirators were condemned to death; three,
however — Princip, Grabeč and Cabrinović — who were minors, had
their sentences commuted to penal servitude, and died in 1917 in a
fortress in Bohemia. They never ceased to maintain that they had
acted independently, and had met Tankosić only when they were
"morally ready" to carry out their project.

2. The Role of Count Berchtola

(23rd July 1914)

Europe was in holiday mood when the tragedy of Sarajevo struck.
The Emperor Francis Joseph was at Ischl, his summer residence, when
Count Paar brought him the news. At first sight the Emperor's reaction
might seem surprising:

A higher power has once again established an order which I unfortunately
found impossible to maintain.[5]

The Emperor was 84. He was of a frigid, precise disposition, a slave
of etiquette and protocol. Constitutional government and obedience
to orders were the code of this monarch whose life had been a succession
of setbacks and tragedies. He had been beaten by Napoleon III in Italy
and by Bismarck at Sadowa. His brother Maximilian, Emperor of
Mexico, had suffered defeat, and was shot in 1867; his only son, the
Archduke Rudolf, had committed suicide at Mayerling in 1888; his
wife the Empress Elizabeth had been murdered in Genevain 1898.
Francis Joseph had retired within himself and bore the burden of his
responsibilities with dignity and arrogance, but not very intelligently.

The aged Emperor was not exactly pleased with his heir Francis
Ferdinand. Francis was of weak constitution, and he suffered from tuber-
culosis; it was only by following a disciplined diet that he managed to
keep alive. He was stern, bad-tempered, difficult and often spiteful.
He easily flew into a passion, and allowed himself to be controlled by
impulse.

It was impulse that led to the Archduke's marriage with the Czech
Countess Sophia Chotek, and the Emperor had agreed only to a morga-

[5] Quoted by Recouly, Le Mémorial de Foch, Paris, 1929 p. 205.

natic marriage, thus eliminating the Archduke's heirs from all claim
to succession. The Countess, however, refused to accept the situation,
and the active scheming of the ambitious couple laid the foundations
of a more authoritarian and dynamic reign. It was known that Francis
Ferdinand was playing with the idea of a Triple Monarchy, and that he
favoured the Austro-German alliance.

William II of Germany, who knew his man and had received the
Archduchess with the greatest honours, pressed Francis Joseph to give
more scope to his heir in his councils of State. It was also common
knowledge that Francis Joseph found official posts for his minions.
Conrad von Hoetzendorf, Chief of Staff, was one of these, and talked
continually of a preventive war against Italy, to be followed by another
against Serbia. Francis Ferdinand and Conrad imagined that the survival
of the Empire depended upon its being more feared than loved by the
races that composed it. Both believed that a salutary lesson was worth
more than any political compromise. From that conception it was but
a short step to imposing the army's views on the government. In 1911
the Emperor was compelled to intervene to settle a difference of opinion
between D'Aerenthal and Conrad concerning policy towards Italy.
The Chief of Staff's warlike notions troubled the aging monarch, and
Conrad was forced to resign.

D'Aerenthal died in 1912, and Francis Ferdinand secured the recall
of Conrad. The Emperor appointed Count Berchtold, an Austrian
aristocrat, to fill the post left vacant by D'Aerenthal's death. Berchtold
had been the Austro-Hungarian ambassador in St Petersburg, and his
only qualification for the post was his vast fortune. Very conscious of
his ancestry, he lived the life of a lord, enjoyed a good table and the
company of pretty girls; he knew scarcely anything, however, about
diplomacy and affairs of state, which he conducted in an off-hand and
easy-going manner. His cultivated demeanour pleased the Emperor,
without offending his heir the Archduke. Berchtold got on well with
Conrad, and did nothing to upset Count Tisza, the Hungarian Prime
Minister. His insouciance shed an atmosphere of serenity, and his philosophy was gleaned from gay parties. As he had little love for work he
delegated his duties to subordinates, and especially to Count Forgasch,
an extremely unhandsome person whose brutal cynicism offset the
nonchalant bearing of his master.

It is therefore clear that, at the beginning of 1914, the Dual Monarchy
was sustained by a very aged, peace-loving, but ill-informed Emperor,
entangled in dynastic regulations and protocol. The Prince, his heir,

was ambitious, somewhat unbalanced, pushed and dominated by his wife. The direction of the country was really under the control of men of high birth, but rather incompetent, who strove to hold out gracefully, and made the best of the minions imposed upon them by the intrigues of the Archduke.

Such was the situation in Vienna when the disappearance of the heir suddenly changed the *status quo*. The Emperor was again thrust into the role of supreme and undisputed head. It remained to the ministers to react.

Berchtold had a choice of two attitudes: he could leave things as they were, or insist on redress by Serbia. Several writers have suggested that Count Berchtold immediately decided to make war on Serbia; but this course hardly seemed in keeping with the psychology of an individual more anxious to wriggle out of a difficult situation than to settle it by the use of force. As a matter of fact, there is no evidence to show what the first reactions of Count Berchtold really were.

One may assume that this minister, like those in a similar position in other countries, gave careful attention to the reports by ambassadors, and read the statements in the international Press. The newpapers and the ambassadors could only report in Vienna the emotion that the whole of Europe had experienced on learning of the tragedy at Sarajevo. The cowardly outrage roused universal indignation; the world could not understand the driving power of those Balkan terrorists, accustomed as they were to settle their accounts by violence. Count Berchtold, therefore, had right on his side, and knew that the world would at once approve the just cause of Austria.

Was it, however, necessary to undertake a punitive expedition against Serbia? Several factors favoured this course. Already in October 1913 Berchtold had suffered a serious diplomatic setback when he had tried to compel the Serbs to evacuate Albanian territory. Then both Germany and Italy, Austria-Hungary's two allies in the Triple Alliance, indicated in Vienna that they would not support an offensive war; Serbia was thus enabled deliberately to ignore the Austrian ultimatum. The Austrian army, mobilized at enormous expense, was forced to return home in disgrace, humiliated and powerless. Furthermore, Conrad, the Chief of Staff, had badly handled that mishap, and vowed that he would never again suffer a similar capitulation.

A splendid opportunity therefore occurred in July 1914 to wreak revenge on the Serbians. One may assume that Conrad encouraged the minister; although he insisted that it was Berchtold who suggested to the Emperor that he should take advantage of the outrage to resolve the Serbian problem.[6]

In any case, the various groups of nations within the Empire were growing restless. Poles, Czechs, Croats and the Rumanians in Transylvaniawere heedful of all the jolts sustained by the Monarchy, and began to wonder if Vienna might capitulate again, thus signifying that the day of liberation was approaching, and that each nation must play its part in shaking the foundations of the central power.

In fact, no decision was reached in Vienna between the 27th June and the 19th July 1914. Berchtold hesitated between his desire for revenge and his determination not to act unless effectively. He had several interviews with Francis Joseph. His first important move after Sarajevo took place on the 5th July, when he despatched Count Hoyos, the head of his Cabinet, to Berlin.

Szögyeny, the Austrian ambassador in Berlin, proceeded to Potsdam, and presented the Kaiser, William II, with a letter signed by Francis Joseph and a memorandum from Berchtold; both documents were conveyed by Hoyos. His purpose was to sound Germany on her intention with regard to the Austro-Serbian dispute. The atmosphere in Potsdam was tense. William II was on the point of embarking at Kiel for his customary summer cruise, and his ministers were endeavouring to get his signature to documents relating to current State affairs. Historians are mistaken when they refer to "a council of war held at Potsdam". The 5th July was a day of hustling. William II was occupied with routine matters connected with the business of being Emperor. He was interrupting his routine to take a holiday, and the reply he gave to Francis Joseph quickened the rhythm of that sensational day.

The Kaiser read Francis Joseph's letter, which ran:

The outrage against my poor nephew is the direct result of the agitation conducted by Russian and Serbian Pan-Slavists, whose sole purpose is to weaken the Triple Alliance and bring about the destruction of my Empire.

According to all the facts previously established, what happened at Sarajevo was not merely the action of a bloodthirsty individual, but the outcome of a well organized plot hatched in Belgrade; and, though it may be impossible to prove the complicity of the Serbian government, there is no doubt that its policy, tending as it does towards the unification of all southern Slavs under the Serbian flag, fosters crimes of this nature. The continuance of this state of affairs constitutes permanent threat to my House and my States.

This threat is aggravated further by the fact that Rumania, despite the alliance existing between us, has entered into friendly relations with Serbia, and permits

[6] Conrad von Hoetzendorf, *Aus meiner Dienstzeit 1906-16*, Vienna, 1926, IV, 109

subversive activities to be carried on within her borders as virulent as those allowed by Serbia.

In consequence, my government must direct its efforts towards isolating and humbling Serbia. The first step in this direction must aim at reinforcing the position of the present Bulgarian government, so that the Bulgarians, whose interests are identical with our own, may be preserved from a return to Russophilism.

If it is appreciated at Bucharest that the Triple Alliance is resolved not to reject an alliance with Bulgaria, but is disposed to invite Bulgaria to reach an understanding with Rumania and guarantee her territorial integrity, it may then be possible to lead her back from the dangerous path into which she has been thrust both by her friendship with Serbia and her rapprochement with Russia. In the event of this endeavour meeting with success, we might try to reconcile Greece with Bulgaria and Turkey. This would result in the creation of a new Balkan alliance under the patronage of the Triple Alliance, whose purpose would be to put an end to the inroads of Pan-Slavism and ensure peace within our States.

But all this will be possible only if Serbia, now the pivot of Pan-Slavistic policy, is eliminated as a political factor in the Balkans.

After this dreadful incident in Bosnia you too must be convinced that it is out of the question to try to smooth out the difficulties existing between Serbia and ourselves; and that the desire of all European sovereigns to maintain a policy of peace will be threatened as long as this hotbed of criminal agitation in Belgrade remains unpunished.[7]

Then the Kaiser read the memorandum which called for a revision of the Triple Alliance's Balkan policy.[8] William II lunched with Szögyeny, and promised the ambassador a reply before he left for his cruise on the 6th July.

The Kaiser was a cultured and courteous man, and quite charming in his personal relations. But the inexercise of his duties he was haughty and curt, arrogant in manner and inclined to military bluntness.[9]

The official side of his character was uppermost when he summoned his ministers to Potsdam to prepare his reply — Bethmann Hollweg, his Chancellor, Zimmerman, his Under-Secretary of State for Foreign Affairs, von Falkenhayn, Minister for War, and his Deputy Naval

---

[7] Die deutschen Dokumente, I, 12; The same text appears in Dipl. Aktenstücke, I, 1.

[8] This memorandum had been drawn up by Count Berchtold's department before the incident at Sarajevo.

[9] The Kaiser's state of mind during those tragic days is clearly revealed in the notes he made in the margin of the despatches from his diplomatic staff. For example, on Tschirsky's report to the effect that the Austrian ultimatum to Serbia had been delayed until after the departure of the French statesmen from Kronstadt, he wrote, "We must have done with these Serbs as quickly as possible . . ." and "What a pity!" On Lichnowsky's report of Sir Edward Grey's proposal to prolong the period of the Austrian ultimatum, he wrote, ". . . It is useless". And "Now or never" was the comment pencilled on a letter from Tschirsky.

Minister Baron Krupp von Bohlen, who joined him in Kiel in the evening of the 6th July.

Meanwhile Hoyos was at the Wilhelmstrasse conferring with Zimmermann. The following day Szögyeny joined them, and all three then called on Chancellor Bethmann Hollweg to hear Germany's reply. This reply reached Berchtold from two different sources. The first one came from Szögyeny: "In so far as our relations with Serbia are concerned the German government holds the view that it is for us to decide what should be done to settle those relations. Whatever our decision may be, we can certainly depend upon Germany, as a friend and ally of the Monarchy, to stand behind us."[10]

The second reply came by way of the German embassy in Vienna. It constituted the text of a despatch from Bethmann Hollweg to Tschirsky: "With regard to Serbia, His Majesty cannot, of course, reach a decision on the matter outstanding between that country and Austria-Hungary, as it is outside his province. But the Emperor Francis Joseph may rest assured that His Majesty, in accordance with the obligations of his alliance and his longstanding friendship, will remain loyally beside Austria-Hungary in every circumstance."[11]

It should be understood that, before signing the despatch, Bethmann Hollweg deleted the words *in every circumstance*, so that Vienna knew nothing about them. This suggests some reservation or prudence on the German side. The German reply, however, as it stood, still remained a signal encouragement to Vienna. Berchtold knew that Berlin would not fail as it had done in 1913. None the less, it seems hardly correct to suggest, as some historians have done, that Germany gave Vienna a blank cheque. The German rulers certainly considered the possibility of an Austro-Serbian conflict degenerating into a European war, because at Potsdam on the 5th July William II envisaged grave European complications.[12] But after his lunch with Szögyeny he expressed the view that:

If it actually came to an Austro-Russian war, Germany, with her customary loyalty, would be at the side of Austria.[13]

After his interview with the Kaiser on the 5th July Falkenhayn wrote to Lieutenant-General von Moltke, Chief of Staff:

[10] *Dipl. Aktenstücke*, I, 7. Telegram 239.
[11] *Die deutschen Dokumente*, I, 15.
[12] *Dipl. Aktenstücke*, I, 6.
[13] *Dipl. Aktenstücke*, I, 6.

His Majesty read to me both the letter and the memorandum and, in so far as the speed of the reading allowed me to form an opinion, neither document convinced me that the Vienna government had taken a firm decision. Both documents painted a very gloomy picture of the general position in so far as the Dual Monarchy is concerned, resulting from Pan-Slavistic intrigues. They also underline the necessity to cut these intrigues short by some kind of prompt action. Neither document refers explicitly to war as a solution; there is rather a suggestion of "energetic" political measures (for example, the conclusion of a treaty with Bulgaria) in which they wish to be certain of the support of the German Empire.

We should have to give them that support, while drawing attention to the fact that it would be primarily the responsibility of Austria-Hungary to take whatever steps her interests demanded.

The Chancellor, who was also at Potsdam, does not appear to think (any more than I do) that the tone of the two documents from the Austrian government — though more resolute than previously — points to any really notable decisions. At least he raised no objection to setting out on his cruise; in fact, it was he who proposed to do so. One may rest assured that no decisions whatever will be reached within the next few weeks.[14]

Nothing is known of the attitude of mind of Bethmann Hollweg during the 5th and 6th July. Witnesses are either too circumstantial or too reluctant. But the erasure made by the Chancellor on the despatch to Vienna indicates only too clearly his prudent attitude, and this must be emphasized. It is known, moreover, that Bethmann Hollweg enjoyed the full confidence of the Kaiser. They liked to recall the period when they both belonged to the same association of students at the University of Bonn, and enjoyed talking of the *esprit de corps* that bound them together. It is not therefore difficult to understand why the Emperor was able to set out on his cruise leaving the direction of the country in the hands of his friend.

Bernadotte Schmitt has carefully studied all the documents in the dossier, and he concluded that the German rulers saw clearly, and accepted, the risk of a general war resulting from their attitude, providing Great Britain remained neutral. This factor constituted an important reservation. We shall, however, follow the American historian, and draw attention to the fact that the Austrian messages which expressed Vienna's irresolution by no means hinted at any imminent action; also that Berlin regarded its reply merely as an element in the general problem.

The German rulers felt that the position was worsening, but refused to admit the imminence of war. Bethmann Hollweg persuaded the Kaiser to set out on his cruise, and it was only on the 18th July that he became

[14] The original of this letter is in the German archives.

anxious to know the itinerary of the imperial yacht, in case any important decisions had to be taken.[15] This state of diplomatic tension was not the first to occur; a previous emergency had arisen in 1913, and now circumstances appeared to favour the consolidation of the Triple Alliance, since European opinion unanimously condemned the Sarajevo outrage.

It followed that the German reply allowed Berchtold to surmount his hesitancy; from the 6th July he lent support to the punitive expedition against Serbia. On the 7th July the Austro-Hungarian Council of Ministers met in Vienna under the chairmanship of Count Berchtold to examine the German reply. Those present included Count Stürgkh President of the Council of Austrian Ministers, Count Tisza, President, of the Council of Hungarian Ministers, Ritter von Bilinski, Minister of Finance, Krobatin, Minister of War, Baron Conrad von Hotzendorf, Chief of the General Staff, Rear-Admiral von Kailer, Commander of the Fleet, and Count Hoyos, as Secretary.

Count Berchtold, announcing the unreserved support of Germany, did not conceal the fact that he was "convinced that a passage of arms with Serbia might result in war with Russia". He believed, however, in grasping this opportunity for a speedy settlement of accounts with Serbia, which might not be possible later on.

Count Tisza declared that he "would never give his agreement to a sudden attack on Serbia without recourse to previous diplomatic action". He asked that terms be placed before Serbia, and that an ultimatum be sent only if she rejected them. "These conditions should be harsh, but not impracticable."

Acceptation of the terms would mean a diplomatic success. Tisza promised to accept the principle of military action in the event of Serbia's rejection. He emphasized, however, that he did not contemplate total annihilation, but merely the humbling of Serbia; first because Russia would never consent to a death struggle, and secondly because, as President of the Hungarian Council, he could never consent to the annexation of part of Serbia.

Tisza was a prominent Magyar lord; serious-minded, moderate, cool and cautious. His task was already prodigious, and the anxiety of a war added to all his other cares was an unpleasant prospect. He was undoubtedly a man of courage, but not committed to extremes. He was

[15] *Die deutschen Dokumente*, I, 67.
[16] *Dipl. Aktenstücke*, I, 8.

above all anxious to prevent Austria gaining control of affairs, and he
endeavoured to keep the Emperor informed personally of his views.
Little by little, however, Tisza came round to a military solution.
The same ministers were convened to a council meeting on the 19th
July 1914. The agenda concerned the fixing of a date for the despatch
of a note to Serbia. Berchtold was eager to push matters through, for
Berlin was growing impatient; but he was careful to suggest that the
date for the diplomatic approach to Belgrade should be the 23rd July
at 5 p.m. This allowed for the departure of the French President, Monsieur Poincaré, from Russia.

Tisza agreed with Berchtold's proposal, knowing perfectly well that
the diplomatic note might lead to war with Serbia. He demanded,
however — and in this he displayed firmness — that the Council of
Ministers should state categorically and unanimously that the Monarchy
entertained no plan of conquest, and had no desire whatever to annexe
a part of Serbian territory.

He stressed that his demand was founded not only on motives of
internal policy, but on an earnest desire to avoid provoking Russia
unnecessarily; Russia would never acquiesce in the destruction of
Serbia. But even in this particular Tisza weakened during the course
of the meeting, and eventually allowed Berchtold to have his way.[17]

The undertaking of a punitive expedition against Serbia was therefore
unanimously agreed in Vienna on the 19th July. But Berchtold failed
to inform Berlin of the decision taken. It was only on the 22nd July
that the German government became aware of the complete text of
the Austrian ultimatum sent to Belgrade on the 23rd.[18] Although the
primary object was to humble Serbia, the Austrians accepted the risk
of a localized war. Tisza was reassured, and was able to write to his
sister-in-law on the 21st July, "The affair can be settled without war.
Please God let it be so."[19]

Bernadotte Schmitt held the view that the leading Austro-Hungarian
statesmen were equally prepared to risk a European war. This was
probably true in the case of Berchtold, but Francis Joseph and Tisza
believed to the end that a general conflict could be avoided. The risk
of a European war was undoubtedly accepted with more lightheartedness
than awareness; and this nonchalance, typical of Berchtold, is revealed

[17] *Dipl. Aktenstücke*, I, 26.
[18] Exchanges had taken place since the 11th July, however, between Vienna
and Berlin concerning the proposed ultimatum.
[19] *Deutsche Allgemeine Zeitung*, dated 17th February 1932.

in the sluggishness of Austrian reaction. Any chance of localizing the conflict lay decidedly in immediate action. The punitive expedition had to be undertaken swiftly to avoid the play of adverse alliances and the reversal of European public opinion. Berchtold was at no time conscious of this fact.

CHAPTER II

THE AUSTRO-GERMAN ALLIANCE

1. Why did the German government reject the proposed international conference?

2. Did the Austro-Hungarian declaration of war on Serbia (28th July 1914) take into account the risk of Russian intervention?

3. Did the German government recognize the risk of Russian intervention (29th July 1914)?

4. What was the real purpose and role of the German General Staff?

5. Did the Austro-Hungarian General Staff decide on its own initiative to mobilize?

1. The International Conference of 26th July 1914

Belgrade had a choice of two replies to the Austrian ultimatum: an acceptance, which would destroy the Pan-Slavistic movement, or a rejection, which would let loose an Austro-Serbian war capable of degenerating into a European war.

Austria-Hungary presented its ultimatum to Belgrade during the evening of the 23rd July, when the French statesmen Poincaré and Viviani had left Russia following a courtesy visit made within the framework of the Franco-Russian alliance.

Berchtold wrote to Francis Joseph on the 14th July: "A personal talk between the ambitious President of the French Republic and His Majesty the Emperor of Russia ... would increase the probability of armed intervention by Russia and France."[1] In a letter dated the 15th July, addressed to Szögyeny, Berchtold emphasized the point: "It would not be wise to approach Belgrade at the very moment when the Emperor Nicholas, who is cautious and a friend of peace, and the prudent Sazonov are exposed to the immediate influence of those two hotheads Izvolski and Poincaré."[2]

[1] *Dipl. Aktenstücke,* I, 19.
[2] *Dipl. Aktenstücke,* I, 21.

Thus the date of delivery of the ultimatum was very carefully studied, though the wording of the document caused a considerable stir in the whole of Europe. The French statesmen and William II were in the Baltic and did not react immediately. It was Sir Edward Grey, Head of the Foreign Office in London, who took the initiative on Sunday, the 26th July. He proposed a meeting with the German, French and Italian ambassadors. Germany refused on the grounds that she did not wish to interfere in an Austro-Serbian matter; the desire to localize the conflict still persisted.

On the morning of the 27th July Sir Edward Grey received a copy of the Serbian reply to the Austrian ultimatum. It conceded everything with the exception of Austrian police intervention in Serbia. Sir Edward immediately summoned the German ambassador Lichnowski, and requested him to ask the German government to intervene in Vienna with a view to causing the Serbian reply to be regarded as a basis for discussion. In St Petersburg the Russian Minister for Foreign Affairs, Sazonov, proposed an Austro-Russian parley for the purpose of drawing up a compromise. Bethmann Hollweg received Sir Edward Grey's proposal and transmitted it to Vienna,[3] and informed the Kaiser of the telegram's contents. William II returned from his cruise in the afternoon of the 27th July, and at once summoned a council to meet at Potsdam.

What happened during the course of this meeting is not known. Suppositions as to what took place are without foundation.[4] The Chancellor no doubt made his point, and the Kaiser did nothing to alter the situation: there would be no international conference at which Austria-Hungary might stand accused before a tribunal. The Minister for Foreign Affairs, von Jagow, placed the latest information before the council, to the effect that the King of England had informed Prince Henry of Prussia on the 26th July that "England would adopt a neutral position in the event of a conflict between the western powers."[5]

The General Staff was then requested to hold itself in readiness to meet every eventuality, and General von Moltke made his final preparations to put into effect the Schlieffen Plan.

Nothing in all this suggested that Germany desired to let loose a European war. On the contrary, the purpose of her refusal to hold an international conference was her loyal support of Austria-Hungary,

---

[3] Bethmann Hollweg made it clear to ambassador Szögyeny that he in no way associated himself with the proposal, but was simply passing it on. *Op. cit.* II, 68.
[4] S. Fay, *The Origins of the World War*, New York, 1929, II, 343.
[5] *Die deutschen Dokumente*, I, 207.

together with a desire to contain within narrow limits the Austro-Serbian conflict. On the 27th July Germany maintained its unconditional support of Austria-Hungary, calmly envisaging the risk of a general war. The important point was, as Pierre Renouvin remarked, should the risk have been regarded as *possible* or *probable?*

2. Declaration of War on Serbia

(28th July 1914)

By the 28th July Austria-Hungary had got used to the idea of a *probable* risk of war. The Vienna government had received a communiqué from St Petersburg dated the 24th July to the effect that "Russia could not remain indifferent to a conflict between Austria and Serbia". It knew very well that an expedition into Serbia would set up a reaction in Russia, and that the interplay of alliances might lead to a European war. Why should it run the risk of a general war from which the Austro-Hungarian Empire had nothing to gain? Apparently the desire to break up the Pan-Slavistic movement still persisted, together with the urge to give an example to the peoples that constituted the Empire. Austrian documents contain no trace of any long-term view of the effect of a general war on the Dual Monarchy. Count Tisza, the most clear-sighted statesman in Vienna, had no wish to increase the number of slavs in the Monarchy, lest the position of the Hungarians be thrown out of balance. As for Berchtold, he considered nothing. Indeed, if he concentrated on the principle that the conflict should be localized, his reaction was so dilatory, and he hesitated so long, that he allowed almost every chance of localizing the conflict to escape him. Furthermore, he relied upon Austria's ally, Germany, whose defection in 1913 had brought about his diplomatic downfall.

The Austrian General Staff anticipated commencing military operations against Serbia on the 12th August. The Germans, who had been kept informed, were growing restless. On the 26th July the German ambassador Tschirsky conveyed the German point of view to Berchtold: "A speedy declaration of war to ward off the danger of unwarrantable interference by all and sundry."[6]

On the 27th July Szögyeny reported that Jagow regretted that "the commencement of military operations had been put off to such a late

---

[6] *Die deutschen Dokumente*, I, 213.

date (12th August.[7] On the same day Berchtold replied: "The declaration of war will be made soon ... The commencement of military operations will not take place until troop concentrations have been completed to allow for decisive action."[8]

It was on the morning of the 28th July that Austria-Hungary declared war on Serbia. Undoubtedly German pressure was decisive in bringing it about, but this belated precipitation still aimed at limiting the extent of the conflict and preventing the intervention of other powers.

3. Germany has Afterthoughts (29th July 1914)

Although approved by Germany, Austria's declaration of war on Serbia set the two allies at variance. Berlin's main preoccupation was to avoid intervention by other powers. On the 28th July the Kaiser telegraphed to the Czar:

> I am extremely disturbed to learn of the impression that Austria's action against Serbia has created in Your country. The unscrupulous agitation pursued in Serbia over the years terminated in a wicked outrage of which the Archduke Francis Ferdinand was the victim. The spirit that led Serbia to assassinate its own king and his wife still prevails in that country. I have no doubt You will agree that it is in both our interests, and indeed that of every sovereign, to insist that those morally responsible for this abominable crime receive the punishment they deserve. Politics play no part in this matter.
>
> On the other hand, I understand perfectly well how difficult it is for You and Your government to disregard the pressure of public opinion. That is why, having regard to the cordial and tender friendship that has bound us solidly together so long, I am exerting all my influence to induce the Austrians to negotiate readily with a view to arriving at an agreement satisfactory to You. I confidently hope that You will assist me in my efforts to straighten out any difficulties that might still arise.
>
> Your sincere friend and devoted cousin,
>
> Willy.

William II did not see Serbia's reply in which she accepted Austria's ultimatum until the morning of the 28th July, on returning from his cruise. He then wrote to his Minister, Jagow: "There is really no further motive for war, but a guarantee is necessary that the promises will be carried out. It might be secured by a temporary occupation of a part of Serbia ... On this basis I am ready to act as mediator in Austria."[10]

---

[7] *Dipl. Aktenstücke*, II, 67.
[8] *Ibid.*, II, 69.
[9] *Die deutschen Dokumente*, II, 335.
[10] *Die deutschen Dokumente*, II, 293.

The Kaiser's ministers did not take his offer seriously, and they continued with their diplomatic tactics of the previous weeks. Meanwhile, Sazonov, the Russian Minister for Foreign Affairs, announced that partial mobilization of the Russian army would begin on the 29th July. Another significant fact was the recall of the English Fleet to its war base at Scapa Flow.

Only then did Bethmann Hollweg react sharply. So far the German Chancellor had been content to let matters take their course, sometimes shielding his Austrian ally. On the 29th July he announced that the continuance of Russian preparations might force Germany to mobilize; but his reversal of attitude began on receiving that afternoon a warning from Sir Edward Grey to the effect that, if Germany and France became involved in the conflagration, Great Britain could not long stand aside. Furthermore, the British minister added a mediatory proposal — that Austria-Hungary should occupy Belgrade and state her intentions.

The Chancellor was horrified, for he had always counted on British neutrality. He endeavoured to resume his links with London, and sent telegram after telegram to Vienna during the night of the 29th to 30th July, urging Vienna to reach an understanding with St Petersburg and accept the British proposal. His concluding telegram, at 4.40 a.m., to his ambassador in Vienna ran: "We must refuse to allow ourselves to be drawn by Vienna into a world-wide conflagration without due reflection and without our advice being heeded."[11]

The same evening Bethmann Hollweg addressed four other telegrams tn Pourtalès, the German ambassador in St Petersburg, asking him to urge Sazonov to exercise patience and avoid "any hostile act against Austria."[12]

The Kaiser, more determined in his attitude, telegraphed the Czar during the night of the 30th July: "If Russia mobilizes against Austria-Hungary, the role of mediator, which I accepted at your earnest request, will be compromised, if not rendered impossible. The whole weight of the decision to be taken now rests on you, and you must bear the responsibility of war or peace."[13]

This telegram held up general mobilization in Russia. By the 29th July, despite the efforts of William II and the belated reversal of attitude of Bethmann Hollweg, the German leaders had already accepted the probable risk of a general war.

[11] *Die deutschen Dokumente*, II, 396.
[12] *Ibid.* II, 380—392.
[13] M. Paléologue, *La Russie des Tsars*, Paris, 1922, I, 33.

4. The Optimism of the German General Staff

When Bethmann Hollweg's telegram arrived in Berchtold's office
in Vienna in the early hours of the 30th July, the Austrian leaders no
longer knew what to think. Did Germany intend to wriggle out?
During the evening of that day Bethmann Hollweg's telegrams again
took up the offensive:

    9 p.m. — "Austria must accept Sir Edward Grey's proposal."
    11.20 p.m. — "Russian military preparations compel us to reach
          speedy decisions."[14]
    2.45 a.m. (31st July) — Transmission of a telegram from the King
          of England proposing the occupation of Belgrade
          to be followed by talks (a renewal of Grey's proposal).

Berchtold was quite at a loss. Why was Bethmann Hollweg applying
the brakes? In the meantime, however, the German Chief of Staff sent
two telegrams to Conrad, his Austrian counterpart:

"Every delay aggravates the situation, for Russia is gaining a lead . . .
Reject the peace proposals from Great Britain. Austria-Hungary's
only chance is to give its support to the European war. She has
Germany's unqualified backing."[15]

And at 7.45 a.m. on the 31st July the following telegram arrived:
"Hold out in the face of Russian mobilization. The interests of Austria-
Hungary must be safeguarded. Mobilize against Russia immediately.
Germany will mobilize."[16]

Conrad took these telegrams to Berchtold, and the Austrians were
reassured. On the morning of the 31st Berchtold told his colleagues:
"I was under the impression that Germany would draw back. I have
now received the most reassuring statement from the highest military
authority."[17]

But what is one to think of this utter contradiction between the
actions of the Chancellor and those of the German Chief of Staff?
"Who is in command in Berlin?" Berchtold exclaimed. The fact was
that events had outpaced Bethmann Hollweg. When he received no
reply from Austria he wrote bitterly. "The machine is moving, and we
have lost our way."[18]

[14] Die deutschen Dokumente, II, 452–456.
[15] Conrad, Aus meiner Dienstzeit, 1906–16, Vienna, 1926, IV, 152.
[16] I. bid., IV, 152.
[17] Die deutschen Dokumente, II, 456.
[18] Die deutschen Dokumente, II, 456.

Moltke was dominated by technical necessities. A short war was the overriding purpose of the German Chief of Staff; the army commanders had no intention of allowing themselves to be outdistanced by their opponents, and the dilatory ways of diplomats quite justifiably caused them some anxiety.

According to Sydney Fay the attitude of the German General Staff proves German responsibility for the war. That is undoubtedly an exaggeration. Moltke's telegram to Conrad forms the basis of Fay's accusation; but if we examine the facts more closely we find that the document was intended for Conrad, not for Berchtold. The German Chief of Staff did not wish his counterpart and ally to allow himself to be influenced by the sluggishness of Viennese diplomacy. Conrad too was dominated by military technical necessity, and he was uncertain whether to mobilize only in the south west against Serbia, or in the north also against Russia. It was Conrad, therefore, whom Moltke urged to lose no time but to mobilize also against the Russians. Conrad went beyond Moltke's intentions when he showed the telegram to Berchtold.

Other historians have asserted that Moltke pushed Bethmann Hollweg into the background; military power in Berlin, it has been suggested, prevailed over political power. In that case Moltke would have knowingly terminated Bethmann Hollweg's reversal of attitude, and imposed a military solution upon the German and Austrian governments.

This deduction is perhaps too rigid. The German historian Gerhard Ritter has emphasized the separate roles of political and military power in Berlin in 1914.[19] On the one hand the Chief of General Staff, von Moltke, was responsible to the Emperor. The government had no authority whatever over military policy, or even the right to see military documents. Chancellor Bethmann Hollweg, on the other hand, though appointed by the Emperor, was responsible to the Reichstag. The military authority was not permitted to interfere in general policy. Any disputes between the two hierarchies were settled out of hand by the Kaiser. This constitutional set-up was quite different from that of France or Great Britain where the *government* was the sole political authority.

Viewed in this light it becomes apparent that the Chancellor played his part fully until the 31st July 1914 — a dangerous, imprudent part

---

[19] Ritter — *Staatskunst und Kriegshandwerk*, Munich, 1954–1960. See also J. Willequet's *La violation de la neutralité belge* — *Reflexions nouvelles. Revue de philologie et d'histoire*, Brussels, 1963.

which Berchtold misunderstood. By the 31st July Bethmann Hollweg
knew that he was playing a losing game; he retired from the scene,
and the lead was then taken over by Moltke. It would be wrong,
however, to conclude that from the 31st July onwards the military
controlled the civil power. Moltke continued to play his role, and sent
telegrams to Vienna and elsewhere; but from that moment it was his
telegrams that assumed prime importance. Moreover, Bethmann stood
aside so as not to incur the reproach of having obstructed the military
in the exercise of their functions.

From the 31st July onwards Moltke's overriding consideration —
accepted by everybody — was that the army should be ready in time.
The German General Staff was certain of victory if the war was a short
one. Moltke hoped for a "thunderbolt" to destroy France. But why
France? Simply because the General Staff recognized the possibility of
a universal conflagration compelling French intervention, and in that
event the defeat of France was necessary so that the army might turn
afterwards towards Russia.

Moltke was a good organizer, but a mediocre tactician. He was a
man of average intelligence and little imagination, and he adhered to
the plan of his predecessor Schlieffen. That plan envisaged the encirclement of the French forces. The German army would make a dash
for the coast, turn the French left wing, and the French army would
collapse in a few weeks. In the interests of speed the Germans had to
press on to Amsterdam (though eventually Antwerp was accepted as
the objective) in the race to the sea. As this plan involved the violation
of Belgian neutrality, it implied the risk of provoking British intervention — as Jagow had observed to Moltke in February 1913: "Are
you aware that your plan involves a violation of neutrality, and a
possible conflict with England?"[20]

Moltke studied this problem which had escaped him, and concluded that it was the only possible plan. The French army had
become too strong to allow the Germans to remain on the defensive in the west until the danger in the east had been warded off.
In the circumstances one is less surprised at the steps taken by
Bethmann on the 1st August, in response to the demands of Moltke
who put into effect his unmodified plan, and kept rigidly to it to the
point of absurdity.

[20] G. Ritter, Der Schlieffensplan : Kritik eines Mythos, Munich, 1956, II, 271,
and Jagow, quoted by Ritter.

In the judgment of the military leaders it was indispensable to cross Belgium by force to ensure the success of the offensive in the west. Political and military interests were in violent conflict. The injustice perpetrated against Belgium was manifest, but the general political consequences of that injustice had to be accepted.[21]

Bethmann was constrained to yield to the demands of the Schlieffen Plan; he therefore bore the brunt of all its errors. To ensure the success of the surprise attack on Liège on D+3 he sent an ultimatum to Belgium and a declaration of war to France, based upon accusations utterly without foundation.

William II, however, clung to the hope of British neutrality. He enquired of Moltke whether, assuming that Britain remained neutral, the General Staff's plans could be modified within a few hours to allow the bulk of the German army to be directed against Russia. Moltke replied that the proper functioning of "his" plan, which had been worked out to the last detail, would be endangered. William II said dryly: "Your uncle would have given me quite a different reply."

Bethmann continued to bear the burden of the consequences which the plan entailed. He lost face in the matter of Belgian neutrality and, by declaring war, he gave Italy and Rumania the opportunity to escape their obligations under the Triple Alliance. The Chancellor gave an account of his actions in the Reichstag on the 4th August in a clumsy speech which Prince von Bülow has condemned harshly:

Before his country and before the whole world the head of the German government − not the French or Belgian government − recognized that by invading Belgium we were perpetrating an injustice, but that necessity knew no law. I shall never forget the moment when I read that speech, for I have rarely experienced such anguish. I understood what children and the common people mean when they say, 'My heart stopped'.

I felt that by this solemn declaration we had at the outset lost touch with all the imponderables, that by this unjustifiably stupid speech we were antagonizing the whole world. And the very evening of that luckless day the Chancellor of the German Empire in his conversation with Sir Edward Goschen, the British ambassador, treated the international treaties on which the neutrality of Belgium was based as a scrap of paper.

Never, since the 15th July 1870, when the words 'with a light heart' were used by Emile Ollivier before the French Legislative Assembly, have more fateful words been uttered. After saying this in a public session of the French Parliament Ollivier had to write a big book in a vain attempt to exonerate himself. It might have been easier for Bethmann Hollweg who allowed his foolish remark to escape him in a private conversation. One does not have to be a Machiavelli to appreciate

[21] Bethmann Hollweg, *Betrachtungen zum Weltkriege*. Berlin, 1923, I, 167.

that if Bethmann, in a second moral collapse, did indeed utter those unfortunate words, reasons of State and the overriding interests of the nation demanded that he shouldrepudiate them immediately and categorically."[22]

5. *Austria-Hungary wavers*

Despite Berchtold's perplexity when faced with the contradictory statements made in Berlin, he felt quite reassured when Conrad showed him Moltke's telegrams. Berchtold did not believe that hostilities against Serbia could now be halted, and Conrad did not want that at any price. The wound left by the failure of 1913 was still smarting. Berchtold called on the Emperor during the afternoon of the 30th July, and on the 31st he made his report to the council of ministers: "His Majesty stated at once that it was impossible to hold up hostilities against Serbia . . . He approved the idea of carefully avoiding outright acceptance of the British proposal, and said that our reply should indicate that we were favourably disposed towards negotiation."[23]

Conrad, notified by Berchtold, replied to Moltke's telegram at 8 a.m. on the 31st: "In accordance with His Majesty's decision, it has been agreed to prosecute the war against Serbia, to mobilize the rest of our army and to concentrate it in Galicia. We request notification of the first day of mobilization in Berlin."[24]

Though Conrad was forging ahead he kept a watchful eye on German activities. Perhaps he too wondered what was behind the apparent contradiction between the telegrams from Bethmann and those received from Moltke.

Following the session of the council on the 31st July Berchtold in his turn left matters in the hands of Conrad. At 12.30 p.m. that day Vienna announced general mobilization, and at 1 p.m. Francis Joseph sent William II a telegram which suggested a shadow of uneasiness: "I am aware of the full significance of my decisions. I have taken them with complete confidence in God's justice, and in the conviction that Your armed forces will rise in their unshakable loyalty to my Empire and to the Triple Alliance."[25] On that day even the aged Emperor allowed himself to be swept along by events.

[22] Prince von Bülow — *Denkwürdigkeiten*, Berlin, 1932.
[23] *Dipl. Aktenstücke*, III, 79.
[24] Conrad, *Aus meiner Dienstzeit, 1906–16*, Vienna, 1926, IV, 150.
[25] *Dipl. Aktenstücke*, III, 49.

CHAPTER III

GREAT BRITAIN AND THE FRANCO-RUSSIAN ALLIANCE

1. What part did the Russian Chief of General Staff play in the decision to announce general mobilization?
2. Did France encourage the Russians to mobilize?
3. Was the irresolution of the British Cabinet a source of encouragement to the Germans?

1. Russian Mobilization (30th July 1914)

Most German historians believe that the general mobilization of Russian forces constituted the starting point of the first world war. But if we take the facts in their chronological order we are confronted with two successive decisions more or less contradictory. Firstly instruc-, tions for partial mobilization were issued from St Petersburg on the 29th July 1914.[1] Secondly, at 4 p.m. on the 30th, the Czar ordered general mobilization. Apparently the latter decision meant a general progressive mobilization. In fact, between the announcement of the two decisions events of primary importance were taking place at St Petersburg.

On learning of the declaration of war on Serbia by Austria-Hungary on the 28th July, the Russian General Staff drew up two edicts for the Czar's signature. The edicts decreed respectively partial and general mobilization. The precious documents were signed by the Czar on the morning of the 29th July — undoubtedly at the same time — and they remained in the custody of General Yanushkievich, Chief of General Staff. Partial mobilization was but a step towards general mobilization, details of which had only recently been perfected by the Imperial General Staff, and involved a cumbersome operation.

The distinction made later between general and partial mobilization was specious. From a technical point of view general mobilization was

---

[1] Covering the districts of Kiev, Odessa, Moscow and Kazan.

the only one possible. The vast size of the country and the disposal
of an army did not permit of any piecemeal operation if millions of
men were to be put on the march.

Did General Yanushkievich wish to hasten Russia's entry into war, or
did he merely put into operation a prepared plan, as his counterparts in
other countries were doing? The evidence of General Dobrorolsky,
Director of Mobilization, suggests what went on in the mind of the
Chief of Staff:

> The way in which things proceed depends as little as possible on the wishes
> of the Chief... A director's main task consists in selecting the right moment, and
> is of very brief duration. His choice is determined by a number of political reasons;
> but, once his decision has been taken, it is final and no reversion of attitude is
> possible: the decision leads automatically to the commencement of war . . .
>   Three forms of military mobilization were possible . . . general mobilization . . .
> gradual mobilization . . . in the case of a war against a powerful and distant neigh-
> bour on whose frontiers an armed force must be built up slowly and progressively
> through lack of railways; partial mobilization . . . in which it is necessary to
> bring to bear the entire armed forces, including the navy, in order to secure a
> victory . . .
>   On the morning of the 24th July between eleven o'clock and noon General
> Yanushkievich, Chief of the General Staff, summoned me by telephone to his
> office at once. He told me that the situation was very grave, and continued,
> 'Austria has handed Serbia an absolutely unacceptable ultimatum, and we cannot
> remain indifferent. We have decided to state this frankly and categorically. Tomor-
> row a brief official announcement will appear in the *Russkii Invalid*, which will
> read: "The whole of Russia follows with close attention the progress of the dis-
> cussions between the Austro-Hungarian and Serbian governments; Russia will
> not stand idly by if the dignity and integrity of the Serbian people, our blood
> brothers, are threatened". Is your department ready for us to announce the mobiliza-
> tion of our army?'
>   I told him it was, and he said, 'Bring me within an hour all the documents
> relating to the placing of our troops on a war footing, covering if necessary partial
> mobilization against Austria–Hungary only. We must avoid giving Germany any
> reason for thinking that this mobilization is a hostile threat to her'. I pointed out
> that there could be no question of partial mobilization; but General Yanushkievich
> again instructed me to bring my report within about an hour based on the decision
> he had made.

The Chief of Staff pointed out to Sazonov that the edict proclaiming
partial mobilization was meaningless.[2] During those few days Yanushkievich played the part of a leader, assuming an air of authority that one
would have thought foreign to him. He had formerly been Director

---

[2] Dobrorolsky, *La mobilisation russe en 1914 (Revue d'Histoire de la Guerre
Mondiale)*, Paris, 1923.

of the Military College, and had held the post of Chief of General Staff since May only. He was forty-four years of age, and felt that his hour had come to play a leading role. He had an affected way of stroking his long, black moustache, and skilfully combined the manners of a courtier with the business of organizing. It is only just to add that he was blessed with remarkable associates. But from the moment General Yanushkievich began to brandish his two edicts the politicians appreciated the danger of the situation.

A few weeks earlier Sukhomlynov, the Minister for War, was boasting that Russia did not want war, but that she was not afraid of it. He was an indolent and depraved individual, engrossed in the whims of a wife thirty-two years his junior; he was surrounded with German and Austrian spies, as disclosed at his trial in 1917. He preferred to maintain an attitude of reserve and leave things to the Chief of Staff.

On the 28th July Sazonov proclaimed partial mobilization for the following day, but apparently the minister was still waiting for some development in the diplomatic sphere. He knew that general mobilization might result in Germany taking the same step, and it seems certain that the purpose of his long conference with General Yanushkievich that day was to try to get him to agree to carry out the mobilization order in two stages. But there is no trace whatever of the interview, and the historian is left to surmise what transpired.

On the following day Pourtales, the German ambassador, visited Sazonov, and advised him officially that "the continuance of mobilization measures would compel Germany to do likewise, a fact that would make war almost inevitable".[3] Sazonov replied that "the measures taken were not directed against Germany".[4]

Just before that interview the minister had seen the Austro-Hungarian ambassador, Szapary, and told him that "an edict would be signed that day proclaiming a fairly considerable mobilization".[5] But during the discussion Sazonov received news of the bombardment of Belgrade by the Austro-Hungarians, and he exclaimed indignantly, "Why continue to talk when you act like this?"[6]

Sazonov still hesitated; he undoubtedly awaited a reply from his French allies who had been informed that morning of the partial mobilization. The news of the bombardment of Belgrade, however,

[3] *Die deutschen Dokumente*, II, 342.
[4] *Die deutschen Dokumente*, II, 343—370.
[5] *Dipl. Aktenstücke*, III, 19.
[6] *Dipl. Aktenstücke*, III, 19.

profoundly modified his attitude. Though he had wished on the previous evening to put general mobilization into effect in two stages, and was awaiting approval from Paris — which did not arrive until the 30th — he now wished to put the second edict into immediate effect and proclaim general mobilization.

The minister called on the Czar and requested his authority to promulgate the edict. But Nicholas II had also altered course. Although on the previous evening he had signed without hesitation the two edicts presented to him by the Chief of Staff, he now hesitated to take the decisive step to promulgate, for he had received the telegram from William II placing on his shoulders the responsibility for peace or war (see p. 28).

The Czar was shocked. He was a man who lacked resolution, and was accustomed to conceal his innermost thoughts. His anxiety to refuse nothing to those who approached him frequently led him into making promises which he did not keep and to ignore advice that he had himself sought. His entourage — including, strangely enough, the Czarina, who was a neurotic and romantic woman — contributed greatly to his tendency to regret every decision he made. It is thus easy to understand that on the 29th July he remained indifferent to the arguments of Sazonov who recommended immediate general mobilization; the Czar merely authorized the promulgation of the edict ordering partial mobilization.

Dobrorolsky states:

> On the morning of the 29th July General Yanushkievich handed me the edict for general mobilization, signed by my master and emperor, and told me to put it into execution. The first day of mobilization was to be the 30th July.[7]

At 9 a.m. on the 29th he went to the central telegraph office with his telegram for general mobilization, and gave orders for its despatch. Half an hour later General Yanushkievich telephoned him and asked him to withhold despatch. It was not until midnight that orders were sent to the four districts as pre-arranged for partial mobilization to begin. Once again Dobrorolsky protested to his Chief of General Staff, and pointed out that the orders would create disruption in the execution of plans that had long been agreed upon. Yanushkievich assured him that His Majesty assumed entire responsibility for the order to mobilize partially.

---

[7] Dobrorolsky, *La mobilisation russe en 1914* (*Revue d'Histoire de la Guerre Mondiale*), Paris, 1923.

By eleven o'clock on the morning of the 30th July everything had again been changed. Sazonov gave in to Yanushkievich's objections, and managed to convince the Emperor. At 4 p.m. Nicholas II, after more inconsistent thinking, authorized general mobilization. Sazonov transmitted the order from the palace of St Petersburg to General Yanushkievich. The argument which finally convinced the Czar was that the suspension of the preparations for mobilization would dislocate the country's entire military organization. We may also assume that French approval of partial mobilization, received during the afternoon, influenced Sazonov in his decision to secure the Czar's confirmation.

Thus, at 5 p.m. Dobrorolsky issued from the central telegraph office the instructions for general mobilization.

"On that same day Sazonov again received the German ambassador, who asked him if Russia was satisfied with Austria's promises not to infringe the integrity of the kingdom of Serbia. 'I replied,' said Sazonov, 'that the declaration was inadequate."

The Minister then dictated the following to Pourtalès, who sent a copy to Berlin: "If Austria, recognizing that the Austro-Hungarian problem is also a European one, declares herself ready to delete from her ultimatum the clauses which affect the sovereign rights of Serbia, Russia will undertake to cease her military preparations."[8]

It should also be noted that on the 30th July Sazonov said to the Czar: "If war breaks out we have nothing with which to reproach ourselves. We have done everything possible to spare the world this distressing ordeal . . . To-day the task of diplomacy is at an end."[9]

General mobilization in Russia resulted in inevitable reactions in Berlin, Paris and London. That day Europe regarded war as inevitable.

2. *France and Russian Mobilization*

On the 29th July, 1914, Poincaré and Viviani returned from Russia, and disembarked at Dunkirk without having halted at Oslo and Copenhagen. On the 27th Paléologue, French ambassador in Moscow, received the following radio-telegram from Viviani, on the liner *France*: "Kindly inform Monsieur Sazonol that France is aware, as Russia is, of the great importance to both our countries of confirming their

[8] *Russian Black Book*, Moscow, II, 292.
[9] M. Paléologue, *La Russie des Tsars*, Paris, 1922, I, 34 (confirmed by Sazonov, *Vospomineniga*, Paris, 1927, p. 219).

perfect understanding in relation to other powers, and of neglecting no effort to find a solution to the dispute. She is, therefore, prepared to give full support to the action of the Imperial government in the interests of general peace."[10]

After that nothing happened. The messages reaching the liner *France* were jammed, probably by the Germans. Poincaré and Viviani hastened to their compartment on the train, where they met the Keeper of the Seals, Bienvenu–Martin, who had been acting as deputy, René Renoult, Minister of Public Works, and Abel Ferry, Under-Secretary of State for Foreign Affairs.

The crowd demonstrated and acclaimed the French statesmen. The ministers who welcomed Poincaré and Viviani were pessimistic, and regarded war as inevitable. Poincaré himself seemed both resigned and full of optimism. He thought that everything should still be done to avoid war, but he expressed his fears in confidence to Renoult when he told him that a settlement appeared impossible.[11]

When the special train arrived in Paris the President received an ovation.

All along the route to the Elysée there were enthusiastic crowds, and the shouting was carried on from street to street. 'Vive Poincaré!' was mingled with 'Vive l'Armée!' and there were occasional cries of 'Vive la guerre!' The Chauvinistic note was, however, far from being general, and it was distinctly a patriotic display and not a war demonstration.[12]

The manner in which the French crowd had accepted the idea of war was remarkable. Poincaré wrote, "I have never experienced so much pain, either morally or physically, in trying to remain unmoved. I found the Elysée deserted. Mme Poincaré is busy in Meuse equipping our country house, and has decided to come to me; but she will not be here until seven o'clock this evening, and in the gloomy solitude of my office I am beset with misgivings".[13]

At five o'clock he presided over an important council of ministers. The overriding question was Russian mobilization. That morning, at 11.15, the Russian ambassador, Izvolsky, revealed that his government had despatched the following telegram: "Following Austria's declaration

---

[10] Poincaré, *Au service de la France*, Paris, 1926, p. 335.

[11] Caillaux, *Mémoires*, Paris (1942–1947), p. 169.

[12] *The Times* of the 30th July 1914 (quoted in French by J. Kayser, *op. cit.*, p. 185.

[13] Poincaré, *Au service de la France*, Paris, 1926, p. 368.

of war on Serbia we shall order mobilization tomorrow in the provinces of Odessa, Kiev, Moscow and Kazan. In bringing this to the attention of the German government we wish to confirm that Russia has no aggressive intentions towards Germany."[14]

Viviani for his part received von Schoen, the German ambassador, and assured him that the "precautionary measures" taken by the French General Staff in his absence were not the expression of belligerent intentions. This information the ambassador passed on to Berlin.[15] Following the interview Viviani spent the afternoon with a friend, and delayed the opening of the council of ministers.

What kind of reply could the French government send to Russia? The ministers knew that Clause 2 of the Franco-Russian military covenant of 1892–93 stipulated:

> In the event of the mobilization of the forces of the Triple Alliance, or any of the powers of which it is composed, France and Russia will, as soon as the fact is announced, at once simultaneously mobilize their entire forces and bring them as near as possible to their frontiers.[16]

In 1913 this dangerous clause was revised to read:

> German mobilization will oblige France and Russia to mobilize their entire forces immediately and simultaneously at the first intimation of the fact, and without the need for any preliminary consultation. This will hold similarly in the event of any belligerent act by the German army against one or other of the allied powers. But in the event of partial mobilization, or even general mobilization on the part of Austria or Italy, prior consultation will be indispensable.

It seems clear that the authors of this clause aimed above all at forestalling a sudden attack by the German army. But in the afternoon of the 29th July partial mobilization of the Russian army was imminent, and France, who had been notified in the morning, was still able to offer her advice. Russia did not exactly consult France within the spirit of the covenant, but she gave a preliminary warning. It is not known precisely what the council of ministers thought; we have only circumstantial evidence on which to rely.

At six o'clock in the evening Malvy, the Minister of the Interior, informed Caillaux, "Russia has asked us if she can mobilize, and we have replied in the affirmative. We are engaged to support her . . . It is understood that Russia will mobilize against Austria only. We

---

[14] Poincaré, *Ibid.*, p. 373.
[15] *Ibid.*
[16] *Third French Yellow Book*, Paris, 1918, No. 71.

have, moreover, recommended that she mobilize with the utmost prudence."[17]

Abel Ferry remarked, "The Russian mobilization must not be stopped".[18]

On the 30th July Izvolsky cabled to Sazonov the following reply (telegram 210): "Margerie[19] has informed me that the French government, without wishing to meddle in our preparations, regards it as eminently desirable that these preparations be conducted as unobtrusively and unprovocatively as possible . . . The Minister for War, Messimy, has told Count Ignatiev[20] that we may state that in the higher interests of peace we agree to slow down temporarily our mobilization measures. While continuing, and even strengthening, our military preparations we shall refrain as far as possible from mass movements of troops."[21]

All these pieces of evidence are consistent, and seem to suggest a common attitude. Another document, though rather suspect, refers to a secret meeting alleged to have taken place at the Elysée on the 29th or 30th July between Poincaré, Viviani, Izvolsky and Sir Francis Bertie.[22] The four men are alleged to have agreed to promise Russia France's support in the event of war following Russian mobilization. If this promise was, in fact, made, it must have encouraged the Russians to mobilize and fostered the launching of war, for the letter of the military covenant still allowed France to escape. But this conversation to which no witness refers is very unreliable. We have to be satisfied with the documents previously quoted, which indicate that France accepted partial mobilization of the Russian army.

The fact was confirmed in a telegram dated the 30th July from Paléologue at the Quai d'Orsay: "This very morning I advised Sazonov to avoid any military step which might offer Germany a pretext for general mobilization. In reply he informed me that during last night the Russian General Staff did indeed suspend certain secret precautions, the disclosure of which might have alarmed the German General Staff."[23]

[17] Caillaux, *Mémoires*, Paris, 1942–1947, p. 170.
[18] French Diplomatic Documents, 3rd Series XI, 262, Paris, 1936.
[19] Political Director at the Quai d'Orsay.
[20] Russian military attaché in Paris.
[21] *Russian Black Book*, II, 290.
[22] The existence and the purport of this interview were revealed to Caillaux by Briand on the 9th February 1932. Perhaps it was merely a case of two vindictive men, thrust out of power, exchanging views.
[23] Telegram sent at 4.31p.m.

At 3.40 a.m., however, a further telegram from Paléologue arrived at the Quai d'Orsay: "According to information received by the Russian General Staff general mobilization of the German army will be ordered tomorrow."[24]

Meanwhile Sazonov confirmed to Pourtalès, German ambassador in Russia, that Russian partial mobilization would be put into operation against Austria-Hungary only. At 11.30 p.m. yet another telegram from Paléologue arrived at the Quai d'Orsay:

In an interview this afternoon between M. Sazonov and Count von Pourtalès the former got the impression that Germany was reluctant to say the final word in Vienna which might safeguard peace. The Emperor Nicholas had the same impression following a personal exchange of telegrams between himself and the Emperor William. Moreover, the Russian General Staff and the Admiralty have received disquieting news concerning German military and naval preparations. In consequence, the Russian government has decided to proceed secretly with the preliminary steps for general mobilization. After informing me of this decision M. Sazonov added that the Russian government will none the less continue its conciliatory efforts. He said repeatedly, 'I shall negotiate up to the last moment'.[25]

This *secret general mobilization* order provides food for thought. The central telegraph office at St Petersburg transmitted the order at 6 a.m. on the 31st July, but by 4 a.m. mobilization notices had been posted on all the walls in the city! The order must have remained secret a very short time. It is scarcely possible to believe that the printing of the notices during the previous evening escaped the observation of the Germans. It was not until 10.43 a.m., however, that Paléologue telegraphed Paris that "general mobilization of the Russian army had been ordered".[26]

It was this final decision to mobilize that hastened the declaration of war. That fact is not disputed; but should war have come so soon? Despite the behaviour of the Russian statesmen which we have already examined, we may still wonder whether France did not precipitate the momentum of war by her encouragement, either direct or indirect. The French ministers' subtle distinction between partial and general mobilization was specious, for either would have achieved the same result.

[21] *White Book*, telegram 306.
[25] *Appuhn et Renouvin, Introduction aux Tableaux d'Histoire de Guillaume II.* Paris, 1923 — telegram 318. (However, Renouvin gives the same number — 318 — to another telegram.)
[26] Telegram 118, distorted in the *French Yellow Book*; cf. Isaac, *Un débct historique : 1914*, Paris, 1931, p. 211.

Even if the Franco-Russian military covenant were not destined to play an inevitable part in the events of the 29th to the 31st July 1914, it is certain that the French accepted and lent weight to Russia's diplomatic and military action. Russia's diplomatic behaviour towards France was correct: every important decision was communicated to the French beforehand, and as soon as possible.

The French ambassador, Paléologue, has been the object of several grave charges. He was accused of having encouraged the Russians to mobilize by promising Sazonov the more or less unconditional support of France; he is alleged not to have informed the French government punctually of the development of events in St Petersburg. Paléologue's attitude certainly laid him open to criticism. While Poincaré and Viviani (the latter was President of the Council and Minister for Foreign Affairs) were returning from Kronstadt to Dunkirk during the 23rd to the 29th July, Paléologue sent very few messages to Paris. He may not have thought it useful to write to those not wholly responsible for affairs, but counted on his friendship with Poincaré. Everything tends to suggest that he relied on the intimacy existing between them, and which the President moreover confirmed by his telegram from the liner *France*, to promise Sazonov the support of the French government. Later, after Poincaré had returned, Paléologue did not report in detail the orders and counterorders of the Czar, and there were long delays between his messages. But he might have agreed with Poincaré to exercise due caution in corresponding with Paris to obviate possible deciphering by Germany. As for the delays in the transmission of messages, they appeared more or less normal. "The usual route from St Petersburg via Berlin," comments Paléologue, "no longer offered security. As a result I had to stipulate that my telegrams be channelled through the Scandinavian and English network, a very complicated route resulting in a loss of time sometimes amounting to six or seven hours."[27]

Poincaré, who carefully examined every publication issued after 1919 on the origins of the war, meticulously weeded out and confounded all the attacks that were made against him. Not even his associates were spared from his niggling criticism; but Paléologue was always exonerated. In his *Mémoires* Poincaré elucidated all the missing texts and distorted documents, but Paléologue escaped every reproach. What Poincaré said about Paléologue was courteous and complimentary, but he refrained from referring to him as his friend, or intimating that

[27] Paléologue, *Vu*, Paris, dated 15th March, 1933.

it was on his insistence that this man whom he trusted should remain at St Petersburg after the 7th January 1914. These personal links between Poincaré and Paléologue are rarely remembered, but they are certainly important. Paléologue must have carried out the President's wishes loyally. The shortcomings of his mission were probably inherent in the superficial side of his character, in the inability of this man from the shores of the Mediterranean to adapt himself to the mists of the Neva region.

The undisclosed aims of Poincaré are more difficult to penetrate. His desire to forestall German aggression, the will to maintain the Russian alliance and to uphold what appeared to him to be the surest guarantee of balance in Europe were the well-known bases of his foreign policy. But did he not encourage the Russians to adopt an intransigent attitude? The French archives have been carefully weeded out, and the report of the conversations at St Petersburg between the Czar and Poincaré on the 22nd July 1914 are among the fragments missing. "I have never forgotten", said the Czar in 1916 to Cruppi, a former French minister, "the determination shown by the President of the Republic when he spoke to me before leaving Russia".[28]

Did this "determination" go so far as to give Russia a free hand? There were no witnesses to say so, and the accusation is too grave to be accepted without proofs; but absolution is too solemn a thing to be bestowed without contrition. The attacks by German historians and the doubts of English diplomats are without foundation, and the conversations of St Petersburg remain an absolute secret.

It must also be mentioned that Poincaré was carried by French public opinion. Several million Frenchmen had subscribed milliards of francs to Russian loans, and considered their interests to be bound up with those of their great ally in the east. The French Press was favourable to the Russian viewpoint and, even though at first public opinion was moved by the tragic death of Francis Ferdinand at Sarajevo, it quickly approved the diplomatic stand taken up by Russia. Most certainly Poincaré did not want war, but, as Chastenet remarks, "Perhaps he did not do all that he could have done to prevent it". There was a time, perhaps after his arrival at Dunkirk, when he became resigned to war.

This feeling of resignation was not peculiar to Poincaré alone; from the 29th July 1914 it affected the whole French population. While Poincaré was in Russia — from the 21st to the 24th July — the ten

[28] Chastenet, *Raymond Poincaré*, Paris, 1948, p. 147.

leading French papers devoted their space to the trial of Mme Caillaux and a mere tenth of their columns to the Russian alliance.[29] But from the 29th July "determination" predominated. For reasons which were inadequately explained the French people had become resigned to war.

It was with genuine relief that the people of Paris on the 1st August 1914 welcomed the false news that Germany had mobilized and that Russia had replied with a similar step. In fact, Russia mobilized first, but Paléologue's despatch took ten hours to reach Paris.

3. The Attitude of Great Britain

Great Britain was certainly a very keen observer of the July 1914 crisis. The reactions of European opinion found a sympathetic chord in the United Kingdom. European indignation at the Sarajevo outrage had its echo in the British Press; so did the reversal of European opinion when Serbia accepted Austria-Hungary's insolent ultimatum. The English were unable to understand the aggressive obstinacy of Count Berchtold.

The Foreign Office, however, was better informed, and the conversations at St Petersburg between the Czar and Poincaré caused uneasiness at 10 Downing Street. British diplomacy quickly sensed that although Germany and France were attached to peace, they had more or less decided not to abandon their allies, Austria-Hungary and Russia. Rather than soothe the Russian and Austro-Hungarian antagonists, British statesmen preferred to ask Paris and Berlin to moderate the tension. London spared no effort to apprise the rival nations of the Continent of their strong attachment to balance in Europe. These warnings were conciliatory, and both Paris and Berlin believed Great Britain would remain neutral.

But the British statesmen were perplexed by the refusal of Germany and Austria-Hungary to agree to the conference proposed by Sir Edward Grey.

Grey had been a member of Parliament since 1885, and a minister since 1908. He was regarded as a wise man, and both ministers and members of Parliament listened to him as to an oracle. Able and prudent counsels issued from his lips. The integrity of Sir Edward reassured England, and his disinterestedness equalled his probity. Almost every

[29] J. Kayser, De Kronstadt à Khrouchtchev, Paris, 1962, p. 175.

week-end the man-in-the-street rejoiced to learn that Sir Edward had gone fishing. When the newspapers announced on Sunday, the 26th July, that the Head of the Foreign Office was at his desk the people of Britain became alarmed — and with good cause, for that week Sir Edward himself lost some of his calm, and knew not what decision to make.

Germany knew that the military agreements reached between the French and British General Staffs in 1906 did not constitute an alliance, and imposed no obligation whatever on the French and British governments. Germany was not unaware that these terms had been perfected by technical agreements that aimed at speedy and effective co-operation in the event of common Franco-British action; but Germany also knew that they were quite susceptible of repudiation by the British Parliament. That is why Bethmann Hollweg agreed to transmit Grey's proposal to Vienna.

The Chancellor telegraphed to William II on the 27th July, "If we reject a limine every offer of mediation . . . England will abandon her attitude of neutrality".[30] But the German leaders were reassured when King George told Prince Henry of Prussia on the 26th July that "Great Britain would remain neutral in the event of a conflict between the western powers".[31]

It was, in fact, not until the 27th July, after Berlin's rejection of the Grey proposal, that the British government became puzzled; for London did not know that Germany, sure of British neutrality, believed more than ever in its own ability to localize the Austro-Serbian dispute, and that it could speed up the result by adopting a firm attitude.

The French government also believed that Britain would remain neutral in the event of a conflagration, and the diplomatic game proceeded without close consultation with Great Britain. Sir Francis Bertie, the British ambassador, visited Poincaré on the latter's return from Russia. "You see, my dear ambassador, I am convinced that the safeguarding of peace between the great powers lies in the hands of England. If His Majesty's government were to announce that in the event of a conflict between Germany and France, resulting from the present dispute between Austria and Serbia, England would come to the aid of France, then there would be no war, because Germany would immediately modify her attitude."[32]

[30] Die deutschen Dokumente, II, 283.
[31] Die deutschen Dokumente, I, 207.
[32] Poincaré, Au service de la France, Paris, 1936, IV, 417.

Sir Francis faithfully transmitted this suggestion to London, but the awaited declaration was not made. Poincaré's deduction was right, and it is probable that if the British Cabinet had made its position clear war might have been avoided. It is well known that the British government wished to remain neutral; but it had no desire to allow France to be overwhelmed.

Appeals also came from Sazonov in St Petersburg, with a view to a precise attitude being taken by Great Britain in favour of her Franco–Russian allies; but these appeals, like those of Poincaré, went unheeded. It was not until the 29th July that Sir Edward Grey informed Berlin that, if Germany and France were drawn into the conflict, Great Britain would not long be able to stand aside. As we have already seen, it was this information which brought about Bethmann Hollweg's reversal of attitude; he feared British intervention, and determined to try *in extremis* to lead Count Berchtold to accept Sir Edward's proposals.

Why did it take Britain so long to make her position clear? Most probably because, as revealed in the British and European Press at the time, opinion had become inured to the idea that war was inevitable, and Britain's leaders, like those of Europe, had come to recognize the irreversible nature of this slow but inexorable evolution leading Europe from peace to war.

Furthermore, Sir Edward's telegram did not by any means state that Great Britain stood behind the Franco-Russian alliance: it intimated that it contemplated intervention in some way as yet undefined. Are we then to think that the attitude of Germany and France, who were prepared to support their allies beyond the extent of their contractual obligations, would have been less firm had the Grey declaration been made sooner? It is quite probable, and Bethmann Hollweg's change of attitude during the night of the 29th and 30th July confirms the hypothesis.

But if Sir Edward's great prudence and reserve expressed the hesitations of the British Cabinet, one may assume that he was interpreting faithfully the opinion of his country. The British government was afraid that a categorical declaration might encourage France and Russia to adopt too determined a stand, not at all desirable in the negotations hoped for. British historians are of the opinion that Parliament would not have approved Britain's entry into the war if the government had laid the matter before it during those last days of July.

It was only on the 4th August, after the violation of Belgian neutrality, that Sir Edward secured, mainly as a result of this new factor, Britain's declaration of war. Undoubtedly the shillyshallying of the British Cabinet accelerated the movement that led to the launching of hostilities; but there is no reason to believe that the British Cabinet did anything but give expression to the profound sentiments of the nation.

CHAPTER IV

THE WAR OF MOVEMENT–1914

1. Was there any real co-operation between the French and Belgian forces?
2. What was the nature of Franco-British co-operation?
3. Was the French Command to blame for the defeat at Charleroi?
4. Did Moltke ensure that unity of command existed between the German armies?

1. Franco-Belgian Military Co-operation

If European public opinion was astonished and deeply touched by Germany's violation of Belgian neutrality, the fact did not surprise the French General Staff. In 1911 General Joffre, the new Chief of Staff, informed the Army Council that it would be eminently desirable in the event of war for the French army to enter Belgium as a preventive measure. This proposal was submitted to Britain who opposed it with a categorical veto, and it was rejected by the council of ministers.

Joffre wrote: On the 27th November 1912, with the consent of Sir Edward Grey, General Wilson visited the French General Staff, and told us that the Foreign Office considered that Belgium hesitated as to what side to take in the event of a Franco-German conflict, but that she seemed inclined to lean towards Germany. Wilson added that if France were the first to violate Belgian neutrality the Belgian army would certainly march with the Germans, and the British government might then be called upon to defend Belgian neutrality. Such a situation might embarass the British government, and General Wilson concluded, "It is, therefore, not in the interests of France to be the first to violate Belgian neutrality".[1]

As French military policy depended on government policy, Joffre and the General Staff had no alternative but to make other plans. Joffre had already foreseen the German plan of encirclement, but he had no idea of the real strength of the German right wing. This failure to appreciate the numerical strength of the right wing was an error of judgment that precipitated the defeat of the French forces in Belgium.

[1] Joffre, Mémoires, Paris, 1932, I, 126.

Joffre had to count on the contribution made by the Belgian army, but military co-operation between the French and Belgian forces had been carefully avoided before 1914 to avoid provoking Germany. It proved extremely difficult to establish that co-operation in a few days. Neither army was prepared for it; no effective liaison did in fact exist between the 4th and 17th August.

Joffre decided "to bring the combined forces to bear upon the point of the German attack", but uncertainty reigned during the early days of the battle; the French army, while seeking to fathom the enemy's manoeuvre, did not get beyond the Meuse.

Joffre considered that the Belgian army could challenge the crossing of the Meuse and thus gain precious time for allied co-operation. If this co-operation could be achieved within a useful period the Belgians would seize an occasion to assault the enemy's flank as it proceeded to the attack of the Franco-British forces. If the Germans proved too strong to allow of this manoeuvre the Belgian army would have to retreat towards Namur, and link up with the left flank of the Franco-British armies.[2]

General Galet has referred to the difference of opinion between the French and the Belgians. Theoretically, and according to the orders conveyed by Colonel Bricard, the Belgian forces were to challenge the Germans to the north of the Sambre and the Meuse.

(But) the Belgian army had already begun to retreat towards the fortress of Antwerp, and it was doubtful whether it could receive sufficient reinforcements from the Allies to enable it to stand up against the enemy.

(From a practical point of view, and after a perusal of the relevant documents) it was evident that no allied reinforcements were in a position to assist us in sufficient strength and in time to enable us to bar the way to the German offensive. The certainty of this disposed of our indecision. Since the Belgian army was isolated we had to persevere in our resolve to retreat towards the fortress.[3]

In fact, Franco-Belgian military co-operation lasted only a short while. General Foch who was responsible for this stated that effective co-operation did exist later at the time of the battle of Flanders (4th October 1914 to April 1915).

A very close unity of command would have been necessary to enable us to see the true position of this difficult battle as a whole; secondly, an active liaison between the unit commanders was essential; and lastly, there should have been a

[2] Joffre, op. cit., I, 245.
[3] Galet, S. M. le roi Albert, Paris, 1931, p. 155.

noticeable spirit of solidarity, an unforgettable brotherhood of arms which would have created a solid bond of friendship between the allied nations for a long time to come. The allied leaders saw each other frequently during the course of the day, but also at the end of the day to keep abreast of each other's activities and prepare the orders for the following day.[4]

That state of affairs, says Joffre, did not exist in August 1914.

The war surprised the Belgian army in the middle of reorganization: it lacked personnel. General de Selliers, the new Chief of General Staff, had but recently been in command of the gendarmes. Belgian public opinion loudly expressed its indignation at the German attitude and its lively sympathies for us. It seems likely that the Belgian government, extremely anxious to preserve its independence, endeavoured to satisfy national feelings; but the military problem that suddenly presented itself was a source of concern, and it seemed that the Belgian army already turned its eyes towards the fortress of Antwerp to which it would retire if Liège fell.[5]

Joffre sent Lieutenant Colonel Brécard to Brussels "to draw the Belgian government's attention to the importance of determining the strength of the German forces on Belgium's eastern frontier, of strongly safeguarding all roads to the Meuse, and establishing co-operation between the Belgian cavalry and the movements of our own cavalry units in the northern region of Neufchâteau".[6]

Brécard's mission brought forth very meagre results. On the 17th August the German right wing rolled back a French cavalry unit, and thrust the Belgian army well back before it. King Albert concluded that he could get no direct support from the Allies, and decided to retire all the Belgian forces behind the fortification at Antwerp. During that period the King experienced some painful moments; he wondered whether it would not be in the interests of Belgium to retain some kind of neutrality in the Franco-German conflict. He wondered whether he might halt at Antwerp without rejoining the Allies, and he settled in a castle situated at some distance from the town between the German and Belgian armies.[7] Queen Elizabeth and de Broqueville, the Prime Minister, persuaded the King that they were convinced Belgium's

---

[4] Foch, *Mémoires pour servir à l'histoire de la guerre, 1914–18*, Paris, 1930, p. 239.
[5] Joffre, *Mémoires*, Paris, 1932, p. 244.
[6] *Les armées françaises* (War Ministry), Paris, 1922, I, 128.
[7] On the 10th August, after the German army had occupied Liège, Germany offered Belgium an amicable settlement. After the battle of the Marne new peace proposals were transmitted to Antwerp by Woeste, leader of the Catholic party. See Wullus–Rudiger — *La Belgique et la crise européenne*, Villeneuve sur Lot, 1942, p. 76.

interests lay in throwing in her lot with the Allies. They pleaded with the King until they persuaded him by the force of their arguments; henceforward he was a loyal and distinguished partner of the Allies.

On the 25th August the sorties from Antwerp made by the Belgian troops confirmed the position taken up by King Albert, and thus the state of war between Germany and Belgium was finally established.

2. Franco-British Military Co-operation

Franco-British military co-operation was just as difficult throughout 1914. The principles underlying this co-operation had been discussed and accepted before the war, but their practical application introduced many difficulties. In any case, the views of the British government and those of its general staff were not identical. The generals, for obvious tactical reasons, wished to submit to the command of the French General Staff, and General Haig went so far as to ask Lord Kitchener, the Minister for War, for authority to submit to Joffre's orders. But Lord Kitchener was anxious to preserve the independence of the British army, and made his position clear in a letter to General French on the 1st September 1914, when planning the route of the Expeditionary Force. He said that the British forces would remain on the line of battle and fall in with the movements of the French army, but would act with prudence and avoid leaving its flanks uncovered.[8] This directive was the cause of many instances of lack of co-operation, some of them serious, especially in the lower commands.

General Foch, who was responsible for British, French and Belgian co-ordination, affirmed that co-operation did exist, and was even fairly good; but one cannot overlook the report made by General French himself on the conduct of the Battle of Mons. He wrote to Lord Kitchener on the 25th August that he was not generously treated by the French command which allowed his retreat to be hampered by considerable enemy forces.

It is fair to add that General French was a mediocre leader with a cantankerous disposition. He had been chosen as commander of the Expeditionary Force on account of his seniority and for having courageously commanded a cavalry unit in the Boer War. He was a fine and valorous leader, but he was soon outpaced by events, and, generally

[8] Huguet, L'intervention militaire britanique en 1914, Paris, 1926, p. 103.

speaking, his relations with the French generals proved difficult. From August 1914 onwards his colleagues Wilson and Haig (the latter became his successor) made commendable attempts to reconcile the French and English points of view, and to establish a measure of co-operation between the two armies.

The French were just as responsible as the English for that absence of co-ordination, for both sides lacked the necessary goodwill towards practical collaboration. Both governments were aware of the deficiency, and Poincaré discussed it with Kitchener at Dunkirk on the 1st November:

> Lord Kitchener came to the rendezvous as arranged. He was a tall man, with a determined face and lively, piercing eyes, and a finely chiselled brow. His nose was a little short and slightly turned up at the end, and his thick moustache curled upwards. He had a strong clean-shaven chin. He was dressed in the khaki uniform of a general, and entered without any pomp and ceremony, but rather with a cordial simplicity . . .
>
> 'I am afraid,' he admitted without beating about the bush, 'that the British army, as yet far too small, might weaken under such a hammering. We count on you to support us.'
>
> Joffre told us that the English had, in fact, just yielded a little ground. They are very brave; but after they have been fighting two or three days they are relieved, and the enemy takes advantage of this to redouble his efforts. General Foch, who also came to Dunkirk to confer with Kitchener and ourselves, complained of the same thing.[9]

The Battle of Flanders, which followed the Battle of the Marne, provided an opportunity for the English and French to profit from their experiences. Together they established a better co-ordination between the three allied forces. General Foch, Deputy Commander-in-Chief, was made responsible for this. It was an unpretentious and sketchy attempt to establish that unity of command which was not to be perfected until 1918, again under Foch.

3. Defeat at Charleroi

The left wing of the French army engaged in Belgium gradually lost touch with the Meuse, and reached the Sambre on the 21st August 1914. It was buttressed by the British army on its left. The second German army un dervon Bülow decided to attack Lanrezac's Fifth Army on both sides of Charleroi. At the same time von Klück's First Army attacked the Expeditionary Force under General French. Von Bülow, by a clever manoeuvre at the very beginning of the battle, cut the French off from

[9] Poincaré, *Au service de la France*, Paris, 1926, V, 407.

the British. General Lanrezac had orders to deliver an attack across the Sambre against an enemy whom Joffre considered numerically inferior. He allowed himself to be ensnared, however, by von Bülow's manoeuvre, which threatened to outflank him on both wings on the Meuse and on the Sambre. That day General Joffre's hope of throwing the Germans back towards the North Sea vanished, and Lanrezac had to beat a retreat with heavy losses. At the same time General French folded up before the onslaught of von Klück.

It was then that Joffre showed his true character. Without allowing himself to be upset by defeat he calmly examined the causes of the set-back in order to learn lessons from them. At the same time he made whatever decisions the situation imposed upon him.

However painful it may be to reveal certain weaknesses, it is incumbent upon me to state fully how things appeared to us then. Too many of our generals proved inferior to the task when put to the trial. In time of peace some of them had acquired a most brillant reputation as teachers and tacticians over a map, but in the face of the enemy they were dominated by the fear of responsibility. My attention was drawn to an utter lack of command in certain large units. I asked to be informed as a matter of urgency the names of all the generals who had not proved to be up to standard. As reports came in to me I examined every case; I then placed at the disposal of the ministry all commanders who in my opinion deserved to be relieved, and I appointed in their places those who appeared most worthy. But faulty leadership in a certain number of units was obviously not altogether responsible for our reverses. It was clear that the principles of attack which we had tried to inculcate into the army before the war had too often been inadequately understood, and badly put into effect. From every point along the front my attention was drawn to tactical errors which had entailed heavy losses, and sometimes nullified the offensive and defensive value of a unit. I was informed that more often than not advance parties joined battle without a real understanding of what an offensive meant and without the support of artillery, so that they fell in mass formation under the blows of enemy artillery. On other occasions a large unit would advance without safeguarding its flanks, thereby suddenly exposing itself to bitter attack. The infantry was almost always pushed into an attack at too great a distance from its objective. Points captured were never consolidated before an attempt was made to win a new objective; so that if the latter attack failed and the troops fell back they even lost the fruit of their first efforts. Above all, co-operation between artillery and infantry was hardly ever achieved. As soon as I appreciated these factors I gave instructions that the armies should organize their attacks prudently, and take the greatest care to ensure liaison between units.[10]

The lesson drawn at the height of battle through the sangfroid of this man who remained completely master of the situation, was un-doubtedly one of the most extraordinary factors of the first world war.

[10] Joffre, *Mémoires*. Paris, 1932, p. 290.

The only criticism of the measures taken by Joffre at the time of the Charleroi defeat came from General Lanrezac, the commander mainly responsible. This general expressed his doubts as to the value of the preparations made, the tactical merits of the operation generally, the absence of liaison, and deplored the chaotic nature of the action. In short, he criticized everything except the command of the 5th Army; but his criticism was too harsh and too personal to be of any real value.[11]

Later, however, Joffre told Minister Loucheur:

Lanrezac became weighed down by the burden of his responsibilities after Charleroi . . . At the time of the Battle of the Marne, when I realized how depressed he had again become, I went to see him, and we both came to an amicable agreement that he could no longer maintain command of his army. A few minutes earlier he had been visibly agitated, but his face immediately assumed a tranquil and contented appearance. On arriving in Bordeaux to report to Millerand who was then Minister for War, he met General Gouraud in the waiting room, and said to him, 'Joffre has replaced me, and he was quite right to do so'. He said the same thing to Millerand.[12]

Later on Lanrezac happened to come into contact with a number of politicians, and the story gradually got around that he had been unjustly made a scapegoat. The criticisms of Lanrezac do not appear to have withstood the test of time. He may even have warned Joffre of some of Bülow's military plans, which the Chief of Staff ignored! On the other hand Lanrezac's enemies were mistaken when they accused him of carrying out a premature retreat.[13]

Joffre's errors rested in particular in his appraisement of the enemy's strength and tactics. But the way in which the Commander-in-Chief succeeded in keeping his armies together to effect an orderly retreat, waging arduous delaying battles as far as the Marne, was certainly a military feat of exceptional merit.

4. Moltke and the Battle of the Marne

To control the operations of the German armies von Moltke estab-lished his headquarters at Luxemburg.

He was of a gloomy disposition and very critical of himself. His health was not perfect, and he disliked constant changes. By nature he was an artist, both a painter and a musician, and was on good terms

[11] Lanrezac, Le plan de campagne français et le premier mois de la guerre, Paris, 1920.

[12] Loucheur, Carnets secrets, Brussels, 1962, p. 135.

[13] Lardemelle, 1914, le redressement initial Paris, 1936, and J. Isaac — Joffre et Lanrezac, Paris, 1922.

with the scholarly Conrad; but he feared intrigue. His bedside book
was Faust, and he was writing a translation of Maeterlinck's *Pelléas et
Mélisande*. He had lived day and night buried in his austere office on the
Königsplatz in Berlin, and so he shut himself up in the girls' school
which was his new headquarters in Luxemburg, and there he stayed.
Until the 16th August he was happy to have escaped from tiresome
visitors and the bustle of his former headquarters at Coblenz. The radio
station, jammed by the transmitter at the Eiffel Tower, did not function
properly, and the Belgians had cut the telephone cables. These may have
been serious setbacks, quite unforeseen in the original plan, but they did
not seem to bother him excessively. The General had confidence in his
plan — the Schlieffen Plan — so minutely prepared, with nothing left
to chance. Mathematically speaking, the French army would be destroyed
within six months.

Until the 25th August the German plan proceeded perfectly. Indeed,
General von Bülow used it intelligently, but his skilful manoeuvre on
the Sambre did not succeed in destroying the French left wing when
Lanrezac broke off the battle to avoid total disaster. On the 27th August
Moltke gave his generals instructions to pursue the French and British
armies. Von Klück, in command of the 1st Army, was given Pontoise
as an objective. Von Bülow, commanding the 2nd Army, was given
La Fère, and von Hausen (3rd Army), Château-Thierry.

The day was not far distant when the French wing would be
broken. Moltke was so sure of himself that on the 25th August he
withdrew two divisions from his advancing left wing, and sent
them to East Prussia to reinforce the troops trying to hold up the
Russian advance.

Von Klück and von Bülow advanced together. On the 26th August
von Klück succeeded in cutting up the British 1st Corps at Cateau, so
that they disengaged with great difficulty. Three days later he stopped
Lanrezac at Guise, but the latter succeeded once more in breaking off
the battle. When von Klück halted at the Marne he had not managed
to hold the French left wing.

Joffre had not remained inactive. On the 4th August he set up his
general headquarters at Vitry le François, where he remained in close
daily contact with his army commanders. Though he managed to take
his meals and his sleep, and interview tiresome visitors, he would none
the less set off at over a hundred kilometres an hour to the headquarters
of his subordinates. Calm and uncommunicative, he scrupulously
examined the reports that reached him from the whole front, and

questioned his associates at length, including his liaison officers, most of whom were remarkable men.

In the early days of September Joffre appreciated perfectly the opportunity offered him by von Klück's error. Since the 25th August he had been forming a new army — the 6th — with troops held in reserve in Lorraine. He brought this army up to his left wing under the command of Maunoury, so that it faced the flank of von Klück's army. Moltke had issued orders that the French forces were to be pursued in the direction of the south east to avoid the fortified area of Paris. But when von Klück got on the move once more and crossed the Marne on the 4th September, Joffre determined to make a general counter-offensive.

On that day he issued his final instructions: "We must take advantage of the situation of the 1st German Army to bring against it the concentrated pressure of the Allied forces on the extreme left." Joffre's decision was influenced by General Gallieni's suggestion to thrust all available troops before the fortified zone of Paris, to link up in the combined push made by the forces of Maunoury and French, together with the 5th Army recovering from its recent retreat and now commanded by Franchet d'Esperey. This offensive, which became known as the Battle of the Marne, was engaged on the 6th September. By the 9th it had become for the Allies "an undisputed victory".

Von Bülow began his retreat on the same day, followed shortly afterwards by von Klück. The two great German armies on the right wing began to fold back on the Aisne. Moltke underestimated the skill of the French commander. He did not think that the 5th Army and the British Expeditionary Force, beaten and worn out by retreat, would still be in a condition to take part in a counter-offensive. He never suspected that the armies in the fortified district of Paris would be able to play any part in the battle. Neither did he know that Joffre, in the middle of the battle for the frontiers, had built up a new army with troops from Lorraine.

It was only on the 4th September that von Moltke learned of this movement of troops from Lorraine. Although he took this into account he could not guess that Joffre would attack everywhere at once with numerically superior forces. In fact, Moltke was at fault in trying to follow the course of the battle 230 kilometres away at his general headquarters in the school. He had given Lieutenant-Colonel Hentsch the care of ensuring personal liaison with von Klück and von Bülow, and allowed his two generals a free hand, relying on Hentsch to make the necessary decisions to ensure co-ordination.

During the evening of the 8th September von Bülow discussed with Hentsch the possibility of an attack in the rear. "In that case," Hentsch said to von Bülow, "retreat would be unavoidable". And at 1 p.m. on the 9th von Bülow gave the order to retreat. At first von Klück hesitated; but in the afternoon he too carried out the order given him by Hentsch to fall back.

Could the German generals have done anything else but retreat? And did Hentsch, as some German historians have said, give the order too early? The German generals themselves did not think so. According to General von Kühl[14], "the commander of the 1st Army (von Klück) executed immediately Hentsch's order to retreat because he had no other choice." Von Klück endorsed that point of view. Von Bülow, though less precise, did not go back on the decision once it had been taken.[15] Lieutenant-Colonel Hentsch claimed that he set out from Luxemburg with full authority to order a retreat *in case of necessity*. Hentsch was a most courageous officer, but he suffered from a deep-seated pessimism. Some witnesses have said that he set off in excellent spirits; others claim that he exceeded his instructions by ordering a withdrawal after it had been decided to hold on at all costs. It is impossible to decide between these two conflicting theories. In any case, Hentsch had received no written instructions, and he did what he considered best. By the time he had returned to Luxemburg at 1.40 p.m. on the 10th September to make his report it was all over.

General von Moltke was too sure of himself; he neglected to safeguard his communications, and committed serious errors of judgement on the eve of the Battle of the Marne. Skilfully organized, and engaged at the right moment by Joffre, the battle was a victory for the French General Staff. Joffre had been compelled to reject his plan (Plan XVII) after the Battle of Charleroi, but Moltke had to abandon his Schlieffen Plan before the river Marne; and when the two Commanders-in-Chief were left to improvise on the field of battle, success went to the one who displayed the greatest military skill.

[14] General von Kühl, von Klück's Chief of Staff, in *Der Marsch auf Paris und die Schlacht am Ourcq, 1914*, Berlin, 1919.
[15] *Mein Bericht zur Marneschlacht*, Berlin, 1919, by General von Bülow. See also W. Muller–Loebnitz's study on Lieutenant-Colonel Hentsch's mission, and *Documents allemands sur la bataille de la Marne*, by L. Koeltz, Paris, 1930.

CHAPTER V

THE WAR OF ATTRITION

1. What was the nature of the quarrel between Falkenhayn and Conrad?
2. Was the role of the military leaders in Germany decisive?

1. Verdun

At the beginning of 1916 the military forces of both belligerents stood more or less equal. Each side was too powerful to allow the other a speedy victory, and too weak to undertake a decisive operation. Each determined to try to wear the other down in a war of attrition, in the hope of changing the balance of strength.

Falkenhayn decided to bring his forces to bear on Verdun, without allowing the forces of the Entente the opportunity to organize the offensive they contemplated. Almost without interruption, from the 21st February until the 30th June, 1916, an immense battle developed around Verdun. Enormous forces were engaged on both sides; more than 56 German divisions and more than 52 French divisions passed through Verdun — nearly three million men. When the battle was over half a million men had been slain: 240,000 Germans and 275,000 Frenchmen.

It is impossible to say what the Germans really aimed at in launching their massive attack. German military historians are of the opinion that the purpose was to destroy sufficient French troops in that sector to weaken the front as a whole; not to make a break-through, but to carry out an encircling operation. On the other hand, French military historians suggest that the Germans really did their utmost to break through, but failed. These opposing views, each firmly supported by documents, may never be clarified; witnesses have failed to bring any conclusive evidence to bear upon the problem. What has been established is that the Germans did not attain their objective, whether it was break-through or attrition.

Joffre had no wish to allow the Germans to gain the initiative, and from the 1st July to the 30th September 1916, he replied with another battle of attrition which developed along the Somme front. That battle did not result in a break-through, and the Germans regarded it as a defeat for the Allies. In reality a large part of the German infantry suffered grave losses on the Somme, particularly among the officers. From this point of view it may be said that Joffre achieved a not unimportant part of his objective.

At the end of 1916 both French and Germans decided to replace their Commanders-in-Chief. Joffre gave place to Nivelle. The western Allies were apparently drawing progressively closer in their viewpoints, and were reaching a better understanding of co-ordination. In Germany Hindenburg took over from Falkenhayn, but consultation with Germany's Austro-Hungarian allies was non existent. This fact deserves to be examined in more detail.

2. *The Quarrel between von Falkenhayn and Conrad*

General von Falkenhayn believed, despite the setbacks at the end of 1914 and throughout 1915, that a decision could be reached in the west. General von Hindenburg, Commander-in-Chief of the German forces on the eastern front, did not share this view; neither did his deputy, Colonel Ludendorff. Hindenburg, still basking in glory after his victory at Tannenberg, did not refrain from criticizing Falkenhayn's plans in the presence of William II.

The Commander-in-Chief refused to give Hindenburg the troops he asked for to "crush" the Russian army; he did not think Hindenburg's plan was the right one to defeat the Russians, who always managed to wriggle skilfully out of his encircling manoeuvres. The result was a somewhat lively animosity between the two generals, and the Emperor, thinking Hindenburg was in the right, was inclined to support his views. Furthermore, Falkenhayn had been receiving numerous appeals for reinforcements from Conrad, the Austro-Hungarian Chief of Staff.

The Austro–Hungarian army won some brilliant successes in the east during 1915, and Conrad considered that the moment had come to bring his efforts to bear in the west, in order to crush the Italian army by the spring of 1916. The Austro-Hungarian commanders were eager to settle a debt of honour with their former Italian ally for its defection to the enemy. Without informing Falkenhayn of the details of his

preparations Conrad withdrew his best units from the eastern front
and concentrated them upon the Italian front. The truth was that Conrad
had no wish to be deflected from his objective by Falkenhayn.
General von Cramon, German liaison officer with the Austro-
Hungarian general headquarters, has since written:

> The two Chiefs of Staff preferred to discuss matters alone, so that the essential
> points of their discussion might not be set down in writing. Furthermore, their
> viewpoints were frequently at variance. These hitches often left one or the other
> with the rather unpleasant impression that their misunderstandings were deliberate
> and not the result of an unfortunate accident. Doubt took root in both their minds,
> and the impression developed that neither had any intention of keeping his word.
> Falkenhayn and Conrad were by nature quite opposite, and their relations lacked
> that touch of mutual understanding that tends to smooth out difficulties."[1]

Falkenhayn was a brisk, dynamic man, and he reasoned rapidly while
ceaselessly sucking a cigar. Conrad was small, slender and refined;
his mouth and eyelid twitched nervously. He liked to take time to
think before reaching a decision. The one conveyed his orders in short,
precise directions; the other drafted long, diligently prepared instructions.

> 'On his own admission,' says 'Cramon,[2] 'Conrad was not made to keep pace
> with Falkenhayn in debate. He therefore gave up expressing his opinions in a
> wordy battle, and waited until he could eventually elucidate his ideas with the
> aid of written notes. Falkenhayn relied on what had been said verbally, and was
> very surprised when a matter settled in conversation reached him again in writing
> and in what appeared to him to be a different form. This gave rise to more dis-
> cussions of a subject assumed to have been agreed upon between them; thus in
> the minds of one or other of the two there gradually developed a really quite
> unjustifiable doubt concerning the good faith of the other.'

The two men were not made to agree. Differences of opinion had
arisen several times in the autumn of 1915 during the Serbian campaign.
On Christmas Eve of that year their personal relations were more or
less broken for a month, and Falkenhayn demanded apologies from
Conrad following a misunderstanding. The Austrian Chief of Staff
decided on the 23rd January 1916 to write a letter of apology to his
German colleague; this improved the atmosphere without obliterating
the effects of wounded pride.
Conrad took advantage of the position to refer once more to his
scheme for an offensive against Italy, and Falkenhayn rejected it as
inopportune. Conrad therefore determined to attack Italy with his

[1] Von Cramon, *Quatre ans aux G. Q. G. austro-hongrois*, Paris, 1922, p. 48.
[2] *Ibid.*

own forces without informing Falkenhayn. In the spring of 1916 these disputes resulted in a paradoxical situation. Falkenhayn was preparing for the great battle of Verdun, and he left Hindenburg but a minimum of troops with which to "force a decision" in the east. Conrad, who was preparing his offensive against the Italian army without having informed Falkenhayn, diverted from the eastern front forces which would have been able to support the manoeuvres of Hindenburg in the south. The two Commanders-in-Chief proceeded without effective co-operation because they distrusted each other. Thus, despite the initial successes at Verdun and Asiago both soon paid dearly for their discord. Their forces were scattered in two directions, rendering them incapable of gaining the victory which concentration would probably have achieved.

The Austrian front broke down in June 1916 before the Russian offensive under Brusilov, and it was only the German counter-attacks under Hindenburg that prevented catastrophe.

3. The Rise of the Dioscuri

In August 1916 William II took an inevitable decision: he dismissed the unfortunate Falkenhayn and placed Hindenburg in command of the army. The Emperor himself was in supreme command in Germany. In the words of Ludendorff,

His Majesty the Emperor was Commander-in-Chief. Supreme power of command over the army and navy rested with him, and all commanders were subordinate to him. The chief of general staff of the army in the field conducted military operations according to the will of His Majesty. In putting plans into execution he remained absolutely independent. No important decisions could be taken without His Majesty's approval. The chief of staff of the army in the field was therefore not invested with absolute authority of command.

The naval chief of general staff, as representing the conduct of the war at sea, was on an equal footing with the military chief of staff. In so far as the war at sea was concerned he had the same rights and duties, and collaboration between the two commanders was always excellent.

The governors general of Brussels and Warsaw were also under the immediate orders of the Emperor, and were subordinate to the Imperial Chancellor. In military matters they fell in with the wishes of general headquarters. The remainder of the occupied territories were under the authority of the Commander-in-Chief (Ludendorff), and therefore of general headquarters. Throughout all these territories the real master was the Commander-in-Chief, the Emperor.

But Ludendorff added:

General headquarters and the Imperial Chancellor were considered as equals. Here again the head that united them was His Majesty. Our contacts with the

Imperial government soon became frequent, and not always pleasant. We did not meet with the eager co-operation we anticipated when we informed the government what the military leaders expected to enable the German people to achieve victory.[3]

When the Kaiser settled the dispute between the politicians and the military in favour of Hindenburg and his loyal associate Ludendorff, he indicated the importance he attached to military leadership. He desired to concentrate into the hands of the "technicians of war" all the means necessary to the conduct of war. In calling upon the services of Hindenburg the Emperor was offering the glorious conqueror of Tannenberg the chance to achieve unity of command in the east and west, a unity which his predecessors had never been able to cement effectually. Furthermore, the Emperor considered that Hindenburg better than anyone else, after having so brilliantly relieved the Austro-Hungarian forces, could create a single inter-allied command to direct the armies of the Central Powers.

Military prestige thus strengthened was faced with a diminished political influence. Chancellor Bethmann Hollweg had to cope with an ever-growing Socialist opposition. Before approving the war estimates the Socialist leaders of the Reichstag required precise details as to the aims of the war, and they opposed the annexationist schemes of the Conservatives. The Chancellor was obliged to depend upon those Socialist elements who were less remote from the Conservative element, and thus incline his policy of national unity towards the centre. Bethmann Hollweg was compelled to yield in words what he wished to withhold in fact; that is to say, a reform of the legislative power. In this parliamentary contest the Chancellor was rarely sustained by the Emperor, whose aim was to avoid anything that might diminish the prerogative of the army.

Within a few months, therefore, Hindenburg and Ludendorff acquired a power without precedent, and the argument over submarine warfare became the occasion of a decisive struggle between civil and military influence.

In February 1916, when unrestricted submarine warfare was about to begin, the Chancellor protested against it. He asked for a few weeks' delay until the beginning of April to give him time for a further attempt to modify the attitude of the United States of America. It was pointed out to him that, considering the United States attitude at the time, nothing could be expected from negotiations,

[3] Ludendorff, *Kriegserinnerungen*, Berlin, 1919, p. 203.

and that there could be no more favourable opportunity to bring the submarines into action than during the period of excitement preceding the American Presidential election. Bethmann was still not convinced; not even by a fear that delay might prejudice the very outcome of submarine warfare.[4]

In the summer of 1916 German and military technicians expressed their conviction that all-out submarine warfare must break down British resistance. If the operation were to succeed it had to commence not later than the 1st February 1917, in order to defeat England within six months.

Chancellor Bethmann Hollweg and Helfriech, Secretary of State for the Interior, fiercely discussed the military proposals. Had not the Allies already a reply to a submarine offensive? Was it not possible that the resistance of the British population might be accentuated rather than destroyed by the pangs of hunger? Could the risk of American intervention be taken lightly?

The army and naval commanders were certain of victory. At his supreme headquarters in Pless on the eastern front the Emperor himself settled the dispute between the politicians and the military leaders on the 9th January 1917.

Chancellor Bethmann Hollweg wrote of the meeting,

I joined the Emperor in the evening of the 9th January to take part in the conference. At the beginning the atmosphere in general was as heavy as it had been during my interview in the morning with the military supreme command. I had the impression of being in the presence of people who were determined not to tolerate any opposition to decisions already taken ... The naval general staff and the military chiefs put forward their demands. I stated that I could not doubt the opinion of the military that war waged on land alone would not end in success. But I added that, in my opinion, the outcome of submarine warfare might well prove a failure; that if we did not achieve the success anticipated we were threatened with the worst possible outcome of the war; that I was convinced the aid eventually given to the Allies by America would outweigh the efforts made by supreme military headquarters. I added that in view of the Allies' reply to our peace offer there seemed little hope at present of peaceful negotiations. I ended by saying that, faced with this situation and the declaration made by Field Marshal von Hindenburg (who was well aware of his responsibilities) to the effect that our military situation permitted us to take upon ourselves the risk of an imminent break with America, I could not advise His Majesty to oppose the views of his military advisers. Thereupon the decision was taken. After about half-an-hour the conference, which no longer had the character of a discussion, came to an end. On the following day the supreme military command requested the Emperor to replace the Chancellor.[5]

[4] Falkenhayn, *Die oberste Heersleitung, 1914–16*, Berlin, 1920, p. 169.
[5] Bethmann Hollweg, *Betrachtungen zum Weltkriege*, Berlin, 1923, p. 256.

Admiral von Capelle, in command of the navy and a friend of the Chancellor, expressed his conviction that total submarine warfare would decide the issue of the war within six months.[6] Ludendorff detailed military reasons in support of the principle, and recalled that the Chancellor eventually expressed his agreement.

The Chancellor's appreciation of the political and military situation was exactly the same as ours. While we were expecting him to draw, with calm precision, the harsh but inevitable conclusion, the Chancellor, true to his character, hesitated. He ended more or less with these words: 'The decision to conduct all-out submarine warfare depends therefore on the results we hope to gain from it; but if the military commanders regard submarine warfare as necessary, I am not in a position to contradict them'.[7]

In short, the Emperor, the Chancellor and the Chief of Staff all accepted the principle of submarine warfare. But the rallying of the Chancellor to the attitude adopted by the military leaders marked an important stage in the development of civil and military influence in Germany. On the 9th January 1917 William II signed the order for all-out submarine warfare. It sealed the capitulation of the political power, for military dictatorship began to dominate events more definitely every day. The Dioscuri were to insist upon unreasonable annexations of territory, inspire and lose a cruel and useless war, and organize in the occupied countries a system of oppression and deportation destined to mobilize world opinion against Germany.

When the military leaders wriggled successfully out of their venture in October 1918, they left the political power at grips with a collapse without precedent in the history of Germany.

[6] Ludendorff, *Kriegserinnerungen*, Berlin, 1919, p. 344.
[7] *Ibid.*, p. 347.

THE CONFUSION OF 1917

1. Was submarine warfare the deciding factor in bringing America into the war?
2. What part did Painlevé play in the 1917 crisis in the French command?
3. What was the significance of the suppression of the mutinies on the French front?
4. Was the failure of the Bourbon–Parma mission due entirely to demands on the part of Italy?

By the end of 1916 neither the Allies nor the Central Powers had won a decisive victory. As in 1915, the opposing forces had achieved a certain balance without the slightest hope of improvement. But in two countries there were ominous signs of collapse: Austria-Hungary longed for peace, and revolution was gnawing at Russia.

The Dioscuri strove to effect a break-through, but without returning to an offensive on land which was undoubtedly doomed to failure. They based their plans on submarine warfare and reorganization of the rear. The French General Staff made preparations for a new offensive, but felt uneasy about the spread of revolution in Russia. In 1917 their great eastern ally retired from the war; at the same time movements that were more or less revolutionary developed in the western countries.

1. The Causes of American Intervention

The entry of America into the war, announced by President Wilson on the 2nd April 1917, compensated for the defection of Russia. Historians have argued at great length to discover the real causes of this intervention.

Bethmann Hollweg considered that American neutrality was due entirely to Anglo-American rivalry, and Ludendorff thought that America had made its choice long before. Lansing, the American Secretary of State, wrote that the entry of the United States into the war was simply the outcome of a long process of events.

Although American public opinion clung to isolationism (the Monroe doctrine) and was extremely anxious to preserve neutrality, the United States did in fact intervene very actively in the European conflict. Exports to the Allies amounted to 924 million dollars in 1914; they rose to 1991 millions in 1915, and 3214 millions in 1916; whereas exports to the Central Powers stood at 169 million dollars in 1914, 11 millions in 1915, and 1159 millions in 1916.[1] As Duroselle observed, the sea belonged to the British, therefore commerce was carried on with the Allies.

Moreover, the Morgan Bank, duly authorized by the American government, agreed in November 1914 to lend the French government 450 million dollars. On the 25th September 1915 the same Bank formed a syndicate to float a loan of 500 million dollars to France and Great Britain. Altogether, in April 1917 the United States lent 2300 million dollars to the Allies and 27 millions to Germany. These facts were known by Germany, and no doubt influenced her decision on the 9th January 1917 to conduct an all-out submarine warfare.

The German objective was to destroy 600,000 tons of allied and neutral merchant shipping a month; this theoretically should drive the Allies into capitulating within six months. The measure involved the danger of letting loose American intervention; but the German military leaders were sure of themselves and convinced that the success of the operation would nullify the risk.

Of course, the Germans calculated wrongly, for American action was swifter than had been foreseen. The United States government was notified of the German decision on the 31st January. Wilson summoned his associates to the White House on the 1st and 2nd February, and presented them with a dramatic view of the situation: freedom of the seas and freedom of trade were seriously affected, and the steps taken by Germany aimed at the destruction of the very foundations of democracy.

Lansing was instructed to prepare for the breaking off of diplomatic relations with Germany, and this became effective on the 3rd February. The decision had the sympathy of the President's closest colleagues. Ever since 1914 Lansing had regarded war between Germany and the United States as inevitable, because of the fundamental contrast between autocracy and democracy; he considered that peace and civilization

---

[1] According to Duroselle (De Wilson à Roosevelt, Paris, 1960); these figures are quoted by Bailey.

depended upon the setting up of democratic institutions throughout the world. House, after several unfortunate contacts with Berlin, had eventually taken his stand with the western powers.

Wilson made it clear to the Senate on the 3rd February that "effective action" might oblige the United States to enter the war; and a number of committees were formed to convince public opinion of the need for a "crusade of democracies". It is also probable that the Banks, anxious to ensure the repayment of the loans they had made to the Allies, and the business men who were interested in maintaining trade with the Allies, took part in this "crusade". It is quite certain, however that these various groups did not bring pressure to bear on Wilson to secure United States entry into the war. The President fulfilled his lofty purpose with an almost mystical sense of moral probity, and there is no evidence whatever to suggest that his decision to take such a grave step was influenced by financial circles committed to the Allies.

On the other hand, American public opinion developed quickly between the 3rd February and the 2nd April 1917. It recognized the danger of accepting Germany's dominion of the sea. America reacted sharply when it became known on the 27th February that two Americans had lost their lives in the sinking of the British ship *Laconia*, that the cargo boat *Algonquin* had been torpedoed without warning on the 12th March, and that three other American ships had been torpedoed on the 19th March. Ships along the eastern coast of America refused to load cargoes; there was an outcry among Middle West farmers and manufacturers who complained of the effects of German submarine warfare.

On the 24th February the British ambassador in Washington handed Secretary of State Lansing a copy of a confidential telegram which the German Secretary of State for Foreign Affairs had sent to the German ambassador in Mexico:

> Zimmermann to Eckhardt — Mexico: 16 January 1917: No. 1658. On 1st February we commence all-out submarine warfare. We shall endeavour to keep the United States neutral . . . In case of failure we shall offer an alliance to Mexico.
> Signed: Zimmermann.

This mysterious telegram was deciphered by the Intelligence Department. The German code had been stolen from the Kommandatur in Brussels (in the Rue de la Loi) by a young engineer named Alexander Szek. He sent it to London on the 15th August 1915 through Major Oppenheim, Deputy Head of the Intelligence Department at The Hague.

This telegram was followed in a very short time by a number of others which managed to reach the State Department.

Taking advantage of the tension that existed between Mexico and the United States, the Germans wished to draw Mexico into war with the United States. Eckhardt offered Mexico the return of Texas, Arizona and New Mexico. Germany even went so far as to hope that Japan would become associated with this anti-American endeavour. Shortly afterwards, however (on the 14th April), Mexico declined the German proposals.

President Wilson was indignant. On the 1st March he decided to communicate the text of the telegram to the Associated Press.[2] This gave rise to a violent reaction of public opinion, and when the President asked Congress on the 2nd April to declare war on Germany, he obtained an almost unanimous vote.

2. Crisis in the French Command

The French General Staff planned an important offensive on the western front to begin in the spring of 1917, and the British agreed in principle. But the Germans, thanks to a skilful strategical manoeuvre worked out by the Dioscuri, carried out a retreat of fifteen to forty kilometres along the whole front during the period 25th February to 4th April, and s ettled down at a prepared base — the Siegfried Line.

General Nivelle succeeded Joffre; the latter had been made the scapegoat of the government who blamed him for the comparative failure of the Battle of the Somme. Despite very strong criticism Nivelle determined to adhere to his plan for an offensive.

Marshal Haig, the British Commander-in-Chief, considered — and stated frankly — that the offensive was difficult and doomed to fialure because it had to be conducted over a scorched earth zone. Nivelle referred the matter to Briand, President of the Council, so that Haig might be induced to co-operate. Two top level Franco-British conferences in Calais and London were necessary before the British government could persuade Haig to associate himself with the Nivelle plan; but this effectively resolved the problem of a single command for the duration of the offensive.

[2] The publication of the telegram caused the Germans to enquire into the origin of the indiscretion. The British government announced through the *Daily Mail* that the telegram had been stolen from a safe in the German Embassy in Mexico.

Moreover, Nivelle's colleagues who had submitted gracefully to Joffre were not reluctant to express strong criticism of their new leader. When this came to the ears of Painlevé, the new Minister for War, he went to see the Commander-in-Chief and discussed the matter: he tried to persuade Nivelle to postpone putting his plan into effect. When the commander refused Painlevé decided to consult the army commanders one after another, and they all re-affirmed their scepticism.

The fact that Painlevé had consulted the commanders placed him in a difficult position; he might have dared to uphold the views of the senior officers, but he could hardly risk the consequent dismissal of the Commander-in-Chief, as this would bring about the fall of the Cabinet. He decided to compromise by putting forward a formula for a limited offensive. Quite rightly this was turned down by Nivelle. All that remained to Painlevé was to break the resistance of the Commander-in-Chief. He pictured an incredible masquerade during the course of which Poincaré, President of the Republic, Ribot, President of the Council, Thomas, Minister of Munitions, and Painlevé himself as Minister for War, would confront Nivelle in the presence of his army group commanders, Micheler, Pétain, Franchet d'Esperey and Castelnau.[3] The meeting took place at Compiègne on the 6th April. Discussion was lively, and Nivelle even offered to resign. At first Painlevé was unbending, but gradually he became more conciliatory. Micheler's approval of the plan broke down Pétain's hesitations, and it was decided to go through with Nivelle's plan. The main result of this deplorable performance in which a Commander-in-Chief was interrogated, criticized and censured by his subordinates was a loss of confidence on the part of the generals in their leader.

The offensive was launched on the 9th April, and by the 5th May it had become a complete failure. On the 11th Nivelle's post was taken over by Pétain.

3. Mutiny on the French Front

The failure of Nivelle's offensive had serious consequences because of the disillusionment it occasioned among the rank and file. The victorious progress they had been promised was limited to an advance of a few kilometres, and entailed losses which, though not considerable, were none the less unnecessary.

[3] On the suggestion of Albert Thomas.

Two regiments stationed at Chemin des Dames mutinied on the 20th
May. When they were ordered to return to the line after a few days' rest,
the men told their officers they would not return. This refusal to march
spread like an epidemic. Within three weeks a number of regiments
had decided to obey no more orders. The military command faced a
difficult situation: if the mutiny was allowed to spread the officers ran
the risk of no longer being able to rely on their troops. In Soissons some
groups of soldiers even talked of marching on Paris.

At about the same time a strike movement developed in the munition
factories behind the line. In May and June 100,000 workers left work
in the Paris district, and the Federation of Metalworkers gave the movement a revolutionary character.

The Painlevé government had a choice of two methods of dealing
with the situation: force or conciliation. On the advice of Loucheur,
Minister of Munitions, and Malvy, Minister of the Interior, they decided
in favour of conciliation. Loucheur, who was in control of the armament factories, said: "I intend to continue a policy of conciliation with
the workers, but the least I must do if I am to carry out my duty towards
those who are in the trenches is to require that the factory workers do
their duty."[4]

The minister endeavoured to examine the wage claims of the workers
with close attention and goodwill, but took no action against the strikers
or the trade unions. He refused to dissolve the *Confédération Générale du
Travail* and the metalworkers' union, and he did not molest their leaders.
His method succeeded, and by October the revolutionary movement
had died out completely.

On the battle front it fell to General Pétain to take the necessary
counter-measures. He became Commander-in-Chief on the 16th May.
On the 20th the incidents at Chemin des Dames took place, and on
the 22nd the leaders elected representatives to present their protests to
the officers in command. On the 25th May a company in the Vosges
refused to return to the line. On the 26th a mutiny broke out in three
infantry regiments due to return to the line along the Aisne; on the
27th troops from Lorraine demonstrated; on the 28th incidents took
place in eight regiments in the Aisne sector; from the 29th to the
31st May serious troubles arose among eight divisions in the Chemin des Dames area; from the 1st to the 3rd June fifteen units
belonging to sixteen divisions became infected; from the 2nd to the

[4] Loucheur, *Carnets secrets*, Brussels, 1962, p. 45.

10th June seven cases of mutiny a day were reported to general headquarters.

From that date, however, the movement began to decline: one incident occurred daily from the 10th to the 30th June; there were seven in July and four in August. Altogether 151 cases of mutiny were counted, of which 110 were serious cases of collective mutiny — two-thirds in the Aisne sector, near Chemin des Dames.[5]

The Commander-in-Chief could have had recourse to disciplinary measures, but in harmony with the government's requests he decided to resort to the minimum of discipline. Pétain preferred to seek a remedy for the evils that were undermining the morale of the troops. He endeavoured to increase gratuities for good conduct, decorations and leave of absence, and to improve rations; he overcame drunkenness, encouraged thrift, and re-organized the administration of billets. Finally, on the 19th May, he issued a memorandum touching upon the "attitude of commanders with a view to a marked improvement in human relationships between officers and men".

The document stated that "a superior must receive a subordinate in a kindly and friendly manner, show a desire to help him to solve his problems, make use of available information and even instigate enquiries . . . The deadly power of fire in the present war does not allow of experiments. The slightest operation demands the most detailed preparation, to achieve which the goodwill of all is indispensable . . . On the other hand, once the groundwork of a scheme has been well planned, a decision taken and the order given, the execution of that order must be pursued with an energy and determination that permit of no compromise".[6]

From May to October, however, 150 men were condemned to death by court-martials, either for mutiny or refusing to obey orders. As a result of reprieves and appeals to clemency the Commander-in-Chief confirmed only seven immediate executions, and the Head of State granted reprieves to all but forty-eight. These were the figures supplied by Pétain's General Staff headquarters; according to other sources of information no more than twenty-three executions actually took place.

The re-establishment of confidence was undoubtedly due to the attitude adopted by the Painlevé government, the General Staff, and especially by Minister Loucheur and General Pétain.

[5] The above details are given by Laure, Pétain's principal assistant.
[6] Laure, Pétain, Paris, 1941, p. 121.

4. Austrian Overtures for a Separate Peace

On the 26th January 1917 Prince Sixt and Prince Xavier of Bourbon–
Parma were at Neuchâtel, in Switzerland, staying at the house of M.
Boy de la Tour (7 Rue du Pommier). Their mother, the Duchess of Parma,
who was also the Emperor Charles's mother-in-law, told them that
the Emperor wished to see them as soon as possible to talk of peace.
Sixt passed his mother a document in which he had set down what he
considered to be the conditions required to induce the Allies to entertain
the idea of peace.

In my opinion the terms must involve the following sacrifices:[7]
1 — The return of Alsace and Lorraine to France without any compensation
    on the part of France;
2 — The rehabilitation of Belgium;
3 — The restoration of Serbia, enlarged to include Albania;
4 — The handing over of Constantinople to the Russians.

The Princes went to Paris, and Sixt and his colleagues drafted a note
to Poincaré who was very interested in the negotiations. They then
returned to Neuchâtel where Charles had sent Count Thomas Erdödy,
a childhood friend. This gentleman said that the Emperor regarded
a secret Austro-Russian armistice as a basis for peace talks, together
with the return of Alsace-Lorraine to France, the independence of
Belgium and the creation of an autonomous Yugoslav state to include
Bosnia Hercegovina, Serbia, Albania and Montenegro, headed by an
Austrian Archduke, and constituted within the framework of the
Austrian Monarchy.

Sixt drew attention to the need to re-build Serbia and to add to it
Albania, and asked for positive guarantees. For a time no headway
was made. On the 15th February Erdödy left for Vienna, and returned to Neuchâtel on the 21st.

On this occasion he handed the Prince a note from Count Czernin,
Minister for Foreign Affairs, who had been made acquainted with the
negotiations by the Emperor. The note was supplemented by secret
comments from the Emperor, which Sixt tore up and burned after
reading them.[8] This was the first occasion of the disappearance of an
essential document.

On the 5th March Sixt went to Paris where he was received by
Poincaré. He showed Poincaré Czernin's note, and also referred to the

---

[7] P. Amiguet, *La vie du Prince Sixte de Bourbon*, Paris, 1936.
[8] S. de Bourbon, *L'offre de paix séparée de l'Autriche*, Paris, 1920, p. 303.

Emperor's secret comments which he quoted from memory. Poincaré appreciated that Czernin's memorandum was considerably modified by the Emperor's comments, because for the first time they took into account both the necessity of making good Belgium's losses and the desire to maintain the Austro-Hungarian Monarchy. Poincaré promised to inform Ribot, President of the Council, and to maintain absolute secrecy. He did not think he should inform France's allies at that stage.[9]

To ascertain the Emperor's intentions the Princes then went to Laxenburg (on the 23rd and 24th March), where they were to meet their brother-in-law in the greatest secrecy.[10]

"After embracing his relatives and discussing family matters Charles talked at length about his plans for a separate peace with the Entente. The sovereign was in uniform. He was too excited to remain seated, and kept walking up and down the room. His frank face, softened by the half-light, betrayed his anxious state of mind. 'I want peace,' he said; 'I want it at any price. The time is quite favourable, for we have all known successes and reverses, and our forces are more or less equal. It is not always great victories that provide the occasion for the best peace . . . It is therefore advisable to come to fair and reasonable terms; and I, for my part, am quite ready to do that."

Prince Sixt interrupted Charles to say that it was impossible to come to any arrangements whatsoever with the Germans who had retired to the Hindenburg line before the threat of Nivelle's offensive, and were at that very moment conducting themselves like savages.

The Emperor admitted that the Germans had no intention of talking peace; with them the dogma of total victory was unshakable His duty as an ally, however, obliged him to try even the impossible to induce Berlin to make a just and equitable peace. He could not sacrifice the Monarchy to the folly of a neighbour, and if that step failed he would make a separate peace. In any case, he proposed not to speak to the Germans about the subject at all until he had ascertained whether they would consider the 'idea of peace' as he visualized it. As far as he was concerned the first and most important point was to arrive at complete agreement with France, and through France with England and Russia, so as to be in a position to say to the Germans, 'We are no longer able to continue to fight for the King of Prussia. We must therefore make the necessary sacrifices, and sign peace immediately'.

Such was the essence of the interview at Laxenburg according to the friends of Prince Sixt. It was a conversation of primary importance, for

[9] R. Fester, "Die Sonderfriedensaktion des Prinzen Sixtus", *Berliner Monatshefte* August, 1937, p. 579.
[10] Amiguet, *La vie du Prince Sixte de Bourbon*, Paris, 1936, p. 120.

it provided the only evidence of the Emperor's desire to sign a separate
peace. There is, however, no official record of the conversation.

Sixt returned to Paris armed with a letter in the Emperor's handwriting which corroborated the secret notes destroyed at Neuchâtel.
The letter clearly showed the Emperor's desire to negotiate, his intention
to come to terms on certain conditions; it was not a proposal but an
examination of the terrain. The letter ran as follows:

I beg of you to inform M. Poincaré, President of the French Republic, secretly
and unofficially, that I shall do everything possible, using my personal influence
with my allies, to support the just claims of France relating to Alsace-Lorraine.

In so far as Belgium is concerned, her sovereignty must be completely restored,
and she will keep her African possessions without prejudice to any compensation
she may receive for the losses she has sustained. As for Serbia, her sovereignty
will also be restored and, as a pledge of our good intentions, we are prepared to
guarantee her a reasonable and natural access to the Adriatic Sea together with
wide economic concessions.

Austria-Hungary on her part will ask, as a necessary and absolute condition,
that the kingdom of Serbia shall suppress and cease in the future all relations with
any society or group whose political aims tend towards a disintegration of the
Monarchy, and in particular Narodna Obrana; that she prevent loyally and by
all means in her power every kind of political agitation, whether in Serbia or
beyond her frontiers, and that this assurance be guaranteed by the powers of the
Entente.

The events which have occurred in Russia compel me to reserve my ideas
on this subject until the time comes for a legal and permanent government to be
set up in that country.

Having thus expressed my sentiments, I ask you in your turn to inform me, after
consultation with France and England, the opinion of those two powers with a
view to preparing a basis of understanding upon which official negotiations may
be entered into and terminated to the satisfaction of all concerned.

Sixt saw Poincaré on the 31st March, and both considered it would
be useful to inform the United Kingdom. He asked Ribot, President
of the Council, for an audience, but he refused to see Sixt. Ribot went
to Folkestone to see Lloyd George, who was of opinion that the negotiations should be continued, but considered that the Italians should
also be informed. To safeguard the secrecy of the conversations, at the
urgent request of the Prince of Bourbon, a meeting took place at
Saint-Jean de Maurienne on the 19th April, where Ribot and Lloyd
George discussed with Baron Sonnino, Italy's Minister for Foreign
Affairs, the course the Austrian overtures should take.[11]

[11] M. Toscano, Gli accordi di San Giovanni di Moriana, Milan, 1936. See also
Ribot's notes in Journal, Paris, Plon, 1936, p. 66.

On the 22nd April Jules Cambon acquainted the Prince with the outcome of the meeting at Saint-Jean de Maurienne: the Italians refused to give up any of the conditions on which they had based their entry into the war, especially those concerning Trieste and the Trentino. On the 23rd April Sixt returned to Switzerland where Erdödy was waiting for him at Zug. He wrote to the Emperor asking him not to break off the conversations with France and England, whatever might be his intentions with regard to Italy.

On the 4th May another meeting took place at Neuchâtel with Erdödy who asked the Prince to return to Vienna. Sixt set out at once, and met Charles on the 8th May. The Emperor did not commit himself in precise terms concerning the concessions he was prepared to make to Italy. He wished to negotiate through the agency of the Entente, and left it to Czernin to prepare the ground on which an understanding could be reached, thus effecting a return to official diplomacy. A communication from Czernin dated the 8th May enquired if the Allies were ready to guarantee "the integrity of the Monarchy", and agreed to a surrender of territory to Italy, but by way of exchange. Once the bases were agreed upon Austria-Hungary would be in a position to enter upon negotiations with the Allies.

Sixt saw Poincaré again on the 20th May and discussed the contents of Czernin's note. But did Count Czernin exaggerate the intentions of his master when drafting his note of the 9th May? The spirit of those intentions, if not the letter, were correctly interpreted by Prince Sixt. Prince Xavier of Bourbon–Parma, who had been present at the Laxenburg talks, wrote in 1961:[12]

> The Emperor did everything he could to initiate peace negotiations. Count Czernin was not only acquainted with the facts, but had been present at the interviews and discussed the details. But he lacked precision; he had a woolly mind, and was temperamentally unreliable.

Did Prince Sixt, *proprio motu* and in his eagerness to reach a solution, influence the insertion of certain clauses into Czernin's note? Here again Prince Xavier reassures us:

> The honesty and determination of the Emperor Charles, my brother's frank and precise explanations to Poincaré and Lloyd George, together with the word of honour given by the parties concerned, are sufficient evidence of the accuracy of the text . . . My brother did not add a single line to the instructions received.

[12] Forty-four years after the event admittedly, but confirming that Sixt's account was a true report of the negotiations.

In any case, Sixt was soon disappointed. He must have been left with a poor impression, for he wrote:

The President of the Republic: a man of lively intellect and very clear-headed; well acquainted with European affairs, and intensely patriotic.
The President of the Council: tired and aging; continually removing and replacing his yellow spectacles. He saw all the difficulties, but nothing else. Above all, he feared Parliament. He had a negative outlook and lacked the will to co-operate.

On the 23rd May Sixt paid a visit to Lloyd George and the King of England. When the King read the document he too became somewhat dubious.

'There can be no question of peace with Germany, of course,' he said. 'Does this really mean a separate peace with Austria alone?'
'That is the essential factor in any negotiation,' replied Sixt.
Would Austria make peace against Germany's will, and despite any pressure from her?
'Yes, indeed,' said Sixt. 'Austria will do so of her own free will, and that is the Emperor's wish. He wants peace on favourable conditions and even without Germany. In fact, I have agreed to take part in these negotiations on condition that they remain unconnected with a German peace.'

Lloyd George envisaged a meeting of the three Heads of State with their Prime Ministers at Compiègne to decide the basis of negotiations, but the conference never took place. Sixt asked Lloyd George for England's reply, just as he had asked for that of France; but he received neither reply, and Charles waited in vain for the result of his tentative efforts.

Sixt was grieved by his failure, and left Paris on the 25th June to rejoin his regiment on the Belgian front. Ribot who had no doubt told everything to Sonnino[13] and applied his *vis inertiae* to stifle the negotiations, stated in the Chamber,

They shall not come hypocritically pleading for peace by devious and shady methods as they did to-day, but openly and on conditions worthy of France.

On the 13th October he was more precise:

[13] Polzer–Hoditz, *Kaiser Karl* — Zurich, 1929. A. Ribot, *Journal et correspondance inédite*, Paris, 1937, p. 167.

Yester day Austria declared her readiness to make peace and satisfy our demands, but deliberately omitted to refer to Italy, knowing that if we heeded her misleading words, tomorrow, when Italy had regained her freedom, she would become our enemy because France had forgotten and betrayed her.

Sixt, commenting on Ribot's speech, described it as the most preposterous lie, the most glaring hypocrisy ever perpetrated by the old felon!

Such were the manoeuvres and schemes of Ribot. The fact still remains that the Prince of Bourbon–Parma in his relations with the Allies often went beyond the literal purport of the messages he transmitted. The only conclusive evidence we have of the accuracy of the "intentions" he endeavoured to negotiate — although no one could suspect the Prince's good faith — is that of Prince Xavier to whose statements we have referred, and his evidence is very definite.

It should be remembered that the Italian demands could quite easily have been met had the negotiations been brought to a happy conclusion. It is, therefore, difficult to understand why France and England should have been prepared to endure another long year of war in support of Italy's doubtful claims, which were exposed to the same diplomatic haggling then as they had been in 1915.

There are innumerable indications, though difficult to verify, suggesting that Italy made independent approaches to Austria-Hungary to enable her to quit the war without consulting the Allies. Trentino and Trieste would have formed the basis of any arrangement made.

Count Armand, of the French Intelligence Department, and Count Nicolas Revertera, two secret agents without ability or mandate, resumed contact at Friburg, and entered into useless and disconnected discussions concerning the compensation to be offered to Italy in exchange for the Trentino and Trieste. These consultations were of no particular interest, but they do corroborate the Emperor Charles's willingness to negotiate over Italy's demands.[14]

Despite all the risks involved in secret diplomacy, it has been suggested that Ribot, urged by sheer political honesty and awareness of his responsibilities, endeavoured to steer the negotiations towards a definite proposal, acceptable to Italy or not. His inaction, to say the least, appears quite unpardonable.

[14] Concerning the negotiations by Armand and Revertera see Revertera's *Historische-politische Blättern für das Katholische Deutschland*, 1922, p. 153, and *L'Opinion*, Paris, July, 1920, pp. 31, 88 and 115. Armand and Revertera made their contacts on the 17th and 22nd August 1917, and again on the 2nd and 18th February 1918.

From the spring of 1917 onwards other secret negotiations took place.[15] The main ones were conducted by Lancken and Briand; they did not get beyond the stage of intermediaries, including the Vatican, and did not progress very far. They were, in fact, "soundings" rather than negotiations. Bearing in mind the aims of the originators — and their aims were always hidden — it seems reasonable to suppose that if these soundings could have led to negotiation a really genuine opportunity existed in 1917 to shorten the war by a year. Even Sixt's mission failed to culminate in talks, for Charles received no reply to his applications. Thus diplomacy proved powerless to renew in time the contacts necessary to the re-establishment of peace. It was probably the same state of affairs–lack of cohesion among the Allies, inefficient co-ordination, absence of the good will necessary to achieve quick results–that Marshal Foch had in mind when he wrote,

Towards the end of 1916 and the beginning of 1917 Germany was at the end of her tether. It required but a succession of well combined operations to overthrow her.

The Battle of the Somme, although fought with a relatively small force of fifteen or sixteen divisions — a fact which obliged us to narrow our line of attack considerably — inflicted immense losses on the enemy, and rapidly wore down his reserves.

Without allowing him any respite we should have mounted a series of well co-ordinated operations, thus achieving victory by destroying what remained of his reserves.

The means at our disposal at that time were certainly not comparable with what we had the following year, but they would have sufficed.[16]

The very people who had been incapable of preventing the outbreak of hostilities in 1914 proved to be just as incapable in 1917 of bringing them to an end, whether in the diplomatic or the military sphere. It was the management side of the war that required reform, and both France and Germany became aware of this during 1917. Germany concentrated on an increasing military power at home, and France on the authority of the government.

The Clemenceau government succeeded in industrializing the building of munitions under the Loucheur ministry, and introducing effective

[15] J. de Launay's *Secrets diplomatiques, 1914-1918*, Paris, 1963.
[16] R. Recouly, *Le Mémorial de Foch*, Paris, 1929, p. 49.

military co-ordination among the Allies by instituting a single military command.[17]

Thus, in these two spheres the Allies surpassed the Central Powers, and forced them to sue for peace in the autumn of 1918.

[17] Orlando's government in Italy and Lloyd George's government in the United Kingdom established a régime of controls. Germany had a succession of "weak" Chancellors, and in Austria the government allowed its power to crumble. By 1918 the Kaiser and the Emperor Charles no longer played any substantial part in the conduct of affairs.

OTHER SOURCES OF INFORMATION
IN PART ONE

The following is a list of the principal works consulted in addition to those named in the bibliography.

Sarajevo

Sarajewski Atentat, Izvorne stenografike (verbatim notes of the trial), Sarajevo, 1954.
Uspomane ucesnika u Sarajevskom Atentatu, by Ivan Kranjceveć, Sarajevo, 1954 (recollections of one of the conspirators).
Der Ausbruch des Weltkrieges, by A. von Wegerer (2 vols), Hamburg, 1939.

The Role of Count Berchtold

Le Comte Tisza et la Guerre de 1914–1918, by L. Lanyi, These, Paris, 1947.
Apparently in both Vienna and Berlin it was assumed that the Central Empires had attained a maximum military power by 1914, and that from then onwards France and Russia must attempt to make up for lost time. It is difficult to estimate the extent of this concern, and we have therefore not gone into the subject.

The Optimism of the German Staff

Der Schlieffenplan : Kritik eines Mythos. Mit erstmaliger Veröffentlichung der Texte, by G. Ritter, Munich, 1956.

Russian Mobilization

Le Général Soukhomlinov, by L. Agourtine, Clichy, 1954.

France and the Russian Mobilization

De Kronstadt à Khrouchtchev, by J. Kayser, Paris, 1962.
Introduction aux Tableaux d'Histoire de Guillaume II, by C. Appuhn and P. Renouvin, Paris, 1923.
Raymond Poincaré, by Jacques Chastenet, Paris, 1948.
Mes Souvenirs, by General Messimy, Paris, 1937.
Journal 1913–1914, by Maurice Paléologue, Paris, 1947.

Les Responsabilités de la Guerre (14 questions), by Raymond Poincaré, Paris, 1930. President Poincaré handed his political documents over to the French Ministry for Foreign Affairs; but he and his widow destroyed his personal papers and notes. His correspondence is scattered far and wide.

The Attitude of Great Britain

Die englische Politik in Juli 1914, by Ernst Anrich, Stuttgart, 1934.
Diary of Lord Bertie of Thame, Volume I, by Lord Bertie, Hodder and Stoughton, London, 1934.

The War of Movement — 1914

Life of Lord Kitchener, Volume III, by Sir George Arthur, MacMillan, New York 1920.
Kitchener, by Sir Philip Magnus, Dutton, New York, 1959.
Le Secret de la Frontière : Charleroi, by Fernand Engerand, Brossard. Paris, 1918.
Lanrezac, by Fernand Engerand, Brossard, Paris, 1926.
Joffre et Lanrezac, by Jules Isaac, Chiron, Paris, 1922.
Erinnerungen, Briefe, Dokumente, by General Helmuth von Moltke, Der Kommende Tag, Stuttgart, 1922.
Joffre, la Victoire du Caractère, by General Demazes, Nouvelles éditions latines, Paris, 1955.
Les Carnets de Gallieni, by General Gallieni, Albin Michel, Paris, 1932.
Souvenirs de Campagne de la Marne en 1914, by General Baron Max von Hausen, Payot, Paris, 1922.
La Marche sur Paris et la Bataille de la Marne, 1914, by General Alexander von Klück.

The Causes of American Intervertion

The Zimmermann Telegram, by B. W. Tuchmann, London, 1959.
Stenographische Berichte über die offentlichen Verhandlungen des — 15. Unter-suchungsausschusses. Berlin, 1919 (2 vols.).

Austrian Overteres for a Separate Peace

La Vie du Prince Sixte de Bourbon, by P. Amiguet, Paris, 1936.
Gli accordi di San Giovanni de Moriana, by M. Toscano, Milan, 1936.
Kaiser Karl, by Polzer–Hoditz, Zurich, 1929.

1914–1918 Period — Works consulted: 178

Controversial Questions	Number of works dealing with the question	Number of works containing worth-while facts	Number of works containing secondary matter	Original testimony contained in the works mentioned in the bibliography	New evidence collected by J. de Launay
1. Sarajevo. Serbian responsibility .	23	13	4	6	—
2. "Provocation" by Count Berchtold	7	3	1	3	—
3. International conference rejected	8	1	3	4	—
4. Serbia's declaration of war . . .	19	1	12	6	—
5. Risks taken by Germany . . .	22	—	16	6	—
6. Responsibility of the German General Staff	11	4	4	3	—
7. Attitude of the Austro-Hungarian General Staff	11	3	5	3	—
8. Russian mobilization	10	4	2	4	—
9. France and Russian mobilization	11	5	2	4	—
10. The British attitude	17	6	8	3	—
11. Anglo–French military co-operation	18	5	4	9	—
12. Franco–Belgian co-operation . .	8	2	3	3	—
13. Defeat at Charleroi	11	3	3	5	—
14. Moltke and the battle of the Marne	11	5	2	4	—
15. The Falkenhayn–Conrad quarrel	10	3	4	3	—
16. The "Dioscuri"	10	9	4	2	—
17. The causes of American intervention	20	9	4	7	—
18. Crisis in the French Command	9	2	5	2	—
19. Mutiny on the French front . .	8	2	2	4	—
20. Austrian overtures for a separate peace	15	6	2	7	1
				88	1

PART TWO

1919 – 1939

CHAPTER I

THE PEACE OF VERSAILLES

1. Did the Allies refuse to support the Rhineland autonomists in 1919?
2. What was the exact amount of German reparations?
3. Was the United States rejection of the Treaty of Versailles due to the intransigence of President Wilson?
4. What were the results of the Franco-Hungarian rupture in 1921?
5. Did the Geneva Conference turn the Soviet Union away from participation in European affairs?
6. What part did President Poincaré play in the 1922 moratorium?
7. What caused the failure of the 1923 Rhineland movement?

1. The Rhineland Autonomist Movement (1919)

After the signing of the Armistice at Rethondes the Allies had to choose between a negotiated peace and an imposed peace; the latter solution prevailed. The decision would have been quite impossible without military guarantees.

On the 1st November 1918 the four great powers accepted the principle of the occupation by Allied forces of the left bank of the Rhine, and in particular Mainz, Coblenz and Cologne. The principle was not questioned later at Versailles. On the 27th November 1918 Marshal Foch drafted a memorandum demonstrating the need to separate the Rhineland from the Reich, of which the new frontier would be the Rhine. Recouly[1] writes:

> The only safe frontier, the Rhine. Whoever controls that crossing is master of the situation. Not only may he repel an invasion without difficulty, but he can carry the war to enemy territory if he is attacked. Any solution which denies the Allies a frontier on the Rhine is a bad one: it would offer a mere pretence of security.

This concept was reiterated by Foch on the 1st January and 31st March 1919; but Clemenceau and the French government, who had

---

[1] R. Recouly, *Le Mémorial de Foch*, Paris, 1929, p. 156.

adopted Foch's security programme, did not make use of Foch's influence, despite the fact that he was Allied Commander-in-Chief, to insist on this condition, which was valuable from the military point of view. The politicians alone discussed Allied policy towards Germany; it was they who made the decisions that were the result of haggling, compromise and surrender. In the face of the protests and warnings of Foch Clemenceau adopted a conciliatory attitude towards Wilson and Lloyd George, and accepted the principle of a temporary occupation of the left bank of the Rhine for fifteen years, with a gradual withdrawal every five years. The idea of an independent Rhineland was therefore abandoned by the Allies, and the politicians at Versailles were content with a temporary occupation.

The views of the German nation were not sought. Much had taken place, however, since William II, fleeing from insurrection, had abandoned his last general headquarters at Spa to seek refuge in Holland, there to live out his life in peaceful exile. Since the 3rd November 1918 revolutionary elements had been at work in Kiel, and a movement of revolt gradually spread towards Hanover, Brunswick, Cologne and Berlin. The beaten German army was retreating with difficulty; Cologne was an important city on their route and train loads of mutinous sailors were to arrive there from Kiel. Military deserters who had thrown away their arms were preparing to welcome the mutineers on their arrival, and the populace took advantage of the confusion to begin looting. The military governor attempted to control the situation by sending troops in the direction of the station, but these were preparing to join the revolution. Already soldiers and workers had formed a soviet and established themselves in the Town Hall. Riot pickets took up their posts on the Rhine bridges and in the signal boxes. By the 9th November the revolutionary atmosphere had reached a climax, although the Kaiser's general headquarters at Spa still tried to maintain control over the situation.

At the Rathaus some members of the soviet were killed, and people clamoured for their burgomaster, Adenauer. He, however, was wrestling with realities. Without any fuss he had set up a non-political committee of assistance which fed and housed the most destitute. The delegates of the soviet wished to make him their leader; but they received no encouragement from Adenauer, who continued his work of providing beds and mobile kitchens.

On the 11th November, the day of the Armistice, Hindenburg knew that his retreating armies had to cross the bridges at Cologne, and

from his headquarters he sent a despatch rider to Adenauer to ascertain
if the road was open. The riot was at its height, but Adenauer sent back
a message to the effect that the march would be carried through in an
orderly manner. He made a simple appeal to the population, and the
troops passed through without any incident. The peace-loving people
of the Rhineland had made their decision: Prussian militarism had led
the country to defeat; Prussian bureaucracy could expect nothing from
the Rhineland.

In October 1918 the archpriest Kaster had established in Cologne a
Committee of the Free Rhine. Its purpose was to found a Rhenish
State. The idea soon became popular, but several prominent Rhinelanders, including Adenauer, considered that if federalism was to be
developed the time was certainly not opportune to demand autonomy.
During this period the Allied forces were settling along the left bank of
the Rhine. They divided it into four zones: the British had Cologne,
the Belgians had Aix-la-Chapelle, the Americans, Coblenz, and the
French, Mainz.

General Mangin was in command of the French sector. Dorten, a
magistrate and attorney at Wiesbaden, wrote of him,

Mangin was a man who would listen with kindly attention, but he was also
a master of the art of questioning and leading the speaker to confide in him. When
he had acquired a grasp of all the details, he came to a rapid conclusion and made
a decision. He had the knack of suggesting his wishes in the form of advice. On
leaving him one had received orders without being aware of it; and those orders
were carried out because they issued from the will of a leader.[2]

Foch's aims were apparently similar to those of Mangin:

His idea was to establish an independent Rhenish republic embracing a
reasonable amount of territory on the right bank. He rejected absolutely the concept
of a Rhenish State forming part of the Reich.[3]

On the 1st February 1919 the Rhineland Parliamentary Commission
assembled for the first time in Cologne to solve the Rhine problem.
Adenauer, who had not offered himself as a candidate, was elected
President. He had already become very popular throughout the Rhineland as a result of his municipal work in Cologne. He devoted a week
to the work of the Commission, and discussed his main concern: to put
an end to Prussian centralized administration by giving greater vitality

[2] Dorten, *La Tragédie rhenane*, Paris, 1945, p. 62.
[3] *Ibid.*, p. 63.

to regional and municipal activities.[4] There were many separatists at this meeting, apart from the Burgomaster of Cologne, who wished to set up a Rhineland State, the dream of the French generals. Adenauer absented himself from the meeting held at Cologne on the 10th February to draft the constitution of a Rhineland Republic. He explained his absence to the Press by saying that he considered the action to be premature. The truth was that Adenauer was not concerned solely with the Rhineland problem, but with the solution of the whole national federal problem. The separatists, however, pressed on. Dorten and his friends prepared in detail a plan for a Rhenish State, and submitted it to General Mangin on the 17th May 1919. The American political delegate, Mr. Noyes, was notified by the General, and he reacted unfavourably in a message to Wilson. The President of America and Lloyd George agreed to insist that Clemenceau refrain from placing the question once more before the Council of Four. The President gave instructions that demonstrations by the autonomists should not be permitted in the American zone (Coblenz), and the British government did likewise.

Only the Belgian and French zones still tolerated the activities of Dorten's movement, and he decided to proclaim the Rhineland Republic on the 29th May at the Town Hall in Aix-la-Chapelle. However, on the morning of the 28th the Belgians, also no doubt as a result of representations by the British, forbade all demonstrations by the autonomists. Dorten then fell back on Mainz where he proclaimed the autonomy of the Rhineland Republic on the 1st June 1919. General Mangin had just returned from Paris where he had been summoned for consultation, and he gave instructions for the proclamation to be displayed.[5] "Clemenceau supports me," he was reported as having said to Dorten; "and that is enough for me."

Senator Jeanneney, Under Secretary of State for War, who had just arrived from Paris on a mission from Clemenceau, asked Mangin to

---

[4] Adenauer's biographer, P. Weymar, says that Adenauer took over the direction of the separatist movement in order to destroy it (p. 44). Dorten is of the same opinion. There is no evidence, however, to confirm this theory.

[5] This was certainly authorized by Mangin. Cf. General Mangin, *Comment finit la guerre*, Paris, 1920, p. 53. Concerning the events of the 9th May he wrote: "If the Rhinelanders desire a special status within the German Republic, they have only to address themselves to Germany. You are supported by the Wilson principle which aims at allowing nations to dispose of their own destiny. Demand the right to be represented at the Versailles conference."

discontinue associating himself with the Rhineland question. Mangin was recalled on the 2nd June. At 3 o'clock in the afternoon of that day Clemenceau declared before the Big Four in Paris: "At the present time I am continually having trouble with generals who exceed their duties and commit faults that I regret."

The Peace of Versailles was signed on the 18th June. It included the recognition by the Allies of a single German State, the removal of administration from the hands of the military authorities, and the setting up of an Inter-Allied High Commission for the Rhine territories, presided over by M. Tirard who was instructed not to concern himself with political matters or German internal problems.

On the 11th October Mangin was recalled to France. Before his departure he assured Dorten that on his return to France he intended to lend his support to the aims of the Rhineland autonomists. It seems, according to Dorten, that Mangin had a stormy meeting with Clemenceau on his arrival in Paris.

'Why did you recall me,' asked Mangin, 'since I acted with your approval?'
'I cannot tell you,' Clemenceau is alleged to have replied.
'Do you wish to suffocate me between two mattresses without listening to me, and without offering any explanation?'
'I cannot tell you anything,' repeated Clemenceau.
'Then I will tell you,' said Mangin. 'You are carrying out the instructions of Lloyd George.'
Clemenceau remained silent, and merely made a tired gesture with his hand. Mangin said later that he regarded the situation as another Fashoda.[6]

2. German Reparations

The Peace of Versailles admitted of a compromise on the Rhineland question, but was inflexible in the matter of reparations. On the 29th October 1918, during the secret conferences that preceded the Armistice at Rethondes, Lloyd George told his associates that he wished to draw attention to the fact that there was one subject upon which the Fourteen Points were silent: the reparations due to the countries that had been overrun and to Britain's merchant navy which had suffered so much

[6] Dorten, *La Tragédie rhénane*, Paris, 1945, p. 83. This evidence is unique, and therefore unreliable. The fact that Clemenceau waited four months before recalling Mangin to France, after relieving him of his post, does perhaps show that the President had originally approved the General's action.

from German piracy. He referred also to the reparations due to the victims of the war.[7]

Although the principle of reparations was accepted on the 4th November, the methods of payment were referred to the Peace Treaty. During the discussions at which the Council of Four were drafting the Peace Treaty, Serbia, Poland and Belgium presented their claims. On the 2nd June 1919 Lloyd George expressed the view of the British experts that they were asking of Germany more than she would ever be in a position to pay; but their criticism was especially levelled at the indefinite and unlimited nature of the debt imposed upon Germany.[8]

These critics questioned the system of German reparations. But various compromises were reached, and the Peace of Versailles ultimately imposed on the Germans included Article 231, which stated: "The Allied governments and their associates declare, and Germany recognizes, that Germany and her allies were responsible for all the losses and damage sustained by the Allied governments, their associates and their peoples in consequence of the war imposed upon them by the aggression of Germany and her allies."

Article 231 therefore laid down

(1) the unilateral responsibility of Germany and her allies in launching the war, and

(2) Germany's financial responsibility in common law in so far as war damage was concerned[9] — in other words, they recognized that it was Germany's duty to make total reparation for all damage. One of the effects of Article 231 was to link responsibility and reparations. It therefore assumed an utterly useless punitive character, since by long established international tradition the vanquished were always expected to pay compensation.[10] Among the appendixes to the Treaty there is even an incomplete scheme for the payment of reparations; the fact is that the Allies were never really sure of the amount of reparations to impose on Germany.

After the 5th April 1919 the Allies became convinced that it was impossible to demand full reparation of Germany, and they had to confine themselves to "damage caused to the civil populations and their pro-

---

[7] J. de Launay's *Secrets diplomatiques, 1914–18,* Paris, 1963.

[8] P. Mantoux, *Les Délibérations du Conseil des Quatre,* Paris, 1955, II, 267.

[9] Cf. E. Weill-Raynal, *Les Réparations allemandes et la France,* Paris, 1948, I, 35 *et seq.*

[10] "Journées de Bergneustadt" organized by the International Commission for the Teaching of History (15th to 17th April 1957).

perty". This really amounted to an attempt to strike a balance between the reparations claimed and Germany's capacity to pay them. Lloyd George declared that he had opposed those who kept saying that Germany could pay the whole cost of the war, but he did not want her to pay less than the utmost possible.[11]

As no definite agreement could be arrived at before the signing of the Peace of Versailles the Reparations Commission was given the task of deciding the amount of the bill to be presented to Germany. In short, the Allies had no desire to apply Article 231 in its entirety; it was, therefore, a question of knowing to what point it could be applied, for the Allies themselves were aware that it was materially impossible to apply Article 231 in full. Another factor was that annexations of German territory were not taken into account in the discussions of reparation questions.

The experts began by finding the cost of the war. Various estimates provided a total of 147 milliard dollars, plus 15½ milliards to cover damage and 15 milliards to cover cost of pensions — a total of 720 milliard gold marks. As it was not possible to claim this astronomic sum from Germany, it was decided to be content with the cost of material damage only.[12]

The French talked of an estimate of actual loss. Klotz, the French Minister of Finance, quoted 450 milliards of marks after having previously put the figure at 800 milliards. The British talked of Germany's ability to pay in thirty years, and quoted the sum of 500 milliards. There followed excited discussions which did not result in any modification of the facts.

It is fair to add that the French and Belgian representatives had to satisfy public opinion that the operations involved in reparations would take several years. Klotz's reply became famous — "Germany will pay!"

On the other hand, the Americans had lent the Allies over nine milliard dollars, of which six milliards were in gold marks, and they had not the slightest intention of cancelling these debts. The losses suffered by the Allies for the common good meant nothing to them.

During the course of the debate the French agreed to reduce the amount claimed by fifty per cent; the English agreed to spread the payments over forty years. On the 20th March 1920 the possibility of a single lump sum payment of 120 milliards of gold marks was discussed.

---

[11] P. Mantoux, *Les Déliberations du Conseil des Quatre*, Paris, 1955, I, 158.
[12] Loucheur — *Carnets secrets*, Brussels, 1963, p. 75.

This figure was suggested by three experts including Loucheur and Keynes. It was not possible, however, to reach agreement on this figure, and a temporary solution was arrived at: a payment of twenty milliards in gold marks before the 1st May 1921, the setting up of a reparations commission to supervise the payments, and to decide before the 1st May 1921 the final amount of reparations to be demanded.

Germany was consulted at a conference held at Spa from the 5th to the 16th July 1920, and eight milliards of marks were paid at the end of that year, but not without strong protests from leading Germans of every shade of political opinion. The Allies came to an agreement on the method of paying reparations, and an ingenious system was perfected. It consisted of putting into circulation a number of Bonds A and B to the amount of fifty milliards of gold marks; Bonds C to the amount of eighty milliards would not be put into circulation until Germany's ability to pay made this possible. That reduced the amount of the credit to fifty milliards, redeemable by means of annuities of two milliard gold marks, plus 26 per cent of the value of German exports, which amounted to approximately three milliards per annum. In forty years Germany would thus have paid 120 milliards gold marks.[13] This was the figure that the Allies finally adopted at the London conference on the 1st May 1921, adding, however, the twelve milliards which Germany had not paid to date.

Germany could quite easily have paid the bill of fifty milliards, but she put forward one obstacle after another. At the end of March 1921 Léopold Dubois, a Swiss Banker, went so far as to suggest the issue of an international loan of fifty milliards which would permit of the total repayment of Bonds A and B, and solve the reparations problem at the same time. For reasons that are difficult to explain the proposal was thrust aside by Simons on behalf of Germany and Loucheur on behalf of France.[14]

The German government found it convenient to blame reparations for all the evils that the people had to endure —

[13] Reparation payments would then terminate in 1962; a somewhat imprudent proposal from a political point of view, because it entailed forcing two generations to pay for the debatable wrongs of the first.

[14] Loucheur — Carnets secrets, Brussels, 1962, p. 81. In 1871 Germany claimed from France compensation amounting to five milliard francs payable in three years. This sum was covered by the issue of a loan which freed France of the debt within two years.

The business man in difficulties; the underpaid teacher; the unemployed worker all blamed their troubles on reparations. The cry of a hungry child was a cry against reparations. Old men stumbled into the grave because of reparations. The great inflation of 1923 was attributed to reparations; so was the great depression of 1929.[15]

Between 1920 and 1934, 164 conferences were convened — an average of twelve a year — to discuss the matter of reparations. It was an insoluble problem, destined to poison international relations between the two wars, and hamper the setting up of a real German democracy. Using the burden of reparations as an excuse for the difficulties encountered in their attempt to reorganize their economy, the Germans succeeded in borrowing from abroad, and especially from the United States of America, about thirty milliards of gold marks between 1924 and 1930.[16] But from 1921 to 1932 Germany paid the Allies twenty-two milliards and 891 millions out of the 132 milliards involved. These payments to the Allies were not allocated to reparations in France and Belgium; they were transferred to the Americans in settlement of war debts. Since the Germans had no desire to re-imburse their foreign creditors either, it may be assumed that reparations profited no one: they merely encouraged the nationalists, who made the destruction of the "chains of Versailles" their first objective.

It is difficult to understand the lack of realism of the statesmen of Versailles. They were in favour of an imposed peace, but failed to proceed to the limit of their principles. They were opposed to nationalism but fostered its rebirth, and were swept along by the public opinion which they ought to have controlled. The German attitude is understandable, not only from the point of view of their desire to take advantage of the disagreements that arose between the Allies, but above all because they rebelled against the one-sided accusation of culpability for the 1914 war. At no time were the Allies able to produce precise proofs to justify their demand of reparations on the grounds of German culpability.

In so far as Belgian reparations were concerned the Germans were at no time reminded of Bethmann Hollweg's speech in August 1914. Bethmann had said,

We have been forced to disregard the justifiable protests of the Luxemburg and Belgian governments. As soon as our military objective has been attained we shall

[15] A. J. P. Taylor, *The Origins of the Second World War*, London, 1961, p. 46.
[16] E. Vermeil, *L'Allemagne contemporaine 1890—1950*, Vol. II, Paris, 1953, p. 88.

make amends for the injustice — I use the word frankly — the injustice of which
we are thus guilty.

Some writers are inclined to think that Germany could quite easily
have paid the reparations demanded,[17] but it seems that the fundamental
error lay in allowing the whole Treaty of Versailles to be doomed merely
because Article 231 was unworkable.

3. The United States and the League of Nations (1919–1920)

President Wilson quite definitely directed international relations from
1917 to 1919. His Fourteen Points constituted the objectives of the war
and the programme for peace. The Allies did not allow themselves to
be robbed of the fruits of their victory, but the Peace of Versailles,
though imposed, owed much to Wilson and his colleagues. The American President had great faith in the League of Nations which he had
helped to create. The League was, in fact, the last of his famous Fourteen
Points, and Wilson defended it vigorously before the Big Four. Clemenceau felt no enthusiasm for this new organization, and Lloyd George
was not really sure whether to support Wilson's enterprise or join
Clemenceau in trying to curb it. Both were aware that the League of
Nations, as contemplated by Wilson, would put an end in Europe to
England's traditional game of balancing France and Germany, and that
it would deprive France of the permanent and unrestricted character of
her guarantees against Germany.

Wilson succeeded in getting "his" League of Nations adopted
despite every objection, because it would destroy the policy of balance
of power which appeared to him, quite wrongly, to be a permanent
source of war. He also thought that the League of Nations would induce
the Great Powers to take the smaller ones into consideration, and consequently foster justice and impartiality in international relations.
Finally Wilson was not entirely satisfied with the clauses of the Peace
of Versailles, because he had to make many sacrifices during the negotiations, and he saw the League as an instrument that would tend to
modify the cold and rigid tone of the text.

On the 25th January 1919 the Peace Conference decided that the
"Covenant of the League of Nations" would form part of the peace
treaties, and on the 28th June it was included in the text presented to

---

[17] Etienne Mantoux, *La paix calomniée*, Paris, 1946.

the signatories of the Peace of Versailles.[18] On the 29th June, that is, as soon as these essentials were adopted, Wilson embarked at Brest on the *George Washington*. He arrived at Hoboken, in New Jersey, on the 8th July, and placed the text of the Treaty of Versailles before the Senate on the 10th for ratification, which required a majority vote of two-thirds. Four out of 47 Democratic senators definitely opposed the Treaty for various reasons, some of which were extraordinary; the remaining 43 supported Wilson.

Of the 49 Republican senators 14 were decidedly against the Treaty; but from the remaining 35 Wilson obtained the 21 votes necessary for ratification. About a dozen Republicans called for a few simple amendments before giving their approval, and about twenty others asked for more substantial modifications. As a dozen supporters were insufficient it was necessary to win over about ten of the more moderate Republicans; but Wilson had no intention of indulging in bargaining. He undertook the almost superhuman task of pushing the text through in its original form — both the Peace Treaty itself and the Covenant of the League of Nations. He summoned the Press and calmly announced that Congress would ratify the Treaty.

Jusserand, the French ambassador, advised him to accept certain amendments, but Wilson told the ambassador that he would not agree to any concession. "The Senate must take its medicine."[19]

But he was opposed by the Republican leader Henry Cabot Lodge.

This Republican was hostile to what public opinion hailed as a great democratic success. Furthermore, he disliked Wilson, who also disliked him. For twenty-three years he had been a member of the Foreign Affairs Committee in the Senate, and had had a much longer political career than Wilson. He was a Doctor of History of Harvard University; rich, cultivated, much travelled and, until the meteoric rise of Wilson, the only American politician to enjoy a great reputation as a specialist in political science. Wilson eclipsed Cabot Lodge, and it grieved the latter. Wilson knew that Lodge was a lawyer who had made a success of his profession, and the great man recalled bitterly that he had been a failure as a lawyer. Eventually jealousy led to an estrangement until, in 1916, Lodge charged Wilson with having hushed up certain details in the *Lusitania* affair, and the President accused Lodge of lying. Naturally enough Lodge always claimed that he did not oppose the Treaty from personal spite. 'My opposition to Wilson,' he said, 'in so far as the war and the League of Nations were concerned, was based entirely on the public interest.' One cannot refrain from thinking, however, that the enmity

[18] The text of the treaties of Saint-Germain, Neuilly, Trianon and Sèvres were similarly dealt with.
[19] Quoted by Duroselle, *De Wilson à Roosevelt*, Paris, 1960, p. 131.

existing between these two men tended to some extent to complicate a problem that was already extremely intricate.[20]

Through skilful parliamentary manoeuvring Cabot Lodge succeeded in gaining time by multiplying obstacles to the ratification of the Treaty. Little by little the supporters of isolationism joined forces with those who could not understand how one could possibly underwrite the imposed Peace of Versailles with the idea of a League of Nations, rejecting crime and injustice; the two conceptions seemed contradictory.

By about the middle of August 1919 Wilson had almost lost the parliamentary battle, and he could no longer hope for victory without mobilizing public opinion in his favour. He therefore made an immediate decision. With the aid of his colleagues he prepared a plan of campaign that included a propaganda tour, leaving out New England which was regarded as unshakable and the southern States already on his side. He had to win over Michigan, Illinois, Indiana, Kansas, Nevada, Utah, Colorado, Iowa, Idaho and California. Between the 3rd and 29th September the President made thirty-six speeches each of about an hour's duration. He made a fatiguing journey of over 3000 miles; though it enabled him to make contact with the people it was conducted under very unfavourable conditions. To the farmers and stock breeders of the Middle West who were discussing enthusiastically the latest victory of the boxer Jack Dempsey, the new heavyweight champion of the world, Wilson recommended a reading of the Covenant of the League of Nations which would defend throughout the world the ideals for which the United States stood. Although the Americans were inclined to defend courageously an ideal of which they were proud, they could hardly be expected to believe in what was still the mere dream of an intellectual, a President with a Utopian outlook!

To inspire the crowd with the fire of his own ardent ideals an orator must be in full possession of physical health and strength; but Wilson was a sick man. The sessions of the Peace Conference in Paris had already weakened him, and on several occasions he had been confined to bed. Even in July he still suffered from dysentery and followed a very strict diet. His doctor (Dr Grayson) strongly advised him against the propaganda tour, which he regarded as suicidal.

Four days after Wilson's return to the White House his wife and Dr Grayson found him lying on the carpet. His stroke had paralysed his

[20] Duroselle, *De Wilson à Roosevelt*, Paris, 1960, pp. 131 and 132. Duroselle's research is remarkable; we have followed it in a number of other points.

left side. On the 17th October an inflammation of the prostate suddenly occurred, and the President's life was in jeopardy. Devoted care and attention brought him through the crisis, and the President began to recover, though he remained too ill to return to his duties. He was unable to follow the development of the parliamentary battle for the ratification of the Peace Treaty.

The President's illness intensified his obstinacy, and he was determined not to yield to anyone. Colonel House, his loyal colleague and political adviser, had played a decisive role since the 1912 election. He brought Wilson the votes of Texas, and never ceased to support him in democratic party meetings and in special missions to Europe, though he held no official government appointment. House, true to his practice of taking the bull by the horns, sent his friend Colonel Bonsal, Wilson's mouthpiece, to Cabot Lodge, to try to work out a basis for compromise. An agreement was reached, and Colonel House himself went to the President with the document which was the crowning achievement of his career; but his request for an audience was refused.[21]

The evolution of American public opinion was followed with interest abroad, and subsequently with uneasiness. Lloyd George sent the former minister, Sir Edward Grey, to Washington — an outstanding personality whose probity and unerring judgment were universally known and respected. Sir Edward's task was to explain to Wilson that England preferred an amended treaty to an outright rejection. Even he was not received at the White House, though Wilson gave a few moments to King Albert of the Belgians who was visiting the United States. Works published since those days reveal that Mrs. Wilson played a particularly disastrous role on that occasion. Edith Bolling was Wilson's second wife, whom he had married in 1915;[22] she was the widow of a Washington jeweller and a fashionable woman. She had an assertive personality, and watched over the President with the greatest devotion. It seems, however that during his illness, from the 17th October to the 19th November, the steps she took to protect her invalid had very grave political consequences. Concerning the passage of his plan through the Senate she kept the President informed of any reassuring news, but did not allow House and Sir Edward Grey to see him lest the invalid became fatigued.

---

[21] It is not known if the President saw the document or whether it was kept from him. There was, in any case, no response.

[22] The first Mrs. Wilson died in 1914. Edith Bolling Wilson died in 1961.

Wilson's silence over the Lodge–Bonsal memorandum was strongly resented by Cabot Lodge, and the Republican leader entered upon the final parliamentary struggle in bitter anger. Wilson rejected *en bloc* the reservations advanced by Cabot Lodge and his friends, who called on the Democratic senators to vote against ratification; thus, on the 19th November 1919 the Treaty was rejected, though a majority agreed to re-examine it.

This new examination began in December. Wilson's friend had failed to secure the President's acceptance of some at least of Cabot Lodge's reservations. The Senate finally rejected the Treaty on the 19th March 1920 by 49 votes to 35. It voted in favour of Cabot Lodge's form of treaty, but again with reservations. The result was that the United States did not join the League of Nations, and signed a separate peace with Germany in August 1921. In the meantime Wilson and the Democrats were defeated at the presidential elections held in November 1920.

4. *The Rupture between France and Hungary*

The appendixes to the Peace of Versailles — Saint-Germain en Laye (19th September 1919) on Austria, and Neuilly (27th November 1919) on Bulgaria — determined the dismemberment of the Austro-Hungarian Empire and the Kingdom of Bulgaria.

The disruption of a system that had been established for many generations gave rise to a tendency towards revisionism among the dissatisfied nations. The wreckage of the Dual Monarchy was divided between Italy, Czechoslovakia, Yugoslavia, Rumania and Poland. While the new Austria and the new Hungary were striving towards stability they experienced grave internal disorder, and both very nearly swung towards Bolshevism. In 1920 a republic was set up in Austria, while Hungary decided upon a Regency, to which the Archduke Joseph of Hapsburg was appointed. This new state of affairs did not put an end to revisionism, and Hungary demonstrated violently against the Treaty of Trianon. Its counter-revolutionary government drafted a monarchial constitution which pointed the way towards a restoration of the Hapsburgs. The Allies, whose function it was to sustain the young States they helped to bring into being, determined to oppose the tendency. On the 3rd February 1920 they published a statement condemning the return of the Hapsburgs. The Archduke Joseph was forced to leave Hungary, and the government was entrusted to Horthy, formerly Admiral of the Imperial Fleet.

The French authorities, however, indicated to the Hungarian diplomats their desire to co-operate with them in finding a solution that would satisfy their claims. Maurice Paléologue, the Secretary General of the Ministry for Foreign Affairs, opened up secret negotiations with Count Csaky. The basis of these negotiations appears to have been the return to Hungary of certain territory, obviously Hungarian, in Slovakia and Transylvania, in exchange for a French interest in the railways and the Bank of Hungary.[23] These negotiations leaked out, and came to the notice of the Czechoslovak and Yugoslav governments, which hastily prepared a military alliance that was signed on the 14th August 1920. Rumania also joined the alliance on the 19th August when Benes, the Czechoslovak Minister for Foreign Affairs, used for the first time the term "Little Entente".[24]

The Emperor Charles I who was living in exile at Prangins, in Switzerland, followed the course of these events with interest. He had continued to maintain indirect contact with French and Hungarian statesmen, and there were many who sympathized with his cause. He did not appear to be deeply disturbed when Paléologue was replaced at the Ministry by Philippe Berthelot in January 1921, although the latter was less inclined to favour Hungarian revisionism. On the 16th February 1921 Charles received news from France:

A well-known and well-informed Frenchman told the Emperor that delay could only weaken the chances of a restoration in Hungary; he said that the Allied governments would certainly protest to begin with, but they could not alter a *fait accompli*. The Emperor was desirous of verifying the news he had received, not through distrust of the bearer of the message, but to avoid any misunderstanding. That is why the stranger referred to left for Paris where he learned that they were ready to accept a *fait accompli*."[25]

Charles sought the support and advice of Polzer–Hoditz, a friend of many years' standing.

'At about this time ,Polzer–Hoditz relates, I was staying on my estate in Slovakia, and the Emperor Charles asked me to proceed to Paris to get in touch with influential statesmen. I was the only one among his personal friends, His Majesty told me,

[23] It seems that during the same period Ludendorff approached the Regent Horthy for the purpose of bringing off a *coup de main* in Austria and Czechoslovakia.
[24] These details are taken from the work by Duroselle, *De Wilson à Roosevelt*, Paris, 1960, p. 36, and Renouvin, *Les relations internationales : 1914–1945*, Paris, 1949 and 1954.
[25] Werkmann, *Der Tote auf Madeira*, Zurich, 1923, p. 116.

who was able to convey accurate information concerning the problems of the ancient Monarchy as well as on matters affecting the future.

It was hinted to me that the mission with which I had been entrusted concerned the restoration of the Monarchy. As this depended on the support of Hungary, I asked the Emperor's messenger to tell His Majesty that, as his personal adviser, I was naturally always ready to carry out his order, but that I considered it my duty to warn him explicitly of the danger entailed in any enterprise of this nature. It was my opinion that any attempt at this juncture to modify the constitutional status of the former territories of the Monarchy was foredoomed to failure. A *coup d'état* that failed would do immeasurable harm to the Monarchist cause. Furthermore, even if the French politicians were convinced to begin with of the justness of the arguments laid before them, we had to be sure that they would not eventually oppose an attempt to restore the Hapsburgs. They might find it impossible to tolerate such an attack on the very "nationality" principle upon which they had sought to rebuild Europe and the world.'[26]

Who was the distinguished Frenchman who had declared that France was prepared to accept a *fait accompli*? The messenger who sought to verify the truth of the statement appears to have been Polzer–Hoditz, but he did not reveal the results of his soundings. Prince Sixt of Bourbon–Parma, Charles's brother-in-law, might have played a part in the affair, but there is no evidence of this. Was Prince Sixt the person to whom Berthelot gave so much encouragement? Berthelot's friends have remained silent on the matter, and Sixt did not mention it.[27]

At Prangins Baron von Werkmann, the Emperor's secretary, pleaded with the Monarch not to embark on any scheme. He pointed out the risks involved if the Regent Horthy were to go back on his word. But Charles's faith in the absolute loyalty of "his" Admiral and the advice of the "distinguished Frenchman" appeared to him irrefutable.

The attempt to restore the Monarchy began to take shape on the 18th February. Charles was at Szombathely, in Hungary, on the 27th March.

The King appeared unexpectedly in the palace of Bishop Count Mikes, with Prince Sixt of Parma, his brother-in-law, after paying a visit to Count Thomas Erdödy in Vienna on Good Friday. Erdödy had lent him his car as far as the frontier. The Count was unaware that His Majesty had left Switzerland, and was extremely surprised when his unknown visitor removed his large driving goggles. Even the Grand Chamberlain, Count Joseph Hunyady, who was in His Majesty's confidence, had not been informed or consulted. At Szombathely the King received

---

[26]Polzer–Hoditz, *Kaiser Karl*, Vienna, 1925, p. 309.

[27]According to other sources Prince von Windischgraetz, one of the Legitimist leaders, overheard the following remark while dining with Briand at the Larue restaurant: "If Hungary succeeds in restoring the Monarchy France would raise no objection."

the submission of the Bishop and all the clergy. He also had an interview with the President of the Council, Count Paul Teleki, who happened to be staying with Count Sigray at the latter's castle. Count Teleki related to me afterwards the outcome of that interview which he summed up in two words: 'Too soon.' (It was Teleki who, without any outside pressure, assumed responsibility for these events, and tendered his resignation in consequence.)

But all Teleki could obtain from His Majesty was his authority to precede him to Budapest to inform me what was happening. He took a different road, and was delayed en route, so that he arrived in Budapest after His Majesty.

I invited Count Sigray to come to the meeting at once, accompanied by my aide-de-camp, and to request His Majesty to be good enough to proceed to the castle. It took me but a moment's reflection to decide to tell the King that the only way out of the difficult situation in which he had placed himself through his own fault was to return to Switzerland as speedily as possible.

A few minutes later I was informed that His Majesty had arrived, having walked the short distance from the castle. We had not met since those ominous days two and a half years ago, when I had had the painful duty of announcing the surrender of the fleet as ordered, and to ask His Majesty to accept my resignation. On that occasion, as on all others, the King expressed his sympathy, and when I conducted him from the office of the aides-de-camp to my own office, he embraced me. He was dressed in the uniform of a Hungarian officer. In a few words he described his life in exile, and expressed the hope that he would soon be re–instated.

I assured His Majesty that to be able to return his throne to him, our crowned King, would be a most happy duty, and that I was ready to defend what I regarded as his legitimate right.

'But Your Majesty must know,' I continued, 'that the very moment I placed power in your hands our country would be invaded by the armies of neighbouring States. They are well armed, and we have nothing to fight with. Your Majesty would then be forced to return to Switzerland, and Hungary would be occupied; the consequences of such a situation are unpredictable.'

When I spoke to him of the attitude of the Great Powers His Majesty told me that he had come with the approval of the Entente. I asked to be informed of the details, and His Majesty mentioned Briand, who was at that time France's President of the Council and Minister for Foreign Affairs.

'Has your Majesty spoken personally to Briand?' I asked.

'No; I have only contacted him through third parties.'

By that he meant the Empress Zita's brother, Prince Sixt of Parma, who was on excellent terms with French royalist circles; but they did not by any means represent the government of France.

· To enable us to examine all these problems thoroughly I suggested to His Majesty that the French High Commissioner in Budapest should enquire if Briand were prepared to give guarantees, on behalf of the Entente, against any consequent action by our neighbours; or at least guarantee the existence of Hungary in its present mangled condition. His Majesty signified his acceptance, and agreed to return to the Bishop's palace at Szombathely to await the reply from Paris.

'If Briand gives us this guarantee,' 'I said, 'I shall gladly return to Your Majesty your ancestral rights. If we receive a negative reply, I shall have to ask Your

Majesty to leave the country at once, so that your presence may not become known.'

Meanwhile, I summoned to the castle M. Fouchet, the French diplomatic representative, and asked him to put to Briand the question I had discussed with His Majesty. The reply was a categorical denial. Briand declared that he had never given his consent to the re-instatement of His Majesty King Charles. Whether this statement was true or not, Briand's reply, which subsequently appeared in the Press, did at any rate represent the French government's official attitude. I learned at a later date, however, that Prince Sixt had discussed the matter with several French generals, including Lyautey and other influential Frenchmen, and that M. Berthelot, Secretary General at the Quai d'Orsay, played a rather ambiguous role, for he was afraid of the Anschluss. Using the Hughes telegraph instrument, which had a special contrivance to prevent a third party from overhearing a conversation, I informed His Majesty the result of my enquiry, and asked him to leave the country as soon as possible.[28]

The ambassadors of Italy, Yugoslavia, Rumania and Czechoslovakia protested to Hungary, and threatened to take energetic action. On the 23rd April 1921, Benes took advantage of the situation to conclude a Czecho-Rumanian military alliance. A further military alliance between Rumania and Yugoslavia on the 7th June strengthened the network of alliances of the Little Entente.

Charles and his wife, the Empress Zita, made another attempt on the 20th October 1921 to restore the Monarchy in Hungary. They arrived at Sopron by airplane, and planned to march on Budapest against the forces of the Regent Horthy. The Regent had them arrested, and they were transferred under Allied instructions to a British ship on the Danube. In the Black Sea the royal couple were transferred to another vessel and taken to Madeira, where, on the 1st April 1922, at the age of thirty-five, His Majesty's unhappy life came to an end.

New treaties were signed between Rumania and Poland (March 1921) and between Czechoslovakia and Yugoslavia (August 1922). The breach between France and Hungary was complete, and the French Republic determined henceforward to regard Benes's patient reconstruction of the Little Entente as the basis of its central and eastern European policy.

The States which remained outside the Little Entente, that is to say, Bulgaria, Austria and Hungary, were dissatisfied with the Peace of Versailles; they therefore turned towards Italy, who was equally dissatisfied, as their natural protectress.

[28] Horthy, *Ein Leben für Ungarn*, Bonn, 1953, pp. 118 to 121.

5. The Genoa Conference (1922)

The main outcome of the Treaty of Versailles, transforming as it did the political *status quo* of Europe, and crushing Germany with the heavy burden of reparations, was to effect a considerable check on international economic relations.

The Cannes Conference, from the 6th to the 10th January 1922, was therefore concerned with re-establishing traditional commercial trends. Despite certain difficulties emanating from France's internal policy, Briand, Lloyd George, Sforza, Theunis and Ishü, in the presence of an American observer, soon agreed to convene in the spring "a great international economic conference for the reconstruction of Europe". The five Allies — France, Great Britain, Italy, The United States and Japan — were invited to this conference, together with Russia, Germany and former enemy States.

It is worth noting that on the 28th October 1921 the Russian government suggested to France, Italy, Japan and the United States that they should hasten the convening of a somewhat similar conference.[29] Moreover, Lloyd George, who was worried by increasing strikes in Great Britain, built great hopes on the Geneva Conference.

Preparations for the conference took place in an atmosphere of feverish excitement. On the 26th February Lloyd George and Poincaré, the new head of the French government (Briand having resigned on his return from Cannes), met at Boulogne to compare their points of view. But Poincaré, who was anxious to form a military alliance with Britain, proved so uncompromising that he could obtain nothing. Thus, from the outset the two principal promoters of the Versailles Treaty were not of one mind.

Nevertheless, experts met on two occasions and tried to clarify the attitude of the Allies. A conference held in Paris during February brought together Russia's creditors, under the chairmanship of Joseph Noulens, former French ambassador in St Petersburgh. There it was learned that the Russian debts in France approximated to eleven milliard gold francs.[30] The amount represented the Russian assets of over a million and a half French shareholders who quite rightly wished to be repaid. It also came to light that big business interests in Great Britain had invested about three milliard gold francs[31] in Russian industry.

29 U. S. S. R. foreign policy documents, 1960, IV, 445–448–477.
30 Worth approximately 3300 million francs in 1963.
31 Worth approximately 900 million francs in 1963.

These enterprises having been nationalized, the French and British capitalists demanded to be reimbursed; damages and compensation in full — such were the maximum demands of the Allied creditors, "in default of which they refused to recognize the Soviet government".

In so far as new investments in Russia were concerned, the Allied government experts summed up their points of view in a note which they drew up in London from the 20th to the 28th March, and entitled, "Conditions under which foreign collaboration and foreign capital may be employed in the work of restoring Russia".

The Germans were also very interested in the Genoa Conference. Chancellor Wirth was an upright man whose policy it was to carry out all engagements entered into. Compared with him Walter Rathenau was a very turbulent character. His ideas were well known, and he expressed them at length to Loucheur on the 12th June 1921:

> To be able to pay, Germany must increase her exports and reduce her imports. But to increase her exports she is faced with the enormous problem of having to find 300 million consumers. How can this be possibly achieved so long as Russia is closed to commerce? All these questions are interdependent, and those who wish to resolve the problem of Germany's payment have no right to separate them'.[32]

He used this same line of reasoning to Lloyd George in London during the autumn. What Rathenau omitted to say, was that he also had in mind Article 116 of the Treaty of Versailles, under which Russia reserved the right to claim reparations from Germany on the same conditions as the other Allies. The Germans were afraid that the Allies might take advantage of the Genoa Conference to present new demands to Germany.

The American government gave the impression that it had no interest in the Genoa Conference. She did not wish to treat with the Russians in the presence of the Europeans, or to confound German affairs with those of Britain and France. But Standard Oil kept a watchful eye on the activities of the Royal Dutch Shell Company in so far as Russian oil was concerned; and, judging by the number of its agents who intervened in Europe, it seemed likely that the United States were ready for a change of attitude.

The political development of the situation in Soviet Russia had created a delicate situation. The government in Moscow had no official

---

[32] Loucheur, *Carnets secrets*, Brussels, 1962, pp. 87 and 187.

relations with Europe, either diplomatic or economic. "While the absence of diplomatic relations disturbed the Soviet rulers, their needs for economic contacts abroad had become very pressing."[33]

On the 15th March 1921 Lenin had attempted a strategic retreat before the Party Congress:

> It was inevitable in dealing with a series of economic questions to beat a retreat in relation to State Capitalism.

Discontented peasants were rallied to the Soviet regime by the N.E.P. — the New Economic Policy. There was no question of a reversal of policy, but of a pause:

> A socialist revolution, in a country where the vast majority of the population is composed of small farmer-producers, is only possible by the application of a whole series of transitional measures which would be useless in countries where salaried workers form the majority of the population under a capitalist system . . .
>
> The conditions under which we have so far lived were created by a war so mad, so unparalleled in history, that our only course was to adopt military methods in the economic sphere . . . We have undoubtedly been dragged along, both theoretically, and practically, further than was necessary.We can therefore retrace our steps a little, without for all that destroying the dictatorship of the proletariat. In fact, we shall in this way consolidate that dictatorship. Its realization will be a matter of practical experience.

From the moment the N.E.P. was adopted commercial relations were established with Britain, and the British Press was delighted. The *Morning Post* declared that Lenin was making giant strides back to Capitalism, the *Observer* stated that freedom of trade might become the grave of Communism in Russia — that Lenin was authorizing the return of capitalists and landlords. But the British journalists were mistaken, for Lenin knew very well what he was doing: "Freedom of transactions means freedom of trade. And whoever says freedom of trade, says return to capitalism . . . Perfection is to know how to keep within bounds".

It was *The Nation* that really saw things clearly. It said that Mr. Lloyd George was mistaken if he imagined that Lenin was an opportunist like himself. Lenin was capable of temporarily yielding ground, and was ready to make use of means which appeared to him to be efficacious;

---

[33] Russian problems had been discussed at Versailles in the absence of Soviet representatives, who had not been invited. Neither had the Russians been invited to attend the Washington Conference in 1921.

but not for a moment did he renounce his fundamental purpose, which was to transform the whole of Russia into a vast field of collective exploitation.[34]

It is none the less true that in Russia Lenin met with serious political difficulties in trying to apply his programme. Trotsky and his group opposed Lenin. The resulting dispute within the bosom of the Party grew violent, and deteriorated in a phase of extremism. During the whole of 1921 Lenin fought hard battles within the Party. Famine struck the population. The internal economic and social problems were innumerable, and every problem called for the personal intervention of Lenin who, from being prime mover of the Revolution, became the organizer of the new Social State.

He lived simply with his wife and sister in a four-roomed flat in the Kremlin. He devoted the greater part of his time to work at his desk, from ten in the morning to midnight, and sometimes until dawn. Brief pauses were allowed for lunch at about four o'clock and the evening meal around eight o'clock. At six he presided over the traditional session of the Council of People's Commissars. Sunday, his only day of rest, he devoted to walking and a nap in the Moscow countryside.

But Lenin, still suffering from a wound received in 1918, could not stand up to this fatiguing routine. On several occasions, when in need of rest, he went to stay at the villa of the writer, Maxim Gorky. Before attending the IXth Soviet Congress on the 23rd December he took a month's holiday, so that he might have sufficient strength to be of the utmost service to the Party. On the 6th December he wrote to Gorky: "Devilishly tired. Suffering from insomnia. I am off to take a rest." On the 16th, to Molotov, Secretary of the Central Committee: "May I please continue my holiday another fortnight in compliance with my doctors' orders?"

Despite all this Lenin presented his report to the IXth Congress, and he was in Moscow when an invitation reached him from Cannes on the 7th January 1922. Lloyd George pressed him to attend the conference in person. Lenin wished to reply at once in the affirmative, but his friends thought otherwise. Some feared for his safety, others for his health, and a motion was passed that Lenin should be asked to abandon his intention to make the journey. On the 27th January the Russian Central Party Executive decided at an extraordinary session to form a

[34] Referred to by F. P. Walters in *A History of the League of Nations*, New York, 1952 'p. 448.

delegation to attend the Genoa Conference. The Committee took no part, but, although Lenin was named as leader of the delegation Chicherin was elected deputy, in case the statesman was not available.

At the Congress of the Metal-Workers Association on the 6th March Lenin said that his health would not stand in the way of his going to Genoa, and that while there he intended to talk with Lloyd George. But at the end of March his doctors were concerned about his condition, and forbade the journey. Once more Lenin visited Gorky, and reduced the scope of his intellectual activities.

Chicherin took charge of the Soviet delegation to Genoa. He was a diplomat of great charm, and accustomed to travelling with Lenin; he was not, however, a first-class statesman. Chicherin, once an exile, had been trained according to western traditions. He wrote in his memoirs: "Every day over the telephone Lenin used to give me the most detailed advice. He was a man of extraordinary versatility and ingenuity, and exhibited these qualities in the manner in which he could ward off an opponent's attacks."

From a distance, therefore, Chicherin maintained Lenin's ideas, which reached him in the form of memoranda and telegrams. On the 1st April the Soviet delegation stopped at Berlin, and, in the course of talks with Wirth and Rathenau, it was agreed that the Soviet and German delegations should maintain contact throughout the conference in Genoa.

The first plenary session of the conference was held at the Palazzo San Giorgio on the 10th April, the Monday of Holy Week. Presiding over their respective delegations were Lloyd George, Barthou (Poincaré's liegeman), Facta (Italy), Ishu, Theunis, Wirth and Chicherin. Altogether twenty-nine European nations were represented. The American ambassador in Rome was present as an observer on behalf of the United States.

The conference marked an important stage in the history of international relations. It was the Soviet Union's first encounter with the West. It was also the first time the world Press had had the opportunity of following the stages of a diplomatic conference, and the number of journalists present was considerable — westerners with a stake in Russian assets were anxious to know at once to what extent their interests were being safeguarded. Observers representing great industrial organizations clustered around the delegations, and held private conferences.

During the first session Chicherin declared:

It is evident that the economic reconstruction of Russia, which is the largest State in Europe and has incalculable natural resources, is an indispensable condition of world economic reconstruction. Russia affirms that she is fully prepared to play her part in solving the problems before the Conference, with all the means within her power — and those means are not inconsiderable.[35]

Chicherin gave more details. He stated that Russia was ready to open her frontiers, collaborate with Western industry, and set up commissions to initiate discussions. Moreover, he proposed a general reduction in armaments and the armed forces — an entirely new and important factor in the history of international relations.

When the western nations asked for repayment of debts and indemnities, the Russians replied with a long memorandum on the 20th April. But Chicherin had already allowed it to be known that Russia also wished to be compensated for the damage caused by Allied military intervention in 1918 and 1919.

Lloyd George dominated the conference room by his personality. Behind the scenes he prepared an agreement with Krassin, the Soviet delegate in London, under which the exploitation of Russian oil in the Caucasus would pass to the Royal Dutch Shell Company. Although the conference drifted into deadlock, important agreements were signed. The Germans were uneasy. On the Saturday preceding Easter Sunday the German delegates gathered in their hotel, and once more went over the groundwork of their policy. It was during this "Conference in Pyjamas" that Wirth and Rathenau decided to sign a treaty with the Russians in Rapallo on the 16th April. Under the treaty the two countries agreed to renounce all claims against each other, and to re-establish normal diplomatic and commercial relations. For Germany this accord was above all political; it enabled her to allow the Allies to suspect a broadening of Russo-German understanding and economic expansion for Russia, who thus succeeded in eliminating her sense of isolation.

The announcement of the Treaty of Rapallo burst like a bomb among the delegations, and the western powers made a strong protest. The uproar settled down, however, when even more sensational news was announced: Lloyd George's agreement with Krassin concerning Russian oil. The Anglo-Dutch company was extremely active behind the scenes. Before the 1914 war it had bought the Rothschild interest in Russian

---

[35] Amedeo Giannini, *Les documents de la conférence de Gênes*, Rome, 1922.

oil,[36] and Henry Deterding had made vain attempts to procure Allied military intervention in the Caucasus in order to recover Anglo-Dutch assets. After the failure of the Wrangel and Kolchak expeditions Deterding decided to do battle in the diplomatic field in Genoa. For several months he had been buying back for a mere song all Russian oil shares on the stock-market, and aimed at becoming the undisputed master of the Caucasian wells.

But when the agreement between Lloyd George and Krassin was announced the Americans reacted immediately. Child, United States representative, mindful of the interests of the Standard Oil Company, declared at once that the United States would accept no other trading policy than that of the open door. Standard Oil, which had also bought up the shares of Nobel Brothers in Caucasian oils in 1914, expected to make the most of those rights. The United States demanded equal rights with Britain.

This quarrel among the oil men brought about the failure of the entire conference. While an opening was being made in the western front by the Soviet's separate agreement with Germany, the Allies were becoming divided once more over oil. The French and Belgians agreed with Standard Oil, and the British dared not disregard the American veto.

On the 20th April the Russian delegation replied with a memorandum to the Allied note. Chicherin offered to pay the debts incurred under the Czarist régime (18 milliard gold roubles), on condition that the Allies paid compensation for the losses sustained as a result of their intervention in 1919 (30 milliard gold roubles). Absolute deadlock had been reached. The conference continued until the 19th May; its only result was an agreement to hold a new conference — the Hague Conference, which lasted from the 15th June to the 22nd July, and went no further in solving the problem of the relations between Europe and the Soviet.

For a while Russia did not join the League of Nations. Her diplomatic and economic relations with the western world remained precarious. France and Britain, rejecting the principle of "peaceful co-existence" — *pacifica convivenza* — recommended by Italy, flung the Soviet Union out of Europe. The League of Nations became an Anglo-French affair.

When Chicherin returned to Moscow Lenin declared:

[36] In exchange for 4 million gold florins worth of Royal Dutch shares and £250,000 worth of Shell shares.

The delegation of the Central Executive Committee has carried out its task well; it has defended the sovereignty of the U.S.S.R., and, by signing a treaty with Germany, has defeated attempts to restore private property and hold us to ransom.[37]

But Lenin was succumbing gradually to his repeated attacks of congestion. He therefore gave up public affairs. Within a few months he became paralysed, and in December 1922 he withdrew from all political activity. He died on the 21st January, 1924.

Stalin had been the Party's general secretary since the 2nd April 1922. The political evolution of Europe might possibly have proceeded differently had Lenin assisted personally at the Genoa Conference. "Peaceful co-existence" might have emerged from that conference, and all the accepted facts of the Treaty of Versailles would have been changed. In any case, the absence from Genoa of the great Soviet statesman is an historical fact of which the consequences are incalculable.

6. The 1922 Moratorium and the Role of Poincaré

On the 12th July 1922 the German Chancellor, Cuno, announced that Germany was unable to execute the settlement laid down under the agreements signed in 1921. Three weeks earlier (24th June) Minister Rathenau had been assassinated by the Nationalists. The inflation of the mark had begun, and the Allies received a letter from Cuno requesting a six months' moratorium.

In France it fell to the President of the Council, Raymond Poincaré, to reply to this request. He and his friends Barthou and Tardieu strongly advocated absolute adherence to the terms of the Peace of Versailles.[38] Poincaré was above all a legal man, inclined to adhere to the letter of agreements and reject any departure that was not authorized and provided for by law. The Treaty contained "imperfections and omissions"; but it existed, and was therefore legally binding. It would be a grievous error to allow even its most insignificant provisions to be suppressed or rendered invalid".[39]

Poincaré conferred with his British counterpart, Lloyd George, and on the 30th July declared himself willing to accept Germany's request

---

[37] Potiemkin, *Histoire de la Diplomatie*, Vol. III, *1919–1939*, Paris, 1947 p. 174,
[38] Poincaré put his point of view in the foreign policy section of the *Revue des Deux Mondes* and the publication *Temps*.
[39] J. Chastenet, *Raymond Poincaré*, Paris, 1948, p. 229.

for a moratorium, on condition that the Ruhr mines were placed at the disposal of the Allies. Lloyd George was not an advocate of the "gage productif" policy, and stated that he was prepared to rely on Germany's ability to pay. The Germans laid the matter before the Reparations Commission, which proposed that the request for a moratorium be accepted without surety. The French delegate, Dubois, who disagreed with France's President of the Council, resigned his post.

An Anglo-French conference met in London from the 7th to the 14th August 1922 to settle differences of opinion, but the stands taken by Lloyd George and Poincaré were irreconcilable, and it was impossible to find a common basis of agreement. The English were ruffled, and took advantage of the situation to ask France to repay their war debts. The demand annoyed Poincaré considerably, and he stated flatly that France would settle her debts when she received her share of the reparations.[40]

After this setback Lloyd George was defeated in the October elections and gave place to a Conservative government under Bonar Law. And Germany still remained without a reply. Cuno repeated his request for a moratorium on the 14th November. On the 9th December the French and British met again in London to study the German request, but no agreement was possible. The delegates present were Bonar Law, Poincaré, Theunis (Belgium), and representing Italy a new man — Mussolini — who had just taken over power following his "March on Rome".

For three days the victors faced each other in the austere surroundings of 10 Downing Street. "No moratorium without security," declared Poincaré. Bonar Law said that England was prepared not to link the settlement of war debts due to the United States with the settlement due from Germany, but she asked for no guarantees. Though Mussolini strove to find a compromise solution he was unsuccessful: the meeting was his apprenticeship as a negotiator on the international plane.

On his return to France Poincaré conferred with Millerand, President of the Republic. Millerand declared that the Ruhr must be occupied, with or without British agreement. Poincaré seemed to hesitate, although he had so far displayed a splendid spirit of resolution. Not that he wished to retreat in order to safeguard Franco-British friendship;

[40] In adopting this attitude Poincaré had the full backing of French public opinion.

his scruples sprung from another source: he was a jurist, and he required a legal right to intervene.

Poincaré waded through documents, searching and ferreting. In his department there was a continual coming and going of files which one by one he stripped of dates, figures and paragraphs that he would quote when the occasion arose. This research provided him with the pretext he sought: on the 30th September the Reich should have delivered to France 50,000 cubic metres of timber and 200,000 telegraph poles. She had delivered only 35,000 cubic metres of timber and 55,000 poles.

Poincaré had given his friend Barthou Dubois's post on the Reparations Commission, and Barthou called a meeting of the Commission for the 26th December to establish Germany's default. A majority vote was taken — France, Belgium and Italy voted for sanctions; Great Britain voted against. The signatories to the Peace of Versailles were notified that under paragraphs 17 and 18, Appendix II, Part VIII of the Treaty, they were empowered to apply sanctions. Poincaré convened another conference in Paris for the 2nd to the 4th January 1923, attended by Bonar Law, Theunis and Poincaré. Mussolini who was not yet quite sure of himself did not attend personally, but was represented by the Marquis della Torretta, a diplomat who wore a perpetual smile.

Theunis and della Torretta agreed with Poincaré who stood firmly behind the principle of guarantees; Bonar Law did not. Poincaré saw himself imprisoned, as it were, by his own formula. If he yielded he would be admiting that the Treaty was unworkable. The text of the Treaty had to be respected, and if agreement was not possible between the French and the British, the only alternative was to record a disagreement.

Bonar Law stated that His Majesty's government, having given the most serious consideration to the French proposals, was firmly of opinion that if those proposals were put into effect, they would not only fail to achieve the desired results, but threatened to have a disastrous effect upon the economic situation of Europe. He said that His Majesty's government very much regretted the existence of a difference of opinion on so grave a matter, but was anxious to assure the government of the Republic that the sentiments of friendship felt by the British people towards the government and people of France remained unchanged.

Poincaré replied in the same vein:

The government of the Republic deeply regrets being unable to agree with the British government on this important question, but thanks the British government for its friendly declaration, and assures it that, despite this difference of viewpoint, the sentiments of the government of the Republic and the French nation towards England remain ever cordial.[41]

On the 11th January a mission composed of Italian, French and Belgian engineers (MICUM), accompanied by three military divisions, entered the basin of the Ruhr, and took possession of the mines and steelworks. The French Chamber approved Poincaré's action by 452 votes to 72 (the Socialists and Communists). The Radicals abstained from voting. This was the first time that the victors, divided in their views, attempted to apply *in toto* the terms of the Peace of Versailles.

Cuno, supported by German public opinion, protested vehemently to the signatories of the Treaty, and ordered workmen and officials in the Ruhr to offer "passive resistance". The Italo–Franco–Belgian mission had to contend with a speedily organized form of sabotage, based upon a general strike and suspension of postal and railway services. Sabotage was encountered almost everywhere: in March alone there were more than eighty cases. Some of the incidents ended tragically; there were, for instance, thirteen deaths at Krupp's on the 31st May. But the carefully chosen members of the mission accomplished their task; the trains were made to run and the factories became active once more.

Lord d'Abernon, British ambassador in Berlin, urged Cuno not to yield, and Lord Curzon, British Foreign Minister, sent note after note to the Quai d'Orsay repudiating the French action. But Poincaré never wavered; in his small, precise handwriting he replied to the British protests point by point, setting out faultless legal arguments to counter the protests.

General Degoutte, commanding the occupation forces in the Ruhr, expelled 145,000 agitators. But passive resistance petered out because Germany could no longer live without the Ruhr. Unemployment spread, the mark collapsed,[42] the whole economic life of the country was halted, and industrialists invested their reserves abroad.

On the 10th August Cuno resigned, and Ebert, President of the Reich, called on Dr Gustav Stresemann to form a coalition government. Confronted with widespread anarchy Ebert announced on the 26th September: "To safeguard the lives of the people and the life of the State we are to-day compelled to relinquish the struggle."

[41] Chastenet, *Vingt ans d'histoire diplomatique, 1919–1939*, Geneva, 1945, pp. 241 and 242.

[42] One dollar was worth 10,000 marks in January 1923; 110,000 in June, 350,000 in July and 4,600,000 in September.

Poincaré won, and work began again immediately. France alone remained the victor of the war.[43] The question now was: would Poincaré take advantage of the situation to initiate the necessary revision of the Treaty of Versailles, as President Millerand advised? Millerand asked Charles Reibel, minister of the liberated zones, to sound Poincaré. But the President of the Council did not wish to exploit his victory. "To talk with Germany would set us at loggerheads with England. I would rather offer my Cabinet's resignation than be forced into that policy."

When Foch was made acquainted with the situation he thundered, "This is a day of decision. It depends on M. Poincaré to make war no longer possible between France and Germany. Mark my words, M. Poincaré holds the victory of France in his hands. If we do not commence talks with Germany at once we shall never regain this lost opportunity". On that day he made an unsuccessful attempt to win over the head of the government. Poincaré remained set in his negative attitude.[44] He had changed since the war; he was now older and wiser, and more inclined to hesitate. He felt that the franc would soon need the support of British finance. An increase in taxation brought about his electoral defeat in May 1924. When he learned the result of the poll he said to his colleagues, "France is too tired to follow me".[45]

7. The Collapse of the Rhenist Movement (1923)

The Rhineland autonomists carried on in secret their movement in favour of an independent Rhineland. The occupation of the Ruhr and the collapse of the mark seemed to favour a renewed effort. At the beginning of April 1923 their leader, Dr Dorten, went to Paris to make contact with leading French personalities and to ascertain their intentions. Dr Dorten's secret wish was to meet Poincaré, and reach an arrangement under which an independent Rhineland would become associated with Poincaré's own plans.

Dr Dorten's sponsor was General Mangin who remained loyal to Marshal Foch's ideas and to all who had supported him in 1919. The General introduced his protégé to Marshals Joffre, Foch, Fayolle and

[43] The occupation of the Ruhr yielded to the Allies 424 million gold marks, of which 364 millions went to France.
[44] Chastenet, *Raymond Poincaré*, Paris, 1948, p. 250.
[45] *Ibid.*, p. 260.

Franchet d'Esperey, and to Generals Marchand and Weygand. All these officers gave Dorten a favourable reception. He was also received enthusiastically by the Committee of the Left Bank of the Rhine and the movement's leaders, Jacques Bainville and Maurice Barrès. A few prominent members of the Press and politics were very encouraging, including Emile Buré, Léon Daudet and Provost de Launay. But Dorten failed to meet Poincaré. Mangin took him to see Loucheur on the 8th April 1923. The Minister noted in his diary that Dorten struck him as being "mediocre", but Dorten appeared to think that Loucheur was sympathetically neutral.[46] Louis Marin and Edouard Herriot gave the Rhenish leader a cautious welcome, and then Poincaré made his position clear — "The President of the Council summoned Mangin, and asked him to send Dorten away at once to avoid his being expelled from France. The General was courageous enough to question the advisability of this step, and added, 'If the French government insists on dismissing Dorten, I believe it my duty to accompany him to the station with the usual official honours.'"[47]

A number of organizations, including the Committee of the Left Bank of the Rhine, favoured Dorten's aims, and they determined to force Poincaré's hand. The President of the Council reacted in his usual way by dividing his opponents. First, he summoned several of Dorten's most enthusiastic supporters, and revealed to them under the bond of secrecy that Dorten was a German spy and a double agent, whose task was to sow discord among Frenchmen. Then Bunau–Varilla, proprietor of the newspaper *Matin*, summoned Dorten and gave him to understand that Poincaré was favourable to his cause, and hoped he would return to the Rhineland to regroup his autonomist forces; he added that Poincaré would give him every possible help.[48] Dorten therefore returned to Wiesbaden convinced that France would support his movement, and he devoted much time to preparing for action on a large scale.

There were two groups in the Rhineland movement during that period: the Activists, of whom Dorten was the leading representative,

[46] Loucheur, Brussels, 1962, p. 122, contains both Loucheur's and Dorten's account of the interview.
[47] Based on Dorten's account; *La Tragédie rhénane*, Paris, 1945, p. 141.
[48] Mangin, *Comment finit la guerre*, Paris, 1920, p. 96, and Dorten, *La Tragédie rhénane*. This interview did take place, but we have only Dorten's account of it. Bunau–Varilla has never commented. The Ministry for Foreign Affairs, when approached by Dorten, denied that Poincaré entrusted Bunau–Varilla with any business whatsoever.

and the Legalists, whose leader, was Adenauer, the Burgomaster of Cologne, who continued to fight for federalism within the Reich. The march into the Ruhr combined with inflation presented the country with crucial problems, multiplied and aggravated day after day. The Rhinelanders became increasingly indignant at having to shoulder the consequences of Prussian policy. Adenauer and Ludwig Hagen, a Cologne banker, perfected a scheme for a bank of issue which, while safeguarding the Rhineland from the bankruptcy that threatened the Reich, would remain linked with the State Bank.

Not all the Activists were grouped under the leadership of Dorten, who remained rather a peace-maker than a real leader. A number of agitators had their own followers, and aimed at a form of Rhenish autonomy resembling that backed by Dorten. Among them was Smeets, a socialist who had the support of the masses, but had broken away from the Social Democrats. Others were Matthes, an extremist with revolutionary tendencies, and Deckers, an ambitious industrialist from Aix-la-Chapelle, but with little backbone.

The Reich government was faced with grave problems. The Cuno Cabinet was forced to resign on the 12th August 1923, and Cuno was followed by Stresemann who lasted only four months. The statesmen in Berlin feared the growing success of the Separatists.[49]

Meanwhile Dorten and his friends were losing precious time. They perfected an autonomous Rhineland banking scheme, which did not receive the support of Poincaré who was inclined rather towards Adenauer's project, since it also enjoyed the sympathy of the United Kingdom. The Americans had left Germany, after transferring their sector in the Coblenz district to France; the British continued to support a unified Germany and stood behind Adenauer; the Belgians, who had accompanied the French into the Ruhr, had no desire, however, to stray too far from the British point of view. It was in the Belgian zone that the Separatists launched their movement. Its progress worried the British, who had no wish to see it spread to Cologne and into the Ruhr. The Belgians were alarmed to see the Francophile movement extending along the Rhine to the north of a line from Prüm to Coblenz, that is to say, the whole length of the Belgian frontier.

A series of discussions took place between a young Belgian politician named Pierre Nothomb, leader in Brussels of the Committee of National

---

[49] On the 30th September serious incidents occurred in Dusseldorf. During a demonstration the police fired on the Separatists, and there were several hundred casualties.

Policy and the Belgo-Rhineland Committee, Colonel de Lannoy, former aide-de-camp to Field Marshal Haig, and Colonel Ryan, British High Commissioner in the Rhineland. As a result of these talks Colonel Ryan became convinced that a Rhenish republic — which England opposed–would present no problem at all if the republic were not entirely dominated by France. According to Baron Nothomb,

Colonel Ryan secured the tacit agreement of his government for us to initiate a movement for the independence of the Rhineland, on condition that it was a northern Rhenish State under Belgian influence. There would be no objection to a southern state under French influence. It was, therefore, desirable to allow a movement to spring into being in the north; but agreement between the French and the "Francophile activists" was a necessary preliminary.[50]

I went to Paris to meet Monsieur Paul Lefaivre, General Mangin and Jacques Bainville at the house of a certain retired diplomat. I pointed out to them that the Rhineland would never become independent if the British and Belgians continued to oppose the idea.

The Belgians would instinctively resist encirclement, and the British would refuse to be separated from the Rhine by a State obedient to France. Eventually General Mangin and Jacques Bainville understood the position, and agreed to make the people in Coblenz and Wiesbaden see sense. All that occurred about the middle of October.[51]

Colonel Reul, one of Baron Nothomb's colleagues on the Committee of National Policy and the Belgo-Rhineland Committee, established himself at Aix-la-Chapelle near the young revolutionaries to act as a friendly political adviser.

On the 21st October Leo Deckers took over the public buildings at Aix-la-Chapelle, and proclaimed the independence of the Rhineland Republic. On the same day Tirard, Inter-Allied High Commissioner for the Rhineland, summoned Dorten to Wiesbaden, and made it clear that the French government favoured the movement. Dorten again saw Tirard on the following day, and informed him that the French government intended to associate itself with the Belgian action, and

[50] This is based on the testimony of Baron Nothomb. No trace can be found elsewhere of this new orientation of British policy.

[51] Again according to Dorten (*La Tragédie rhénane*, p. 162), the French at first refused to participate in Nothomb's scheme. On the 20th October they agreed on condition that they might later raise the question of the division of the Rhineland into several States. Mangin's son wrote disparagingly of the scheme — "The rather confused dream of a mind that casually overlooked eleven hundred years of historical evolution." L. Z. Mangin, *La France et le Rhin*, Geneva, 1945, p. 106.

---

that M. Poincaré had given instructions accordingly. The time was ripe, for all Rhenish organizations to act in unison. A provisional government composed of their representatives would be recognized *de facto* by France.[52]

The early success of the Aix-la-Chapelle putsch had two results. To begin with the Belgian Ministry for Foreign Affairs made no comment. Furthermore, Matthes took over "power" in Coblenz at the head of a free corps — "Freies Rheinland" — and endeavoured to seize control of public affairs throughout the whole of north Rhineland. A quarrel then occurred between Dorten and Matthes, which resulted in a division of territory: the north Rhineland went to Matthes and the south to Dorten.

Matthes then attempted to suppress the movement in Aix-la-Chapelle. A quixotic commando unit, conveyed in special French trains, proceeded to Aix on the 2nd November with the intention of crushing the Rhineland Republic. The commandos were soon overpowered by Belgian troops. In view of the international scandal and chaos that resulted, the Belgian government was unable to follow closely the development of events during those hectic days, and allowed its soldiers to break up the northern republic and crush the Activists in the south.[53]

Matthes's forces rapidly disintegrated. The tension in Berlin had relaxed since the 26th September, and Stresemann ordered the end of passive resistance. Dorten endeavoured to gather together the last of his available forces to form an autonomous government at Bad Ems. On the 22nd December Tirard once again summoned Dorten to Coblenz.

The President of HCJTR, High Commissioner for the French government, informed me that France had given Britain an undertaking that she would put an end to the Separatist movement; and he added that he had received very precise instructions on the subject obliging him to take action *manu militari* against any resistance by the Rhinelanders, should they refuse to evacuate public buildings.

With regard to my person the head of the French government stipulated that I was to be handed over to the Prussian authorities to be tried under common law.[54]

[52] Dorten, *La Tragédie rhénane*, Paris, 1945, p. 166.
[53] This is based on the testimony of Pierre Nothomb. Britain sent a note to Brussels and Paris on the 31st October, pointing out that she would not recognize a Rhineland Republic.
[54] Dorten, *La Tragédie rhénane*, Paris, 1945, p. 192. Tirard's tactful account is not quite accurate.

Tirard did not carry out the last instruction, and Dorten left the Rhineland on the Ist January 1924 for Nice, where he remained under house arrest.

Some little time elapsed before the Separatists really appreciated that their movement had finally collapsed. On the 12th February 1924 a group of strongly armed Nationalists undertook to drive out the representatives of the "autonomist movement" who were still installed in the law-courts at Pirmasens. The Separatists, about forty in number, refused to quit the building and barricaded themselves in. At 6.30 in the morning the Nationalists began to fire on the building; they forced their way into the ground floor which they sprinkled with thirty-three gallons of petrol, and set fire to it. The fire rapidly took hold of the building, and the Separatists, suffocated by the smoke and suffering from burns, surrendered one by one. As they came out of the building they were massacred with hatchets and knives. Several of the bodies were hurled back into the blazing mass. Schwab, the "Commissioner of the Autonomous Palatin Government," shot himself in the head rather than surrender to the Nationalists.

During this demonstration of savagery the French forces maintained a "strict neutrality". According to General Mordacq, who was responsible for that area, the officer commanding the troops on the spot wished to enforce order. It appears, however, that a representative from the High Commission informed the officer that he had just received from Paris — that is to say, from the government — orders not to intervene, but to observe strict neutrality.[55]

The massacre at Pirmasens was long remembered, and France lost face as a result of the incident.

[55] General H. Mordacq's *La Mentalité allemande*, Paris, 1926.

CHAPTER II

THE UNITED STATES OF EUROPE

1. Was Stresemann sincere?
2. Did the Thoiry talks result in anything concrete?
3. Was the failure of the United States of Europe plan due to the growth of nationalism?

1. Stresemann's Sincerity

Although it was Ebert who announced the end of "passive resistance", it was Gustav Stresemann, the new Chancellor, who had taken the decision.

Stresemann merits closer study. His fragmentary writings were intended to serve as the groundwork of his *Memoirs* which he began to write in 1928. The notes were collected by his secretary, Heinrich Bernhard, and published in bulk without amendment. Everything tends to prove the reliability of the work; though the notes sometimes lack cohesion, we may none the less be sure that, had the Chancellor himself been able to complete the work, it would have proved a reliable account.

The arguments of Stresemann's opponents can, in the main, be summed up in one letter: the one dated the 7th September 1925 and addressed to the Kronprinz:

In my view Germany's immediate foreign policy has three main objectives . . . the solution of the Rhineland problem . . . the protection of the ten or twelve million Germans who now live under a foreign yoke . . .[1] the re-adjustment of our eastern frontiers — the taking over of Danzig and the Polish corridor, and an alteration in the frontier of Upper Silesia; then, as a long-term plan, the union of Austria and Germany . . .

But the first point I mentioned is the most important — the liberation of our country and the removal of occupation forces from our soil. The first essential is that those who are now throttling us release their hold. That is why German policy must at the outset adopt the method followed, I think, by Metternich in Austria in 1809: resort to subterfuge and avoid important decisions.

[1] The Saar, Czechoslovakia and Poland.

I trust your Imperial Highness will not wish me to enlarge on this subject at present. I am, of course, bound to be discreet; if V. A. I. is going to give me the opportunity to discuss these matters with him — and they will soon become urgent — I gladly place myself at his disposal.[2]

The above letter breathes an obvious atmosphere of sincerity. But if the programme outlined is compared with Stresemann's other statements, in which he appears to be ready to consider a Franco-German rapprochement as the basis of his European policy,[3] one is forced to question the honesty of this German statesman.

Beginning with this dual attitude of Stresemann the Nationalists criticized his weaknesses and double dealing to their hearts' content. The complexity of the Chancellor's personality had its origin in his youth. He was born in Berlin on the 10th May 1878, the son of a tavern-keeper on the Köpenickerstrasse. He was, therefore, of humble birth, and spent a lonely youth entirely engrossed in study, apart from one or two romantic outbursts. He admired the 1848 Liberals and, despite police regulations, used to lay flowers on their graves.[4] As a student he lived in Berlin and Leipzig, and chose as the theme of his thesis at the university the subject, "The small scale beer trade in Berlin: a typical example of industrial centralization". He devoted all his leisure to reading, the editing of students' magazines and fencing with other students.

The degree of doctor was conferred on him at the age of 23, and he joined the board of the German chocolate manufacturers' association at Dresden; there his talent for organization and publicity made him a brilliant success. He helped to create the German manufacturers' union, and others soon followed his example. Similar associations came into being in Thüringen and Württemberg. When these associations amalgamated in 1895, Stresemann was appointed Vice-President of the new organization — the Bund der Industriellen, a post he retained until 1919.[5]

His mind was absorbed in schemes for the protection of manufacturers, especially the smaller concerns, and at the age of 26 he joined the municipal council in Dresden. Shortly afterwards he was elected member of the Reichstag. Stresemann soon became one of the leaders of the National Liberal party where he specialized in export matters and foreign

[2] Stresemann, Les papiers de Stresemann, Paris, 1932–1933, Vol. II, p. 113.

[3] Ibid. Vol. III, p. 62, for instance.

[4] In 1923, loyal to the ideal of his early youth, he made a speech in honour of the 75th anniversary of the 1848 revolution.

[5] The year in which the Reichsverband der deutschen Industrie was founded.

policy. He also defended the interests of the middle classes and strove to safeguard them against industrial monopoly.

He was defeated in the elections of 1912, but held a seat in East Friesland at the end of 1914, one of the strongholds of the National Liberal party. From the moment he entered the German parliament he found himself torn between the two ideals of his youth: Nationalism and Liberalism. Throughout the war he worked strenuously for the victory of "mighty Germany"; he gave his backing to total submarine warfare and absolute power for the army; and he fought for the maintenance of the Monarchy. In support of such principles he cast his votes. He condemned barrack-room savagery, the evils of bureaucracy, and he never forgot the arduous conditions under which businesses like his father's laboured.

His objective gradually took shape in his mind: a constitutional Monarchy, guided by great ministers with a liberal outlook–men like Prince von Bülow. But all these hopes were dashed to the ground when Germany was vanquished. It is easy to imagine that 1919 must have been a year in which this stimulating spirit with the constructive outlook was forced to examine his conscience. Undoubtedly the result of that examination was the vote he and his party cast against the ratification of the Versailles Treaty. He was one of the last to leave the hall of the Reichstag when it was overrun by the revolutionaries.

The private life of Stresemann followed the same pattern as his public life. When his college days were over he had a disappointing love affair: perhaps he aimed too high; or a dream may have been shattered. Shortly afterwards he married and lived a regular, humdrum life, from which he escaped into his study to read Goethe and Napoleon. By 1919 this man, divided between ambition and Utopia, torn between Nationalism, and Liberalism, was ripe for a great destiny. As leader of the National Liberal party he believed in the usefulness of negotiation and organization. He succeeded in bringing about the merger of the National Liberal and Democratic parties, and founded the Deutsche Volkspartei, a party of the centre.

Stresemann was nominated Chancellor on the 13th August 1923, and remained Chancellor, either by right or in fact, until his death in 1929. He managed to restore normal relations between France and Germany. Although he never lost his dream of a "mighty Germany", he at once set about restoring confidence in international relationships. His first act as Chancellor was to bring about the end of passive resistance (26th September 1923), and by this single stroke he disposed of Poincaré's objective: a return to the policy of forcing Germany to carry out the engagements entered into in 1921. Henceforward it became a question of assisting Germany to re-establish its economy; Stresemann was therefore able to secure on the 24th October a re-examination by the Reparations Commission of Germany's ability to pay.

General Dawes, a former American administrator, was entrusted by the Commission with the task of framing a new scheme for the payment of reparations. The Dawes Plan resulted in a reduction of the total arrived at in the 1921 agreements. It was agreed that Germany would pay between one and two and half milliards of gold marks within five years. To offset this arrangement, which Stresemann accepted, Germany received an initial loan of 800 million gold marks, and secured a decision to evacuate the Ruhr between July 1925 and January 1926.

In the sphere of foreign politics Stresemann proposed to the French in 1925 a German guarantee of France's eastern frontiers. This meant a definite recognition of France's annexation of Alsace-Lorraine. To begin with Poincaré regarded the offer with suspicion; but the proposal gained ground, and was seriously considered by Aristide Briand after the fall of Poincaré in the 1924 elections. Briand was also in favour of a Franco-German rapprochement, and took advantage of the opportunity to arrange an international conference at Locarno from the 5th to the 16th October 1925. Together Briand, Austen Chamberlain, Stresemann, Vandervelde and Mussolini endeavoured to replace the imposed Peace of Versailles by a negotiated peace which guaranteed the frontiers of all the signatories. Stresemann reiterated his profound conviction that Germany was not "guilty" of the war — and no one contradicted him.

The signing of the Pact of Locarno marked an important date in post-war diplomatic history. For the first time the French and British agreed to a revision of the treaty which had never realized the stable peace expected of it. Also for the first time German response was really sincere in these negotiations.

For Stresemann Locarno was a milestone in his life. He failed to secure a formal declaration acquitting Germany of guilt for the war, but he repeated his demand on the occasion of Germany's joining the League of Nations. The question was evaded by the Allies who saw in Locarno an opportunity to preserve and maintain the Peace of Versailles, once a number of desirable amendments had been introduced. As for the Germans, they considered that Locarno offered them a chance to work round the treaty, and put an end to the state of affairs created by the *diktat* of Versailles. The Allies, however, had no wish to carry their policy to its logical conclusion and deal with the Germans as equals. The old misunderstanding remained, and it persisted for another year, until Germany joined the League of Nations on the 4th September 1926.

France found it possible to believe in that "universal peace" promised by Briand; and Germany believed that the concept of a "mighty Germany" within a pacified Europe was once again realizable.

There is nothing in all this to suggest that Stresemann deceived anyone by concealing his true intentions. The German statesman obviously did not hide his conviction that Germany was not guilty of the war; he did not cover up his desire to secure the evacuation of the occupied zones, or his hope of making Germany great. The Chancellor desired to achieve his aims by peaceful methods, and the fact the Nationalists made him the object of their violent attacks is a point in his favour.

2. The Conference at Thoiry (17th September 1926)

A financial crisis was rapidly developing in France. Once again Poincaré took over the leadership of the country, but he retained Briand as Foreign Minister. French foreign policy lacked coherence: Poincaré — the principal supporter of the Treaty of Versailles — had placed his foreign policy in the hands of the very man who strove for revision of the Treaty.

Immediately following Germany's entry into the League of Nations — an event that had been brought about by Briand — the German Chancellor, Stresemann, expressed a desire to meet Briand privately. He suggested that the meeting took place at at Ferney-Voltaire, but Briand's colleagues[6] arranged the rendezvous at the Hotel Léger, in Thoiry, Savoy, a few kilometres from Geneva. To outwit the journalists Briand and Stresemann left Geneva by different routes at 11 o'clock on the morning of the 17th September 1926. Stresemann made the journey by motor launch, and Briand by car.

Their lunch lasted from 1 o'clock to 5.30, and three persons were present — Briand, Stresemann and a Monsieur Hesnard, a cultural attaché at the French Embassy in Berlin, who acted as interpreter. In the course of time this gentleman returned to France, and became Dean of the Faculté des Lettres, in Grenoble. He died in December

[6] Monsieur Peycelon especially, and not Loucheur, as some writers have thought.

1936. His papers, left to his widow, contain no reference to the conference at Thoiry.[7]

There exists no reliable trace of the conversation at Thoiry, except perhaps the menu found among Stresemann's papers:

> Hors d'œuvre variés
> Aspic de Foie gras
> Truite sauce bleue
> Poulet Henri IV
> Canard truffé braisé au Porto
> Petits Pois fernière
> Perdrix rôtie sur Canapé
> Fromage — Fruits
> Vacherin glacé

This succulent menu must have kindled a communicative atmosphere between the men; M. Seydoux summed it up as follows: "At Thoiry Stresemann said that everything in dispute between France and Germany might be contained in a liqueur glass."

Stresemann left a brief note of the conversation, a one-sided and very sketchy account, which should be treated with caution. According to Stresemann the talk at first touched upon secondary matters. Briand observed that a military manual in use in the national organization known as Stahlhelm (Steel Helmets) seemed very militant and vindictive. Stresemann expressed his surprise that the French army still occupied so much residential accommodation in the Rhineland.

Then Briand spoke of Poincaré, who, he said,

has never cultivated the company of his fellow-men. He began by spending his time surrounded by files at the law-courts, and then among old political documents. He was a man who followed his train of thought tenaciously, and knew every sentence of every memorandum. But he was ignorant of the sentiments of the French people, and had not the remotest idea of the spirit demanded by the changing times.

Stresemann said that, whatever the sensationalist Press in the capital might say, the German people approved his foreign policy.

All this suggests that so far the conversation had not touched upon anything really important. But the basis of the discussions had a bearing on the essential facts of Franco-German relations:

[7] However, Hesnard did hand Briand some notes that evening; Briand's biographer, Suarez (*Briand*, Plon, Paris, 1938), found them among Briand's papers. They are very vague in content.

[8] Stresemann, *Vermächtnis* Berlin, 1932–1933, III, 10.

(1) The payment of reparations to France;
(2) France's evacuation of the occupied territories.[9]

On these particular points Stresemann's memorandum is more concise:

> Monsieur Briand stated his conviction that partial solutions were useless, because they always harboured new dangers. His intention was to resolve once and for all every question outstanding between France and Germany. He asked me to tell him frankly whether, once these problems had been solved, I thought we might also enter upon financial agreements with France. He then went into details, saying that he envisaged not only the restitution of the Saar, but bringing to an end the occupation of the Rhine.[10]

Stresemann is alleged to have replied:

> 'Assuming that our Cabinets approve our action, let the experts set to work at once, so that early next year we may seek agreement on all these matters with the other nations concerned; then, by the 30th September 1927 at the latest, all foreign troops should have left the Rhineland.' (Briand nodded his assent.) 'I take it, therefore, that it is not a question of reducing the period of occupation, but of immediate and total discontinuance.'

Apparently the two ministers spoke of possible financial loans: 300 gold million marks for the purchase of the Saar mines (foreshadowed by the Treaty of Versailles), and one milliard gold marks to cover Germany's obligations. Both promised to discuss these matters with their associates in their respective governments.

> Later, on the 23rd November 1926, Stresemann confirmed before the Reichstag that the evacuation of occupied territory and the settlement of the Saar question were discussed at Thoiry, in relation to certain financial co-operation from Germany, and in particular with the release of part of the German State Railway bonds issued following upon the Dawes Plan.[11]

The talks at Thoiry came to nothing, because they were not very realistic. No French government at that period could defy public opinion to the point of agreeing to evacuate the Rhineland and the Saar. In any case, Poincaré's Cabinet succeeded in stabilizing the franc, and had no further need of German advances.

[9] Suarez found no trace of the second item in Hesnard's memorandum.

[10] Stresemann, op. cit., *Volume* III, p. 2. The Hesnard memorandum that Suarez discovered emphasizes the fact that Stresemann's position was that of a petitioner, and he did not approach the question of the evacuation of the Rhineland and the Saar.

[11] Hirth, *Stresemann*, p. 185, Paris, Ed. des Portiques, 1930.

The fact that no one really knew what Briand and Stresemann had promised each other fostered suspicion among their opponents at home. That was the danger of secret diplomacy. On the other hand, the personal contact between the two men was eventually to prove fruitful.

On the 21st September, before leaving Geneva, Stresemann made a speech to the German colony, in a beer house. It was the kind of speech that he had not been able to make before the League of Nations, "When we are reproached for having been morally responsible for the war, we reply: It is not true".[12]

In December 1926 Briand saw Stresemann in Geneva, and told him that for the time being it was necessary to shelve the schemes discussed at Thoiry. The German government had appointed a special committee composed of the Ministers of Foreign Affairs, Finance and Economics, together with the President of the Reichsbank, to put the Thoiry proposals into effect. They were now compelled reluctantly to suspend their activities. In consequence, 1927 was a year of waiting.

On the 26th August 1928 Stresemann was in Paris. One of his associates wrote an account of the event.

When he got off the train he looked pale and weary; he even found it difficult to stand up and face the photographers. All who had known him formerly had the impression that his days were numbered, for he was unable to make a step without experiencing pain. His voice was faint, his cheeks hollow, and he looked extremely wan. He was forced to rest for several hours, and it was only in the evening that he arrived at the Quai d'Orsay, where he had a conference with Briand lasting more than an hour. He found it impossible to take part in the demonstrations that had been arranged to celebrate the signing of the pact.[13] The doctor who accompanied him — Professor Zondek — forbade all exertion, especially attendance at the banquet which was to follow. Stresemann therefore took a drive in the Bois de Boulogne. It was the first opportunity he had had to sample the charms of Paris, to admire the life and bustle of France's capital. He would have preferred to see its beauties a little closer, but his two day's stay was so taken up with official duties that he had to be content with a few short drives, enabling him to glimpse the outstanding sights of Paris.

At 11 o'clock on Monday morning, the 27th August, took place the most significant event of the visit — the first conversation between Stresemann and Poincaré. On the occasion of Stresemann's meeting with Briand, the German Minister had worn a lounge suit, but when he called on Poincaré he marked the official character of his visit by presenting himself in the Rue de Rivoli in morning

---

[12] Stresemann, *op. cit.*, p. 16. Poincaré protested at once that Germany *was* responsible: the lawyer in him would not allow the validity of that claim to be discussed.

[13] The Briand–Kellogg Pact.

coat and top hat. He was received on the steps of the Ministry of Finance by M. Vermeil, of Strasburg University, who was Poincaré's interpreter. This gentleman conducted Stresemann to the President of the Council, whose office was situated on the first floor. The conference had been arranged to last an hour, as Stresemann had to be careful to avoid any strain. When the hour had passed Professor Zondek, who was waiting in an anteroom, had a message passed to Stresemann reminding him that it was time to take his leave.

But the French President and the German Foreign Minister had so much to say to each other that the time allowed by the doctor was extended by twenty minutes.

On leaving the Palace of the Louvre Stresemann declined to make any statement on what had passed between himself and Poincaré. It is impossible to say what might have been the impressions of these two men who, without knowing each other personally, had used strong official language to each other for five years across their frontiers! In an article written subsequently for the *Nación* of Buenos Aires Poincaré described Stresemann as being "bathed in perspiration"; the effort demanded by conversation, he wrote, tired Stresemann very much.

"One day the Communist member Béron maintained in the Chamber of Deputies that the Alsace question was discussed between Poincaré and Stresemann. The President of the Council interrupted, and flatly denied the statement, without, however, saying what exactly was discussed.[14]

Neither Professor Vermeil nor Dr Schmidt, who acted as interpreters, left any notes of the talks. We were unable to obtain details from Professor Vermeil.

Dr Schmidt's account of the meeting was given twenty years after the events.

One might have supposed that the two men would feel bitter towards each other, for the memory of the unconditional surrender demanded by Poincaré and the passive resistance of 1923 was far from having been extinguished.

An extraordinary tension reigned in Poincaré's office when these two eminent representatives of their countries began to speak. Poincaré opened the talks, in the slightly broken and rather monotonous voice of an old man, by putting a few personal questions to Stresemann. But the conversation remained very formal and restrained.

When Poincaré asked Stresemann what question was uppermost in his mind, the German Minister replied, "The Rhineland". But he added:

"Above all I am concerned with Franco-German relations. My desire is that our two peoples shall live like good neighbours, and I know that the majority of the German people have the same wish."

[14] Hirth, *op. cit.*, 217.

"I am willing to believe that this is your desire", Poincaré interrupted; "but are all Germans of the same mind? Is it not true that some university teachers are talking against France? Anti-French demonstrations take place in your country, do they not?"

The conversation then turned to the questions of Alsace and a possible Anschluss with Austria:

"Such a trend would altogether compromise a policy of peace", declared Poincaré.
"In Germany we know very well", Stresemann replied, "that an Anschluss could amount only to a mere gesture . . . The German government does not regard the matter as a reality. But the people will never cease to love Austria, and that affection will never be condemned. Austria is part of our life", he added warmly.
Poincaré did not press the point.

With regard to war debts Stresemann said:

"We must settle our European financial problems once for all, for this is a matter that is keeping all our countries cut off from America."

Poincaré nodded, and went on:

"The first thing necessary is a rational settlement of the reparations problem. Why has Germany not yet put forward the promised proposals?"

Stresemann made no reply. Then the two ministers discussed the influence of the German Romanticists on European culture as opposed to the American way of life.

"Stresemann was in excellent form" wrote Schmidt, "and Poincaré listened, ascinated. The ice had begun to melt."

But then an usher entered the room. Poincaré said to Stresemann, "Your doctor wishes to remind you of the time, Monsieur le Président".
"He must wait a little longer," replied Stresemann.
Ten minutes later the doctor sent another reminder by way of a sharp note. The conference was therefore brought to an abrupt conclusion.[15]
Stresemann left a brief note.[16] M. Poincaré complained about the rumours current in Germany concerning a forthcoming Anschluss

[15] Paul Schmidt, *Statist auf diplomatischer Bühne 1923–1935 : Erlebnisse des Chef-dolmetschers im Auswärtigen Amt mit den Staatsmännern Europas*, Bonn, Athenäum ed., 1949, p. 151.
[16] Stresemann, *op. cit.*, III, 265.

with Austria. Stresemann assured him that the question did not then arise. On the other hand, he called for a solution of the occupation problem. Poincaré replied that the problem was not linked with the Locarno agreements; the occupation of German territory remained a guarantee for the payment of reparations; at Thoiry it had been right to link these two questions independently of the others.

This conversation, however, was no more productive than the one at Thoiry had been. It was not until the advent of the Young Plan on the 7th June 1929 that the anticipated evacuation of the Rhineland (from September 1929 to June 1930) occurred in conjunction with a new system for the payment of reparations; this time, however, it was extended until 1988.

3. The Failure of Briand's United States of Europe (September 1929)

Aristide Briand had a vague idea that the solution to Franco-German problems was to be found on a higher plane, by thrusting aside the quarrels of individuals, avoiding the antagonisms of parties, and escaping from the deadlock to which public opinion had led the two countries.

Imperturbably the French Minister pursued his concept of an international rapprochement.

Briand came from a Breton family.[17] He had been thwarted in his choice of a career, for he wished to be a sailor; when his uncle was drowned his parents decided to choose a less arduous profession. He met with occasional frustrations as a result of spite in the early days of his career at the bar, but they merely tended to reveal his basic qualities which gradually asserted themselves: a profound horror of injustice and a great love of humanity. Though he had the tenacity, the obstinacy of the Breton, Briand retained the deep-seated character of the Celt — a meditative disposition, a constructive approach, but no sense of organization.

In a small farmhouse in Cocherel, on the banks of the Eure, he perfected his plans; with his carefully-chosen colleagues, especially Loucheur and Berthelot, he put his schemes into effect. As the years went on he grew more and more impatient at not being able to find a far-reaching solution to the Franco-German problem. His friend

[17] He was born in Nantes on the 18th March 1862.

Loucheur, who considered that the solution had to come from an expanded economic market, regarded the whole problem as an essentially economic one.

While productive capacity has increased, consumption and purchasing power, far from developing, have diminished. European industry must be organized according to what is known as the horizontal method, that is to say, on the basis of individual industries. Agreements and combines will to some extent solve the problem of Customs barriers, and will bring about a simultaneous increase in salaries, a fact which will restore to post-war Europe the consuming power it enjoyed before the war."[18]

This economic conception of Europe, which manifested itself as early as 1925, was more specifically defended by other industrialists. In Luxemburg Emile Mayrisch, founder of ARBED, succeeded in setting up an international agreement for steel, under which the metallurgists of Germany, Belgium, France, Luxemburg and the Saar met periodically, and agreed to apportion their products.[19] But these accords were not enough. Briand's ambition was to give this new European economic policy a scope which measured up to his own conception. There was a moment when this expansion seemed to have been achieved in the Coudenhove–Kalergi idea of "Pan-Europe". It began in 1922, and met with little success at first, though it gathered strength in time. Coudenhove-Kalergi sprang from some of the noblest families in Europe. Born an Austro-Hungarian, he was of Dutch and Greek ancestry, and of Czechoslovak nationality. Beginning with Press campaigns, followed by a book which had a great success, he called for the creation of a European Union to be named "Pan-Europe".

With certain reservations the idea won the approval of Benes and Stresemann, while Briand regarded the Pan-Europe conception as a means of realizing the United States of Europe of which he had dreamed. The French Minister warmly welcomed Coudenhove, and had many talks with him. Coudenhove wrote of his relations with French Statesmen:

I had an interview with Briand on the organization of a European committee in France. As numerous top-ranking French statesmen had declared themselves in favour of Pan-Europe, I requested Briand to propose one of them as President

[18] Loucheur, *Carnets secrets*, Brussels, Brepols, 1962, p. 160. This idea foreshadowed the Schuman Plan and the Common Market.

[19] It is worth noting that Mayrisch himself appreciated the necessity of not limiting his international agreement to steel alone. He established a Franco-German board to collect information; its purpose was to facilitate a cultural rapprochement between the two countries. Several meetings were held at Colbach, in Luxemburg.

of the French board. He did not choose Herriot or Painlevé, but Loucheur — a choice which surprised me.

Louis Loucheur was rather like an elegant and pleasant brother of Molotov. He was exceptionally intelligent and dynamic; he aspired to wealth and power as a means for action and the exercise of influence. In a Soviet state he would have made an excellent People's Commissar. Under the Third Republic he wished to be both minister and millionaire. In his right hand Loucheur held the reins of economy and in his left the trump card of politics. Firmly established in these two spheres, he was in addition proprietor of the Paris paper *Le Petit Journal*, over whose policy he exercised absolute control.

His profound knowledge of economics made him almost indispensable in the Council of Ministers. In this domain he occupied first place as adviser to his friend Briand, who did not understand much about economics. Loucheur was of an ardent and eager disposition; he worked hard and quickly. The French committee was set up in no time. The vice-presidents were chosen from the leaders of both left and right — Léon Blum and Joseph Barthélémy, the great jurist who became Minister of Justice in the Vichy government.

Loucheur had no illusions, and he did not hide the fact from Coudenhove, who wrote:

After we had set up our committee Loucheur said to me, 'We have a good committee, and we can add as many names as we wish. Do not imagine, however, that it will be of any help whatever to us in the realization of Pan-Europe! Once a year the members of our committee will appear at our general assembly, unless, of course, they excuse themselves from attendance. But, as far as Pan-Europe is concerned, they will do absolutely nothing, and all will go on as before. If you really wish to win over France to Pan-Europe, you must enlist the support of the industrialists. Only if you succeed in persuading these gentlemen to exchange their nationalist outlook for a European outlook can you possibly hope to gain France to Pan-Europe'.

Loucheur soon gathered together the French leaders in industry, and persuaded them to set up a second committee. This economic committee was composed of twenty leading businessmen representative of all branches of industry: Théodore Laurent and Lambert Ribot (steel), Gabriel Cordier and Louis Marlio (aluminium), Peyerimhoff (coal), Robert Hecker (electricity), René Fould (marine dockyards), Duchemin (chemicals), Gilet (silk), Dubrulle (woollens), and so on. It was agreed to the formation of a German committee as a counterpart to the French one, and thus open the way to Pan-European economic talks between the two governments.

I experienced no difficulty in forming the German economic committee, which was composed as follows: Geheimrat Duisberg and Carl Bosch (chemicals), Hermann Bücher (electricity), Dr Paul Silverberg (coal), Albert Vögler and Ernst Poensgen (steel), Richard Heilner (linoleum), Hermann Lange and Richard Gütermann (silk), Ludwig Roselius (Sanka coffee), and the Bankers Stauss, Herbert Gutmann and Carl Melchior.

Under the chairmanship of Loucheur the Pan-European Economic Council met several times in Paris. Despite the perfect cordiality that reigned over their exchange of views, the ideas of the German and French representatives differed fundamentally. In fact, the Germans wished to seize the French market, while the French, without bothering much about exports, defended their home market against foreign competition. But Loucheur was not only a brilliant president; he was a skilfull negotiator. He proposed the formation of European combines between French and German industries in the same productive field. Through the protection afforded by the combine French industry would have safeguards similar to those guaranteed by its own Customs barriers; on such a basis the abolition of those barriers in the interior of Europe would become possible, combined with the setting up of a great European market.

In the eyes of Loucheur this economic policy was impossible unless preceded by a convention between Germany and France, which would dispel the danger of war, and provide control of inter-European combines by an organization within the bosom of the League of Nations; the latter would prevent any infringement that might entail an increase in the cost of living.[20]

Loucheur promulgated the idea by pen, by conferences, by a work of research on problems of international economic co-operation — an idea which foreshadowed the coal-and-steel corporation to be realized twenty years later. Public opinion continued to develop an interest in Pan-Europe. With Coudenhove's co-operation Robert Bosch, a prominent German industrialist, founded an international association for the development of Pan-Europe; the purpose of the association was to gain the financial support necessary for action.

Robert Bosch was a self-made man. He was brought up the hard way, having begun life as a precision mechanic. In 1905 he was among the first European manufacturers to introduce the eight-hour day. His factories having worked on munitions during the whole of the 1914–18 war, he decided to devote part of his war profits to the construction of the Neckar Canal, which cost 13 million marks, and part to cultural and social enterprises (7 million marks). He also gave his attention to the housing problem, and created a richly endowed building society. Furthermore, he looked to a better mutual understanding between Germany and France, and from Germany gave his support to the efforts being made in France by Loucheur.[21]

Coudenhove endeavoured to unify all this good-will and channel it into a common effort. He organized a Pan-European congress for 1930. A beginning had been made on the 14th January 1938, when a small committee was set up composed of Loucheur, Coudenhove, Bücher, Mayrisch and Heinemann. This committee met in Paris or Brussels at the end of February to agree on the main features of the

[20] Coudenhove–Kalergi, *J'ai choisi l'Europe*, Paris, p. 166 *et seq.*
[21] Heuss, *Robert Bosch*, Tübingen, p. 523 *et seq.*

programme of the conference and to discuss the measures to be taken; additional members were then added.

Coudenhove accepted Loucheur's proposal that the terms of reference be defined as follows: To study the conditions under which the economic solidarity of European nations can best be realized.

During 1928 and 1929 Loucheur gave Coudenhove strong support in the organization of his congress, and without any apparent fuss Loucheur became responsible for the launching of the scheme. On the 1st September 1929 the opportune moment had arrived, and Briand made his famous appeal before the Tenth General Assembly of the League of Nations:

> During the last few years I have been associated with a movement to popularize an idea that has been described as noble, though perhaps to save it from being deemed foolhardy. The idea was born many years ago; it has haunted the imagination of philosophers and poets, and has enjoyed a considerable *succès d'estime*. It has blossomed in men's minds as the result of its own excellence, and has come to be regarded as filling a need. Propagandists united to disseminate the idea, to make it penetrate further into the souls of nations, and I confess that I have been one of those propagandists. I believe that among peoples who are geographically grouped as are the nations of Europe there should exist a sort of federal bond. It is this bond that I should like to see established. Naturally the association would function in particular in the economic sphere, for that is the most pressing problem. I think it can be made to succeed. I am also sure that from the political and social points of view this federal bond may be beneficial, without infringing upon the sovereignty of nations who become members of such an association.

In this way Briand exercised caution in presenting his scheme. It has been suggested that he was more anxious to please than to succeed. But this is not true, for he and his friend Loucheur had pondered long over the scheme, and he had to employ great tact in touching upon the sovereignty of States, which was being challenged for the first time. None the less, this diffident and diplomatic speech had the effect of a bomb. During a luncheon at the Hôtel des Bergues on the 9th September the twenty-six European delegates asked Briand to draft a memorandum on the subject, so that they might consult their governments. Briand presented the memorandum on the 1st May 1930, and it was agreed that replies should reach Paris before the 15th July.

During the winter Pan-European propagandists were dispersed all all over Europe. Herriot and Coudenhove in particular spoke in Vienna, Berlin and Prague, and secured ready approval of their cause, including the support of Stresemann and Benes. Others, among them Poincaré and Mussolini, were non-committal, but even their neutrality was welcome. On the 17th May 1930 the Pan-European Congress, organized by Coudenhove and Loucheur, opened in Berlin. Logically, the intensive, radiating publicity that surrounded the effort should have culminated in success; but at the end of 1929 two unexpected eventualities jeopardized the whole enterprise. Stresemann died on the 3rd October and, in New York, quotations on the Stock Exchange slumped on the 24th October. By a stroke of fate Briand lost the German spokesman who alone was capable of responding to France's offer, and Loucheur saw his economic proposals crash against the confusion of an unprecedented economic crisis.

Despite the reception given to Chancellor Wirth, despite also the cordial discussions between the French expert Daniel Serruys and Robert Besch, the Berlin congress was doomed to failure. The British representatives, Amery and Churchill, marked time, though they were most favourably inclined towards the Pan-Europe idea: Europe had to push ahead, but for imperialist reasons Britain was prevented from participating.

Loucheur then travelled to eastern Europe where also the reparations problem had poisoned the atmosphere. After friendly talks in Prague with Masaryk and Benes he arrived in Bucharest on the 28th May 1930, where the Rumanian parliament gave him an official reception. He said that the agricultural crisis raging in Eastern Europe as the result of surplus production had to be resolved by an increase in consumption; and to achieve that an economic organization of Europe on the plan outlined in Briand's memorandum was essential. There was no question of French hegemony.

The Rumanian parliament gave Loucheur an ovation. He explained to King Michael that the only possible solution lay in concerted action by European States. When he stopped at Budapest on the 30th May he was received by the Regent, Horthy, and Count Bethlen, President of the Council, to whom he spoke in a similar strain: a conference should be called to prove the necessity of burying past quarrels and turning the eyes towards the future; Hungary and the Little Entente must come together to examine factors which united them rather than conduct a Customs tariff war; they must work together in a European economic union.

In Belgrade on the 2nd June he made similar approaches to the King of Yugoslavia, and received a no less enthusiastic welcome.[22]

---

[22] Loucheur, *op. cit.*, pp. 163 *et seq.*

One by one the replies of the various governments reached Briand in Paris. Apart from Yugoslavia, which approved without reservation, the replies of most of the countries were conditional. Hungary wanted a revision of the Versailles treaties; whereas Rumania demanded guarantees that the terms of the treaties would be respected; Lithuania raised the question of Vilna; Poland asked that the concept of security be more precisely defined, but Norway and Sweden preferred not to discuss it. Switzerland and Portugal had no desire to weaken the position of the League. Most important of all, Great Britain had no desire to have to choose between Europe and the Commonwealth; Britain gave a formal, but courteous, refusal.

On the 8th September the European delegates to the League of Nations entrusted Briand with the task of raising the matter on the agenda of the eleventh Assembly — which he did on the 11th September. There followed a debate as to whether politics should take precedence over economics, or vice versa. When the oratorical wrangling had ended the 26 delegations declared themselves ready to co-operate with France in solving the European problem within the framework of the League of Nations. On the 16th September a committee of investigation was established to study the question of the United States of Europe, and to make a report. The committee assembled on the 17th under the chairmanship of Briand, and on ten other occasions until 1932, when Briand died; and still nothing had been achieved.

It is debatable whether Briand's proposal ever had any chance of being accepted. Perhaps Germany's parliamentary majority might have been more favourable in 1928 (before Stresemann's death). It is possible too that economic conditions at that period might have permitted Britain to co-operate; that is, before the Wall Street crash. Perhaps also the League of Nations was powerless to lead such a grandiose project to a successful issue. There will never be a reliable reply to all these questions. Apparently the timing was unfortunate, but Briand's proposal deserved a better fate. His objective investigation demonstrated clearly that when public opinion, politics and the economic situation all favour the implementation of an idea, its realization must follow within a short time, if it is not to decrease in popularity or even forfeit its chances of success altogether. It would be false to suggest that the rise of nationalism was an obstacle to success; but Briand's proposal constituted the last attempt by the most moderate men of Versailles to put an end on an international scale to the dissensions of the member nations of the League.

CHAPTER III

THE RISE OF FASCISM

1. What was the nature of the plans for a preventive war during the period 1933–1934?
2. Did Röhm instigate a plot against Hitler?
3. What was the extent of Hitler's responsibility in the assassination of Dolfuss?
4. What part did Mussolini play in the Marseilles outrage?
5. Was fraud involved in the conduct of the Saar plebiscite?
6. Did Laval give Mussolini a free hand to conquer Ethiopia?
7. Why did the Hoare–Laval plan fail?

1. The Preventive War Against Germany (1933–1934)

With the disappearance from the scene of the men who had striven to put into effect the provisions of the Treaty of Versailles, the fundamentals of diplomacy were completely altered. In France Briand and Loucheur were dead, and Poincaré no longer played a part in the political life of the country. Barthou alone remained of the old brigade of the Great War. In Germany Stresemann was dead; in the July 1932 legislative elections his party lost seat after seat, and almost disappeared from the Reichstag. The Nazi Party, by winning thirty-five per cent of the seats, had gained entry into the Chancellery in a nationalist coalition government (30th January 1933).

This growth of nationalism in Germany was a source of uneasiness to neighbouring countries. The French and British had more or less renounced reparations at the Lausanne Conference in 1932,[1] and Germany had only to pay three milliard gold marks to settle the account — a sum which, in any case, she never paid. In consequence, Britain and France decided not to pay any more of their debts to America, a fact which tended to thrust the Americans more and more towards isolationism.

[1] It was impossible for Germany to pay the annual sums agreed under the Young Plan in July 1932.

France and Britain, defenceless, stripped of all guarantees, found themselves left alone to restrain the vengeful nationalism of Germany, determined as she was to overwhelm Europe. But Europe possessed one strong man — Mussolini. The head of the Italian government had at that time reached the pinnacle of his glory. He was a small man, but stood erect; by nature he was energetic and precise, and he brought an enquiring mind into his occasionally dramatic behaviour: "His sunburnt features betokened in turn anger, disdain, determination and cunning; to all of which must be added the quality of eloquence and a capacity for mimicry; and his large, dark brown eyes seemed at times ready to burst from their orbits when he spoke . . . He never used an unnecessary word, and all his speeches could be printed at once without amendment.[2]

In a speech in Turin on the 23rd October 1932 the Duce launched the idea of a Four Power Pact, made up of Germany, France, Italy and Great Britain, the purpose of which was to contain German ambitions within the framework of a general organization. The scheme was welcomed by the four nations concerned, but it greatly disturbed Poland and the Little Entente; they were afraid the pact would enable the great powers to dispose of smaller nations according to their whims. Yet the Four Power Pact was buried even before it was signed.

Since a limited understanding proved to be impracticable, it became necessary to turn once more to the League of Nations, though on a broader basis. Some statesmen considered that disarmament was the key to the problem, and a disarmament conference composed of sixty-two nations assembled in Geneva in February 1932. But when Germany was refused equality of rights she walked out of the conference, but returned in December when France, Britain and Italy formally agreed to equality of rights. After various difficulties relating to procedure Hitler announced on the 14th and 19th October 1933 that Germany finally withdrew from the disatmament conference of the League. Thus Germany was more free than ever. From 1930 to 1933 the secret rearming of the Reich developed rapidly, and reached its maximum in April 1934.[3]

---

[2] P. Schmidt, *Statist auf diplomatischer Bühne 1923–1935 : Erlebnisse des Chefdolmetschers im Auswärtigen Amt mit dem Staatsmännern Europas*, Bonn, Athenäum ed. 1949, p. 123.

[3] Castellan, *Le réarmement clandestin du Reich (1930–1935)*, Paris, Plon, 1951, p. 505. The determination to re-arm sprang from the army, and had the backing of Hindenburg *ibid.* p. 530.

Poland more than any other country felt that German re-arming was directed against herself. Moreover, German military and semi-military circles did not hide their hatred of the new Poland and their determination one fine day to retrieve Danzig and the Polish Corridor. In fact, several incidents occurred during 1933.[4]

Marshal Pilsudski, that magnificent champion of the new Poland,[5] appreciated the dangers of the situation, and decided to make the first move. In April 1933, in the course of secret negotiations that have never been brought to light, he suggested to France the idea of a preventive war against Germany. While rumours were current of a *coup de main* by German commandos at Danzig, two representatives of the Danzig senate, Rauschning and Creiser, arrived in Warsaw during the spring of 1933 with the object of finding a solution to the problems in dispute.

Marshal Pilsudski spoke his mind without beating about the bush: "I am extremely pleased that you chosen have the one reasonable way of looking at our mutual relations. I trust you do not come here as enemies, because that would end badly — worse, in fact than you may imagine."[6]

According to Rauschning, Pilsudski even suggested a preventive war. The French government did not respond to his proposals, and he turned towards Germany. Wysocki, Poland's ambassador in Berlin, sought an interview with Hitler, and met him on the 2nd May 1933: "Poland and Germany remained hostile to each other ... The Press (i.e. the Nazi Press in Danzig) stated that the re-union of the free city of Danzig to Germany was merely a matter of time once Hitler had taken over power".

Hitler's reply was that "Neither he himself, nor any member of his government had ever done or said anything at all which might give rise to such concern. The Reich government has no intention whatever of interfering with existing treaties".[7]

Colonel Beck, the Foreign Minister, was then entrusted by Pilsudski with the task of sounding the statesmen in Geneva on the occasion of the disarmament conference to ascertain whether any direct understanding with Germany was at all possible. But the leaders of the German

---

[4] *Op. cit.*, p. 467.
[5] Pilsudski was really Commander-in-Chief, but he took over the reins of government during a difficult period.
[6] Beck, *Dernier rapport: Politique polonaise 1926–1939*, Neuchâtel, La Baconniére, 1951, p. 27.
[7] Polish *White Book*, Document No. 1.

delegation in Geneva, Goebbels and von Neurath, themselves invited
Beck to talk to them. Colonel Beck wrote:

The three of us met at the Carlton Hotel, at the top of the hill overlooking
the site of the new buildings which were to house the League of Nations. Dr
Goebbels at once said that the new German leader desired above all to put order
into the Reich's relations with other countries; he was convinced that former
German policy had been encumbered with errors harmful to the interests of the
German nation. For my part, I repeated what Marshal Pilsudski had said in his
talk with Stresemann in 1921.

Goebbels immediately showed interest in my observations, insisting that Hitler
himself regarded a direct understanding between two parties to be much more
likely to contribute to the improvement of a situation than all the confabulations
of Geneva. And then, to add emphasis to the hostile nature of the discussions going
on within the League of Nations, and perhaps also as an expression of his disap-
pointment with his journey to Geneva, he opened the window, pointed to the buildings under construction, and declared, 'Schauen Sie, Exzellenz, das ist der Ruinen-
berg vom Völkerbund'.[8] We shall find no basic settlement in this modern Tower
of Babel.[9]

A German-Polish pact was signed on the 26th January 1934. It covered a period of ten years, and aimed at avoiding the use of force to solve
differences arising between the two countries. Poland thus regained her
freedom of action in relation to France, believing that by herself she had
safeguarded her independence.

In the west of Europe Belgium had been asking herself the same kind
of questions. As she was nearer to France and Britain she did not bother
to find answers; but her Foreign Minister, the Comte de Broqueville,
considered two possible courses: the application of legal methods or a
preventive war. Speaking of the latter de Broqueville said in the Senate
on the 6th March 1934:

In my view this remedy is the worst of all evils. To suggest it one would
have to be mad or inspired by criminal tendencies. I repeat that there is one way
only to prevent Germany from re-arming, and that is immediate war; but I refuse,
for my part, to hurl my country into such a venture.

I have bitter feelings, just as you have, about the situation in which we find
ourselves at present. It is the consequence of a great delusion, created by the men
who drafted the Treaty of Versailles without paying sufficient attention to the
lessons of history . . .

To the south of Europe Mussolini was reinforcing his network of
friends and followers; among other things he signed agreements with
Austria and Hungary in March 1934. It displeased him to see Hitler

[8] "Look, Excellency; these are the ruins of the League of Nations".
[9] Beck, *op. cit.*

giving support to the Austrian Nazis while he himself was financing
Starhemberg's Heimwehr, an altogether different nationalist movement. He summed up his views in the *Popolo d'Italia* of the 13th May
1934:

> The situation is extremely grave . . . I feel that no power on earth can prevent
> Germany from re-arming. There is only one way to deal with it — a preventive
> war. This is envisaged as a possibility in certain quarters, but the French people are
> not in sympathy with such a course. The occupation of a part of German territory
> would meet with such opposition to-day that a preventive war would soon become
> a real war, which would last a long time and involve immense sacrifices in men
> and money.
>   If we discard the notion of a preventive war, and allow an arms race to develop,
> then undoubtedly at a given moment in history a new war will be let loose, splitting
> the nations of Europe into two camps facing each other in a death struggle.

We cannot be quite sure whether Mussolini was making a proposal,
perhaps just the hint of a suggestion; it was certainly the disillusioned
conclusion of a clear-sighted statesman. Von Neurath and Suvitch, the
latter Mussolini's Foreign Minister, both regarded an improvement in
German-Italian relations as an urgent necessity. A meeting between
Hitler and Mussolini, the first of a long series, was therefore arranged for
the 14th June 1934. The two men did not know each other; they had
never had any contact, either direct or indirect.[10]

The meeting took place at Stra, in the Villa Pisani, formerly the
residence of the Doges of Venice. Hitler and Mussolini talked while
walking in the park, and then sat on the lawn. Hitler spoke almost
continually, and Mussolini, who knew German fairly well, made it a
point of honour to understand everything without the aid of an interpreter. In the photographs of this meeting Hitler wore an anxious look, and
Mussolini seemed disillusioned. The outcome of this "dialogue de
sourds" disappointed both men; the burning subject of the moment
— Austria — was not even mentioned. When Mussolini gave an account
of the interview to his wife, Donna Rachele, he wrote: "Hitler talked a
great deal, and often in an excited tone of voice, bubbling over and
making all sorts of exaggerated statements. He is a man who finds
difficulty in controlling himself. My conclusion of the talks is simply —
nothing doing!"[11]

---

[10] The financial support that Mussolini is alleged to have given to the Nazi
Party is a myth.

[11] Rachele Mussolini, *Ma vie avec Benito*, Cheval Ailé, Paris, 1948, p. 107.

2. *The Blood Purge of June 1934*

Hitler's Storm Troops — the S.A. — gave him many anxious moments even in Germany herself. This private army that had been so useful to him in the conquest of power continued to disturb the life of the country. Once the objective had been achieved these tens of thousands of men, who had for years been encouraged to create disorder and anarchy, had to be kept employed. Violence, disturbances and destruction of all kinds occurred everywhere. Nazism was in the throes of a crisis. While Hitler was gradually leading his comrades to the threshold of power, the Cabinet of which he was the Chancellor contained so far no more than two Nazi ministers — Goering and Frick — and the excesses of the Storm Troopers were jeopardizing everything.

Moreover, he was encountering difficulty in regrouping the S.A. Their leader, Röhm, envisaged the fusion of the Reichswehr with the S.A., and already visualized himself as War Minister. But, of course, the Reichswehr, who had regarded the S.A. favourably during the period when those auxiliary forces made it possible to circumvent the provisions of the Treaty of Versailles, certainly had no wish to find themselves under the authority of Röhm.

Later — on the 13th July 1934 — Hitler said of the S.A. before the Reichstag: "Complaints against the S.A. multiplied during April and May. Their Commander-in-Chief (Röhm) attempted to deny the facts, and treated these grievances as underhand attacks against his Storm Troopers. Dissatisfaction was developing within the party itself, and the S.A. were becoming more and more isolated.

"As a result of these incidents heated discussions took place between the commander and myself, during which, for the first time, I began to entertain doubts about the man's loyalty. From May onwards there was no possible doubt about it. Röhm cherished ambitions the realization of which would have resulted in the most serious upheavals. But I found it hard to believe that stories which I imagined were based on loyalty were merely a lie. In any case, I always hoped to spare the movement and the S.A. the shame of a public scandal; I thought I should be able to remove the danger without violent controversy".

Röhm was a difficult man to get on with. The Reichswehr regarded this ex-officer as a man who resisted authority. He had been a brilliant soldier in 1914, and left the army as a captain after having been wounded several times. He remained in the army less than two years after 1919. From the outside he stirred up trouble among his former comrades, joined the Nazi party, quarrelled with Hitler and, in 1924, headed a German mission to Bolivia. When he returned to Germany he joined Hitler once more, and gradually formed the Strom Troopers into a well organized militia; but they were more inclined towards rebellion and riot than well-disciplined semi-military civic duties. The Reichswehr were continually complaining to Hitler about the excesses of the S.A. The Chancellor needed the support of the army at the time Hindenburg took over, but he was extremely reluctant to take action against those who had helped him to power.

Röhm allowed it to be understood that the S.A. was on the point of being disbanded, and rumours very unfavourable to Hitler were circulating to this effect. Then the opposition raised its head. Von Papen, the Vice-Chancellor, made a sensational speech at Marburg on the 17th June; he described the taking over of power by the Nazis, and referred to his disappointed hopes:

> We certainly did not foresee that the abolition of parties would result in the setting up of a complete dictatorship, revolt against the law, the rights of the individual and of the Church, the crushing of all who opposed such methods and their being openly treated as reactionaries. We had hoped, with the assistance of the National Socialist movement, to substitute an efficient organization for the crippled régime we had previously. But we certainly had no intention of establishing a totalitarian State.[12]

Eventually von Papen asked Hitler to break with the extremists in his party who were distorting his ideas. Goebbels reacted immediately by forbidding the broadcasting of the speech. Von Papen then reported to Hitler, and offered to resign; upon which the Führer launched into a violent tirade of invective against the insubordination of the S.A., who were only complicating his task more and more. He declared that he would be compelled to make them see reason at any cost. Hitler asked von Papen to delay his resignation until he could accompany him to Neudeck to see Hindenburg. Von Papen agreed, but the visit was continually postponed.

Von Papen's "fling" encouraged the leaders of the opposition, and Schleicher, former Chancellor, together with a few generals who had been members of the Steel Helmets, began to speak openly of a crisis in the Nazi Party; the names of persons who might be concerned in a Cabinet reshuffle were whispered within the Party. Hitler's entourage kept him informed of some of these tiresome rumours, no doubt magnifying the facts to the point of suggesting a conspiracy.

---

12 Von Papen, *Der Wahrheit eine Gasse*, Munich, 1952.

It was only on the 29th June that Hitler reached a decision. On the 28th he had gone to Essen to be present at the wedding of Gauleiter Tergoven; he left there to visit the labour camps in the Rhineland. During the afternoon of the 29th he arrived at the Hotel Dreesen, in Bad Godesberg, where he enjoyed an occasional rest with a former wartime colleague. There is no evidence to suggest that he really thought any plot was under way. Hitler maintained later that all he intended to do was to relieve Röhm of his command, imprison him and his senior officers, and call the others to order.

Goebbels then arrived in Bad Godesberg, and came to warn Hitler that the S.A. in Berlin had received orders to rejoin their units. The news was unfounded, but it seemed to substantiate the rumour of conspiracy that was in the air. Before leaving Berlin Hitler had given instructions to Himmler and his SS, also to Goering and his special police, to hold themselves in readiness for any eventuality; but so far those instructions had nothing to do with a purge. At about one o'clock in the morning two alarming messages arrived from Munich and Berlin, and were passed on to Hitler.

Hitler had a conversation with Goebbels, and then decided to take immediate action.[13] During the night of the 29th to 30th June he took a plane for Munich, accompanied by Goebbels. At dawn on the 30th he unexpectedly entered the Hotel Hanslbauer where Röhm was staying, in Wiessee, near the Bavarian lake Tergen. He found the S.A. leader fast asleep. Hitler gave him a dressing gown, and someone offered him a revolver which Röhm thrust aside. The S.A. leader was then taken to Munich prison where two SS officers subsequently came and shot him in his cell. Several of Röhm's lieutenants were similarly eliminated.

In Berlin Himmler and Goering had not been idle: 150 SA leaders were assembled and summarily shot, together with a few unruly members. Papen's three colleagues, Jung, Bosc and Klausener, who had assisted him in drafting and disseminating his Marburg speech, were eliminated either in prison or in their offices. Gregor Strasser was arrested and shot in prison; General von Schleicher and his wife were murdered in their villa near Berlin.

Hitler himself stated that sixty-one people were killed, among them nineteen S.A. leaders; but at least five times this number were killed.

---

[13] The rumours spread by Otto Strasser to the effect that Goebbels kept in touch with Röhm until the 20th June have never been substantiated.

When giving an account of this "purification" Hitler made no attempt to prove the existence of Röhm's "plot". The references he made to "foreign collusion" were aimed at the French ambassador, François–Poncet. Following a protest from the Quai d'Orsay the Wilhelmstrasse sent a note to Paris confirming that the suspicions directed against the ambassador had proved to be entirely without foundation.[14]

The Führer made an immediate report to Hindenburg, and received a telegram of approval from the aged president on the 2nd July:

"By your initiative, determination, and your courageous personal intervention you have frustrated high treason. You have saved the German people from a great danger, and I wish to express my profound gratitude."

The army Commander-in-Chief, von Blomberg, also expressed his satisfaction on the 3rd July.

François–Poncet held the view that Marshal Hindenburg could not have drafted the telegram to Hitler, nor would he have willingly agreed to the text; but there is nothing to confirm this theory. The Marshal's colleague, Meissner, who published his reminiscences in 1950, remained convinced that the plot was a reality.[15] Röhm's conspiracy, if it did exist, was never properly worked out, and could not by any means have exploded in such a short time. Undoubtedly Hitler thwarted a possible revolt. He was pressed into action by the Reichswehr, and afterwards received the approval of Hindenburg. The official Nazi version of a carefully prepared conspiracy is quite false.

3. The Assassination of Dolfuss (25th July 1934)

For the world Austria was a test case. Anschluss schemes had never ceased to flourish since 1919, and everyone knew that one day the question would again arise as a grave problem.

Until 1934 the problem had never been solved to Germany's advantage, because France, Great Britain and Italy did not wish it. The important question was: Would they succeed in opposing the Anschluss indefinitely?

[14] François–Poncet, Souvenirs d'une ambassade à Berlin (Sept. 1931–Oct. 1931) Paris, Flammarion, 1946.
[15] Meissner, Staatssekretär unter Ebert–Hindenburg–Hitler : Das Schicksalsweg des Deutschen Volkes vom 1918–1945 wie ich ihm erlebte, Hamburg, Hoffmann, 1950, p. 364.

Louis Barthou, France's Foreign Minister, Poincaré's last follower and the last loyal supporter of the Treaty of Versailles, was busy trying to pick up the threads of French alliances and friendships. In April 1934 he went to Warsaw; in June he was in the capitals of the Little Entente — Prague, Bucharest, Belgrade — to try to establish a kind of eastern Locarno pact, as a protection against growing German nationalism. These negotiations worried Hitler who feared encirclement, and it is possible that this fear intensified his desire to smash the French diplomatic manoeuvre.

Austria was also a source of anxiety to Germany, because the government in power expressed determination to defend Austria's independence at any cost. The soul of resistance was Chancellor Dolfuss — a small, but determined and energetic man.

Hitler set about undermining Austria from within by rendering support to the Austrian Nazis. Theodor Habicht, a member of the Reichstag, was despatched to Vienna as an inspector of the Austrian Nazi party. An Austrian Nazi, Dr Alfred Fravenfeld, installed himself in Munich where he was in charge of the daily radio messages from Austria. For several months the Austrian Nazis had been conducting a reign of terror, and tension was increasing almost hour by hour. Eventually, on the 25th July, at midday, a Nazi putsch flared up in Vienna. Two groups of SS in Austrian army uniform, totalling 154 men, surrounded the federal chancellery in Ballhausplatz and the broadcasting station. An unknown announcer declared that Chancellor Dolfuss had resigned, and the group at the Ballhausplatz proceeded to occupy the government offices. Dolfuss's associates were locked in, while the SS rushed on the Chancellor himself and shot him down. Dolfuss was wounded in the throat, and died about six o'clock in the evening on a couch, where his assassins had left him. To the end he refused to sign a document of resignation.

The Austrian army, obeying the orders of Dr Schuschnigg, who was forthwith nominated Chancellor by the President of the Republic, reacted at once. Within a few hours they overpowered the rebellious SS and arrested them. By midnight the putsch had failed, and Hitler was present that day at the Wagner Festival in Bayreuth. Two of his officers kept him informed hour by hour of the news from Vienna, and he was enabled to follow the whole development of the putsch from his box at the theatre.

Friedlinde Wagner – Wagner's grand-daughter — was a witness of these events. She subsequently wrote that the Führer was very excited about what had happened, but managed to control his joy while in the restaurant; he was able to order dinner with his customary care. He remarked that it was advisable for him to show himself for at least an hour, in case people connected him with events in Vienna.[16]

Mussolini reacted vigorously by bringing up five divisions to the Brenner Pass. At that period the Duce was spending a holiday with his family in Riccione, where Madame Dolfuss and her children had joined Mussolini's wife. The Austrian Chancellor himself was expected to arrive any day.[17] Moreale, the Press attaché of the Italian Embassy in Vienna,[18] informed the Duce immediately, and asked for his instructions. It was on the Duce's orders that Moreale warned the Austrian police who cut all telephone communications with the outside world. The new Chancellor, Schuschnigg, and Vice-Chancellor Stahremberg had the conspirators arrested, and thirteen of them were hanged. Hitler's responsibility was not proved during the trial of those concerned in the putsch.

Such were the basic facts. Did Hitler order the Vienna putsch and the execution of Dolfuss? That question occupied the attention of the judges at the Nuremberg trials, and they were able to establish the following facts:

1. Habicht was the instigator of the putsch (Goering's evidence)

"At one time the leader of the Austrian party was a man named Habicht from Wiesbaden. I saw him only once; I never knew him before that. Prior to the Dolfuss affair he allowed the Führer to believe that the Austrian army was ready to act on its own initiative, either to overthrow the government or force it to agree to the Anschluss. If the army took this action should the party in Austria support it? If the army did move in this direction it would obviously be necessary, according to the Führer, to give it the political support of the party. However, the whole thing was nothing but a trick, because the Austrian

---

[16] See Friedlinde Wagner, *Heritage of Fire*, New York, 1945 p. 125.

[17] It is noteworthy that the onus of announcing the sad news to Madame Dolfuss fell upon Mussolini himself. She returned to Vienna immediately where she received a poor welcome from her relations. She later left again for Riccione, looking worn and dispirited. Madame Dolfuss took with her the ancient key of the city of Venice which had been preserved in Vienna, and, since Dolfuss had intended to offer it to the Duce, she presented it to him herself. She also handed Mussolini a letter in which Dolfuss recommended his children to him. Shortly afterwards Madame Dolfuss emigrated to the United States of America.

[18] The ambassador was away.

army had no thought of attacking its government. It was a minor action by the Wehrmacht–Standarte, composed of former members of the Austrian Wehrmacht — men who had either resigned or had been discharged, and had joined the party.

"It was on the basis of this false information that Habicht undertook the affair in Vienna. I was at that time with the Führer in Bayreuth; he sent for Habicht, and reproached him indignantly for having deceived, duped and misinformed him. The Führer very much regretted the death of Dolfuss, for it had created a difficult political situation for the National Socialists, especially in relation to Italy."[19]

2. Dr von Rintelen was to take over power

The person who had announced over the Vienna radio, under the threat of the rebels, that Dolfuss had resigned, added that Dr von Rintelen had been appointed Chancellor. Rintelen was Austrian ambassador in Rome; he had a personal interest in the Thyssen firm, and had arrived from Rome on the 23rd July. His unexpected return is proof of the intentions of the organizers of the putsch, but is not proof of the personal responsibility of Hitler.

3. The German ambassador was in league with the rebels

Messersmith, American ambassador in Vienna, said in his evidence that Dr Rieth, German ambassador in Vienna, maintained contact by telephone with the rebels, who had occupied the Chancellery during the afternoon of the 25th July; he also visited them and brought them safe-conduct permits to enable them to escape to Germany in case the putsch failed. Dr Rieth, Messersmith said, was in direct and constant touch with the Austrian Nazi agents, as well as with those of German origin; it was, therefore, impossible for him not to be aware of all the details. Messersmith added that senior members of the Austrian government told him after the putsch that Dr Rieth had had dealings with von Rintelen, and that the Nazis had a plan to replace Dolfuss by von Rintelen in the event of their success. Dr Rieth might not have given his personal support to the scheme, but he was undoubtedly aware of it, and agreed to its being carried out.[20]

---

[19] Nuremberg Documents, IX, 317.
[20] See the written evidence of Messersmith, United States ambassador in Vienna, in the Nuremberg Documents (PS 1760; USA 57).

Although Rieth was probably involved, Hitler repudiated his action on the 26th July, by saying that Rieth was wrong to meddle with a matter that concerned Austria only.

4. The strange attitude of Dr Goebbels

According to the diary of Mr. Dodd,[21] the government expressed its satisfaction in a Press announcement at 11 p.m. on the 25th July at the fall of Dolfuss, adding that it would result in the emergence of Greater Germany. When the news of the event reached Berlin, the German Ministry of Propaganda forbade publication, and managed to get possession of those newspapers already in circulation.

On the 26th July Goebbels announced that the German government had played no part in the putsch and the frightful tragedy resulting from it. According to Messersmith, the American ambassador, it appears that at the end of June Goebbels told Cerrutti, the Italian ambassador, that a Nazi government would be installed in Vienna within a month. This evidence is very circumstantial; but if it is true it proves that Berlin was aware of what was happening.

This accumulation of evidence in no way proves Hitler's personal responsibility. In any case, the Führer reacted swiftly and cleverly. He recalled Habicht and Dr Rieth, and repudiated their activities; and, as we have seen, he made the best use of propaganda. Was he, however, kept informed of the details of the putsch, or did Habicht, given a free hand, overstep the mark? Did Hitler really regard the coup as altogether an Austrian matter, or did he simply back down when faced with Mussolini's immediate reaction?

It seems that the absence of any evidence of Hitler's guilt was not the result of his Machiavellian tendencies. Moreover, the selection of the date for the coup was particularly unfortunate, for Hitler was seeking a rapprochement with Mussolini, and the state of affairs at this period only tended to bring Dolfuss and the Duce closer together.

On the 26th July Hitler wrote to von Papen, who had only just survived the Blood Purge of the 30th June:

We very much deplored, and have repudiated, the assassination of the Austrian Federal Chancellor — a deed which, without the least fault on our part, has rendered more tense an already delicate situation in Europe.[22]

[21] United States ambassador in Vienna. Nuremberg Documents (PS 1760; USA 57).

[22] Nuremberg Documents, II, 359.

The Führer also telephoned von Papen who continued to remain shut up in his house in Berlin:

Herr von Papen, you must set out immediately for Vienna as minister pleni-potentiary. You cannot refuse; the situation is alarming.

To which von Papen replied, 'After what has passed between us I cannot understand your proposal. Why has the situation become so alarming all at once?'

'Do you mean to say you don't know what has happened?'

Then, in an excited tone of voice, Hitler explained the whole business, adding hysterically, 'It's another Sarajevo!'[23]

Von Papen accepted the new mission, and went to Bayreuth. His task consisted of peacefully preparing the way for the Anschluss, a mission which he brought to a successful issue; and Hitler, after his repudiation of the rash Dr Rieth, found the repair work of the smooth von Papen of inestimable value. It helped the Führer to reassure the world that he had had no hand in the assassination of Dolfuss.

As for Mussolini, he was bitterly disappointed to have been the only one to react against the putsch; but he was never caught again!

4. Mussolini and the Marseilles Outrage
(9th October 1934)

On the 27th September 1934 four men sat in the refreshment room on the Lausanne railway station, talking eagerly and glancing surreptitiously around. All four belonged to the O.R.I.M., a Macedonian revolutionary association; the members of the Ustava branch, known as the "Ustashis", were professional terrorists. Their local leader was a man named Kraemer (Kwaternik) who came from Italy as representative of the Ustava leader, Ante Pavelić, on whose behalf the men were given instructions and money.

On the 28th September the four men — Nowak, Benes, Malny and Kaleman — crossed the French frontier at Valorbe in the Paris express. On their arrival in the capital they split into two groups. Nowak (Pospiril) and Benes (Raich) remained in Paris to accomplish their mission, if Malny (Krail) and Kaleman (Georgniev) did not succeed in Marseilles.

Malny and Kaleman took the train again in Marseilles, and got out at Aix-en-Provence, where they stayed until the 9th October at the Hôtel Moderne, a small hotel in the Avenue Victor Hugo. They behaved very politely, and

[23] Von Papen, *Der Wahrheit eine Gasse*, Munich, 1952 p. 245.

allowed everyone to believe they were merchants. Between two "business deals" they took their meals in the town, as their small hotel had no res- taurant. A few days later Kaleman received a visit from a pretty young woman named Maria Voudrof; she brought him some rather bulky parcels, which anyone might have thought contained presents or merchandise.

Malny and Kaleman settled their hotel bills on the morning of the 9th, and took the train from Marseilles. Maria, meanwhile, had disap- peared. During the morning and early afternoon the news-boys selling the Paris-Midi and the Paris-Soir on the boulevards were shouting out the headlines: their papers announced that Croat terrorists living in Berlin had planned an attempt on the life of King Alexander of Yugo- slavia who was due in Marseilles that day. But no one took much notice of this sensational piece of news.

However, Louis Barthou, the French Foreign Minister, who was to welcome the King, became apprehensive. He telephoned Pietri, Minister for the Navy, who was to accompany him:

I do not feel very well, my friend, and would rather you went alone to Marseilles; after all, the King will pass through very quickly. I have spoken to Doumergue about it, and he agrees with me.[24]

Pietri later telephoned Barthou:

My principal secretary, Rear-Admiral Odend'Hal, informs me that, as my role is to welcome the King at sea, it is hardly fitting for him not to be met by a member of the government when he comes ashore. If you do not come, I shall not be able to go aboard — which I ought to do as Minister for the Navy.[25]

Barthou therefore went to Marseilles. Before leaving he received a few members of the Press, and told Geneviève Tabouis that someone had apparently discovered that some anarchists had organized a coup in Marseilles.[26]

At eight o'clock that evening Barthou and Pietri boarded the night train for Marseilles. On their arrival the following morning Pietri went on board the launch to greet the King on the royal warship Dubrovnik. Barthou welcomed the King at the Quai des Belges, and the group drove slowly along La Canebière towards the Prefecture. Barthou and General Georges accompanied the King in the car. Jevtic, the Yugoslav Foreign Minister, followed in another car with Pietri.

[24] Francois Pietri, Sous mes yeux Alexandre de Yougoslavie est assassiné, published in L'Histoire pour tous, No. 16, August, 1961.
[25] Geneviève Tabouis, Vingt ans de suspense diplomatique, Paris, 1958.
[26] ibid.

Suddenly, when they were abreast of the Stock Exchange, on the Place Puget, a man rushed towards the royal car shouting " Long live the King!" He jumped on the running board and fired some shots. The King was instantly killed, and both Barthou and General Georges were seriously wounded. The chauffeur managed to catch the assassin by the coat, while Piollet, the Chief of Police, who was on horseback beside the royal car, struck him with his sabre. As the man fell he fired at random into the crowd, killing a policeman and a woman and wounding others. The assassin was then trampled under foot by the crowd.

Barthou died of loss of blood on the way to the hospital, because none of the police had thought of giving him first aid. General Georges hung between life and death for five months. When the doctor examined the body of the assassin he found on him the tattooed sign of the Ustava — a skull and cross-bones, with the words, "Liberty or Death". His Czechoslovak passport bore the name of Kaleman. He was heavily armed: he carried grenades, cartridges and revolvers. Such were the contents of the parcels delivered by Maria Voudrof. The police managed to stop Nowak and Benes at Thonon les Bains at the moment they were attempting to return to Lausanne, and they arrested Malny at Melun.

During the preliminary investigation it was learned that the four men were under the orders of the Leader of the Ustashis, Ante Pavelić, a Croat lawyer who preferred to attempt by force what could not be won through parliament — an autonomous Croat State, which the Serbs refused to grant. He was subpoenaed to appear as witness. Italy was asked to issue an extradition order against Pavelić, who had been arrested in Turin with Kwaternik on the 18th October. Mussolini rejected the request.

The fact that Mussolini "protected" Pavelić in this way has led writers to believe that the outrage at Marseilles was perpetrated under his orders. There is no evidence to substantiate the accusation.

The Yugoslavs formally accused the Hungarians before the League of Nations of having been the instigators of the crime. Apparently Mussolini did support and encourage the Ustashis in their efforts to create turmoil in Yugoslavia; but it was only in April 1941 that Mussolini met Pavelić for the first time. Rosenberg's department also seems to have supported Pavelić, who was in Berlin on the 8th October. The Hungarians welcomed the Croat political refugees in Janka–Puszta, and quite possibly a number of Ustashis were amongst them. No one has ever succeeded in putting forward anything but circumstantial evidence. Laval went so far as to offer the Hungarian delegation at the League of

Nations a way out of the difficulty in a speech that was really incomprehensible.[27]

It would be an exaggeration to suggest that the Ustashis wished to eliminate both Alexander and Barthou. Their odium was directed against the King; they had nothing against Barthou and his policy. King Alexander's journey to France merely offered them a favourable opportunity, since previous attempts in Yugoslavia had failed. Moreover, Mussolini at that time was seeking a rapprochement with France, and he hoped to reach an agreement with Barthou which would undoubtedly offer colonial possibilities. A few months earlier the Duce had given Hitler a rather cold welcome, and he relied upon French co-operation to avert the Anschluss.

Everything tends to suggest that the outrage was entirely the work of the Ustashis who, in this instance as in others, sought to muster support in any quarter whatever, but especially in Rome and Berlin.

Kaleman's three accomplices were condemned to hard labour for life; and it was only in 1941 that Germany made France release them. At that period "General" Kwaternik, having arrived in Zagreb with the German army, proclaimed Croat independence, and on the 13th April Pavelić was appointed head of the new Croat State, to which Mussolini offered the Duke of Spoleto as its king, though the latter had no wish to take possession of his kingdom.

5. The Saar Plebiscite (13th January 1935)

Pierre Laval succeeded Louis Barthou at the Quai d'Orsay. In January, 1935, when the plebiscite was due to be held in the Saar, the new minister caused all French propaganda to cease in the territory under international control.

Barthou was buried on the 14th October 1934; Laval's orders were issued on the 16th. On the morning of the 17th André Fribourg, the French representative and Vice-President of the Foreign Affairs Commission, visited the Minister and told him,

"I have stopped everything; action in the Saar is at an end. I wish to make peace with Germany".[28]

This evidently foreshadowed a reversal of French foreign policy as practised by Briand and his successors since Versailles: a shifting away

[27] Miklós Horthy, *Ein Leben für Ungarn*, Bonn, 1953, p. 146.
[28] André Fribourg's account in *Le Fait du Jour*, p. 15, Paris, 21st May 1945.

from international negotiation and a movement in the direction of bilateral conversations. Laval wished to superimpose "his" foreign policy — a strange admixture of pacifist realism and sharp practice. He was an innkeeper's son from Auvergne, a barrister, but a self-made man who believed only in himself and his destiny. He was a young opportunist cleaving to the Socialist Party from which he had emerged shortly after the war; but he did not embark on any clear-cut political course which would oblige him to reveal his convictions. He supported Clemenceau and Caillaux, Tardieu and Briand, but never to the point of committing himself to loyalty.

Impecunious and scheming, he gradually built up a tidy fortune which he paraded in his native Auvergne. A pacifist and a self-seeker, the ideas he brandished on technical questions suffered from over-simplification, though he had a preference for diplomacy; he imagined that he could talk to Hitler, Stalin or Mussolini in an easy-going and informal manner, as he might to any one of his constituents.

Hitler had declared that the Saar was the only outstanding problem between France and Germany; so Laval decided to make a clean sweep of securing peace with Germany. The Saar was a gift which he presented as a lure to encourage Franco-German amity.

In fact, it did not seem that the result of the plebiscite could possibly be unfavourable to Germany. Indeed, the Saar, seventy-two per cent Catholic, was unhappy about Nazi philosophy, but the Saarlanders belonged to the German dioceses of Trier and Speier, and their bishops intervened in favour of Germany on the 6th January 1935. The Socialists, led by Max Braun, a courageous but headstrong man, were but a minority. The weak resistance of the Francophile elements was swept aside by a wave of Nazi propaganda. Under the direction of Spaniol, leader of the *Deutsche Front*, and his successor Bürckel, and with the financial assistance of the industrialist Hermann Röchling, every possible means of dissemination were used: books, leaflets, radio, theatres, cinemas and the Press. Young Saarlanders were made welcome in Germany, in the *Arbeitsdienst*, and trained for the "struggle for the Saar". The *Winterhilfe* — Winter Relief — also played a part in the propaganda effort.

To precipitate events Bürckel was reduced to employing terror tactics: the hesitant Saarlanders were invited, with threats if necessary, to join the *Deutsche Front*. The Nazis seized the opportunity to recall to mind the incidents of Pirmasens and the way the French had forgotten their friends.

The financial support available to the Francophile organizations was not comparable with that at Bürckel's disposal, and Laval therefore decided to withdraw his backing. On the 6th and 10th November 1934 Laval received Koster, the German ambassador, and spoke to him about the Saar. There is no trace of the conversation, but it is likely that Laval declared his lack of interest in the Saar, and that his aim was Franco-German rapprochement.[29]

After these talks German propaganda was left with a clear field in the Saar. On the 3rd December, under the chairmanship of Baron Aloysi, Italian delegate to the League of Nations, a Franco-German agreement was signed providing for a payment by Germany of 900 million francs to cover outright purchase of French credits and property in the Saar. Laval as good as sold the Saar before the plebiscite took place. The German victory on the 13th January was certainly huge: 477,119 voted for return to Germany, 46,613 in favour of the *status quo*, and 2124 for union with France; in other words, ninety per cent voted for Nazi Germany. But we may be sure that the number of votes in favour of the *status quo* might have been infinitely greater had French propaganda been brought into action under normal conditions.

With one exception all observers were of the opinion that, despite previous pressure, the voting was unquestionably free and properly conducted. The one exception was André Fribourg, Vice-President of the French Commission for Foreign Affairs. When the polling was concluded he drew attention to some curious facts.

Two witnesses of the plebiscite were questioned. One of them, John Knittel, at that time on the staff of the *Journal de Thann*, followed the whole campaign.

'I witnessed the plebiscite,' he said. 'For several days before the voting took place, and for two days afterwards, I was staying in the Saar, or, occasionally at night, at Forbach, which is a few kilometres from the frontier. In consequence, I was in Saar territory every day during the vital period. My records and notes on the subject were either destroyed or stolen by the occupants of my flat and my office during the 1939–45 war. But I can well remember that the opponents of National Socialism, who operated in favour of Saar autonomy, and in particular J. Hoffmann who, after the end of the second world war, became President of the Saar Council, were sure that some of the results were falsified. During the night preceding the plebiscite I personally conveyed to safety in French territory Hoffmann's wife and children, who very rashly had remained in the Saar during the plebiscite period.

[29] The French representative in the Saar, Moraze, was not even notified by Paris of the change of attitude that had occurred.

'All my fellow-countrymen are well acquainted with Saar territory and the Saarlanders; they, as well as serious-minded observers, are of the opinion that the overwhelming majority of the Saarlanders voted for union with the Third Reich. This position was obvious long before the plebiscite. A little underhand work did nothing to change the National Socialist psychosis that had broken out among the population of this territory.'[30]

The second witness was Gabriel Perreux. He was in the Saar as a correspondent of the *Paris-Midi*, and he told us:

The falsification of the plebiscite was apparent to me in a number of details that were quite possible, if not probable . . . I heard it said in the Saar that the right conditions for a plebiscite were not achieved; that it ought to be postponed until conditions were more stable. I added that such a decision would have the irritating effect of straining relations between France and Germany. In my opinion it was imperative to hold the plebiscite on the date decided, but the League of Nations should have taken steps to ensure honesty and freedom of choice . . . To have safeguarded the preparation and proper carrying out of the plebiscite an international police force would have been indispensable.

I had a feeling at that time (November 1933) that there was a possibility of fraud . . . Historically I could not have been certain; it was rather a moral conviction.[31]

The testimony of the above two witnesses should be compared with A.J.P.Taylor's statement:

They (the Saarlanders) knew what awaited them in Germany: dictatorship destruction of trade unions, persecution of the Christian churches. Yet, in an unquestionably free election, 90 per cent voted for return to Germany.[32]

Let us return to the statements of André Fribourg who described the scrutiny of the ballot held in the Wartburg (in Saarbrücken), where the ballot boxes were taken in the evening of the 13th January. They were conveyed by lorry under military escort.

The Wartburg was guarded by ten or so British soldiers and twenty uniformed police who were members of the German Front. The boxes were deposited between ten o'clock and midnight, and taken to the vaults under the supervision of Commander Hennessey of the League of Nations, the Countess von Roedern and two members of the Deutsche Front. They remained there without supervision from ten in the evening till 4 p.m. the following day, the 14th. The boxes were unbelievably fragile, having been constructed carelessly by a Hitlerian carpenter in Saarbrücken. The locks that secured them were shoddy.

[30] Evidence collected by the author on the 10th April 1962.

[31] Evidence collected by the author on the 12th April 1962. Cf. also G. Perreux's *Saar, 13th January 1935*, Editions des Portiques, Paris, 1934.

[32] A. J. P. Taylor, *Origins of the Second World War*, p. 86.

About twenty young people arrived from Berlin — perhaps by coincidence — ostensibly to set up loudspeakers in the Wartburg to announce the result of the ballot. Contrary to the regulations they went inside. A certain official of the criminal police department named John, whose business was to remain on the premises until the votes had been counted, showed in his report that it would have been an easy matter to falsify the ballot. He wrote that everything seemed to have been organized to make falsification easy; that the foreign soldiers were drunk; that on the 14th January he saw in the prohibited part of the Wartburg about thirty SS men disguised; that he tried to discover their identity, but had to beat a retreat with his colleague Hartel because of their threatening attitude. He added that, to all appearances, these men had spent the whole night in the house, and that the cellars containing the ballot boxes were not guarded. John reported everything to his superiors, but they took no action; the Germans warned him not to magnify an unimportant affair, and to abandon all investigation if he valued his life.

In addition to all this it appears from the statements of various witnesses that a quantity of forged voting papers were printed; large central heating stoves, with their fires alight, stood in the cellars beside the fragile ballot boxes. It seems clear, therefore, that there would have been no difficulty in replacing the real ballot papers by false ones and destroying the former in the stoves. Brandstetter, the SS man from Frankfurt-on-Main, who had been drinking, declared on the evening of the 16th in the Saarautomat Restaurant, Bahnhofstrasse, Saarbrücken, that he had been unjustly treated. It had not been worth the trouble, he said, to help to burn the ballot papers in the Wartburg, because he had not received the official appointment he had been promised; he added that he would tell everything if his name were kept secret. Rhode, the Swedish President of the Plebiscite Commission, refused to allow Max Braun and the other Saarlanders who supported the *status quo* to assist in the scrutiny of the ballot. He threatened to imprison Gebelein himself if he made a protest against the inaccuracy of the electoral lists. According to John, the policeman, the government commission received a detailed account of the falsification of the plebiscite a week previously; but the commission took no action, since every-one, including France and Laval, seemed to have but one desire: to finish with the Saar as soon as possible and to avoid any difficulties. When one considers that after the scrutiny the ballot papers were destroyed with questionable haste, one cannot fail to be influenced by this combination of extraordinary coincidences"[33]

[33] The evidence of Gauthier Gebelein, at that time director of the French newspaper *Saar-Chronik*, corroborates the statements made by André-Fribourg. He adds one or two important details. The head of the SDN police, Commander Hemsley, an Englishman, was alleged to be on rather friendly terms with the opponents of the Nazis, and was relieved of his post. He was replaced by Major Hennessy, a member of Mosley's Fascist movement. Instead of returning to the United Kingdom after the plebiscite, Hennessy took up residence in Coblenz. His deputy, the Norwegian Captain Ly, was subsequently put in charge of Quisling's personal guard. According to Gebelein, Attema, a Dutch official who was also a member of the Plebiscite Commission, stated in Forbach on the 15th January, before three witnesses, "that he knew exactly how the German Front had faked the plebiscite".

We cannot be absolutely certain from this accumulated evidence that trickery actually took place. When we conducted an enquiry in the Saar itself we did not come across the account of John, the policeman, and no doubt all the proofs were destroyed. We should remember, however, that the statement by A. J. P. Taylor and most commentators, that the plebiscite was conducted under normal conditions, is probably exaggerated. The Saar plebiscite produced results conformable with the wishes of the Saarlanders, but it was indicative of Nazi methods, and revealed Laval's personal views in so far as foreign policy was concerned. There seems to be nothing to show that the French, or foreign observers, or even the League of Nations drew from the affair the conclusions which the circumstances demanded.

6. The Rome Agreements (6th January 1935)

Laval made his second attempt to modify French foreign policy in January 1935. The Duce also declared in Milan on the 6th October 1934 that nothing fundamental stood in the way of an entente with France. This speech resulted in an easing of the political situation shortly before the death of Barthou, and should logically have led to a Franco-Italian agreement; but after the outrage in Marseilles everything fell to pieces.

Laval decided to return to the talks, and visited Rome in January 1935, without even waiting to gauge the effects of his new policy towards Germany following upon the Saar plebiscite. Agreements were signed between France and Italy on the 7th January; under them the privileged status of the Italians in Tunisia was to be progressively abolished between 1945 and 1965, and Italy would receive in exchange 114,000 square kilometres of desert in Eritrea and a share in the Djibouti–Addis Ababa Railway. France and Italy also agreed to work together to meet any possible threat to Austria.

The exchange brought very meagre advantages to France, but it emphasized Mussolini's colonial aspirations. A more serious matter, however, was that on the 6th January 1935, during a dinner at the Farnese Palace, Laval might have given Mussolini a free hand to invade Ethiopia. There is no doubt whatever that Laval desired a rapprochement between France and Italy. It is probable that he wished to offer the Duce a gift as a sign of his good will, along the lines adopted in relation to the Saar question. Such a course would be in harmony with the political

cynicism of the French Minister: his gift would naturally be at the expense
of another country. The Italians apparently entertained no doubt at
all about the free hand given to Mussolini. Badoglio spoke to Gamelin
about it,[34] and De Bono confirmed the impression when he said that
the Duce had not renounced his extensive rights in Tunisia for a piece
of desert.[35] On the 24th December 1938 Ciano told Perth, the British
ambassador,

> It is not true that the Laval–Mussolini agreement was confined to economic
> matters; France was aware of Italy's programme for territorial conquest.[36]

Mussolini himself stated on the 29th September 1935 to Alfred Mallet
of the *Petit Journal* :

> In the talks concerning colonial matters Monsieur Laval upheld France's
> economic rights in Abyssinia, in the region covered by the Djibouti–Addis Ababa
> Railway.

It is true that Mallet was a friend of Laval's, and that by this statement
the Duce was able to shield his partner who was being attacked in
France. But the French denied that Laval gave Mussolini a free hand.
Herriot said that when Laval rendered an account of his Rome mission
before the Council of Ministers, he said absolutely nothing about
Ethiopia.[37] Flandin, who had been President of the Council since the
8th November 1934, said that Laval, who often spoke to him in confidence, mentioned nothing about it; and when Flandin later succeeded
Laval as Foreign Minister no Italian statesman ever claimed to have been
given a free hand.[38] Indeed, Laval himself declared in the Chamber on
the 27th December 1935: "By a waiving of France's economic claims
I agreed to give Italy the right to demand concessions in the whole of
Ethiopia, providing our existing rights were respected . . . I felt justified
in thinking that Italy would use this freedom of action for peaceful
purposes only."[39]

Ciano went so far as to refute Flandin's objections.

[34] Salvemini, *Mussolini diplomatico*, Paris, 1931, p. 177.
[35] MacCartney, *Italian Foreign and Colonial Policy, 1914–1937*, London, 1938,
(p. 299).
[36] Ciano, *1937–1938 Diario*, Bologna, 1948, p. 313.
[37] E. Herriot, *Jadis*, Vol. II: *D'une guerre a l'autre, 1914–1936*, Paris, 1952,
p. 493.
[38] Flandin, *Politique française (1919–1940)*, Paris, 1947, p. 104.
[39] Pierre Laval, in the Chambre des Députés on the 27th December 1935.

"In May 1935 I had a conversation with Flandin, who advised me on the best method of launching the war by fomenting rebellion against the Negus."[40]

Naturally enough there exists no written account of the meeting between Laval and Mussolini at the Farnese Palace. A subsequent exchange of letters took place between the two men, but the correspondence was destroyed in June 1940 with the Quai d'Orsay records. Generally speaking historical commentators are reserved in the conclusions they draw of the interview. It is commonly accepted that the agreement was a verbal one, and that it went beyond a mere implication. It is also certain that the Italians acted in every respect as though an agreement had been reached. After the talks at the Farnese Palace the Duce spoke and acted as though he could count upon France's neutrality, and Laval seemed to have gone to extraordinary lengths to ensure Franco-Italian friendship.

Italy's determination to embark on aggression in Ethiopia must not be under-estimated, but one may suspect that Laval's encouragement was the determining factor. The easing of the tension which Laval envisaged was accomplished on the occasion of the dinner at the Farnese Palace, and it seems certain that the Duce must have spoken plainly enough of his "projects" to give Laval the opportunity either to approve or discourage them. No evidence exists to suggest that Laval raised any strong objection.

The officials who accompanied Laval to Rome have said that the Minister allowed them to prepare the text of the agreements, but that he took upon himself the actual discussions with the Duce. Laval acted alone, without consulting his colleagues; he looked upon agreements as of a secondary nature, and entered into discussions of other questions with the Duce. We may deduce from his customary practice that he alone on this occasion "negotiated" with the Duce.

If we compare the organized enthusiastic welcome accorded Laval on his visit of the 7th January with the cold reception given to Eden in the preceding spring, when the British Minister endeavoured to dissuade the Duce from attacking Ethiopia, we may conclude that Laval to some extent responded to the Duce's hopes. And the undisguised purpose of the Duce during that period was to ensure that France and possibly England — would leave him free to act in Ethiopia.

---

[40] Ciano, *op. cit.*, p. 313.

Without doubt the true facts touching upon this vital episode of
international relations will never come to light; but despite lack of
evidence the "diplomatic methods" of Laval, who pledged France
to a new foreign policy without the approval of his government,
were manifestly lacking in prudence and fraught with dire consequences.

7. The Hoare–Laval Plan

On the 3rd October 1935 Mussolini hurled his forces into Ethiopia,
and the campaign lasted until the 5th May 1936. On the 7th October
the Council of the League condemned Italy, and on the 18th November
economic sanctions were agreed upon. However, Pierre Laval and
Samuel Hoare, the French and British representatives, excluded iron,
steel, copper and oil from the list of materials whose delivery to Italy
was forbidden; a fact which rendered the policy of sanctions ineffectual.
    France and England tacitly recognized Italy's right to some kind of
colonial expansion at the expense of Ethiopia. This derogation was a
real threat to collective security, for there appeared to be no grounds
for departing from the code of the League. The fact that the leading
members of the League recognized in certain cases "the right of the
strongest" was a source of grave concern to the small nations.
    The activities of Laval became more and more disturbing, and public
opinion began to react. The French Minister perceived which way the
wind was blowing, and became anxious as the Ethiopian campaign
dragged on. On the 8th December 1935 he submitted to Mussolini a
compromise solution prepared in conjunction with Samuel Hoare.
Once again Pierre Laval utilized his new methods. Alone, without the
support of his administration, ignoring his country's allies and the
prerogative of the League, he undertook to resolve the Italo-Ethiopian
conflict on a man-to-man basis.
    The compromise, known as the Hoare–Laval Plan, offered Italy
two-thirds of Ethiopia; that is to say, a little more than the territory
conquered by the Italian army, with the possibility of effecting the
peaceful colonization of the remainder of the country. In exchange
Ethiopia would continue to remain independent, appreciably extended
by access to the sea in Eritrea — described by the British as a camel
corridor. Mussolini, who no doubt accepted the plan as a basis for

discussion, had no time to go into it, for his troops were not advancing as quickly as he had hoped.

Laval had the plan initialled, and intended to present the League Assembly with a *fait accompli*, thus imposing it upon the Negus. But that manoeuvre also failed.

Indeed, on the 19th December a debate took place in the British House of Commons during which Prime Minister Baldwin asked for a vote of confidence. On the 14th the British government had published a White Paper giving details of the attitude adopted by the government and the facts leading up to it. Several Cabinet Ministers opposed Samuel Hoare, among them Anthony Eden, Lord Privy Seal, who represented Britain at the League of Nations, and Duff Cooper, Secretary of State for War. Behind Baldwin stood Chamberlain, Chancellor of the Exchequer, and Runciman, President of the Board of Trade. Together they prepared to defend the Hoare–Laval Plan.

Anthony Eden was the leader of the Young Conservatives. He was thirty-seven, and had been a brilliant success at Eton and Oxford. For several years he had been the son-in-law of an administrator and brother-in-law of the President of the Westminster Bank. He was a brilliant young member of Parliament and liked by the British public. Handsome, well-dressed, a lover of art and photogenic, he enjoyed the support of the élite of both sexes in Geneva. He vigorously defended the principles of the League, and discussed them with his friends in Paris and London; among whom were Alexis Leger, Secretary General at the French Foreign Ministry, and Sir Robert Vansittart, Permanent Under Secretary at the British Foreign Office. Both upheld the traditional diplomatic code, and were a little unhappy at having been "outflanked" by their ministers. They gave their support to Eden, but the parliamentary victory in the Commons was far from being won.

The bomb burst on the 17th December 1935. The *Daily Telegraph* published an article by Pertinax giving the essentials of the Hoare–Laval Plan. It roused British public opinion which was shocked by the hypocrisy of the plan. A flood of indignation swept over Samuel Hoare who immediately resigned; while the Labour Party, which at first favoured appeasement, decided to vote against the Hoare–Laval Plan, described as a flagrant violation of the Covenant of the League and a betrayal of the Abyssinian people.

On Thursday, the 19th December, Baldwin made a long hypocritical speech in the Commons. He explained that Sir Samuel Hoare went to Paris to open up negotiations. During the whole of Sunday there had been no liaison between him and the Cabinet, who were unaware of any agreement having been made. At breakfast on the following Monday the Prime Minister received a letter from Sir Samuel Hoare in which the Cabinet was urged to endorse what he had done, as he considered his action was necessary at that time. Baldwin added that he now felt that he should have recalled the Minister, and that it might be considered he had shown weakness in not doing so. It was a mistake which implicated the whole Cabinet, but for which he held himself principally responsible.

He told the Commons that the government had been inclined to let the League of Nations reach a decision on the Paris plan; it was now clear, however, that those proposals no longer obtained, and his government would make no attempt to revive them.

After the debate Eden was appointed on the 22nd December to replace Sir Samuel Hoare at the Foreign Office.

In France Laval was challenged by Paul Reynaud on the 27th December, but succeeded in holding his ground before a divided Right.[41] On the 9th January 1936 the complete text of the Hoare–Laval Plan was published by Geneviève Tabouis in the *Oeuvre* and by Pertinax in the *Echo de Paris*.[42] The Radicals then decided to walk out of the government, and Laval was forced to resign on the 23rd January; Flandin then took over the Quai d'Orsay, in the Sarraut Cabinet.

Who was guilty of the indiscretion that enabled Pertinax and Tabouis to "torpedo" the Hoare–Laval Plan? Among the names suggested was that of Alexis Léger, who was later to win fame as a writer under the name of Saint John Parse; others were Pierre Comert, head of the Press division at the Quai d'Orsay, and Quilici, diplomatic editor of the Havas Agency. No proof of their involvment was ever brought forward.

Andrè Giraud, who wrote under the name of Pertinax,[43] began his career in London before 1914 as correspondent of the *Echo de Paris*. The articles he published in that paper after the war were generally pro-British and favourable to the League of Nations, whose tenets he defended strenuously in the foreign policy review *Europe Nouvelle*, subsidized by the Lazard Bank.

[41] Paul Reynaud's interpellation is contained in his work, *La France a sauvé l'Europe*, Paris, 1947, p. 161 *et seq*.
[42] This was the text that Pertinax had written for the *Daily Telegraph*.
[43] He was born in Bordeaux in 1882.

Geneviève Tabouis,[44] Jules Cambon's niece, began her career in Petite Gironde in 1924, and published regular news reports in the *Oeuvre* and the *Sunday Times*. She has since written that,

> Pierre Laval had imposed strict silence on the Quai d'Orsay. Every publication, forecast or reference to the result of tripartite negotiations were strictly forbidden. — 'Otherwise,' Laval told his Press agent, Pierre Comert, 'everything is done for'.
> But the temptation to publish details of the arrangements concerning the partition of Ethiopia was too strong for two Paris journalists of whom I was one. Perhaps, I thought, it might be possible to save Ethiopia after all; to take a stand against the Duce's scoring off the League and its fifty-four member nations; to defend the basic principle of the League to maintain the integrity of the territory of member States against being automatically abolished by such actions.[45]

The hopes of Madame Tabouis were dashed. Despite the torpedoing of the Hoare–Laval Plan Mussolini succeeded in conquering the whole of Ethiopia by using appropriate methods.[46] As for the Franco-Italian rapprochement attempted by Laval, it remained but a memory after Nazi Germany, watching the progress of events, took a firm stand against the Hoare–Laval Plan; thus Germany frustrated the Anglo-French-Italian accord which could burgeon only at Germany's expense.

[44] Geneviève Lequesne, born in Paris in 1892.
[45] Geneviève Tabouis, *Vingt ans de suspense diplomatique*, Paris, 1958, p. 253.
[46] Poisonous gases.

CHAPTER IV

IMMEDIATE CAUSES OF THE SECOND WORLD WAR

1. What exactly was the scope of the "Hossbach Protocol"?

2. What was the real purpose of Germany's intervention in the Spanish Civil War?

3. Was the French Air Force out-classed in 1938 by the forces of other countries?

4. What was the attitude of the Soviet Union towards the Munich agreements?

5. Did France give Germany a free hand in the East?

6. Why did the Anglo-French-Soviet negotiations fail in 1939?

7. What were the true aims of the Soviet Union at the time of the signature of the non-aggression pact?

1. The Hossbach Document (5th November 1937)

What were Hitler's true aims and ambitions?

On the 5th November 1937 he summoned several of his principal colleagues to the Chancellery — Blomberg, Minister for War, von Neurath, Minister for Foreign Affairs, Raeder, Naval Commander-in-Chief, Goering, Commander-in-Chief of the Air Force, Fritsch, Commander-in-Chief of the Army. Friedrich Hossbach, a Staff Colonel, was also present; his task was to ensure liaison between the Nazi Party and the Services.

A few days later Hossbach summed up the details of the meeting in a document that was produced at the Nuremberg Trials. This document reveals that Hitler did most of the talking. He first drew attention to the importance of the conference, during which he wished to acquaint his colleagues with his sentiments and experience resulting from four years of government. He asked that, in the event of his death, his statements should be regarded as his last will and testament.

Hitler considered it essential for Germany to conquer "living space" in Europe. He said that Germany's aim was to seek in Europe rather than beyond the seas territory rich in basic raw materials, and that objective had to be obtained within one or two generations. He reminded his audience that the history of the Roman and British Empires both demonstrated that all territorial expansion must be accomplished by running risks and breaking down resistance.

He went on:

> The question that Germany has to answer is: In what direction can we accomplish most at the least cost? The German problem can be solved only by force, and this is always accompanied by risk . . . If the considerations which follow are inspired principally by our decision to use force with the risk that force involves, there only remains for us to answer the questions 'When?' and 'Where?'

In reply to the first it was agreed that,

> As the Fuhrer was growing older, there could be no question of postponing the launching of operations to some time in the distant future. The solution must come between 1943 and 1945 at the latest.

The reply to the second question was,

> Our first objective, if we are drawn into war, must be to conquer Czechoslovakia and Austria simultaneously, in order to dispose of any threat on our flank if ever we advanced towards the west.

Hitler's comment on these statements was that he was personally convinced that England, and perhaps even France, had secretly written off Czechoslovakia, having recognized that one day the question would be settled by Germany. A counterstroke by France without the backing of Great Britain seemed highly improbable. As for Italy, she would never react so long as the Duce was alive. The ideal moment for action would undoubtedly come during a period of social unrest in France. Another favourable opportunity might arise out of a possible dispute between France and Italy, when the attention of these two powers would be diverted to the Mediterranean. Hitler believed such a conflict might burst in 1938, and would emanate from the international tension caused by the civil war in Spain. It might even bring about British intervention, a circumstance which would leave Germany's hands free in Central Europe.[1]

At the end of Hitler's statement von Neurath declared that a Franco-Italian conflict did not seem likely in the near future, or even possible. Blomberg observed that Czechoslovak defences were not insignificant,

---

[1] The full text of the "protocol" is contained in the Nuremberg Documents (PS 386).

and should not be underestimated. Fritsch ventured to express a doubt as to an early conflict between the western powers, but added that he was quite sure that such a conflict would not immobilize all the French forces, and so leave the Franco-German frontier open.

The Hossbach document constituted one of the basic pieces of evidence in the Nuremberg Trials –

Hitler's obvious intentions with regard to Austria were, in fact, realized four months after the conference; less than a year afterwards the first part of Czechoslovakia was conquered, and Bohemia and Moravia were overcome in their turn a few months later . . .
The Tribunal is of the opinion that the account given by Lieutenant-Colonel Hossbach is a reliable report of the proceedings of the meeting; and those who were present knew perfectly well that Austria and Czechoslovakia would be annexed by Germany at the first opportunity.

The investigations at the Nuremberg Trials revealed, however, that Goering did not believe at the time that Hitler really intended to attack Austria and Czechoslovakia, and that the sole object of the conference was to exert pressure on Fritsch to expedite re-armament. Raeder for his part came to the conclusion, with Fritsch and Blomberg, that Hitler did not really intend war; he would have preferred a "political solution" of the German problem.

It is of primary importance to know whether, as the Nuremberg judges thought, Hossbach's account was a faithful interpretation of Hitler's intentions. We have questioned Colonel Hossbach (who is to-day a general), and he has given us the following information:

I did not draft minutes during the conference that took place in the Reich Chancellery on the 5th November 1937; but subsequently, on the 10th November, I wrote a manuscript account of it.
It was only after the war had ended that I learned that a certain Colonel Count von Kirchbach, who had to go through some military files moved from Berlin to Liegnitz, made a typewritten copy of my manuscript account. This copy was later sent by one of my relatives to the British military government in Germany. Undoubtedly it was through the intermediary of the latter that the document reached Nuremberg. It was frequently referred to in subsequent post-war literature by the inaccurate term 'the Hossbach minutes'.
My original manuscript account, which I never saw again after November 1937, was not, for reasons which I have stated in my book, *Zwischen Wehrmacht und Hitler 1934–1938*, a literal account of Hitler's statement of the 5th November 1937. I had never been in a position to form an opinion as to any premeditated intentions on the part of Hitler, because the comments he made to those present were quite new to me.

The second question put to Hossbach was: Does the Hossbach document prove Hitler's aggressive intentions towards Austria and Czechoslovakia?

At first sight it seems — and Hossbach confirmed this — that the document should not be taken literally. Hossbach went on to say:

> As to whether the document presented to the international Tribunal at Nuremberg and alleged to be the typewritten copy of my original account of the 10th November 1937, really constitutes 'proof' of Hitler's intention to make war, I can only repeat the remarks already made in my memoirs; that I cannot say with certainty whether the 'document' is an absolutely accurate and literal reproduction of my original account. I consider, however, that on the whole it is a correct reproduction of the contents of my manuscript version. General Beck, who was at that time military Chief of General Staff, saw my original account, and made some critical comments on the 12th November 1937. They are quoted on pages 80 to 82 of Professor W. Foerster's book, *General Ludwig Beck — Sein Kampf gegen den Krieg;* [2] these comments confirm that my manuscript account of the 10th November 1937 agrees in its essentials with the typewritten copy made by Colonel Count von Kirchbach in 1943, if that is the document to which you refer. The contemporary evidence of Colonel Beck, who was profoundly conscious of his responsibilities and whose close collaborator I was, sheds some light on his reaction to the contents of my account.

> Hitler was a very difficult man to see through. He was anything but consistent, and not entirely proof against outside influence. But had he really determined by the 5th November 1937 to run the risk of war to realize his fantastic ambitions, which were in any case irreconcilable with admitted facts and actual possibilities, either political or military? The reply to this question will no doubt keep historians and psychologists busy for a long time to come.

A third question arises: What was the full significance of this document? In point of fact, the only people who appeared to have taken it seriously were the judges at Nuremberg The General Staff did not regard it as a basic document, nor did the German generals build any plan upon these preliminary statements. Did they reveal, as some have suggested, the innermost thoughts of the Führer? In that case, was it not strange that he should have revealed himself in such precise terms to five people of consequence, of whom only one — Goering — was in his confidence?

According to Goering it was essentially a matter of exercising pressure on Fritsch to push forward with a more realistic re-armament programme Up to that time Hitler had only the backing of Schacht in his re-armament policy. He required the backing of the Army, Navy and Air Force; he also needed some diplomatic camouflage. He therefore thought it

[2] Isar Verlag, Munich, 1952.

advisable to treat those responsible a little roughly; and if he failed to convert them to his ideas he would know that their co-operation could not be depended upon.

Goering was present to support him, and in the months that followed he helped to get rid of the "lukewarm". Schacht was at loggerheads with Goering; he had therefore been given leave of absence on the 5th September 1937, and Hitler accepted his resignation on the 8th December. Funk took over Schacht's post in January 1938; and on the 25th Blomberg resigned following a scandal adroitly manoeuvred by Goering and Himmler. Goering at once presented Hitler with a file purporting to prove that Fritsch was a homosexual.[3]

The army commander was thus relieved of his command. On the 4th February Ribbentrop, Nazi ambassador in London, replaced Neurath, and the post of Oberkommando der Wehrmacht (OKW) was created, concentrating all military power in the hands of Hitler. Funk took charge of economy, Goering of the Four Year Plan, and Ribbentrop took over Foreign Affairs: all three became Hitler's loyal and obedient collaborators.

Domestic policy was therefore the underlying motive of the November conference; it was a strategem to enable the Führer to take over absolute power. He did not express his innermost thoughts before the lukewarm, but he cornered them, so that they were forced either to submit or resign. Then, and then only, could he and his party associates perfect a programme of aggression in which Austria would be the first victim.

The Nuremberg judges and numerous commentators were perhaps in error in treating the Hossbach document as proof of Hitler's determination to let loose a war. This proof must be sought in Hitler's actions after that date; the Hossbach document is merely the story of one episode in the overall picture.

2. Germany and the Spanish Civil War

The Spanish civil war broke out on the 16th July 1936. It ended on the 31st March 1939 with the victory of the rebels, the Nationalist forces commanded by General Franco. The Nationalists estimated that

---

[3] Hossbach, who was present at the time, had warned Fritsch, and was in consequence removed from his post immediately.

they lost 110,000 men, the Republicans 175,000. About 25,000 civilians were killed, and 125,000 persons were executed.[4]

A decisive victory was impossible during the early months of the war, as the forces facing each other, Nationalists and Republicans, were more or less equal. On the 19th July 1936 the Republican Prime Minister, Giral, sent a telegram to Léon Blum, the President of the French Council, asking for aid: "Caught unprepared by dangerous military forces. We ask you for immediate military and air support. Fraternally yours, Giral."[5]

The French government agreed to grant aid and, despite attempts made to maintain secrecy over their intervention, news of it spread very rapidly, and drew protests from well-known journalists, among them Kerillis and Churchill. The Nationalists then called on Mussolini for help. On the 25th July Franco's emissaries presented their request to Count Ciano, and the Duce decided in their favour on learning of French intervention. The Spanish officers then proceeded to Berlin to present a similar request to von Neurath; but they met with a refusal, despite the sympathy felt by Admiral Canaris for Franco. Goering also supported the Spanish request, and succeeded in getting Hitler to receive the Spaniards in Bayreuth on the 26th July, where he was attending the Wagner Festival. Hitler agreed to aid the rebel movement for several reasons: he was anxious to divert the attention of the western powers from German re-armament; he needed Spanish iron ore, and he was glad to acquire a new ally.

For somewhat similar reasons the U.S.S.R. agreed to support the Republicans. As a result volunteers from many countries joined in the war from one side or the other. The Spanish civil war thus provoked a European diplomatic war, though most countries favoured non-intervention. The German and Italian Foreign Ministries, as well as those of France and Britain and many other countries, seriously discussed the signing of a non-intervention pact, although they all continued to send air support to the belligerents. German and Italian airmen were enthusiastically acclaimed in Seville, while French airmen were being applauded in Barcelona.

Eventually, Germany, the U.S.S.R., France and Great Britain joined the non-intervention pact, but aid was continued indirectly or dishonestly. It went on increasing, and in January 1937, 7000 Germans

[4] H. Thomas, *The Spanish Civil War*, London, 1961, p. 633.
[5] *Commission d'enquête*, Vol. III.

and 14,000 Italians were in Nationalist Spain; 24,000 foreign volunteers arrived from France.

The battles were fierce, and the progress of the Nationalists was very slow: the siege of Madrid lasted two years. While the Russians were eager to avert the defeat of the Republicans, the Germans had no wish to see the Nationalists crushed. The demand for reinforcements sent by General von Faupel, who remained in Salamanca and maintained liaison between Berlin and the Nationalist army, was not acceded to; but the Italians sent another 15 000 men into Spain. However, at a meeting in Rome on the 20th January 1937 between Goering, Mussolini and Ciano, Germany and Italy both agreed that the Spanish conflict should not degenerate into a world war.[6]

During the course of the battle for Guadaljara, on the 18th March 1937, the 30,000 Italians commanded by General Roatta suffered a severe defeat.[7] The Italians and Germans gradually decided to return to non-intervention; but Mussolini was deeply committed in Spain, and felt the need to gain a victory.

After the Spring of 1937 the German attitude underwent a definite change. On the 12th July von Faupel managed to negotiate an economic agreement with the Nationalists, under which Germany would receive raw materials as payment for war debts, together with an annual interest of 4 per cent. Germany agreed to assist with the reconstruction and industrial rehabilitation of Spain. The Italians on the other hand continued to strive for military victory, and, by October 1937, 60,000 Italians were serving in Spain.

Hitler then prepared for action in Austria and Czechoslovakia. He considered extending, by force if necessary, Germany's *Lebensraum*, and began to intensify re-armament as a preparation. The Spanish war served as an excellent opportunity to distract the attention of the West. Several German diplomats[8] saw in this interminable conflict which they wanted to prolong the chance of creating serious tension between France and Italy, and subsequently between Great Britain and Italy. Such dissensions would not only stand in the way of closer relations between Italy and the Franco-British amity, but would inevitably bring Italy closer to Germany. Hitler finally adopted this attitude in the autumn of 1937. He decided to make no further efforts in support of

[6] Weizsäcker, *Erinnerungen*, Munich, 1950, p. 113.
[7] The casualties were 2000 killed, 4000 wounded and 300 prisoners.
[8] Among them Weiszäcker *(op. cit.)* and von Hassell, German ambassador in Rome. See also German Archives, I, 172.

the Nationalists, but would encourage Mussolini to do so. German diplomats then entered into negotiation with Jordana, Franco's Foreign Minister, to secure mining concessions.

Meanwhile the Nationalist forces alone broke down the resistance of the Republicans. An Italian terror raid on Barcelona on the 16th March 1938 did nothing to hasten the end, or to give Roatta the show of victory so much desired by the Duce.[9] At the end of 1938 the international brigades withdrew. On the 22nd May 1939 the German forces, including the Condor Legion, left Spain, and on the 21st May 20,000 Italians embarked at Cadiz. By the end of June no more German or Italian forces were left in the country.

German intervention had been well timed, well worked out and capably handled. It altogether fulfilled Hitler's expectations. In Berlin he reviewed the 14,000 men of the Condor Legion, and expressed to them his entire satisfaction. In addition, German diplomacy had given strong support to the master in forging the Rome–Berlin Axis on the battlefields of spain, and at very little cost.

3. The French Air Force in 1938

In the spring of 1934 Marshal Balbo undertook a mass flight with his squadron over foreign territory. The tour, which fired the imagination of the youth of Italy, included a flight over France. Every government whose permission had been sought authorized Balbo to fly over their territory, but the French displayed a touch of fastidiousness in arranging for an escort of French fighters to accompany the Italian squadron. The French airmen took up their positions punctually and precisely over the Alps, but they were incapable of keeping up with Balbo's planes which were, however, standard models. It was the first opportunity the French military air force had had of comparing itself with a foreign air force. Apparently the contrast by no means absorbed the attention of the French authorities.

Two organizations were concerned with the development of the French air force: the Conseil Supérieur de la Défense Nationale and the Comité Permanent de la Défense Nationale. Pierre Cot, the Air Minister, had on several occasions insisted on the need to increase the sums allocated to aviation and to sign an air agreement with the U.S.S.R. But no one listened to him.

---

[9] Franco disapproved the raid, and it took place without his authorization.

Pierre Cot was an outstanding minister. Trained in dialectics by the Jesuits, he showed his true character in Catholic Action, and as a barrister he gave evidence of exceptional talent. When he moved over from the National Coalition to Briand's Radicals he showed an interest in the development of the Soviet air force, and aspired to create in France a parachute regiment and units of airborne troops. Pierre Cot himself made a courageous parachute jump from the Tour de l'Exposition in Paris; he did not, however, pursue his aims resolutely. France lagged behind the other powers in building up its air force, and although Pierre Cot wished to see the French force equipped with the most modern planes, he lacked the determination necessary to achieve his objective.

Supported by the theories of the Italian General Douhet, a number of specialists discussed the usefulness of dive-bombers to work in conjunction with fighter planes on the battlefield. They worked out brilliant theories on the technique of combining air operations with armoured vehicles on the ground, but no experiments were ever carried out. At about the same time the Germans were trying out their air force in the Spanish civil war, and Cot proved incapable of attaining his target of 1700 planes in 1937. His successor, Guy La Chambre, managed to carry through a part of his plan to have 2400 planes in 1938.

No lesson was drawn from the war in Spain, but Guy La Chambre, in order to satisfy everybody, manufactured a general utility craft — the Potez 63 — which was a combination of the fighter, bomber and reconnaissance plane.[10] No constructive debate on the question of the air force was ever conducted in the French parliament, and Bossoutrot, President of the Commission de l'Aéronautique in the Chamber, himself a former airman, confined his efforts to supporting the two Ministers Cot and La Chambre in their attempt to secure an allocation of 39 milliard francs to the air force for the period 1933 to 1939.[11]

General Vuillemain was appointed to the post of General Chief of Staff of the Army Air Force. He had been a junior artillery officer who re-enlisted in 1914, and had joined the air force as a volunteer. He won

[10] The importance of co-operation between aircraft and armoured vehicles was borne out during the war in Poland. The conclusions drawn by the French Military Mission in Poland should have claimed attention; and an account of the usefulness of those planes appeared in an article by J. de Launay, *Le Monde en Guerre*, published in Paris, J.-B. Janin, 1945, p. 50; but little notice was taken of the warning.

[11] Bossoutrot's predecessor was Laurent-Eynac.

fame as a pilot and built his career upon personal prestige. General Vuillemin does not appear to have been an exceptional man, considering that he was appointed to a post that demanded a profound instinct for organization. His ministerial colleagues no doubt found it convenient to lean upon an airman who enjoyed universal esteem, however ill-qualified to carve out an "air policy" which they had hoped to reserve for themselves. Vuillemin was incapable of organizing the air force; he could not create an efficient French offensive and defensive plan. This distinguished pilot, who would certainly have been able to give an example of courage, proved unsuited to the business of direction and organization entrusted to him. In 1943, however, reverting to his glorious past, he went to North Africa and joined the air force as a Lieutenant Colonel in a French fighter unit.

In August 1938 when the tension between Germany and Czecho-slovakia was reaching a climax, Vuillemin went to Berlin to return the visit that the German Air Chief of Staff had made in 1937. On his return to Paris Vuillemin gave an account of his journey to Georges Bonnet.

The General told us of the very cordial reception Hitler and Goering had given him. His conversation with Hitler was unimportant; the Chancellor reminded him briefly of the solidarity which bound together ex-servicemen of the world. It was Goering who broached the subject of Czechoslovakia. He remarked that 'the pact between France and Czechoslovakia should come into operation only if the latter were the victim of unprovoked attack. And this was not the case; Czechoslovakia was provoking Germany by conducting an intolerable persecution of the Sudeten Germans'. General Vuillemin, who knew our views in the matter, replied firmly, 'If Czechoslovakia is attacked France will go to her assistance'. And there the conversation ended.

General Vuillemin was particularly impressed by his visit to the airplane factory, and by the rhythm and speed of production. The Messerschmidt factory at Augsburg was at that time building, at the rate of 180 a month, planes of a speed exceeding 500 kilometres an hour; Junkers were producing 600 engines a month, and this output could easily have been trebled by employing three shifts working twenty-four hours. Those were only a few examples... General Vuillemin recognized the power of the German air force, revealed by the quality and quantity of the material; he was in no doubt that the Germans were technically ahead of France. Their armament and flying techniques placed German fighters and bombers well ahead of production in other European countries.

The General's visit only intensified the concern he had expressed to the Comité Permanent de la Défense Nationale a short while previously. He said to me, 'Alas, if war were to break out the French air force would be destroyed in two weeks. We have nothing but old planes whose speed does not exceed 300 or 350 kilometres an hour. Our air force is completely out-classed by the German air force which has a guaranteed average speed of 500 kilometres an hour, that is to say, 200 kilo-metres an hour faster than our own. If war broke out, and I had to put these antiquated planes in the air I should feel obliged to have them piloted by my worst airmen, because I should most certainly be sending them to their deaths. My best airmen would have to be saved for the distant future when we might have modern planes capable of fighting on equal terms with the enemy.'

Vuillemin did not reserve these observations only for his chiefs. With incredible carelessness he repeated them to the Czech ambassador in Paris, American ambassador Bullitt, and many others.

It seems, therefore, that the French air force in 1938 was decidedly out-classed by foreign air forces generally, in particular that of Germany. The responsibility for this state of affairs was shared by the French parliament, the government and Air Force General Headquarters. It is fair to add that the pacifist sentiments of the French people did not create the kind of atmosphere conducive to the building up of a strong air force. Air power, as an essentially offensive weapon, did not appear to demand any special attention from a nation whose mind was focused on the defensive.

Moreover, the opposing sides were well informed as to their respective air forces. The Germans had 3500 planes at their disposal, of which half were bombers. The British had 700 fighters and 620 bombers. The Czechoslovak force was not unimportant: it consisted of 300 bombers and 300 fighters. The French were capable of putting 1250 planes into the air, 800 of which were more or less out-of-date.[12]

A few observations on these figures are relevant. Even though some of the German machines may not have been of the latest type, the numerical strength of the Luftwaffe exceeded the forces of its rivals by about 500 planes. Belgian neutrality, which had once again been formally recognized on the 14th October 1936,[13] deprived British planes of easy access to the Ruhr, since their range was still inadequate. On the other hand, it seems surprising that the western powers failed completely to take Russia into account. For, although 2000 Russian planes were locked up in the Far East, the Soviet still had 4000 machines ready to intervene, and about 3000 of these were quite comparable with the Luftwaffe.

The problem was to make Czechoslovakia "Soviet aircraft carrier", so that Russian planes could land on Czechoslovak aerodromes. Thus

[12] These figures are given by the French expert Pierre Sorlin.
[13] The announcement of Belgium's return to a policy of independence played a considerable part in persuading the Czechoslovak statesmen to reconsider their former determination to resist at any cost.

based the Soviet air force could reach Germany's strategic points. Since the spring diplomats had many times discussed this proposal.

Requests to fly over Poland and Rumania had been rejected by the governments in Warsaw and Bucarest. The Rumanian government, however, pressed by France, agreed on the 11th September 1938 not to oppose flights over its territory. In fact, the West preferred to do without Soviet intervention in Czechoslovakia. Taking into account the strength of the opposing forces, "the inadequacy of the West's strength in pursuit planes, combined with the fear of bombing attacks, greatly influenced the decision of the French and British governments".

All this partly explains the temporizing attitude of the French and British at the time of Munich. Prior to that date they had studied the balance-sheet of their resources; having been forced to recognize their serious deficiency in aircraft, they decided to gain time and postpone the risk of an uncertain war, even at the price of capitulation.

4. Russia and the Munich Agreements

As France and Britain were not prepared in September 1938 for war they were ready to capitulate at Munich.

But they took this step not only because militarily they were unprepared, but because public opinion both in France and Britain was opposed to war. The really black spot in the negotiations entered into by Chamberlain is to be found in his mission of the 20th September, when the British and French had to compel Benes, the Czechoslovak President, to agree to the Sudetenland being united with Germany.

The "Anglo-French proposals" arrived in Prague during the afternoon of the 19th September. The Czech Cabinet deliberated the whole day, knowing that the suggested transfer of territory implied removal of the country's entire military defence, and, in consequence, all political balance in central Europe. After a futile protest Benes explored the possibilities of resistance, which was the alternative.

Oreste Rosenfeld, a friend of Léon Blum, furnished the following details of those events:

Relations between President Benes and the Czechoslovak ambassador in Paris were not good. As Benes had a great regard for and confidence in Léon Blum who, when President of the Council, had expressed categorically France's liability in regard to Czechoslovakia, he wished to enter into direct talks with him. To this end he sent to Paris his Minister Necsas, a member of the Czechoslovak Social

Democrats. So far as I can recall he was Minister of State Insurance, or Labour, an I think he died in 1939 or 1940.

On his first visit the Minister was accompanied by Hubert Ripka, editor-in-chief of Benes's newspaper; he was a friend and confidant of the President, and Léon Blum and I had known him for several years. He and I were good friends. As the former President of the Council happened at that time to be in the country, about forty-five kilometres from Paris, it fell to me to receive the personal envoys of President Benes. I later took them to see Léon Blum. It was agreed that the Minister would visit Paris every week, and that I would keep him informed of the situation in France in relation to the German-Czechoslovak dispute. In an emergency he could telephone me, preferably at my home and at night.

In fact, he returned two or three times, and also telephoned me on several occasions. On one of his journeys he showed me on a map the concessions that Czechoslovakia was prepared to make; they included the transfer to Germany of certain districts with a Sudeten majority. The territory in question faced Czechoslovakia's line of defence. During the night of the 10th to the 20th September 1938 I received an urgent message from Prague. I no longer remember whether it was the Minister or M. Ripka who spoke to me. I may have spoken to them both, because we had two messages — the first at three in the morning and the second at five.

The three o'clock caller said, 'I am speaking from the President's palace. The meeting of the government has been postponed because the President wishes to consult you before taking a final decision. We wish to reject the Anglo-French proposal. If Hitler attacks us we can hold out for two weeks. May we hope that during those two weeks of unequal combat a change of heart might take place in French public opinion and in the attitude of the French government, which would permit France to stand by her pledges to us and come to our help? President Benes requests that you consult Messieurs Léon Blum and Edouard Herriot urgently. We shall call you again in two hours . . .'

I knew very well what reply I should have to give Prague, since we had no hope whatever of persuading the Daladier government to reverse its decision; moreover, public opinion, and even a group within our Socialist party — the SFIO — were ready to support the government through fear of war.

However, as a matter of duty, I at once telephoned Léon Blum. He called me back three quarters of an hour later, and instructed me to tell Prague that Czechoslovakia could not rely upon such a sudden change of attitude on the part of France and her government.

At five in the morning I received the call from Prague; feeling sick at heart I julfilled my painful duty. As a result the Czechoslovak government capitulated.[14]

It is noteworthy that a number of German writers have stated that Hitler informed Chamberlain on the 22nd September that he had had the telephone conversations between Rosenfeld and Benes recorded[15] —

[14] The author received these details from O. Rosenfeld on the 26th February 1962.
[15] We cannot accept the story that Mandel and Reynaud pressed Benes to hold out. But see H. Nogueres, *Munich*, Laffont, Paris, 1963, p. 154.

"I have the discs" Hitler is alleged to have said. The German Chancellor wished to bring pressure to bear on Chamberlain by showing him that the Paris "warmongers" were urging Benes to resist. The evidence of Rosenfeld as quoted above disposes of the Führer's bluff, and illustrates his methods of everlasting blackmail.

International trade union organizations had already decided to support Benes, but for reasons which it is difficult to unravel twenty-four years after the events, they made no approach to the Czechoslovak President.[16]

Léon Jouhaux went to Washington, called at the White House on the 20th September, and drew Roosevelt's attention to the gravity of the Czech crisis. The interview was probably not unconnected with the telegram Roosevelt had sent to Benes, Hitler, Chamberlain and Daladier, urging them in the name of humanity not to break off negotiations, but to seek out a peaceful, just and constructive solution to the questions under dispute.

Who were the real opponents of the Munich agreements? In Paris they were the Popular Democrats, the Communists and such journalists as Henri de Kérillis (the *Epoque*), Georges Bidault (the *Aube*), André Tardieu *(Gringoire)*, Geneviève Tabouis (the *Oeuvre*), Emile Buré (the *Ordre*) and Wladimir d'Ormesson *(Le Figaro)*. But these brilliant journalists were not truly representative of a public that really did not want war.

On the 21st September Churchill and his friend General Spears attended a dinner at the Ritz, in the Place Vendôme, Paris, in an attempt to bring together the forces opposed to capitulation; among those present were Reynaud, Mandel and Champetier de Ribes. The question discussed was how to bring about a reversal of attitude in the Daladier Cabinet through the mass resignation of the supporters of resistance.[17] But those ministers did not resign, aware no doubt of the peaceful aspirations of the electorate.[18]

In London the Labour Party, represented by Attlee and Greenwood, and the Liberal Party, represented by Archibald Sinclair, were opposed

[16] It seems very likely that the visit which Jouhaux and Schevenels paid to Benes on his private estate, forty-five kilometres from Prague, was undertaken on the 10th October, that is to say, after the main events referred to.

[17] According to Reynaud, Churchill advised against resignation. Reynaud maintained that the three ministers offered their resignation to Daladier on the 22nd September; but when Daladier told them that their resignation implied desertion they agreed not to press the matter.

[18] The "Grand Orient de France", at its session of the 20th September, stated that "war solves nothing".

to the Munich agreements, and supported Eden, Churchill and their friends;[19] but their protests met with little response among the British people, although the nation was not subject to military conscription.

To-day the true attitude of the Soviet Union towards the Munich agreements is better known, although very few documents are available to permit us to form an opinion. It is none the less possible to draw some kind of conclusion and take a note of a few relevant facts.

1. The U.S. and S.R. distrusted Chamberlain's representatives

Russia's traditional distrust of the West re-appeared when Chamberlain took the initiative in trying to resolve the Sudeten problem through a personal talk with Hitler. To some extent this suspicion was justified, for no one in Prague, Paris or Moscow knew the real intentions of the British Prime Minister in regard to existing treaties. Apparently the Soviet rulers immediately suspected a western plot aimed at turning Hitler towards the east.

2. The U.S.S.R. was prepared to intervene to help Czechoslovakia

Litvinov, Foreign Affairs Commissar, expressed his point of view quite clearly on the 21st September 1938 in Geneva:

We are determined to fulfil our obligations under the pact, and render assistance to Czechoslovakia and to France by whatever means at our disposal. Our military commanders are ready to parcitipate immediately in a conference with French and Czechslovak military leaders, to consider what steps the situation demands.

It should be noted that intervention was conditional upon parallel action by France. This seemed quite a logical attitude involving no risk for Russia, because, as Beloff observes[20], Moscow did not believe the western nations would take a firm stand. Apparently, however, the Soviet Press did not at any time prepare public opinion for a war in support of Czechoslovakia. Yet was it not precisely in the interets of the Franco-British-Soviet coalition to arrest, without going to war Hisler's contemplated agression?

[19] Though Duff Cooper did not resign until the 1st October.

[20] Beloff, *The Foreign Policy of Soviet Russia, 1929–41*, New York and London, 1947, p. 165. It might be mentioned here that it was France who requested that the Russo-Czechoslovak pact of 1935 should allow France to intervene before Russia. The French had no wish to be drawn into war by the Russians as they had been in 1914.

3. In principle the U.S.S.R. favoured an international conference

When Roosevelt suggested on the 28th September convening an international conference to solve the German-Czech dispute,[21] Soviet Russia welcomed the proposal. Litvinov had already said on the 21st;

> It is necessary to make every effort to ward off an armed conflict, and we consider that one of the steps conducive to this aim would be to convene at once a conference of the great powers in Europe, and other States idterested, in order to agree on some collective action.

The Soviet reply of 28th the September likewise refered to a conference of all interested parties.[21a]

Chamberlain, however, was opposed to such a large conference; and the British Prime Minister had no wish to engage in talks with the Russians and Poles. He therefore asked Mussolini to intervene as mediator. The Duce caught the ball on the bounce, for the idea of a four power pact was familiar to him. He too was anxious to keep the Russians out of Munich; he hoped to postpone the threatening European conflict and facilitate the solution of the Danubian problem to Italy's advantage, without bringing the Russians into the discussion. Another important factor was that Benes looked towards Paris and London rather than towards Moscow, and he did not hope to offer resistance with the support of Russia alone. This factor is certainly not insignificant.

There was some delay in advising the Soviet government of the progress of events in Prague. And, when Prague finally capitulated on the 30th September, the Soviet ambassador, Alexandrovsky, learned of the proposals for capitulation and the fact itself almost at the same time. Thus Soviet Russia was never really asked by Prague to intervene.

4. The capitulation at Munich was badly received by the Soviet Union

Documents published by the Soviet government lay stress upon the important military precautions taken along Russia's European frontiers. It had been decided without the U.S.S.R. to upset the political equilibrium of central Europe, and the Soviet feared that French and British pacifism might lead those two countries to divert the German threat towards the east, whatever might be the consequences for the Soviet Union.

[21] According to Georges Bonnet.
[21a] U.S.S.R. foreign policy documents, 1960 IV, 391–92.

Potiemkin, Deputy Commissar for Foreign Affairs, said to Coulondre, the French ambassador, on the 30th September; "What have you done, my poor friend? As for us, I cannot see anything but a fourth partition of Poland".[22]

Litvinov committed to his diary the bitter observation that the Poles also had buried Czechoslovakia, and added that it was a rare example of political stupidity.[23]

5. The Pact of Paris (6th December 1938)

After the Munich agreement of the 30th September Chamberlain again met Hitler, man to man. They carried on a rambling conversation on disarmament and the Spanish problem; when the atmosphere became less strained the British Premier came round to the object of his visit. He made a proposal to Hitler. "It would be helpful to both countries and to the world in general if they could issue some statement which showed the agreement between them on the desirability of better Anglo-German relations, leading to a greater European stability."[24]

Chamberlain drew a draft from his pocket. It ran: "We are resolved that the method of consultation shall be the method adopted to deal with any other questions that may concern our two countries, and we are determined to continue our efforts to remove possible sources of difference and thus contribute to assure the peace of Europe".[25]

Hitler accepted the proposal with delight, and they both signed what has been called the Anglo-German Declaration. When Chamberlain returned to London he waved the document in his hand before an enthusiastic crowd. "I have it!" he exclaimed amidst frenzied applause.

Daladier, who had been very depressed throughout the Munich interview, returned to Paris uneasy. On his arrival at Le Bourget he expected the worst, especially when he saw the crowds. Georges Bonnet, who was waiting for him at the airport, reassured him quickly, and both crossed Paris amidst acclamations.

[22] Coulondre, *De Staline à Hitler : Souvenirs de deux Ambassades (1936–1939)* Paris, 1950, pp. 156 to 164. Russian historians hesitate to accept this solitary piece of evidence."

[23] Litvinov, *Notes from a Journal(1926–45)* London, 1955. The authenticity of Litvinov's diary has sometimes been questioned. The Minister's remark, however, is in keeping with his state of mind at the time; he expressed similar sentiments to many other people.

[24] A. J. P. Taylor, *Origins of the Second World War*, p. 186.

[25] *Ibid.*

When Bonnet returned to the Quai d'Orsay he learned through the evening papers of the signature of the Hitler–Chamberlain declaration. He spoke to Daladier on the telephone, but the President knew nothing about it. Corbin, the French ambassador in London, was asked to obtain information; but the Foreign Office knew nothing either. Apparently Chamberlain's spontaneous effort surprised Daladier and the French ministers, who were somewhat upset. Some there were who observed that, although Germany may have promised never again to make war on England, nothing had been said about France and the Alsace-Lorraine question.

The ambassadors in London and Berlin were asked to find out, and they reported very favourably on both Chamberlain and Hitler.

On the 13th October François–Poncet wrote to Bonnet:

We should try to get Hitler to express in writing his recognition of France's frontiers, and give an undertaking not to violate them, or do anything without prior consultation that might affect the relations between the two countries.[26]

The ambassador then went to see Hitler:

During the evening of the 17th October the Chancellor asked me to call and see him as soon as possible, and placed one of his personal planes at my disposal. Accompanied by Captain Stehlin I went by air the following day to Berchtesgaden, and arrived about three o'clock in the afternoon. From there I was taken by car; not, however, to the villa at Obersalzberg where the Führer was staying, and where he had previously received me, but to a remarkable place where he liked to spend some time when the weather was fine.

In the distance the place looked like a kind of observatory or a little hermitage, perched 1900 metres high on the edge of a cliff. It was reached by a winding road of about fifteen kilometres distance and cut into the rock. The bold contour of the road said as much for the skill of the engineer, Todt, as for the strenuous work of the men who, in three years, had carried out the gigantic task. The road terminated at a long subterranean passage which plunged into the ground, and was shut off by a heavy double door made of bronze. At the end of the tunnel an enormous lift, of which the interior was covered with copper, awaited the visitor. By a vertical shaft, 110 metres in height and cut into the rock, he was raised to the level of the Chancellor's quarters. Here was an even greater surprise. Facing the visitor stood a spacious, solid structure, consisting of a long balcony supported by Roman columns and an immense, round hall with windows. Enormous logs burned in a broad fireplace, and in the centre of the room was a table surrounded by some thirty chairs. There were several lateral rooms, elegantly furnished with comfortable armchairs. Through the bay windows all around the room the gaze plunged, as from a plane in flight, upon a vast panorama of mountains.

[26] Bonnet, *Défense de la Paix*, Vol. II: *Fin d'une Europe*, Geneva, 1948, p. 24.

At the bottom of the amphitheatre one could see Salzburg and the surrounding villages, and as far as the eye could reach an horizon of chains and peaks, and meadows and forests clinging to the mountain slopes. Near the house, which appeared to be suspended in space, rose up a sheer, overhanging wall of naked rock.

The whole tableau, bathed in the half-light of an autumn evening, was wild, awe-inspiring, almost a delusion. The visitor wonders whether he is dreaming, and where he might be. Was this the Castle of Montsalvat where dwelt the knights of the Holy Grail, or a Mount Athos, the shelter of a cenobite wrapt in meditation, or the palace of Antinea set up in the heart of Atlas? Was it perhaps the realization of one of those fantastic drawings with which Victor Hugo decorated the margins of the manuscript of the Burgraves, or the dreamland of a millionaire, or merely the haunt of brigands who came there to rest and store their treasures? Was it the work of a normal mind, or of one tormented by the folly of splendour, the obsession of dominion and solitude, or a prey to fear?

But there was one striking detail, no less important than everything else to anyone who seeks to understand the psychology of Adolf Hitler; the slopes, the openings to the tunnels and the approaches to the house were well guarded: they were protected by nests of machine guns . . .[27]

The conversation between Hitler, François–Poncet and Ribbentrop was courteous and friendly. The Chancellor said that he was disappointed by events following the Munich agreement, by the threats and criticism uttered against him in England. He said he was in favour of a Franco-German declaration, and instructed Ribbentrop to prepare the text.

On the 5th November 1938 the draft was taken to Bonnet by the German ambassador, Count Welczeck. Despite the unfortunate incident of the 7th November, when a Jew assassinated von Rath, a secretary at the German Embassy in the Rue de Lille, Ribbentrop's journey to Paris, after being somewhat delayed, was fixed for the 6th December. The French Council of Ministers approved the text of the declaration on the 23rd November, with the proviso that it should change nothing in France's existing scheme of alliances.[28]

Ribbentrop arrived in Paris on the 6th December 1938.

Tall, with hard features and a stilted gait, elegant to the point of affectation — such was Ribbentrop as he appeared to me when, dressed in a black morning coat and preceded by ushers, he entered my office at the Quai d'Orsay. He sat in the armchair reserved for visitors, with Count Welczeck seated beside him. I sat at my desk opposite him, and Monsieur Léger sat near me. The conversation was carried on without an interpreter, because Ribbentrop's French was fluent.

[27] *Yellow Book*, Item 18.
[28] According to Zay and de Monzie, Bonnet more or less "dragged" an approval from the Council. See de Monzie's *Ci-devant*, Paris, 1941, and Zay's *Souvenirs et Solitude*, Paris, 1945.

It was the German Minister who spoke first. He was always affable in a social atmosphere, but returned to his naturally brusque manner immediately one approached general problems affecting European politics. On those occasions he spoke with imperturbable self-confidence, of which he had an unlimited supply, especially when he referred to the large nunber of tanks, guns and divisions that Germany possessed. He had borrowed from Hitler his method of trying to smother his listener with an interminable speech which allowed no room for questions or interruptions, and made conversation, or any exchange of views at all, very difficult. One had to exercise a great deal of patience and goodwill in bringing him back to the subject, and obtaining the explanations one required of him.[29]

After a general survey of the situation the two ministers signed the following declaration:

1. The French and German governments share the conviction that peaceful and good neighbourly relations between France and Germany constitute one of the essential elements in the consolidation of the European situation and the maintenance of general peace. In consequence, the two governments will use all their powers in this direction to ensure the development of relations between their two countries.

2. The two governments state that no territorial problem remains in doubt between their countries, and they solemnly recognize as final the frontier between their countries as at present outlined.

3. The two countries are resolved, subject to their special relations with third Powers, to maintain contact on all questions affecting their two countries, and to consult each other should the subsequent development of such questions threaten to lead to international difficulties.

From the wording of this document two possible interpretations confronted each other in July 1939. On the 1st July Bonnet received ambassador Welczeck, and pointed out that "the Franco-German declaration (Art. 3) cannot be regarded as affecting France's special relations with Eastern Europe".[30] Consequently, any modification of the *status quo* in Danzig would result in the operation of the Franco-Polish Pact.

On the 13th July Ribbentrop replied to the French observation of the 1st; "That is not correct. I expressly drew attention to the fact that Eastern Europe constituted a German sphere of interest".[31]

[29] Bonnet, *op. cit.*, p. 36.
[30] *Yellow Book*, Item 150.
[31] *Yellow Book*, Item 163.

On the 21st July Bonnet wrote to Ribbentrop: "At no time, either before or after the declaration of the 6th December, could it have been possible for the German government to think that France had relinquished her interest in Eastern Europe".[32]

From these two versions a whole series of interpretations are possible. If we keep to the facts we must remember that there exists no account of the Bonnet–Ribbentrop conference that preceded the signature of the declaration, other than the accounts of Bonnet and Ribbentrop; and Léger and Welczek have left nothing in writing. Bonnet denied having given Germany "a free hand in the east". He had no authority from the Council of Ministers to do so, and the wording of the declaration (Art. 3) made particular reference to the "special relations with third Powers".[33] Ribbentrop wrote: "In December 1938 . . . I signed the Franco-German non-aggression pact with Bonnet; it implied that France ceased to retain any interest in her eastern alliances".[34]

Less important witnesses are divided between the two interpretations. On Bonnet's side, Lebrun, President of the Republic, regarded the misunderstanding as due to the fact that the persons concerned did not speak the same language. Coulondre, ambassador in Berlin, thought it sprang from the fact that France regarded the declaration as a "receipt", and Germany as a treaty. Noël, French ambassador in Warsaw, said that the wording was clear, and certainly made provision for alliances, but that the behaviour of Bonnet was vague and ambiguous.

For Ribbentrop, Kordt said that the French Minister had stressed France's desire to devote herself henceforth to her internal development and her empire. Schmidt, the official German interpreter, declared that some reference made by Bonnet to the recent Czech crisis was taken by Ribbentrop to be a pledge relating to future action. But Bonnet denied quite definitely that Schmidt, who was a member of Ribbentrop's staff, had taken part in the conversation at all. Abetz, who also supported Ribbentrop, left an account of what had occurred, but made no mention of "a free hand in the east".

Perhaps it will never be possible to reconstruct the Bonnet–Ribbentrop conference. One has to be careful not to exaggerate the scope of the agreement reached; but, with the lapse of time, this Franco-

---

[32] *Yellow Book*, Item 168.

[33] Bonnet, *op. cit.*, Vol. II, p. 47 *et seq.*

[34] J. von Ribbentrop, *Zwischen London und Moskau : Erinnerungen und Aufzeichnungen*, 1953 p. 148. Ribbentrop made use of Léger's notes to draft his telegram of the 14th December (*Yellow Bork*, Item 32).

German declaration certainly seems to have been inopportune. It by no means improved the relations between the two countries, and did not fail to worry the countries of eastern Europe. The Polish ambassador in Paris remarked, "France is too weak not only to break off her eastern alliances, but to stand resolutely by them".[35] Comnene[36] has described the extent to which this agreement upset the Little Entente.

Great Britain and Poland had been kept informed of the progress of the negotiations. At a period when France was increasing the pace of her re-armament against any eventuality, it was obvious that the strengthening of her diplomatic alliances should also have been in full swing; but the Paris declaration only made France's allies feel uneasy. In order to draw near to Germany France had not hesitated to weaken her links with the Little Entente.

The fact that the two ministers' statements contradicted each other is perhaps due to the differences in their characters. Bonnet was above all a legal man. At forty-nine years of age this eminent councillor of state was skilled in the art of conducting a negotiation in such a way as to lead men and events to conform with his own plans. As a native of Périgord he had a shrewd mind. He had cultivated the knack of rounding off corners and facilitating relations.

It was Bonnet who wanted the Pact of Paris, and he so arranged matters that the proposal came from Hitler himself. Possibly, in his dogged anxiety to gain time in favour of peace, he did not foresee the consequences of that negotiation. Might it not have been better on the eve of war to strengthen the alliances with the small nations, rather than drag from Hitler a promise of peace which could compromise even further the work of Briand and Barthou — a work already shaken by Laval?

Ribbentrop was an altogether different kind of man. At that time he was forty-five years of age. He had completed his education in Metz, in Switzerland and in London. When he left college he went to Canada, where for two years he worked as a railway employee and then as a bank clerk.

On the outbreak of the first world war he was in Canada, whence he returned to Germany in September 1914 and fought in Turkey. In 1919 Lieutenant Ribbentrop was aide-de-camp to General von Seeckt, and accompanied him to Versailles. By then his commercial career had

[35] *Documents polonais relatifs à l'Histoire des origines de la guerre*, 1ere série, Berlin, 1940, p. 11.
[36] N. P. Comnene — *Preludi del grande dramma*. Roma, 1947, p. 411.

commenced; he became German representative of Henkell, the champagne firm. In 1925 he got himself adopted by an aunt who had no heir, so that he might become *von* Ribbentrop, and eventually married the daughter of his employer, Henkell. After being introduced to von Papen with whom he struck up a friendship, he set up a small foreign policy office on Nazi party lines under the direction of Rosenberg. He learned how to make himself indispensable to the Führer through his knowledge of English and French. Thus he built up a career by his skill as a courtier, being careful to anticipate and put into effect the wishes of his master. His conceit and obsequiousness bored even his colleagues, and his snobbery annoyed everyone who came into contact with him; it gratified the Führer, however, who appreciated this zealous and obedient servant.

One can quite imagine that while Ribbentrop was engaged in the Paris talks he remained the slave of his Führer, and still more so when he contradicted Bonnet in July 1939. When questioned at the Nuremberg Trials on his attitude during this period he aways maintained that he had obeyed the Führer. A week before the meeting in Paris he began the first negotiations with Poland on the subject of Danzig. Perhaps he already wished to induce the French to abandon their interest in Poland. But the talks with the Poles took place in a favourable climate, and it was less important then to eliminate French interest than it became in March 1939, when the Poles adopted an inflexible attitude.

After the examination of evidence and documents we feel that if the question of "a free hand in the east" was present in the mind of the German Minister (a matter which engrossed the Führer in *Mein Kampf!*), it was not definitely put to Georges Bonnet. The interpretation of the Paris agreements based upon the confidential conversation that preceded them was undoubtedly a diplomatic manoeuvre on the part of the Germans.

6. *The Failure of Anglo-French-Soviet Negotiations (April–August 1939)*

The Danzig dispute began to grow acrimonious from about the 15th March 1939. When Chamberlain gave Poland Britain's pledge on the 31st March, he hoped to fix the limits of German expansion.

The Western Powers knew well that the danger of war was nearing its peak, and they set about drawing up a balance-sheet of their friends and allies. Since 1936 Belgium had returned to her position of neutrality.

The sympathies of Spain, weakened as she was after the civil war, were with the Axis. Italy had already bound herself to Germany. The Little Entente, after the desertion of Czechoslovakia, welcomed German trade missions, preferring to be on cordial terms with its most powerful neighbour than to rely on vague promises from Paris and London. Poland, isolated and threatened, was still tied to the Franco-Polish alliance of 1921.

On the 13th April France hastened to confirm that that alliance still held, and the French and British governments gave their pledge to Rumania and Greece. On the 12th May Britain signed a mutual assistance pact with Turkey, and France did the same on the 23rd June.

On the 3rd April Hitler had signed an order appointing the 1st September as the date of the attack on Poland. It was not a final decision, but a date appointed for the completion of military preparations. The order was, of course, secret, and not known to the statesmen in Paris and London. France and Britain desired to buttress their guarantee to Poland by an alliance with Russia. As Moscow had protested to Berlin on the 19th March against the annexation of Bohemia and Moravia, the moment seemed opportune to renew ties with the U. S. S. R.

But the Russians were extremely suspicious. The Munich agreements and the talks in Paris between Bonnet and Ribbentrop had ultimately convinced the Russians that the Western Powers were seeking to divert German expansionist aims towards the east.[37] The Russians were, however, ready to reconsider the problem of eastern Europe as a whole. If they were to be asked for help, they wished to discuss all questions touching upon Russia's traditional sphere of influence: they agreed to discuss Danzig on condition that the Baltic States, Bessarabia and the Straits were dealt with also.

But those were matters which the French and British had no desire to include; they even declined to touch upon them — despite the urgent appeal by Churchill:

The worst folly, which no one proposes we should commit, would be to chill and drive away any natural co-operation which Soviet Russia in her own deep interests feels it necessary to afford.[38]

[37] Cf. the statement by Manuilsky at the Communist Party Congress on the 11th March 1939, quoted by Duroselle in Les frontières européennes de l'URSS 1917–1941, p. 276, Paris, 1957.
[38] Quoted by A. J. P. Taylor in The Origins of the Second World War, p. 225.

And Lloyd George said:

If we are going in without the help of Russia we are walking into a trap. It is the only country whose arms can get there . . . If Russia has not been brought into this matter because of certain feelings the Poles have that they do not want the Russians there, it is for us to declare the conditions, and unless the Poles are prepared to accept the only conditions with which we can successfully help them, the responsibility must be theirs.[39]

Chamberlain viewed an alliance with Soviet Russia with the greatest aversion. He thought more about avoiding war than winning it.

Gregorio Gafencu, Rumanian Foreign Minister, who was making an exploratory tour of western countries in search of information, refers to the view expressed by Lord Halifax that:

With regard to the Soviet Union the British government did not share Mr. Churchill's optimism or the illusions of the Labour Opposition. He seemed to have noticed a certain reticence on the part of Russia; she went her own way, and was in no hurry to accept the programme of aid that was offered her. Moreover, the British government was obliged to take into account Poland's objections and, to a lesser degree, those of Rumania. As far as Lord Halifax could see, those two countries, having a common border, wished to remain aloof from a policy which exposed them to inevitable danger. He was determined, however, to overcome every obstacle, for Russia's support was indispensable if the unbridled ambitions of Germany were to be held in check.[40]

In short, the western nations desired the support of the U. S. S. R. in the Danzig affair, but in no other matter. They offered nothing in exchange, and refused to treat with Moscow on any other question whatsoever. They altogether failed to recognize the traditional aims and spirit of Russian diplomacy. It is not true that Soviet Russia was dilatory in regard to western approaches. A. J. P. Taylor has stressed the rhythm of the negotiation, as shown in Foreign Office documents:

The British made their first tentative suggestion on 15 April; the Soviet counter-proposal came two days later, on 17 April. The British took three weeks before designing an answer on 9 May; the Soviet delay was then five days. The British then took thirteen days; the Soviet again took five. Once more the British took thirteen days; the Soviet government answered within twenty-four hours. Thereafter the pace quickened. The British again tried in five days' time; the Soviet answer came within twenty-four hours. The British next needed nine days; the

---

[39] Op. cit., p. 226.
[40] Gafencu, Les derniers jours de l'Europe, Paris, 1947, p. 139.

Soviet two. Five more days for the British; one day for the Russians. Eight days on the British side; Soviet answer on the same day. British delay of six days; Soviet answer the same day. With that the exchange virtually ended. If dates mean anything, the British were spinning things out, the Russians were anxious to conclude.[41]

There is other evidence to show that the British and French handling of the matter was very casual; it was as though they had no faith in the results.

Could the Soviet agree to negotiate with the west a pact dealing exclusively with the pledge to Poland? The French Foreign Minister, Georges Bonnet, thought so. Instead of treating the affair in an off-hand manner as the British were doing, he submitted a note to Moscow on the 14th April:

> In the event of France and Great Britain finding themselves at war with Germany as the result of action on their part to render assistance to Poland or Rumania, the victims of unprovoked aggression, Soviet Russia would immediately come to their aid. In the event of Russia finding herself at war with Germany as the result of action on her part to render assistance to Poland or Rumania, the victims of unprovoked aggression, France and Great Britain would immediately come to her aid.

This agreement naturally implied the right of passage for the Red Army across Polish and Rumanian territory, and the Russians said so to England and France.

A leading Foreign Office official, William Strang, then proceeded to Moscow to speed up the negotiations;[42] he broke his journey in Warsaw, where Colonel Beck warned him in confidence against Soviet Russia's lack of sincerity. Beck was sceptical about anything positive resulting from the talks, and he refused to join in them.[43]

Molotov, the Soviet's new Foreign Minister, endeavoured to state precisely the scope of the guaranteee asked for by Russia. A political agreement was on the point of being reached on the 24th July, and it only remained to arrive at a satisfactory conclusion on military matters. The Russians entertained a secret hope that the generals would prove

[41] A. J. P. Taylor, op. cit., p. 231.

[42] It was Halifax who should have gone to Moscow, on Molotov's invitation, but he was too busy. Eden, the Under-Secretary of State, offered to take his place, but Chamberlain refused.

[43] J. Beck, Dernier Rapport: Politique polonaise, 1926–1939, Neuchâtel, La Baconnière, 1951, p. 202.

more realistic than the diplomats. Molotov intended to open the military negotiations in Moscow on the 1st August.

The military mission was then set up. For France it was led by General Doumenc, and for Great Britain by Admiral Plunkett. The British Admiral received no written authority to deal with any subject whatever. It is noteworthy that for the sake of prestige he had insisted on the mission making the journey in a warship, a decision that added three days to the voyage. General Doumenc's terms of reference authorized him "to deal with all military questions". His instructions were not precise; but France's choice of Doumenc was a good one, because he was shrewd and flexible, and skilled in diplomatic negotiation.

The military mission arrived in Moscow on the 11th August. Already on the 4th the German ambassador, von Schulenburg (an impartial witness), who was visiting Molotov, reported to his Minister, von Ribbentrop, that Russia was ready to treat with the Western Powers if they accepted her demands. In point of fact, Molotov was growing impatient. He had waited ten days for the arrival of the military mission, and this new delay only tended to increase his suspicions. He wondered what the real intentions of the Western Powers were: could they be trying to manoeuvre German aggressive inclinations towards the Soviet?[44]

Marshal Voroshilov received the military mission on the 12th August. While the Russians endeavoured to draw up plans and state figures, the western diplomats, who had been given limited powers, made vague statements in an attempt to avoid revealing "military secrets". Voroshilov learned enough, however, to appreciate that Britain intended to land no more than five divisions on the European continent, and that the Poles would be crushed within two weeks. Doumenc also said that the Germans would confront France with no more than forty divisions when they attacked Poland.

On the 14th August Voroshilov put the vital question: Would the Poles allow Soviet forces to cross their frontier? Doumenc wished to find out at once by sending his deputy, General Valin, to Warsaw. On the 16th August Paris refused permission, but sent Captain Beauffre, who left on the 19th — losing another five days — to put the question to the Polish army commander, Marshal Rydz-Smigly. The Marshal did not commit himself, but replied: "With the Germans we run the

[44] Yet Molotov was unaware of the latest secret Anglo-German contacts (Wohltat–Hudson).

risk of losing our freedom; with the Russians we should lose our soul".[45]

Voroshilov lost patience. Having received no reply by the 17th August, he adjourned the talks until the 21st.

General Doumenc sent a long explanatory telegram to Paris: "There is no doubt that Russia desires a military pact, and does not wish us to present her with a meaningless document. Voroshilov affirmed that every question could be dealt with without any difficulty whatever, as soon as what the Russians call the "cardinal question" has been answered".[46]

When Beauffre returned to Moscow with his fanciful message, Doumenc was helpless, and the meeting of the 21st August was cut short. Daladier sent Doumenc the following telegram: "You are authorized to sign the military covenant, in agreement with the ambassador, in the best interests of all concerned, and subject to the eventual approval of the French government".[47]

Doumenc wished to acquaint Voroshilov with the contents of the telegram, but Voroshilov avoided him. They met during the evening of the 22nd, and the Marshal said to Doumenc,

> The question of military co-operation with France has been raised for several years, but a solution has never been reached. Last year, when Czechoslovakia was being destroyed, we waited for a sign from France; our forces were ready, but the sign never came ... The government, the country, the whole nation wished to help Czechoslovakia, and carry out the obligations implicit in the treaties ... The French and British governments allowed the political and military discussions to drag on indefinitely. That is why we cannot exclude the possibility that certain political transactions may be taking place ... We must have a definite reply from the governments of those countries (Poland and Rumania); we must know if they agree to allow our troops to pass ... If the Poles had replied in the affirmative, they would have demanded to be present at these talks.[48]

By the evening of the 22nd it was all over: the Anglo-French-Soviet negotiations had failed. The Russian reversal of attitude occurred on the 19th August, but until that date everything suggested that the Russians really wished to negotiate with the western powers, and to join them in giving guarantees to Poland and Rumania.

[45] Paul Reynaud, *La France a sauvé l'Europe*, Paris, 1947, p. 587.
[46] Reynaud, *ibid.*
[47] Reynaud, *op. cit.*, p. 588.
[48] *Ibid.*

7. Did Russia Really Intend to Provoke War? (23rd August 1939)

We have referred to Russia's distrust of the western powers,[49] and the inability of the London and Paris governments to negotiate the military aid agreement which the Soviet sincerely desired.

The truth was that London never really wished to reach an understanding with Moscow, and the negotiations did not assume a more positive shape until France decided to take the initiative, followed half-heartedly by Great Britain.[50]

The Russians endeavoured to ascertain Hitler's intentions. The first contacts between them and the Germans with a view to improving their relations dates from the 17th April 1939. Further talks took place on the 17th May. On both occasions the Soviet discussed economic matters only. On the 20th May Molotov received von Schulenburg, the German ambassador, who agreed to resume the talks in relation to trade; but Molotov pointed out that, if they were to succeed, the talks should be conducted "in the appropriate political atmosphere". As Molotov did not state precisely what he meant, Berlin thought it was a trick, and endeavoured to keep to the economic sphere.

None the less, by the 23rd May Hitler had decided to attack Poland. He laid his cards on the table before his military leaders who had been summoned to the Chancellery; "There can be no question of sparing sommoned tn the Chancellery:

> There can be no question of sparing Poland. We have only to decide when is the opportune moment to attack her. We cannot rely upon a repetition of the Czech affair; this will mean war. We must isolate Poland, and it must be done effectively... The isolation of Poland is a matter of political ingenuity.[51]

Two days later, on the 25th May, Weizsäcker and Gaus, the legal expert on foreign affairs, were asked by Ribbentrop to "normalize" German-Soviet relations.[52] Moreover, Schulenburg was instructed to notify Molotov that Germany had no aggressive intentions to-

---

[49] Stalin's distrust was expressed in unmistakable terms in his speech before the XVIIIth Congress of the Party on the 10th March 1939. For the complete text see, *Les questions du léninisme*, by J. Stalin, Moscow, 1947.

[50] The idea that French diplomacy at that period adopted a follow-my-leader policy with regard to Great Britain in quite untrue.

[51] Lieutenant Colonel Schmundt's report; Nuremberg Documents, XXII, 471.

[52] See Shirer, *The Rise and Fall of the Third Reich*, London, 1960 Vol. I, p. 529.

wards the Soviet, but wished to maintain normal relations with the Union.

Hitler delayed the despatch of this order — which might have provoked mirth in Moscow — for everyone in Berlin believed that the French and British were on the point of clinching their negotiations with the Soviet.[53] It was Hilger, the commercial attaché at the German Embassy, who conducted the talks; Molotov and Schulenburg met on the 29th June, but discussed general questions only. Prior to this — on the 14th — the Soviet ambassador in Poland had told Count Szembeck, Poland's Secretary General for Foreign Affairs, that no one need anticipate an armed conflict in Europe.

In short, up to the 24th July, when the Anglo-French-Russian political negotiations came to an end and were replaced by military discussions, the Soviet had done nothing to facilitate a real Russo-German rapprochement. The shrewd Molotov kept himself informed, and the door remained open forany possible negotiations.

Events were accelerated from the 3rd August onwards: Ribbentrop in Berlin and Schulenburg in Moscow referred for the first time to zones of influence. The Russians were annoyed by the dilatoriness of the west. They probably knew — for it was no secret in London — that Chamberlain regarded any protraction of the Moscow conversations as a means of delaying, and possibly destroying, Hitler's schemes. But Molotov still refused to commit himself; Schulenburg told Berlin he was convinced that Moscow was going to treat with the French and British if they were prepared to accept the Russian demands. "Only with considerable effort could we bring about a complete reversal of Soviet government policy".[54]

A complete change did come over the Russians on the 12th August, when Voroshilov received the Anglo-French military mission, and learned that it had no powers and was ill prepared to negotiate. It was also on the 12th August that Astakhov, chargé d'affaires in Berlin, saw Ribbentrop and told him that the U. S. S. R. was ready to discuss political questions by stages, and he suggested that the negotiation should take place in Moscow.

Hitler discussed the matter at Obersalzberg throughout the whole of the 13th August. He knew that it was only two weeks to the 1st

---

[53] German Archives, VI.
[54] *Ibid.*

September, when his army would be ready. He could not await the results of a negotiation "by stages".

On the 14th August Ribbentrop instructed Schulenburg to advise Molotov that he was "ready to pay a return visit to Moscow to present the Führer's point of view to Stalin. I am of the opinion that personal contact only can effect a change, and it should not be impossible in this way to lay the foundations of a definitive settlement of Russo-German relations".[55]

Molotov was informed of Ribbentrop's communication on the 15th August, but had no wish to hasten matters. On the 16th Ribbentrop requested that a date for his journey be decided as speedily as possible. On the 18th Molotov mentioned for the first time a "non-aggression pact". On the 19th, when Hitler and Ribbentrop were quivering with impatience, the date for Ribbentrop's visit was at last arranged: the 26th August. At the same time Molotov sent Schulenburg the draft for a non-aggression pact.[56]

Hitler was not satisfied. He telegraphed Stalin on the 20th August, requesting him to see Ribbentrop on the 22nd or 23rd: "I accept the draft of the non-aggression pact proposed by your Foreign Minister, but I consider it urgent to clarify a number of points as soon as possible. The tension between Germany and Poland has become intolerable, and a crisis may occur at any moment".[57]

On the 21st August Stalin agreed that Ribbentrop should come to Moscow on the 23rd. What happened is well known. Ribbentrop went to Moscow, signed the non-aggression pact and secret protocols settling the spheres of influence of the two countries.[58] But on the 22nd August Hitler finally decided to attack Poland, and Halder made an entry in his diary for the 23rd August: "D-Day definitely fixed for the 26th".[59]

Western observers have expressed conflicting views about the behaviour of Russia. We may reject the over-simplified theory that after

[55] The German Archives, VII.
[56] The published versions of the minutes of the meeting of the Politburo on the 19th August are unreliable, and hardly credible. See Beck, *Dernier rapport : Politique polonaise 1926–1939*, and Heydecker's *Le Procès de Nuremberg*, 1961.
[57] The German Archives, VII.
[58] The secret protocols were prepared in Moscow "thoroughly, but quickly" by Dr Gaus. (interviewed by *Le Monde*, Paris, 19th February 1949 issue.
[59] Halder's unpublished diary was consulted at the Hoover Library. D-Day was postponed by several days because the Führer hoped to secure the neutrality of England.

Munich Soviet Russia sought only to come to terms with Nazi Germany. There are no grounds for this theory.

The second suggestion is that Russia allied herself with the highest bidder, after having waited until the last moment the outcome of two contingencies. That also is not true. We have seen that until the 12th August, when Doumenc admitted his inability to reach an agreement, the Russians hoped for a pact with Great Britain and France; only then did Russia seek a pact with Germany. The accusation that she ran with the hares and hunted with the hounds is not worth examination. The Russo-German contacts before the 12th August meant no more than did the Anglo-German contacts during the same period.[60]

A third suggestion, which implies a Machiavellian attitude on the part of Stalin, is that the Soviet Union deliberately sought to provoke conflict in Europe, allowing her to act as umpire in the eventual struggle between Hitler and the West. There is no evidence to substantiate this version, and to-day the theory is unacceptable.

On the other hand, documents exist which show that Stalin was uneasy about the western powers; he was aware of Russia's unpreparedness and of Germany's bellicose intentions — confirmed by Hitler in his telegram to Stalin dated the 20th August.

Stalin also believed that some day Hitler's aggression would be directed towards Russia, and he hoped to control for as long as possible the circumstances which might set the German forces in motion. "We have secured peace for our country", he said, "for a year and a half, as well as the opportunity to prepare our forces for defence, in the event of Fascist Germany attempting to attack our land in violation of the pact".[61] Stalin felt that the Soviet Union was isolated, and all these were good reasons for wishing to preserve peace on Russia's frontiers. When, therefore, on the 12th August he was forced to renounce his hope of an Anglo-French-Soviet agreement, which might have avoided a European conflict, he turned — though very slowly — towards Germany.[62]

[60] The Hudson–Wohltat talks.

[61] Vladimir Potiemkin, *Histoire de la Diplomatie, Vol. III, 1919–1939.* Stalin's agreement of the 23rd August, under which Poland was abandoned to Hitler, thus turning him towards the West, is comparable with the Munich agreement which was intended to turn Hitler towards the East by abandoning Czechoslovakia to him.

[62] Hitler precipitated the momentum because he had already decided by the 1st September to attack Poland.

One must be careful not to confuse Soviet intentions with the consequences of Russian diplomacy. Their intentions were peaceful. What country could have guessed at the martial madness of Hitler at that period! The will of the Nazi leader dominated everything, and propelled Europe towards catastrophe. What remains a mystery is that the German people should have remained so docile as to allow this false prophet to carry them along to ruin. Public opinion had obviously been perverted by dictatorial methods.

OTHER SOURCES OF INFORMATION IN PART TWO

The following is a list of the principal works consulted in addition to those named in the bibliography.

The Rhineland Autonomist Movement

La France sur le Rhin — Douze Années d'Occupation sur le Rhin, by Paul Tirard Plon, Paris, 1930 (518 p.).
La Tragédie rhénane, by Dr J. A. Dorten, Laffont, Paris, 1945 (271 p.).
La France et le Rhin, hier et aujourd'hui, by Ct L.-Z. Mangin, Ed. Milieu du Monde, Geneva, 1945 (212 p.).
(The work consists of Mangin's notes.)
Le Mémorial de Foch, by Raymond Recouly, Ed. de France, Paris, 1929, (307 p.).
(Foch's confidential papers.)
Konrad Adenauer, by Paul Weymar, Munich, 1955.
We are indebted to the colleagues of Chancellor Adenauer for some valuable documents dealing with this subject. Most of the memoranda relate to the Rhineland separatist movement, and are to be found in the Hoover Institute, Stanford (Caalifornia.

German Reparations

Les Réparations allemandes et la France, by Etienne Weill-Raynal (his main work), Nouvelles Editions latines, Paris, 1948 (3 vols).
Von Versailles bis Lausanne, by Hans Ronde, Kohlhammer, Stuttgart, 1950 (210 p.).
Les Délibérations du Conseil des Quatre, by P. Mantoux, CNRS, Paris, 1955 (2 vols).
We have also made use of the unpublished shorthand notes of the Big Four conferences which preceded the signing of the armistice (29th October to 4th November 1918). These documents are the personal property of the author.

The United States and the League of Nations

Woodrow Wilson, by A. C. Walworth, New York, 1958 (2 vols).
The Life of Woodrow Wilson 1856–1924, by Josephus Daniels, Philadelphia, 1924 (381 p.).

Woodrow Wilson, The Man, His Times and His Task, by W. A. White, Boston, 1924 (527 p.).
The Senate and The League of Nations, by Henry C. Lodge, New York, 1925.
Woodrow Wilson As I Know Him, by Joseph P. Tumulty, Garden City, 1921 (553 p.).
My Memoirs, by E. B. Wilson, Indianapolis, 1939.
The Woodrow Wilsons, by E. W. MacAdoo, New York, 1937.
Duroselle *(op. cit.)* has a very complete bibliography. He has produced an indispensable work which we have followed on a number of points.

The text of the amendments put forward by Cabot Lodge is well known. Details may be found in Daria Hasiuk's thesis, *On the refusal of the United States to become a member of the League of Nations,* Louvain, 1957.

The Rupture between France and Hungary

Philippe Berthelot, by Auguste Bréal, Gallimard, Paris, 1937 (249 p.).
This biography is the work of Berthelot's closest friend.
Kaiser Karl, by Polzer–Hoditz, Amalthea Verlag, Vienna, 1925.
The author was a close friend of the Emperor Charles.
Der Tote auf Madeira, by Baron Karl von Werkmann, Zurich, 1923.
The author of this account was the Emperor Charles's last secretary.
Kaiserin und Königin Zita, by Emy Gehring, Franz Reisinger, Wels, 1961.
We have questioned His Imperial Highness the Archduke Otto of Hapsburg, who was kind enough to throw some light on our comparative study of the various sources of information.

The Genoa Conference

Les Documents de la Conférence de Gênes, by Amedeo Giannini, Rome, 1922.
Lénine, by Gerard Walter, Paris, 1950.
Histoire de l'URSS, by Louis Aragon, T. I., Paris, 1962.
A scientific study of Lenin's life is in course of preparation by the Moscow Institute of the History of Marxism and Leninism, and has therefore not yet been published. Concerning the instructions given to Chicherin we have taken account of *Stati i rechi po voprosam mezhdunarodni politiki,* by Chicherin, Ed. de littérature sociale et économique, Moscow, 1961 (515 p.). Cf. especially page 284.
The diary of Lenin's departmental secretaries in *Voprosy istorii K P SS No. 2,* Moscow, 1963.
The notes of the 21st November 1922 to the 6th March 1923 appear in volume 45 of the complete works of Lenin, which have not yet been published.
See *Documents de la politique étrangère de l'URSS,* Moscow, 1960, Vol. IV, concerning the year 1921, and Vol. IV, concerning the year 1921, and Vol, V, concerning the year 1922.
The unpublished memoirs of Lyubimov and Erlich, former members of the Soviet delegation in Genoa.
Chicherin's recollections of Lenin are to be found in his *Vos pominannia o V. I. Lenine,* Gos politizdat, Moscow, 1957.

194

1919–1939

A number of Lenin's directives to Chicherin are to be found in Lenin, *Sur la politique extérieure de l'Etat soviétique*, the Institute of Marxism–Leninism, Moscow, 1960 (592 p.). See especially pp. 474, 475 and 484.

We have also made use of the notes of Alberto Pirelli (1919–1932) to whom we are extremely grateful.

The Collapse of the Rhenist Movement

See the work by Mangin to which reference is made at the end of Chapter I. We questioned Baron Pierre Nothomb who was kind enough to look through his notes and select documents relative to the period in question.

Other Belgian statesmen had planned to form a Belgian–Rhenist federation. On this subject see, *Le Rhin et la Question d'Occident*, by R. de Briey, Brussels, 1922, and especially, *Belgique et Rhénanie*, by N. Wallez, Brussels, 1923.

The Preventive War against Germany

Le Réarmement clandestin du Reich, by Georges Castellan, Plon, Paris, 1954 (572 p.).
Die Präventivkriegspläne Pilsudskis, by Hans Roos, in *Vierteljahreshefte* No. 3 (344 p.), Munich, 1955.
Ma Vie avec Benito, by Rachele Mussolini, Cheval-Ailé, Paris, 1948 (255 p.).

The Blood Purge of June 1934

L'Assassinat de Röhm, by André François-Poncet, published in *L'Histoire pour Tous*, No. 12, Paris.
The two following works deal with the role of Goebbels:
Goebbels, by Curt Reiss, Hollis and Carter, London, 1949. A French translation (670 p.) was published by Fayard, Paris, 1956, see p. 251 *et seq.*
Goebbels, by R. Manvell and H. Fraenkel, p. 179 *et seq.* Laffont, Paris, 1960 (425 p.).
The official Nazi version of the subject may be found in:
Histoire de l'Armée allemande, by Jacques Benoist-Mechin, Albin Michel, Paris, 1938 (672 p.). See Vol. II, p. 554 *et seq.* This edition has subsequently been revised and corrected.

The Assassination of Dolfuss

Heritage of Fire, by Friedlinde Wagner, New York, 1945.
The author's personal experiences.
A description of the friends and "traitors" in Dolfuss's entourage will be found in:
OEsterreiche Sendung im Donauraum, by E. Ludwig, Staatsdruckerei, Vienna, 1954 (356 p.).
Dr Ludwig was during the period in question Chancellor Dolfuss's closest associate, and we discussed these events with him. He introduced us to the Ballhausplatz district of Vienna. This enabled us to reconstruct the events which took place there, and was of great assistance in the detailed preparation of this chapter.

Mussolini and the Marseilles Outrage

Sous mes yeux Alexandre de Yougoslavie est assassiné, by François Pietri, in *L'Histoire pour Tous*, No. 16, Paris, August 1961.
Vingt Ans de Suspense diplomatique, by Geneviève Tabouis see pp. 205–215, Albin Michel, Paris, 1958 (408 p.).
We have seen some of the documents relating to the trial of the Ustashis.

The Saar Plebiscite

The Saar Plebiscite, by Sarah Wambaugh, Harvard University Press, 1940 (498 p.).
A scientific study of the question.
Geschichte der französischen Saarpolitik, by Harold Martin, Bonn, 1934 (103 p.).
A Nazi version.
Pourquoi la Sarre retourne a l'Allemagne? by Max Weber, Editions Mondiales, Paris, 1936 (32 p.). Written from an anti–Nazi point of view.
Die Saar von Genf, by Helmut Hirsch, Bonn, 1954 (96 p.). Also anti-Nazi in tone.
Le Plébiscite de la Sarre, by Georges Passe, Loviton, Paris, 1935 (275 p.). This work was the author's thesis for his Doctor's degree.
La Sarre et le Plébiscite de 1935, by Fernand Wiedemann, Presses Modernes, Paris, 1935 (159 p.). This work also was the author's thesis for his Doctor's degree.
The following works deal with the part played by Laval:
Pierre Laval, by Alfred Mallet, Amiot Dumont, Paris, 1954 (2 vols).
Pierre Laval cet Inconnu, by Maurice Privat, Fournier–Valdès, Paris, 1948.
We have collected at first hand the evidence of Jean Knittel and Gabriel Perreux.
See also:
Le Fait du Jour, by G. André-Fribourg, Dupont, Paris, 1946.
La France et le Problème sarrois, by G. Gebelein, OFE, Paris s. d.

The Rome Agreements

The works concerning Laval mentioned above.
Mission à Rome, consisting of the memoirs of Lagardelle, Plon, Paris, 1955 (308 p.).
The work sheds no new light on events.

The Hoare–Laval Plan

The biographies of Laval already mentioned.
See also:
Vingt Ans de Suspenss diplomatique, by G. Tabouis (p. 253).
The work contains some chronological errors.

The Hossbach Protocol

General Hossbach was interviewed in connexion with these events.
Madame von Ribbentrop's notes *(Verschwörungen gegen den Frieden*, Leoni, 1962) contain nothing new.

Germany and the Spanish Civil War

The Spanish Civil War, by Hugh Thomas, London, 1961, is an indispensable work.

The French Air Force in 1938

We have questioned M. Georges Bonnet on this subject, and we have taken into account a number of documents produced at the Riom trial. Pierre Sorlin, in *Forces aériennes françaises*, Paris, November 1958, has provided a statement of the technical resources available.

From the point of view of ground forces, against the hundred or so French divisions along the Alsace frontier the Germans opposed no more than twelve divisions, and they were badly protected because the Siegfried Line was still under construction. Undoubtedly this fact must be borne in mind when seeking reasons for the opposition of the German generals to intervention in Czecho-slovakia.

It is not true to say that the year's respite gained at Munich enabled the Western Allies to re-establish a balance of forces with Germany. The Siegfried Line was completed during the period between the Munich conference and the beginning of the war. The production of armoured vehicles did not proceed more rapidly in France than it did in Germany (cf. Conquet, *L'Enigme des Blindés*, Paris, 1956), and in May 1940 the numbers of tanks engaged in the battle for the West were more or less equal. By comparison with 1938 the extent to which French air power was surpassed in 1940 was overwhelming. From October 1938 onwards the British alone produced sufficient fighter planes to enable them eventually to win the Battle of Britain.

Russia and the Munich Agreements

We have taken account of:

Nouveaux documents pour servir à l'histoire de Munich, Prague, 1958.

We have questioned MM. Georges Bonnet, Gregorio Gafencu, Oreste Rosenfeld and Walter Schevenels.

The *Necsas* papers in Prague corroborate the evidence of Rosenfeld.

Fierlinger, the Czechoslovak ambassador in Moscow, also records some reluctance on the 17th and 29th September on the part of the Soviet Union to take part in war.

The first telegram from Alexandrovsky (whether Benes capitulated or continued to resist alone, and the attitude of the U.S.S.R. with regard to these alternatives) reached Moscow at 5 p. m., and was decoded at 6 p.m. The second telegram (Benes did not expect a reply; he capitulated) arrived in Moscow at 5.45 p.m. Alexandrovsky had already informed Moscow on the previous evening, "Benes regards help from Moscow as a last extremity against Hitler's aggression, a form of suicide for the Czechoslovak middle class".

To follow the development of the Soviet Press we studied the August and September 1938 issues of *Pravda* and *Izvestiya*.

Concerning the attitude of the British statesmen we consulted the valuable work of V. Polyakov, *Angliya i Myunkhenskii Sgovor*, Academy of Sciences, Moscow, 1960 (335 p.), and A. Nekrich, *Vnechnaya politika Angliy, v Gody vtoroi mirovoï voïny, 1939*, Academy of Sciences, Moscow, 1963 (530 p.).

The Pact of Paris

Ci-devant, by A. de Monzie, Flammarion, Paris, 1941.
Munich, by H. Noguères, Laffont, Paris, 1963.
Souvenirs et Solitudes, by J. Zay, Paris, 1945.
    We also interviewed MM. Georges Bonnet, de Saint-Hardouin and Dr
Paul Schmidt.
    The question of Dr Schmidt's presence during the talks has not been touched
upon. Dr Schmidt stated that he was present, but that he translated nothing
into German. Monsieur Bonnet said that the conference was attended by von
Ribbentrop and von Welczek, Bonnet and Léger. Document R. M. 265 of
the German records refers in the English edition to Schmidt's attendance,
but the French edition apparently contains an erroneous interpretation.
Noguères's explanation *(op. cit.,* p. 358) does not seem to be the
satisfactory answer. The enquiry conducted by Dr Cuénot in *Historia,* Paris,
November 1963, provides some useful details as to the motives behind von
Rath's assassination.

The Failure of Anglo-French-Soviet Negotiations

We questioned M. Georges Bonnet and General Doumenc.
See also:
Carrefour, by General Doumenc, Paris, 21st May 1947.
    We also took into account a work in Russian entitled, "History of the Great
Patriotic War of the Soviet Union" (48–3907. I).
    Doumenc did his best, but was thwarted by the French government. Moscow
rejected the German proposals as long as the possibility of reaching agreement
with the Western powers remained (p. 176 *et seq.*).
Recherches internationales à la lumière du marxisme No. 12.
    This work contains the text of the Anglo-French-Soviet talks of August 193 9.
The proceedings of the meeting of the Politburo on the 19th August 1939 was
undoubtedly invented by the *Revue de droit international No. 3,* Geneva, 1939,
No such document exists in the Soviet archives.

Did Russia Really Intend to Provoke War?

The Incompatible Allies, by G. Hilger and A. G. Meyer, Macmillan, New York,
1953.
See also Dr Gaus, interview in *Le Monde,* Paris, 19th February 1949.

1919–1939 Period — Works consulted: 414

Controversial Questions	Number of works dealing with the question	Number of works containing worthwhile facts	Number of works containing secondary matter	Original testimony contained in the works mentioned in the bibliography	New evidence collected by J. de Launay
21. The Allies and the Rhenist movement	12	1	9	2	1
22. The amount of German reparations	24	19	2	3	1
23. The Franco-Hungarian rupture	11	5	4	2	1
24. Failure of the Rhenist movement	16	7	5	3	1
25. The United States and the League of Nations	19	4	13	2	—
26. Lenin and the Geneva Conference	17	7	7	3	—
27. Results of the Thoiry talks	19	5	11	3	—
28. The 1922 Moratorium	13	7	6	—	—
29. The sincerity of Stresemann	35	7	23	—	—
30. Failure of the United States of Europe	22	7	11	4	—
31. The preventive war	7	5	2	—	—
32. Hitler and the assassination of Dolfuss	45	15	27	3	2
33. Mussolini and the Marseilles outrage	27	6	19	2	—
34. The Röhm conspiracy	34	11	22	1	—
35. Fraud in the Saar Plebiscite	17	4	13	—	2
36. Laval gives Mussolini a free hand	42	11	22	9	—
37. Failure of the Hoare–Laval Plan	42	12	28	2	2
38. Cause of German intervention in Spain	19	7	10	2	—
39. The Hossbach Protocol	16	4	11	1	1
40. French air strength in 1938	17	4	4	9	2
41. The U.S.S.R. and the Munich agreements	27	16	4	7	4
42. A free hand in the East	32	18	4	10	3
43. Anglo-French-Soviet negotiations	42	26	9	7	2
44. Russia and the War	46	35	9	2	—
				82	20

PART THREE

1939 – 1945

CHAPTER I

THE BLITZKRIEG

1. Did the Germans deliberately provoke incidents along their frontier with Poland (Ist September 1939)?
2. Was there a diplomatic reason for the retreat from the Warndt?
3. Was General Manstein the creator of the plan of the offensive in the West?
4. Did the German invasion of Norway cause an Allied invasion to miscarry?
5. Can we regard the withdrawal of the British Expeditionary Force from France as a headlong retreat?

1. "Operation Himmler"

"Tonight for the first time, Poland's regular army opened fire on our territory. Since 5.45 this morning we have been firing back".

Those were Hitler's words on the 1st September 1939. They were spoken during a speech at the Kroll Opera House, for the Reichstag had been burned down a few years previously by "unknown persons", and not yet rebuilt. But the members of the Reichstag, complete with unifom — black shirt, breeches and high boots — applauded to bringt the horuse down and sang "Deutschland über alles". The most importan duty of the Reichstag members, summoned from time to time to hear a speech by the Führer, was to sing the traditional songs, "Deutschland über alles" and "Horst Wessel Lied".

Nobody doubted the Führer's word, and it is surprising to find that of the 441 leading works published on the Second World War, fourteen deal with the origins of the war, but do not discuss or take into account the Führer's statement.

The three leading French statesmen of the day — Georges Bonnet, Foreign Minister, Robert Coulondre, ambassador in Berlin, and Léon Noël, ambassador in Warsaw — made no protest against the official German version of the "frontier incidents" caused by the Poles.

It is true that Bonnet endeavoured once again to snatch at the threads of peace which, on this fatal 1st September, were breaking one

after another. He talked that day over the telephone with François–
Poncet and Léon Noël; he took care to advise Ciano that the French
government was favourable to his suggestion to convene a conference
on the 5th September to "revise the clauses of the Versailles Treaty, the
causes of the German-Polish conflict," and to ascertain from Colonel
Beck if Poland accepted the principle of such a conference. Robert
Coulondre began to pack his bags. He destroyed his codes and confidential papers, and never thought of trying to prove the truth of
Hitler's words.

At ten o'clock in the evening, after having uttered a few more lies, in particular
that German territory had been invaded in three places by the Polish forces, he
(Ribbentrop) told me that he was going to transmit to the Führer at once the
message that the French government intended to fulfill its obligations to Poland.[1]

Léon Noël was startled out of his sleep:

A few minutes after 6 a.m. the sirens sounded, and drew me painfully from a
light sleep. There seemed to be no doubt as to what had happened. However,
while dressing quickly I enquired the position from the Warsaw police on the
Embassy telephone. The police said they did not know. General Faury's aide-de-
camp, whom I had awakened, called his staff officer. His reply dashed our hopes
to the ground: since dawn the German forces had been attacking Poland.[2]

What was even more surprising, the Polish leaders, caught no doubt
in their last minute preparations, did not think it necessary to disprove
Hitler's statements.

Beck in his notes dictated in Rumania in the Autumn of 1939 said
simply: "The German version that Polish forces had attacked the
Gleiwitz Station, which the Reich used as an excuse for attacking, was
a complete fabrication".

Count John Szembeck, Deputy Secretary of State at the Foreign
Office, made no reference to any *casus belli*. General Anders, who later
described the Polish campaign, does not mention it either. Yet the
"Polish regular army" who opened fire over German territory on the
1st September 1939 were Germans!

Everything began around the 10th August 1939, which proves that
while for three weeks Hitler was engaged in diplomatic conversations
that could end nowhere, he was also planning his justification in the
eyes of the world. Admiral Canaris, head of the Abwehr branch of the

---

[1] Coulondre, *De Staline à Hitler : Souvenirs de deux ambassades 1936–1939*,
Paris, 1950, p. 308.

[2] Léon Noël, *L'agression allemande contre la Pologne*, Paris, 1947, p. 469.

O.K.W.,[3] received a visit from Jost, the Führer's aide-de-camp, with an order which Canaris thought strange: he was to procure some Polish uniforms.[4] Canaris went to see his chief, General Keitel, on the 17th August. As head of the O.K.W. Keitel was one of Hitler's executives. He was also a colleague of General Beck, Chief of Staff in 1933; he had insinuated himself into the good graces of Field Marshal von Blomberg, the Minister for War, whose daughter had married Keitel's eldest son in 1937.

When the scandal of Blomberg's second marriage burst in 1938, Keitel was the first to receive the confidential dossier on the new Frau von Blomberg, and refused to keep it. Rather than harm himself vis-à-vis the Himmler clique he allowed the scandal to take its course. Keitel was a cringing and obsequious individual. His services were rewarded by the Führer who, when he had dismissed Fritsch, set up the O.K.W. to replace the War Ministry and the post of Chief of General Staff. Keitel, though submissive before Hitler, was arrogant in his dealings with subordinates; in this way he managed to remain at the head of the O.K.W. until 1945.

When Canaris went to see him, and told him that he had to procure some Polish uniforms, Keitel asked, "For what purpose?" Long afterwards Keitel related, "We were both convinced it was for something illegal. As far as I can recall, I told him then that I did not approve of such actions, and advised him to have nothing to do with it . . . I believe I told Canaris that he could avoid the difficulty by pretending that he had no Polish uniforms. He had only to say that he had none, and the matter would then be closed".[5]

Such was Keitel's account seven years later at Nuremberg, but Canaris noted in his diary on the 17th August 1939 that Keitel told him, "If that is the Führer's order there is nothing to be done".[6] In any case, Canaris gave in, and placed 150 Polish uniforms at the disposal of Heydrich, head of the SD;[7] and General Halder made the following entry in his diary on the 17th August: "Canaris; countersigned, Section

---

[3] Abwehr means counter-espionage. The O.K.W. was the German High Command.

[4] This account is to be found in the Canaris papers (Nuremberg Documents, PS 795).

[5] This account was given by Keitel on the 4th April 1946 before the Nuremberg tribunal, when he was shown the details given in the Canaris papers (Nuremberg documents, X, 534).

[6] Ibid., PS 795.

[7] SD — Sicherheitsdienst: Security Branch of the Nazi Party.

I, Himmler, Heydrich, Obersalzberg, 150 Polish uniforms with acces-
sories for Upper Silesia".[8]

Heydrich was a man of exceptional intelligence. His reputation was
damaged by his past: as a student naval officer on the cruiser *Berlin* he
had to resign his commission as a result of misconduct. He aspired to
play a leading part in affairs, and he succeeded in doing so in the Nazi
Party which was not too strict about morals.

To carry out what has been described as "Operation Himmler"
Heydrich called on the services of Mehlhorn and Naujocks, two men
whose adventurous lives read like a book of fiction. Oberführer SS
Dr Mehlhorn sprang from a good middle class Saxon family. He began
his career as a barrister in Dresden, but his profession did not satisfy his
ambitions. He was a very clever organizer with little faith in the
"Thousand Year Reich" idea, but he soon made a bid for the Nazi
Party. He joined the SS where his ability led him into the SD. He was
entrusted with the secret supervision of manufacturers, artists, journalists
and the police, and he placed at the disposal of Heydrich invaluable
information on the whole of German cultural and political life. Dr
Mehlhorn, despite his ability, remained unsettled. He found it difficult
to endure the iron rule of Heydrich, and occasionally carried on intrigues
against him. Schellenberg, another of Heydrich's associates, wrote in
his Memoirs:[9]

On the 26th August 1939 an oppressive heat lay heavily on Berlin. During the
afternoon Dr Mehlhorn telephoned me, and asked if I was free that evening.
He wished to speak to me urgently on a personal matter, and did not think it
wise to come to my office. We therefore met at eight that evening in a quiet little
restaurant; it was, in fact, a rendezvous used by my counter-espionage branch:
from the cook to the head waiter every member of the staff had been chosen from
among my agents.

I noticed at once that Mehlhorn appeared profoundly disturbed and depressed. I
let him take his time, without pressing him with questions. He spoke of nothing in
particular during dinner, and I waited patiently. When the meal was over we went
by car to the West End. Berlin was a magnificent city at that time, and at the height
of its wealth and power. The attractive shop windows were flooded with light;
multicoloured electric signs sparkled; there were bustling crowds and endless lines
of traffic. In a word, life was gay and brisk, as it is in times of peace.

I was going to take Mehlhorn into a small bar, and I was looking for a place
to park, when he asked me to continue driving. He said he needed fresh air and

[8] Halder's diary (The Hoover Library).
[9] This account from Schellenberg's Memoirs, published eighteen years after
the events, corroborates his statements at the Nuremberg Trials.

to be away from crowds. We therefore drove towards Lake Mannsee, situated between Berlin and Potsdam. There we got out, and began to walk. Mehlhorn was more relaxed, and began to talk, but more or less to himself. Now and again a gust of wind came from the direction of the lake, and rustled the leaves in the tall trees; then silence reigned again, except for the voice of my companion.

"Mehlhorn spoke quickly, in broken sentences, and almost ceaselessly. 'There's going to be war. Impossible to avoid it any longer. Hitler made his mind up a long time ago; you must know that. Everything is ready. Even if Poland or the Western Powers attempt conciliation at the last moment — even if Italy intervenes — nothing can change Hitler's basic plans. At the very best it might mean a short delay, that's all!'

In a voice becoming increasingly agitated he told me that Heydrich had revealed to him — much to Mehlhorn's surprise — Hitler's secret orders. Before the 1st September, if possible, an absolutely unimpeachable *casus belli* had to be established; a case which would constitute a complete vindication before history, and would brand Poland in the eyes of the world as an aggressor against Germany. To that end he had planned to dress troops in Polish uniforms, and send them to attack the radio station at Gleiwitz. Hitler had instructed Heydrich and Admiral Canaris, head of the military information branch, to carry out the operation. The order so upset Canaris that he managed to get well out of the venture, and Heydrich remained in sole charge. On instructions from Keitel the Polish uniforms were to be provided by the O.K.W. — the commander in chief of the armed forces.

I asked Mehlhorn where he would find the Poles to wear these uniforms. 'That is the trouble,' he replied. 'It is the most diabolical part of the scheme: the *Poles* will be condemned men from the concentration camps. They will be equipped with genuine Polish arms. The men have been promised that those who come out alive will be given immediate freedom. But who would dare to believe such a promise?'

Mehlhorn paused, and then added, 'Heydrich has given me command of the operation . . .' He gripped my arm. 'What am I to do?' he asked. 'Heydrich has given me this mission in order to get rid of me; I know it. He wants me dead! What can I do?'

It was my turn to remain silent. At length I said, 'The whole business is sheer madness. One cannot fabricate world history in this fashion. The affair could never be kept secret; at any rate not for long. Somewhere, in some way or other, it will be disclosed. You must definitely get out of it. Invent some excuse. Pretend you are ill; or simply refuse. Whatever happens, it is better to refuse than face the consequences of accepting!'

The following day Mehlhorn faced the worst crisis of his career. He was courageous enough to refuse the mission. He excused himself by saying that his state of health would not allow him to carry out such an exacting task with the hundred per cent efficiency required to guarantee complete success. At first Heydrich would not accept this excuse, but Mehlhorn held out despite his chief's threats. Fortunately Heydrich was over-burdened with work, and eventually accepted Mehlhorn's excuses; but within ten minutes of doing so he appointed him to a lower post in the East, and a very difficult one.[10]

[10] Schellenberg, *Mémoires*, Paris, 1957, pp. 63–65.

In point of fact, Mehlhorn was charged with the task of organizing the terror in Poland.

The whole Gleiwitz affair then fell on the shoulders of Alfred Helmut Naujocks. This young SS officer of the SD acquired the knack of things in Slovakia, by dropping a few political and diplomatic bombs here and there. He had remained faithful to the SS since 1931, when, as a student at Kiel University, he took part in brawls with the Communists.

When questioned by the judges at Nuremberg he told the story of the "Gleiwitz adventure".[11]

"About the 10th August 1939, Heydrich, chief of SIPO and the SD, personally instructed me to sham an attack against the radio station at Gleiwitz, near the Polish frontier, and make it appear like an attack carried out by the Poles. Heydrich said to me, "We must have material proof of these Polish attacks, both for the foreign Press and German propaganda'.

I received an order to proceed to Gleiwitz with five or six SD men, and there to await a message in code from Heydrich concerning the launching of the attack. I was to take over the broadcasting station, and hold it long enough to allow a German-speaking Pole, who would be placed at my disposal, to broadcast a message in Polish. This message, Heydrich told me, would say that the hour of the German-Polish war had struck, and that the Polish forces were going to crush all resistance on the part of the Germans. Heydrich also told me at that time that he expected Germany would launch an attack against Poland within a few days.

I went to Gleiwitz, and waited there two weeks. I then asked Heydrich to authorize my return to Berlin; but I was ordered to remain in Gleiwitz. Between the 25th and 31st August I went to see Heinrich Müller, Chief of the Gestapo, who happened at that time to be in Oppeln which was quite near. In my presence Müller discussed with a certain Mehlhorn a plan for a frontier incident which would create the impression of a Polish attack on the German forces. Approximately a company of German soldiers was to be used. Müller said that he had twelve or thirteen condemned criminals who would be dressed in Polish uniforms, and left dead on the spot to prove that they had been killed during the attack. For this purpose they would be given fatal injections by a doctor in the service of Heydrich; following which wounds would be inflicted on them by firearms. After the incident, members of the Press and other persons would be brought to the spot, and then a police report would be drafted. Müller told me that he had instructions from Heydrich to place one of these criminals at my disposal for the Gleiwitz affair. The code by which the criminals were referred to was "Preserves".

The Gleiwitz incident in which I participated was carried out the evening before the German attack on Poland. As far as I can remember war broke out on the 1st September 1939. At noon on the 31st August I received a telephone call from Heydrich giving me the code word for the attack, which was to take place at eight o'clock that evening. Heydrich said, 'In order to execute this attack you must ask Müller for the "Preserves." I did so, and instructed Müller to bring the

[11] Deposition dated 21st November 1945 Nuremberg Documents, PS 2751.

man near to the radio station. When I took the man over I had him stretched out at the entrance to the station. He was alive, but quite unconscious. I tried to open his eyes. From his appearance I could not tell whether he was alive or not; but only from his breathing. I saw no wounds inflicted by firearms, but his face was smeared with blood. He was dressed in civilian clothes.

In pursuance of orders we took possession of the radio station, transmitted an announcement lasting three or four minutes over a relief transmitter, fired a few revolver shots, and went off.[12]

All the statements of witnesses, their examination and cross-examination, which took place at Nuremberg, suggest that Naujocks's evidence is reliable. General Lahousen, an associate of Canaris, stated that "the other SS witnesses who took part in the operation were eliminated; in other words, killed".

If we examine the foregoing evidence a little closer we shall find that they contain merely a few errors of detail. If it is likely that Mehlhorn began to be concerned with "Operation Himmler" on the 27th August, and managed to get out of it only on the 28th — after his conversation with Schellenberg — it is hardly credible that Heydrich should have given his orders on the 10th August, assuming that Heydrich became seriously involved only on the 17th. But the depositions were made six years after the event, and Naujocks might have made an error of a few days.

The only way to throw some light on these events, was to question Mehlhorn and Naujocks; but we were unable to trace them. Mehlhorn had disappeared, and Naujocks avoided our search. Naujocks left the SD in January 1941, after having taken part in the Venlo affair and operation Bernhard. Heydrich sent him to Russia as Wafen SS. He returned wounded, and then served in Brussels in the economic branch of the German military administration in Belgium, under Dr Reeder, from September 1942 to September 1944. He surrendered to the Americans on the 19th October 1944. He gave evidence at Nuremberg, was classed as a war criminal, and escaped from prison shortly before his trial. The police of several countries have never been able to find any trace of him.[13]

The matter has been sufficiently investigated, however, to show that the Germans were the cause of the incidents[14] on the Polish frontier on

[12] The announcement was in Polish to the effect that the Poles had attacked (*ibid.*, IV, 250).

[13] The account of his escape may be found in *Zwischen Krone und Kerker*, by Prinz Schaumburg–Lippe, Wiesbaden, 1952.

[14] Another "incident" occurred at Hohenlinden, but details are lacking.

the 1st September 1939. So that Germany might be exonerated from responsibility for the launching of the Second World War, Hitler did not hesitate shamelessly to manufacture his own *truth* to vindicate himself before the world.

2. *Daladier's Secret*

The Franco-Polish military covenant of the 19th May 1939[15] provided that: "France would launch an offensive against Germany with the bulk of her forces on the fifteenth day after the first day of French general mobilization."

General Gamelin explained, however, that "*les* gros de ses forces" was not at all the same as "*le* gros de ses forces".[16] If "le gros" meant the whole French army, "les gros" would mean just a third, say, about forty divisions; it was quite a subtle inference, and one which, according to Gamelin, had not escaped the Poles.[17]

Hence, "les gros" began to advance on the seventeenth day of mobilization. But on the 17th September the Polish campaign was virtually at an end, and the Russians began to enter the eastern side of Poland. The French army was content to occupy the forest of Warndt, in the direction of Saarbrücken, to the great astonishment of the Germans, especially Keitel: "We always expected the Western Powers, or at least the French, to attack during the Polish campaign. We were very surprised that in the west, apart from a few skirmishes between the Maginot Line and the "West Wall", nothing happened; I know quite definitely that along the whole western front, from the Netherlands to Basle, our total strength was five divisions, excluding the small forces occupying the fortifications on the West Wall. Thus, from the point of view of military operations a French attack during the Polish campaign would have been opposed by a weak screen of German troops, and not a real defence".[18]

Tippelskirch, a German military historian attached to the O.K.W., expressed a similar opinion:

[15] This was complementary with the Franco-Polish Treaty of the 19th February 1921.

[16] There is in French a subtle distinction here between the plural and the singular; both *les gros* and *le gros* may be translated as *the bulk, the mass* (Translator's note).

[17] Gamelin, *Servir*, Vol. II, Paris, 1946, p. 421.

[18] Nuremberg Documents, X, 538.

The Poles were therefore abandoned to their fate, and what happened was exactly what Hitler had anticipated. The French were content with a few local raids in the zone separating them from the West Wall. The Wall did not every-where follow the bends in the frontier, but was as straight as possible. It would, therefore, have been an easy matter for the French, allowing for the caution which the Germans had been ordered to exercise, to occupy two sections of terrain that jutted out — the Warndt forest to the south-west of Saarbrücken, and another projection of the frontier between Saarbrücken and the Palatinate forest. An attack in the latter zone was carried out on the 13th September, and for a time the Germans feared that a break-through was imminent at Deux-Ponts; reserves were urgently brought up behind the threatened sector.

After the end of the Polish campaign the Germans brought up three formations from the east. The pressure of these forces caused the French on the 3rd October to evacuate the greater part of the frontier territory they had previously occupied. They had no wish to expose their forward troops to partial defeat; they therefore withdrew as far as, and even slightly behind, their own frontier. The Germans followed, and were very surprised to find how badly the French tactical positions were disposed.[19]

Similarly, Jodl stated:[20] "That we did not break down in 1939 is entirely due to the fact that, during the Polish campaign, the 110 French and British divisions in the west remained absolutely inactive before 23 German divisions".

What was the cause of this inactivity on the part of the French army? Numerous political, psychological and military reasons have been put forward, all of which did undoubtedly play some part in events. It seems, however, that one fundamental military reason must be accepted: the French army believed in the efficacy of defence. This sacrosanct principle, inherited from the 1914–18 war, had become the unshakable doctrine of French military leaders, especially under the influence of Marshal Pétain, the hero of positional warfare — a doctrine which no one dared to demolish.[21] This tenet Gamelin had made his own. That was why no offensive plan had been prepared by the French General Staff against the possibility of a German invasion of Poland. The de-ployment of military forces, the organization of reserves and fighting material demanded a plan of mathematical precision, studied in detail. No such plan was ready on the 1st September 1939, and it was not possible for the General Staff to improvise one during the fever of mobilization.

---

[19] Tippelskirch, *Geschichte des zweiten Weltkrieges*, 1951, p. 29.

[20] Nuremberg Documents, XV, 365.

[21] All the works by French military experts published at this period, including Colonel de Gaulle's *La France et son armée*, mention Marshal Pétain.

The swift and easy advance of the French forces in the direction of Saarbrücken was, therefore, an improvisation. It stopped when the O.K.W. quickly brought to the west the forces made available on the 27th September by the fall of Warsaw.

The political situation itself had undergone a change. The fifth partition of Poland had become a *fait accompli* under the Russo-German treaty of the 28th September 1939. And the French found themselves engaged in a war launched, not by loyalty to the Polish alliance — they had already broken faith with Czechoslovakia in 1938 — but because their British allies had suddenly become aware of the Hitler danger about which they had scarcely bothered up to then. No doubt the war was inevitable; but France had entered into it under adverse conditions, without the effective support of the British,[22] without the possibility of American intervention, while the Russians had promised Germany they would remain neutral.

At the end of the Polish campaign, when France found herself facing Germany alone, French politicians could not fail to ask themselves the question, Why? Even French public opinion was bewildered by the "phoney war". Flandin expressed this attitude of mind when he said: "The war has no longer any purpose, for Poland, which we should have saved, has been conquered."[23]

And certain politicians, among them Laval, already contemplated possible bargaining and compromise.[24]

On the 28th September 1939 Moscow and Berlin published simultaneously a declaration, signed by Molotov and Ribbentrop, affirming that it was in the interest of all peoples to terminate the state of war existing between Germany, Britain and France. The two governments also stated their determination to direct their efforts towards that end. Two French Communist leaders, Arthur Ramette and Florimond Bonte, then wrote to Daladier on the 1st October to ask that,

> the peace proposals about to be made to France be examined with the object of establishing a just, loyal and lasting peace as soon as possible, which all our fellow citizens desire from the bottom of their hearts.

This made Daladier think.

[22] On the 11th October there were still only four British divisions in France — 158,000 men.
[23] De Launay, *Le Monde en Guerre*, 1956, p. 65.
[24] *Ibid.*

'He was a particularly complex individual,' wrote de Monzie; 'debonair but distrustful, shy but vehement, incapable of breaking a circle of habits, but capable of becoming enthusiastic about himself, without, however, developing self-assurance . . . Whenever he spoke, and above all when he was cogitating, Daladier heard two voices'.[25]

At Daladier's side there was Gamelin — a man of short stature and a plump face. He created an impression of thoughtfulness and level-headedness, but he was shy; and as he spoke he would turn away his eyes, and unconsciously play with the buckle of his belt. According to him it was most important to economize one's resources, not to waste them. He believed that present-day wars might best be compared with the wars of siege of the eighteenth century.[26]

These two were not the men who would take the initiative in the new politico-military form of warfare. The French government asked the British to avoid the aerial bombardment of German military objectives, so as not to provoke reprisals. As for Hitler, he had withdrawn to Obersalzberg to think; and there on the 26th September he received a Swedish businessman named Dahlerus. Their conversation took place in the presence of Marshal Goering. Dahlerus had seen Forbes, a member of the British legation at Oslo, and had gained the impression that in Great Britain a desire for peace was gaining ground, and that use might be made of this attitude to bring the war to an end. The Swedish businessman thought it possible to gamble on British self-interest, for all that Britain wanted was an opportunity to save her face.

This point of view appealed to Hitler; he told Dahlerus he would be quite ready to open secret negotiations under which he would undertake once for all to respect Belgian and Dutch territory, as well as the Franco-German frontier. He repeated that Germany had no further territorial ambitions in the Balkans, but only commercial interests. He was prepared to include all these promises in a European treaty. It was considered that the Queen of Holland might be asked to patronize the peace conference, and try to secure the services of General Ironside to open up preliminary secret negotiations.[27]

A similar report reached Hitler on the 2nd October from Guariglia, the Italian ambassador in Paris, through Attolico, to the effect that the majority of French ministers favoured a peace conference which would enable both Britain and France to save face. This report probably interpreted the feelings of the habitués of the salon of Madame Georgette-Jean Brunhes, frequented by Guariglia and a few French ministers,

[25] A. de Monzie, *Ci-devant*, Flammarion, Paris, 1941, p. 99.
[26] De Launay, *op. cit.*, p. 62.
[27] The German Archives, VIII, 138.

including A. de Monzie. It was on the strength of this information that Hitler launched his great peace offer of the 6th October. Daladier's reply on the 7th was negative, but did not exactly close the door: France desired real guarantees of peace and general security. Chamberlain's reply of the 21th October was abrupt: he had no confidence in Hitler's promises. That gentleman's self-respect had been damaged beyond repair.

But Daladier's attitude merits closer study. He did not accept the "no separate peace" put forward by the British. He maintained his friendly relations with the parliamentarians who desired peace; he refused to agree to the military offensive demanded by Britain. In this hazy and uncertain atmosphere Daladier made a decision: on the 17th October he gave orders that all troops be withdrawn from occupied German territory.

Was there any diplomatic motive behind this retreat from the Warndt forest? A possible interpretation is that "in order not to compromise the chances of peace, Daladier gave secret orders to Gamelin on the 17th October to withdraw his forces from the forest of Warndt, which had been conquered at great cost since September".[28]

In any case, the troops engaged were amazed to receive this unexpected order to withdraw, since it appeared useless and ill-timed.

On the 30th September the Commander-in-Chief suggested to the War Council that he should "bring back all covering troops to our frontier, and withdraw the bulk of our forces behind the Maginot Line". But in order to conceal the withdrawal, light units were to be left in contact in their present positions "to deceive the enemy". These units would be instructed to fold back before aerial attacks, to show that bombs were dropping in empty space. The war council approved the proposal, and decided to "get rid of the difficulty we have in the Saar". Thus the conquering of this terrain, which had been given so much publicity, became another sore point. The orders were given at once, and the withdrawal was carried out without any trouble.[29]

If we are to draw any conclusions from these events we must return to the two authors of the decisison: Gamelin and Daladier. General Gamelin's account is as follows:

Our troops had penetrated deeply into the angle formed by the Siegfried Line, between the Vosges and Saarbrücken . . .

[28] De Launay, *op. cit.*
[29] Goutard, *1940, La guerre des occasions perdues*, 1956, p. 122.

If we were to fulfill our duty of safeguarding for as long as possible the integrity of our territory, it was out of the question to maintain in front of our line of organized resistance (the Maginot Line) advance troops who might soon have to become a rearguard force carrying out a possible retarding action . . .

It was, therefore, imperative to withdraw to our frontier the forces facing the Siegfried Line. It was also essential to maintain the utmost secrecy. French public opinion could not fail to be disturbed when we had to admit that we had withdrawn . . .

We decided to go and see President Daladier, and put before him in detail the considerations to which I have just referred. I knew only too well that this solution would distress the President of the Council. Our propaganda had made a great fuss about our having penetrated into Germany . . . The President was, therefore, apprehensive about the reactions of French and world opinion.

General Gamelin told Daladier that if they succeeded in falling back without mishap, they could congratulate themselves on having "bluffed" their opponents. The President eventually came round to the view of General Gamelin. In fact, he approved the order to carry out the withdrawal.[30] Apparently there was no diplomatic advantage in deciding to pull out; but Gamelin was not to know anything about reasons of state.

Daladier has left no account of these events. It is known that at the beginning of November 1939 Emile Roche, who was one of his friends, discussed political problems with P. H. Spaak in Brussels; but Emile Roche denied that the conversation had any bearing on mediation by Belgium.[31] Daladier continued to hesitate for several months between peace and war instead of planning an offensive operation.

As we were anxious to ascertain Daladier's intentions, we put to him the following question: "Was the order issued by General Gamelin the result of a directive by the government, because it was anxious to avoid any obstacle to a possible negotiation for a peaceful compromise by way of an international conference?"

President Daladier gave the following reply:

The withdrawal of the French forces towards their frontier on the 17th October took place after an order of General Gamelin which I approved. It was based on the fact that there was every reason to expect a German military offensive in the west after Poland's defeat. You will find all the necessary details in the work by General Gamelin.[32]

Daladier's vague answer is comparable with General Gamelin's involved account. In the absence of any other evidence, and in view of

[30] Gamelin, *Servir*, Vol. III, Paris, 1947, pp. 85–90.
[31] De Launay, *Secrets diplomatiques 1939–1945*, Bruxelles 1963, p. 22.
[32] De Launay, *ibid.*

the information at present available, this war secret will remain im-penetrable. Daladier, or the conscience of a Daladier at that time divided between contradictory considerations, could alone enlighten us.

This uncertainty does, however, prove that western democracies were anxious to the very last not to let any opportunity escape which might avert the cataclysm of a world war — a war that could not solve any existing international problem.

3. The Manstein Plan

On the 10th October 1939 Hitler transmitted to his generals Directive No. 6, which instructed them to prepare a plan of operation in the west, which would allow for a march through Belgium, Holland and Luxemburg.[33]

Some time previously Hitler had read to his generals a memorandum in which he recalled to them the basic principles of strategy: not to lose themselves in the conquest of towns or territory, but to destroy the opposing army; to concentrate their forces on a single point of attack and reduce their forces on other points. With these few principles Hitler showed his determination to join the ranks of the great captains of military history, while Daladier and Gamelin were moving in the very opposite direction. Hitler's capacity for decision and his sense of attack appeared on every line of that document.

The generals left the room stupefied. During the next few days they raised objections which were swept aside. Then they conspired to remove Hitler from power; but they were irresolute, and did not know how to set about it.

Hitler fixed the date of the offensive as the 12th November; on the 7th he postponed it for three days. The date was postponed fourteen times until the 10th May 1940. The reasons were on the whole connected with adverse weather reports, but above all it was because the plans were not ready.

Fall Gelb — Operation Yellow — hastily prepared by the O.K.W., was simply a re-hash of the Schlieffen Plan: advance of the right wing along the coast as far as Normandy, turning towards the east below Paris to encircle and destroy the French forces by cutting them off from the British.[34]

[33] Nuremberg Documents, XXXIV, C–062.
[34] *Ibid*, XXX–PS 2329.

The plan naturally allowed for the invasion of Holland and Belgium, to avoid a clash between the French left wing and the German right. In any case, the French responded to the hopes of the German generals by forming the "Dyle Theory",[35] which allowed for a considerable outer flank movement into Belgium — an obvious target for encirclement. But Hitler ignored it. The *Fall Gelb* was loosely knit, and it provided for almost any eventuality. But a circumstance occurred that jeopardized the operation.

On the 10th January 1940 Major Rheinberger, a Luftwaffe Staff officer, was given a special mission to transmit to General von Bock, commanding Army Group B, the detailed plan of the advance through Belgium, which was to be undertaken by the Sixth Army. The plan included, as a variation from the Schlieffen Plan, an attack on Ghent by parachute troops. Rheinberger had arranged to celebrate some kind of anniversary on that day at the Münster Casino, and, in consequence, missed his train. A friend of his, Major Hoeneman, helped him out by offering to take him by plane. He accepted the offer, and emplaned at Münster in a Fieseler Storch which set off for Cologne. The weather was bad, and two hours later the pilot, mistaking the Meuse for the Rhine, made a forced landing at Mechelen on the river Meuse.

A Belgian military historian named Jean van Welkenhuyzen has since met Rheinberger who confirmed the story. When the major was forced down he made a dash for the nearest hedge, and set fire to his precious papers. But Belgian troops in the vicinity came up, and quickly put out the fire which had scarcely touched the documents. The Belgians then took the two airmen and the documents to the nearest military post. A Belgian officer got the major to sit down, put the papers on a table, and took off his greatcoat. As soon as the officer's back was turned Rheinberger seized the papers, and threw them into a lighted stove, with such haste that he burned his arm. The Belgian officer saw the movement, rushed to the stove, and withdrew the papers which had been partly burned.

We have since been able to trace those papers, and found them in the same conditions that they were in when the officer took them from the stove.[36] There were ten typewritten sheets and two fragments of a Michelin map of the region around Givet-Floreffe. The sheets were

---

[35] De Launay, *ibid.*, p. 64.

[36] We are indebted to the "Service Historique" of the Belgian army for a sight of these documents.

half burned. They contained instructions relating to reconnaissance missions and aerial landings to be undertaken by the 2nd and 3rd Air Units in conjunction with Army Group B. They also included details of the zones to be bombed (the Dinant sector) and the conditions of the defences in the territory situated between the Meuse and the French frontier. In addition, they contained a valuation of landing possibilities to the west of the Meuse.

It was clear from the papers that the Low Countries and Luxemburg figured within the area of operations. It was also evident that the Germans were well acquainted with the Belgian and Allied defence plans, and that they counted on encircling and destroying the largest possible groups of the French army.

At 11 o'clock that night General van Overstraeten was advised by the commander of the 2nd column of the discovery of the documents. He had the translation in his hands by the following morning, and King Leopold was informed. The King decided to notify General Gamelin and the British and Dutch Chiefs of Staff. General van Overstraeten wrote:

> On my return to the Palace I received Colonel Hautcoeur at 5 p.m.; he was deputizing in the absence of General Laurent, French military attaché. I had known this fine officer a long time; he had been my pupil at the military college. I said to him, 'Something new has cropped up. Written details of primary importance concerning German plans have come into our possession. These details are incomplete, as the original papers were partly burned. They are sufficient, however, as you will be able to judge for yourself,[37]

On the 11th January van Overstraeten handed a summary of the papers to the French military attaché. Hautcoeur left for Paris at once to take the summary to Gamelin. The Commander-in-Chief, after summoning all the army commanders to a conference in Paris for the 19th January, asked for a complete copy of the documents seized, because he considered that the Intelligence Branch, accustomed as they were to dealing with this kind of material, would provide a better interpretation. The Belgians would not comply with the request.

Moreover, Berlin did not know what the seized documents contained. At the request of the O.K.W. the Abwehr instigated an immediate enquiry. Seelen, Commissioner of Police at Maastricht, reported that Rheinberger did not succeed in burning the papers, and that they were now in the hands of the Belgians.

[37] Van Overstraeten, *Albert Ier, Léopold III : Vingt ans de politique militaire belge (1920–1940)*, Brussels, 1949.

When the Abwehr report reached Goering he flew into a violent temper. In front of his assistants the Reichsmarschall declared that he intended to resign. On reflection, however, he found a scapegoat in General Kuhne whom he made responsible for the whole business and transferred to an inferior post.

At the same time the O.K.W. informed the Foreign Minister, who immediately got in touch with Bülow-Schwante, the German ambassador in Brussels. On the 11th January the ambassador asked Minister Spaak to allow the prisoners to be visited. When the Belgian General Staff was consulted permission was at first refused; later they thought better of it, no doubt to gain information, and authorized the visit for 10 a.m. on the 12th January.

General Wenniger, German Air Attaché in Brussels, after being duly lectured by Goering, was sent especially from Berlin to visit the two men. The Intelligence Branch had hastily installed a few microphones in the visitors' room. But General Wenniger was suspicious: in order to jam any possible recording he took the precaution of tapping the table with his pencil whilst questioning the officers. When the interview was over, Wenniger returned to Brussels, reported to the ambassador, and left for Berlin. Bülow-Schwante telegraphed Ribbentrop at 1.25 on the afternoon of the 12th: "Rheinberger confirms that the mail was burned, and reduced almost to nothing, but he cannot say more".[38]

This obscure reply annoyed Ribbentrop; he wished to be the first to be informed. At 9 p.m. on the 12th January he telegraphed to Brussels: "Send detailed report immediately of the conversation Wenniger-Rheinberger and of the destruction of the baggage".[39]

Bülow sent off the reply from Brussels at 4.40 a.m.: "Rheinberger informed Wenniger that his baggage was destroyed, and that the remaining fragments could be held in the palm of the hand ... It was impossible to identify the bits when pieced together ... Wenniger will arrive in Berlin to-day to make a personal report to the Air Minister".[40]

One can imagine Ribbentrop's anger. At eleven o'clock on the morning of the 13th January a conference was convened at the Air Ministry in Berlin. It was attended by Goering, Bodenschatz, Jeschonnek and Jodl who questioned Wenniger at length. Later Jodl made an entry in his diary, "Account of the conversation of the air attaché with the two

[38] German Archives, VIII, 528.
[39] The German Archives, VIII, 529.
[40] *Ibid.*, VIII, 531.

airmen who had made a forced landing. Conclusion: destruction may be regarded as certain".[41]

In point of fact, as we have seen, what remained of the papers did allow the Belgians to make certain deductions relating to various troop movements. Berlin was informed by Bülow. But Paris did not believe an attack was imminent. The conference of commanders-in-chief on the 12th January concluded that the information did not suggest an imminent offensive.

But on the 17th January Spaak summoned ambassador Bülow, and declared angrily:

"The documents found in the plane contain proof of Germany's aggressive intentions. They did not refer merely to a general operational plan, but they contained detailed instructions which lack only the date of the invasion."[42]

Bülow passed the message on to Ribbentrop, and it puzzled him. In the meantime — and this is the main point — Hitler postponed the invasion of Belgium. On the 13th January he abandoned the execution of Operation Yellow "on account of weather conditions".[43] But the O.K.W. postponed its plans for an offensive until the spring, because it believed that its project had been partly discovered.

By a fortunate coincidence Hitler's luck changed. On the 17th February 1940 he attended a dinner in honour of some recently promoted generals, and the commander of the 38th Army Corps had the audacity to approach Hitler, and vigorously defended some of his ideas in relation to strategy. He said that so far he had never been able to see that his ideas reached Hitler personally, because they had to be transmitted through the "usual channels".

The general was Erich von Manstein. He was the son of a general of artillery, and his name at birth was von Lewinski. At the end of the first world war Manstein was a captain, and his career on the General Staff was uneventful.[44] In 1933 he was a colonel, in 1938 a lieutenant-general, and he was appointed general of infantry in 1940 at the age of fifty-three. He had been adopted by his uncle, General von Manstein, who had taken part in the 1870 war and was Hindenburg's nephew on

[41] Nuremberg Documents, 1811 — PS.

[42] Nuremberg Documents, XII, 1220. See also German Archives, VIII, 544.

[43] After the 10th May 1940 the two German prisoners were transferred to France, then to England, and eventually to Canada.

[44] Under General Beck, Chief of General Staff, his early career was influenced somewhat when his chief fell into disgrace.

his mother's side. Von Manstein was an extremely gifted officer, bubbling over with new ideas. In 1939 he was von Rundstedt's Chief of Staff. Von Rundstedt at that time was in command of Army Group A and, having been director of the Military College, had retired at sixty-three years of age after the Czechoslovak affair. Recalled in 1939, he led the Army Groups which conquered Warsaw during the Polish campaign. Von Rundstedt had a high opinion of von Manstein, but considered it advisable to restrain the youthful ardour of his impetuous second in command.

Manstein dissected Operation Yellow, and found in it two fundamental flaws:

1 — Attack on the lines of the Schlieffen Plan was organized in such a way as to terminate in a frontal battle, which should be avoided at all costs;

2 — The operation completely lacked the advantage of surprise.

Hence Manstein's own proposal — firstly, to hurl armoured divisions through the Ardennes, which was difficult terrain where the French would undoubtedly offer very weak resistance; secondly, to profit by the element of surprise resulting from the attack, by carrying the break-through as far as the Lower Somme, and take the Allied armies in the rear.

Von Manstein wrote a detailed account of his proposals[45] and of his criticism of Operation Yellow. We now know that he had judged rightly in assuming that the French would put up a fairly weak defence in the Ardennes because the forest itself was a natural obstacle. For the French point of view we collected the evidence of General Corap on the essential points of the plan. Because of his family's objections his diary was never published, despite his express wish that it should be. Corap's testimony corroborates what precedes.[46]

Von Manstein's idea, when passed through normal military channels to Halder and Brauchitsch during the winter of 1939–1940, was not accepted. But after the General's talk with the Führer on the 17th February 1940 Hitler accepted his plan enthusiastically; and on the 24th, in a directive from the O.K.W., the new plan for the campaign in the west was finally adopted.

At Nuremberg Goering declared that the plans for the campaign in the west were exclusively Hitler's. He consulted his generals, co-

---

[45] Von Manstein, *Verlorene Siege*, Bonn, Athenaum Verlag, 1955, p. 91.
[46] De Launay, *op. cit.*, p. 84.

ordinated and synthesized their ideas; but the dominating plan was his alone.

> Keitel also testified that: The extent of Hitler's study of general staff books military treatises, works on tactics and strategy, would have been regarded as amazing even for a professional officer; he had a really extraordinary knowledge of military matters. Even throughout the night he would study the voluminous general staff works of Moltke, Schlieffen and Clausewitz, and from such books he derived his knowledge.[46]
>
> Otto Dietrich, his Press liaison officer, was a secondary witness. He said that: Hitler conceived this plan of campaign, and made the final arrangements: and it developed accordingly. It was he who decided troop movements and the strength of the offensive. There is no doubt, however, that he based his plan on the scheme presented to him by von Manstein.

This testimony is rather important, because in June 1940, after the victory in the west, the staff of Dr Dietrich broadcast to the world that the Führer was, with the technical collaboration of Jodl, the *sole* author of the plan of operations. This non-verified information, partially contradicted to-day by Dietrich in the above remarks, still serves as the basis of historical accounts.

It seems, however, that the "Manstein idea" developed a little differently. Jodl noted in his diary on the 13th February 1940:[48]

> The Panzerdivisionen must be concentrated in the direction of Sedan. The enemy does not expect our main effort to be in that area. The documents seized from the airmen have convinced the enemy that we are interested only in the possession of the Dutch and Belgian coasts . . .
>
> I drew attention to the fact that the attack on Sedan was a manoeuvre, the success of which lay in the lap of the gods of war. If the French attacked to the south, it would be necessary to carry out a turning movement towards the south.
>
> But the Führer persists in believing that the enemy will not attack at all; or, in any case, will not do so automatically. The news from Holland and Belgium could be so alarming from the very beginning that the enemy might decide to do nothing.

In short, starting from Manstein's idea Hitler elaborated an operational plan which was considerably improved by Jodl and Halder, who drew up from that plan all the directives for carrying it out.

---

[47] Nuremberg Documents, I, 621.
[48] Nuremberg Documents, XXVIII, PS-1809.

The idea of dropping paratroops over Ghent was cut out, probably because the details had been discovered by the Belgians; it was replaced by a paratroop attack in Holland. The special project for the investment of Eben Emael was conceived by Hitler himself; he had had the whole operation set up on a model fort at Hildesheim as far back as November 1939.

The victory in the west was Hitler's masterpiece of strategy, and has placed him in the ranks of the world's greatest leaders in military history.

4. Exercise Weser

On the morning of the 9th April 1940 Bräuer, the German Minister at Oslo, had the Norwegian Foreign Minister — Halvdan Koht — awakened at nine o'clock — Ribbentrop was very precise in these matters — and read to him a long memorandum inviting Norway not to offer resistance to the German forces.

This memorandum, on which Ribbentrop's staff had worked relentlessly since the 2nd April,[49] explained that the sole aim of the military operation was to protect the north against the occupation of Norwegian bases by Britain and France. Germany, therefore, hoped that Norway would offer no resistance.

By 5.52 a.m. Bräuer was able to transmit to Berlin a negative reply from Norway. The King and his government left Oslo hastily to organize a resistance which lasted until June 1940. This campaign cost the Germans 5000 men; the French, British and Norwegians also lost 5000.

Were the Germans responsible for the invasion of Norway? Or were France and Britain responsible, as Ribbentrop said? The question may be answered by a study of the documents published since the war. Two main phases have to be considered: the drawing up of the plans and the decision to invade.

1 The drawing up of the plans

Hitler first conceived a landing in Norway on the 10th October 1939. The man who discussed it with him was Grand Admiral Raeder. Since the 1914–18 war the German navy had been haunted by the fear of

---

[49] Especially Hitler's interpreter, Schmidt. He not only had to translate a memorandum for Denmark, but both memoranda into Italian for the Duce, together with a letter to the Duce to keep him informed. See Paul Schmidt, *Statist auf diplomatischer Bühne 1923–1935 : Erlebnisse des Chef-dolmetschers in Auswärtigen Amt mit den Staatsmännern Europas*, Bonn, 1949, p. 481.

encirclement. During that period a network of minefields pinned down
Germany's finest ships, cornering them in Jutland and tightening the
blockade around Germany.

Radeer was anxious to focus the Führer's attention on this danger,
and occasionally he succeeded; but Hitler was always busy with the
offensive in the west, and kept the dossier pending.[50] It is fair to add
that the Grand Admiral showed the Führer both the advantages and
disadvantages of the operation. He stressed that the maintenance of
strict neutrality on the part of Norway would be the better solution.

Raeder was not the man to commit himself without due reflection.
He had been chief of staff to the last commander-in-chief of the Imperial
Navy. After the Great War he published two works on cruiser warfare,
and had rebuilt the German navy at tremendous effort. Only by sheer
ability did he contrive to get round the terms of the Treaty of Versailles.
He had also to contend with his country's politicians, for no one but
Hitler was prepared to heed him. His twofold objective in 1939 was to
safeguard "his" navy by shunning any reckless adventure, and to ensure
access to the open seas to obviate a repetition of the errors of 1914.

In November 1939 Germany became for the first time anxious about
the Allied blockade. Her apprehension concerned the supply of iron ore,
of which two-thirds of German requirements came from the Kiruna
mines in Sweden. The iron ore was imported by way of the Baltic,
but, owing to the ice, the only practical route was overland through
Norway, by ship from Narvik and conveyance along the coast, inside
Norwegian territorial waters all the way. Thus it was sheltered from
Allied ships and planes.

This stratagem was quickly discovered by the Allies, and Churchill
asked the War Cabinet's approval to lay mines in Norwegian waters.
Chamberlain and Halifax, however, rejected the proposal to avoid
violating Norwegian neutrality.[51] The question was raised again in
Paris when the Allied Supreme Command met on the 5th February
1940. The subject at issue was the despatch of an Anglo-French expeditionary force to Finland, and the Allies examined the advantages of
occupying the Kiruna mines en route. No final decision was taken,
however; Daladier and Chamberlain had a policy — the policy of
blockade — but refused to put it fully into operation.

[50] Information concerning a possible paratroop landing in southern Norway
by the British was passed to Raeder by Canaris. Nuremberg Documents, –XIV, 90.
[51] Churchill, Memoirs, Vol. I, Part II, p. 145.

Raeder on the other hand made a further step forward on the 11th December when he received Quisling. Raeder stated,[52]

On the 11th December Schulte-Mönting, my Chief of Staff, informed me that Major Quisling from Oslo, former Norwegian Minister for War, was seeking an interview (through a certain Herr Hagelin), to give me a report on the Norwegian situation.

Hagelin, as I said before, had been recommended to my Chief of Staff by Herr Rosenberg who had known him a long time. I regarded as very valuable any information I might receive from such a source on the situation in Norway, and I expressed my readiness to see Herr Quisling.

I saw him that morning, and he described the Norwegian situation in detail; his government's relations with Great Britain, and particulars concerning the British plan for a landing in Norway. He presented the last fact as a particularly urgent matter; from what he said the danger was imminent. He even endeavoured to hazard the latest date for the operation: he thought it would take place before the 10th January, because after that date the political situation would be favourable. I told him that the political situation did not concern me, but I should try to give him the opportunity of presenting this account to the Führer. As for me, I was interested only in the military and strategical position, and I was able to tell him at once that any attempt undertaken between the 11th December and the 10th January would fail on account of the winter conditions and through lack of time.

However, I regarded his report as of such consequence that I told him I should try to arrange for him to inform the Führer personally, as this news might impress him.

I went to see Hitler at noon the following day and told him about my conversation with Quisling. I asked Hitler to talk to him, and see what impression he made on him. I also told Hitler — and this appears in one of the documents — that such a matter required a great deal of prudence. One could never know to what extent a party leader might be seeking merely to promote his party's interests. Our enquiries should therefore be conducted very carefully, and I drew the Führer's attention again to the risks involved in attempting to occupy the Norwegian coast, and the disadvantages that could result. In short, I put the matter to him objectively from those two points of view.[53]

Hitler received Quisling on the 14th December. Quisling explained how he could be of use to the German forces in the event of a landing. No trace remains of this conversation,[54] but it had the effect of con-

[52] Nuremberg Documents-XIV, 97.

[53] *Ibid*, XIV, 97.

[54] Quisling returned to Oslo with a gift of 200,000 gold marks *(Führer Conferences on Naval Affairs*, British Admiralty, London, 1947, p. 104). It seems that Hitler told Quisling that he had no wish to violate the neutrality of the Scandinavian countries (Otto Meissner, *Staatssekretär unter Ebert–Hindenburg–Hitler : Das Schicksalsweg des Deutschen Volkes vom 1918–1945 wie ich ihm erlebte*, Hamburg, 1950, p 533). Quisling's trial (September 1945) revealed that the Norwegian Führer also provided the Germans with a great deal of military information.

vincing Hitler. He gave orders to the O.K.W. that very day to prepare
a plan for the invasion of Norway, either on a friendly basis or by force.

The plan was finished by the 13th January 1940. Beginning with this
material a detailed instruction intended for the three arms of the Service
was perfected by the O.K.W. under the title "Exercise Weser" (Weser-
übung). The instruction was ready by the 1st March.

On the 17th February an incident occurred in Norwegian territorial
waters. A German auxiliary cruiser, the Altmark, returning from South
America, broke through the British blockade, and hugged the Norwegian coast on the way to Hamburg. The vessel carried three hundred
British sailors as prisoners.

When Churchill learned this he sent the British destroyer Cossack
which tackled the Altmark, still in Norwegian waters. The British
sailors were taken off and repatriated to England. The Norwegians
protested against this violation of their neutrality by the British; but
Hitler concluded that the Norwegians were incapable of enforcing
respect for their neutrality, and asked the O.K.W. to hasten the completion of Exercise Weser. On the 21st February Hitler put Falkenhorst
in command of the expeditionary force.

Since January 1940 the Allies had brought pressure to bear on Norway
to reduce her iron ore exports to Germany. The intentions of the Allies
were "mixed". Gamelin told Daladier on the 15th January that this
pressure, "if cleverly handled, was likely to incite the Germans to
armed reaction, which would justify our own intervention".[55] But
apart from the attack on the Altmark the Allies took no further action.
Reynaud, the new President of the Council, wished to expedite matters;
but despite an urgent request from him the British refused to violate
Norwegian neutrality.[56] Reynaud wished to win the battle for iron ore
without delay.

Daladier and Reynaud had nothing in common.

L. O. Frossard, a former minister, said that they differed in every respect — in
their deep-seated characteristics, their ways of doing things, their mental outlook,
their exercise of authority and their methods of conducting the war. Reynaud made
quick decisions with a self-assurance that suggested lack of reflection. Daladier
acted slowly, and his hesitating manner never quite deserted him. Reynaud would
gladly have ruled from the market square, whereas Daladier was cautious and secre-

[55] Reynaud, La France a sauvé l'Europe, Paris, 1947, II, 25.
[56] The British reply is the subject of a note by Reynaud, dated the 27th March,
in the Commission parlementaire d'Enquête. See Reynaud, Ibid, p. 351.

tive. Reynaud reproached Daladier for what he had omitted to do; Daladier instinctively dreaded what Reynaud was about to do.[57]

2. The decision to invade

Hitler made his decision on the 1st March 1940, although several more setbacks occurred. Goering, who had not been informed, flew into a passion; but that was appeased by the 5th March. The O.K.W. continued its preparations. Jodl, however, made an entry in his diary on the 13th March: "The Führer has not yet given the order for Exercise Weser; he is still looking for extenuating circumstances".

But Raeder explained that Hitler wanted a pretext rather than a justification for his action, because the order of the 1st March was irrevocable. It was absolutely necessary to ward off British attacks, safeguard the transportation of iron ore, and extend German naval and air bases against Britain.[58] Preparations for executing Exercise Weser began immediately, and terminated about the 20th March. On the 26th Raeder revealed that, according to information at his disposal, an invasion by the British was imminent.

Reynaud, meanwhile had found a strong ally in the eager and impetuous First Lord of the Admiralty, Winston Churchill, who, on the 8th April at last obtained authority to lay mines in Norwegian territorial waters. This decision was arrived at in London on the 27th March as the result of an understanding between the military commanders, and Norway was notified on the 5th April.[59] Hitler reached his decision on the 2nd April, and by the 3rd German supply ships were already at sea. Ribbentrop had been informed on the previous day, and instructed to cover up Exercise Weser as diplomatically as possible.[60] When the Allies were laying their mines on the 8th April the German troop ships were already north of the obstructions!

The Germans disembarked in Norway on the 9th. The French expeditionary force, the Audet Division, which was intended for Norway, was still in the Jura. The small British force was ready to leave. The British speculated that Germany would take action against the blockade

[57] De Launay, Le Monde en Guerre, p. 68.
[58] Nuremberg Documents-XIV, 90.
[59] Trygve Lie — Leve eller do Norge in Krig, Oslo 1955, p. 91.
[60] Up to that date the German diplomats had been told nothing of the move. See Weizsäcker, Erinnerungen, Munich, 1950; Schmidt, Statist auf Diplomatischer Bühne, Bonn, Athenaum Verlag, 1960; Ribbentrop, Zwischen London und Moskau : Erinnerungen letzte Aufzeichnungen, Leoni am Sternberger See, Druffel Verlag, 1953.

of iron ore, and assumed that they might invade Norway to re-establish their lines of communication; in that event an Anglo-French force would occupy Narvik and cut off the passage of the ore.

The examination of documents therefore suggests that the opposing forces had twice made plans for operations in Norway, for both sides considered Norway incapable of defending her neutrality. Hitler alone, however, decided to invade, on the instance of Raeder, and to some extent of Quisling. "Conscious of my responsibility," said Raeder, "I continued to acquaint the Führer with the advantages and disadvantages of the operation, and I knew the Führer would base his decision upon the facts I presented to him ... It is therefore evident that, to a certain extent, I was responsible for the whole business".[61]

The Allies may have worked out their plans without burdening themselves with Norwegian neutrality, but they cannot be said to have put their plans fully into execution concerning Norway apart from laying mines. If the Germans had not made a landing it seems very probable, despite the intentions of Reynaud and Churchill, that the British and French would never have disembarked an expeditionary force in Norway. On the part of Germany there were definite plans, an order issued and a diplomatic justification; on the part of the Allies there existed the desire, the impulse, but when they were put into execution they became a reply to German action rather than an independent expression of initiative.

Grand Admiral Raeder made a full admission of the part he had played. His naval operation was, in any case, a magnificent success, and he was proud of it.

5. Lord Gort's Retreat

The plan of operations in the West was undertaken with extraordinary success. As foreseen by the "Doyle Theory" a considerable mass of French and British forces advanced through Belgium to join the Belgian and Dutch armies.[62] A strong Panzer column, passing through the Ardennes, severed the hinge of the French army near Sedan. It advanced very quickly into the breach, and on the 16th May Guderian was already one hundred kilometres to the west of Sedan.

---

[61] Raeder. Nuremberg Documents.
[62] J. de Launay, *Le Monde en Guerre*, Paris, 1956, pp. 56–78.

On the 16th May Churchill, who had been Prime Minister since the 10th, hastened to Paris to see Gamelin. "Where are the reserves?" he asked Gamelin. The latter replied helplessly, "We have none left."

Hitler was amazed at his success. He too wondered where the French reserves were. Halder wrote in his diary on the 17th May: "The Führer is very excited. He is concerned over his successes, and hesitates about running further risks. He wishes to hold us back, because he is anxious about his left flank". On the 18th Halder made the following entry: "The Führer is anxious about the southern flank. He grumbled that we are ruining the whole operation and risking defeat. He prefers to hold up the advance to the west".[63]

Brauchitsch had failed to put into position a flanking detachment to the south, and was instructed by Hitler to comply at once. But the French did not anticipate any counter-movement, and on the 20th May Guderian was in Abbeville; the armies in the north were surrounded. On the 19th Gamelin decided that the armies in the north would attack in a southern direction; that very evening, however, Reynaud replaced him by Weygand.[64]

It is hardly likely that the operation contemplated by Gamelin could have succeeded, but, in any case, the change of commander-in-chief entailed a loss of three precious days. Only on the 21st May did Weygand adopt Gamelin's plan, and in the meantime the German armoured forces had managed to consolidate their positions. As Foch's former associate Weygand enjoyed great military prestige.[65] Since 1919 he had accomplished important missions in Poland, Syria and Turkey, and his name alone was an inspiration. When Reynaud put him in command of the forces, Weygand left Syria on the 17th May, and journeyed to Paris. There he cancelled Gamelin's plan, and joined the northern front to study the position on the spot.

While his plane flew over the Somme it was hit by tracer bullets from German fighters, and Weygand had to make a forced landing at Calais. From there he proceeded to Ypres, where an Allied conference had been called for the 21st May.

What happened at that vitally important conference, and were all the army commanders present? Weygand has left his account of the

[63] Halder's Diary (The Hoover Library).
[64] Reynaud demanded the dismissal of Gamelin on the 9th May 1940. See de Launay, *op. cit.*, p. 75.
[65] Weygand was 73.

conference,[66] and other writers have left their versions, which vary considerably.

Our attention was drawn to this by the Burgomaster of Ypres when we were questioning him in 1940, a few months after the conference. Gort, Leopold III, van Overstraeten, Michiels, Billotte and Weygand were all received by the Burgomaster, and Weygand stated that he had "not been able to meet Lord Gort". The one essential fact that deserves attention is that Weygand wished the armies in the north to launch an offensive in a southern direction, along the line Arras-Saint Quentin, while the French forces approaching from the south were to join them. His idea was to persuade the army commanders to co-operate in this project, but he had to convince them personally, and induce them to play a part in his plan.

But in a congested area, overcrowded with civilians fleeing towards the coasts, communications were extremely difficult. The army commanders had no desire to leave their headquarters for long periods. As a matter of fact, Weygand was already in Ypres with King Leopold III and his two associates, General van Overstraeten and General Michiels, when General Billotte arrived late at the town hall. Lord Gort did not arrive until eight in the evening, when Weygand had already left.

General Weygand asked King Leopold to withdraw the Belgian army to the river Yser, in order to ensure a better cover to the east and south east. General van Overstraeten, as military adviser to the King, pointed out the disadvantages of the withdrawal: the base would be too restricted; the rear would be paralysed by a million fleeing refugees; there were problems of equipment and supplies. Above all the troops were tired, and could hardly undergo another retreat.

While Weygand was refuting these objections Billotte arrived, and explained to the Commander-in-Chief the Belgian army's interest in holding the line formed by the river Scheldt and the Terneuzen Canal. At about six in the evening Weygand left — he had to be in Paris on the following day — and, as the military historian Bernard observes,[67] "To keep this appointment Weygand sacrificed his contact with the commander of the B.E.F., the main object of his visit to the north".

While the conference was proceeding at Ypres, Gort, who had engaged all his reserves, paid a visit to his three corps commanders. At

[66] Weygand, *Mémoires*, Tome III, p. 114.
[67] H. Bernard, *La guerre et son évolution à travers les siècles*, Tome II: *De 1939 à ajourd'hui*, Brussels, 1957.

4.45 p.m. he ordered them to fall back on the defences along the Franco-Belgian frontier during the night of the 22nd to 23rd May.

At eight o'clock that evening Gort arrived in Ypres, and met King Leopold in the Burgomaster's office; Billotte and van Overstraeten were also there. It became clear that the operations in which the British Expeditionary Force was engaged did not admit of any immediate action within the framework of Weygand's plan; but Billotte made an inventory of the forces and equipment available, and noted the plan to be put into effect.[68] After thus taking stock of the situation, they made two decisions which Weygand learned only later:

1 — The Allied forces would be withdrawn to Valenciennes and the French Scheldt, that is to say, to the French frontier as far as Halluin, Lys; and the Belgians would fall back on the Lys, instead of holding the Scheldt;

2 — Four to six divisions would be earmarked for the offensive in the south. Billotte was to take charge of this arrangement, and pay special attention to co-ordination.

Billotte set off for his headquarters during the night, but was killed in a motor accident at Reninghelst, and that tragedy put an end to the co-ordination of the armies in the north. According to Lord Gort, General Blanchard succeeded Billotte as commander of the 1st French Army Group, and probably also took over his task of co-ordination, although this appointment was never officially confirmed.[69]

In the meantime Weygand — who had not himself seen Lord Gort, but had charged Billotte to reach an understanding with him regarding the participation of the B. E. F. in the Weygand plan -- returned to Paris. He made his journey from Ypres to Dunkirk by car, where he was bombed, and by destroyer from Dunkirk to Cherbourg; he then proceeded by car from Cherbourg to Paris.

On the 22nd May, at his headquarters in fortified Vincennes, in brilliant sunshine, he gave an account to Reynaud and Churchill of his visit to Ypres.[70]

The German armoured corps had opened up a corridor twenty-five kilometres wide from Sedan to Abbeville, and the encirclement of the northern armies was almost complete. Weygand expounded his plan:

[68] H. Bernard, *ibid.*

[69] See the London Gazette Supplement dated 10th October 1941.

[70] The account is based on the minutes of the meeting drawn up by Captain de Margerie (quoted by Reynaud, *Au cœur de la mêlée (1930–45)*, Paris, 1951, p. 147).

The Commander-in-Chief is of the opinion that there can be no question of expecting the French, English and Belgian formations still in the north, comprising more than forty divisions, simply to retreat towards the south in an attempt to join up with the bulk of the French army.

Such a manoeuvre would be doomed to failure, and those forces would be rushing to certain destruction. The situation demands, on the contrary, that, protected by the Belgian army which would cover them, first to the east and subsequently to the north, the available French and British forces attack in the south in the region of Cambrai and Arras, and in the general direction of Saint Quentin, so as to fall on the flank of the German armoured divisions in the Saint Quentin–Amiens pocket.

At the same time the French army under General Frère, centred to the south of the Somme in the region of Beauvais, must push towards the north in order to accentuate the pressure on the enemy's armoured sections in the region of Amiens, Abbeville and Arras. The essential aim is to submit these elements to continual pressure; to prevent the German armoured divisions from assuming the initiative, to keep them continually on the move, to inflict losses on them, and threaten them from the rear.

This is the only way in which the withdrawal of the Belgian armies may be successfully carried out.[71]

Weygand's plan was, in fact, founded on a completely fictitious picture of the situation. General Frère's forces were not concentrated in the south, as Weygand said, but dispersed over a wide area, and had to be reassembled. The principal role fell to the armies in the north — an offensive with a view to a breakthrough. Another factor was that in the north the Allied armies lacked co-ordination.

Major Ellis[72] has given numerous examples of this lack of co-ordination; the fact that they also lacked air cover was no mean consideration. The air component attached to the B. E. F. had been forced to evacuate numerous aerodromes as a result of the German advance, and liaison with the French air force no longer existed.[73]

We questioned at some length General François d'Astier de la Vigerie, Commander-in-Chief of the air forces on the north-east front, and we have studied his operational notes. He told us that he had received an order "to support the operation, but was given neither a time nor a line of attack". D'Astier made fruitless attempts to link up with his British counterpart, who, moreover, knew nothing of what was happening.

The attacking forces on which Weygand depended did not, therefore, exist on the terrain as he imagined, and the timetable on which he

[71] Margerie; referred to by Reynaud, *op. cit.*
[72] Ellis, *The War in France*, H.M.S.O., 1953, p. 96.
[73] Macmillan, *The Royal Air Force in World War II*, London, 1950, II, 54.

depended did not exist either. The date of the offensive — the 22nd
May — could not be settled with General Frère who first had the task
of concentrating his attacking forces. And General Gort, who thought
the attack must come from the south and not the north, awaited instructions from General Blanchard, from whom he had received no news
since as far back as the 23rd.

Weygand, however, continued to work things out on paper, and the
messages exchanged between Reynaud and Churchill were full of
inaccuracies based on details emanating from the Commander-in-Chief.
Every now and then Churchill expressed amazement on finding that
the information received from Gort did not tally with that received
from Reynaud regarding the Weygand plan.[74]

While the Commander-in-Chief was saying that the forces under
Michiels, Blanchard and Gort could be saved only if they were "inspired"
with a fierce determination to make a break-through (24th May), the
situation in the field had undergone great change.

General Gort went to see Blanchard, and told him that if they were
to carry out the task assigned to them under Weygand's plan, they
should attack in the south with two British divisions, one French
division and the French cavalry corps. Both generals considered that
such an operation could not be put into effect until the 26th May at the
earliest. Gort asked Blanchard to enquire from his G. H. Q. how the
operation could be synchronized with the attack coming from the
direction of the Somme, which apparently was still being prepared.
General Gort also impressed on the Secretary of State, as well as
Blanchard, that the main effort should come from the south. He pointed
out that a sortie was all that could be expected from the forces in the
north.

Gort subsequently stated that he had received no information of any
kind whatever as to the disposal of his forces, or the position of the
enemy's forces in the gap; nor did he receive a time-table of any
projected attack from the south. On the 24th May he had not only to
prepare a counter-attack to the south (to operate on the 26th), but
also to prepare to reinforce the length of the canal. He instructed Lieutenant General Sir Ronald Adam, commanding the Third Army, to
continue negotiations with General Blanchard and General René
Altmayer, commanding the French 5th Corps, with a view to perfecting
the plan of counter-attack.

[74] Reynaud, *Au coeur de la mêlée (1930–45)*, Paris, 1951 p. 151, *et seq.*

The final plan envisaged a counter-attack by five divisions, three French and two British, under the command of General Altmayer. The primary object was to establish during the evening of the 25th May bridgeheads to the south of the Scarpe, so that the main attack might be launched on the following day against Plouvain–Marquion–Cambrai. Sir Ronald Adam, with three divisions (two English and one French), would proceed to the east of the northern section of the canal; General Altmayer with two French divisions would advance along the west of it, his right being covered by the French cavalry corps. The attack was never carried out.[75]

On the 25th May the Germans further developed their encircling movement, and pressed in upon the Belgian and British forces. In the evening both Gort and Blanchard thought that the counter-attack towards the south had over-reached itself, and both feared the collapse of the Belgian army; although in the confusion of battle they did not manage to meet personally until the morning of the 26th May.

At 10.30 a.m. on that day Gort returned to his Headquarters, where he found a telegram from the Secretary of State instructing him to prepare to fold back the B.E.F. towards the ports. The same morning Blanchard received a message from Weygand authorizing him to act to the best advantage to safeguard the honour of his units. That evening Gort received a telegram from the War Office to the effect that the Prime Minister had been given details of the situation, and the strength of French military resources in a conversation with Reynaud. Obviously the French could not attack from the south with sufficient strength to enable them to link up with the armies in the north. All that Lord Gort could do in the circumstances was to fall back to the coast. The telegram said that Reynaud would inform General Weygand, who would no doubt issue orders accordingly. Gort was therefore authorized to withdraw to the coast in liaison with the French and Belgian armies.[76]

Consequently, on the 27th May, Lord Gort folded his forces back towards the channel ports. On the 28th the Belgian army surrendered. On the 30th the remainder of Blanchard's and Gort's armies embarked at Dunkirk.

The falling back of the B.E.F. was carried out under bad conditions, but this by no means suggests anything in the nature of a flight or disordered retreat at any time.

---

[75] See the Supplement to the London Gazette, dated 10th October 1941.
[76] *Ibid.*

Thus, from an examination of documents and the evidence of witnesses it seems that the ring around the northern armies could not have been breached without executing an extensive and well planned manoeuvre to the south of the Somme, and unless it had been possible to maintain communications in all circumstances.

The replacement of generals (Gamelin–Weygand and Billotte–Blanchard) at such a time can be regarded only as catastrophic.

The violent criticisms expressed against the retreat of the British forces and the so-called "betrayal" of Lord Gort, magnified moreover by German propaganda, bear no relation whatever to historical fact.

CHAPTER II

THE WORLD WAR

1. Did Hitler really intend to invade England?
2. Did Admiral Canaris influence Spain's decision not to intervene in one space the war?
3. Does the Barbarossa Plan show Hitler's clear determination to attack the Soviet Union?
4. Did the Russo-Japanese pact give Japan a free hand?
5. Did Roosevelt have prior knowledge of Japan's intention to attack Pearl Harbour?

1. Operation Sea "Lion"

Apparently Churchill was never in any doubt about Hitler's desire to make a landing in England. Is it true that Hitler really intended to invade England, or did he never give the matter serious thought? The question has not yet been cleared up.

An enormous amount has been written on Hitler's political aims when, on the 24th May 1940, he ordered his armoured divisions to halt before Dunkirk, instead of pursuing to the end the encirclement and destruction of the northern armies.[1] Hitler over-estimated the strength of the French army, and feared a violent counter-attack on the Somme; perhaps also — although this has not been proved — he had no wish to inflict a defeat so serious and so humiliating upon the British as to compromise his chances of negotiating an ultimate peace.[2]

In point of fact, after his victory over France at the end of June 1940 the Führer was perplexed. Up to the 1st July he still thought he could make peace with Great Britain. He had clung to this old dream for nearly twenty years, and had often referred to it, especially in *Mein Kampf*; he considered that an Anglo-German entente could form the

---

[1] Rundstedt, despite his statements to the contrary to Shulman and Liddell Hart after the war, took this decision in conjunction with the Führer.

[2] William Shirer has analysed this question in detail in his *Rise and Fall of the Third Reich*, p. 117, Secker & Warburg, London.

basis of a new world peace. Because his peace overtures by way of secret diplomacy[3] had been rejected he entered into a very long discussion with his associates of the O.K.W. On the 2nd July he ordered the O.K W. to begin preparations for a landing in England. He laid stress on the fact that this was a project and not a directive; consequently no date had been decided upon. Moreover, it was absolutely essential that definite air superiority be achieved beforehand.

On the 7th July he received Ciano in Berlin, and informed him that no final decision had been reached.[5]

From the 11th July onwards Hitler began to summon his military advisers to Berchtesgaden. Raeder came first. He was of the opinion that invasion should be the last resort. He did not think it possible to repeat the Norwegian operation, and expressed his conviction that England could be compelled to sue for peace when the Luftwaffe had achieved victory in the air, and when the submarines of the Kriegsmarine had secured victory at sea.

Raeder's visit was followed by that of Keitel, Halder and Jodl; they brought their problems to Hitler on the 13th July, and pleaded that they could fulfil their task only after an expeditionary force had been landed on the other side of the Channel. These reservations nearly succeeded in convincing the Führer who enjoyed breaking down obstacles. On the evening of the 13th he wrote to the Duce:

> The repeated proposals I have made to England have been treated with such scorn that I am convinced any further appeal will result in rejection.[6]

The Führer issued "Directive No. 16", which was to be "Operation Sea Lion" on the 16th July:

> As England, despite the hopelessness of her military situation, continues to show no intention of coming to terms, I have decided to plan a landing operation, and, if necessary, to put it into execution.
> The object of this operation is to eliminate the British capital, in so far as it is a base for carrying on the war against Germany, and to occupy the capital should military necessity require it.

The directive still remained conditional, for Hitler had not yet come to a decision. He still wished to leave the door open to Britain, and, on the 19th July, he made his final offer of peace before the Reichstag:

---

[3] See de Launay, *Le Monde en Guerre*, Paris, 1956, p. 24.
[4] *Führer Conferences on Naval Affairs*, Admiralty, London, 1947.
[5] Ciano, *L'Europa verso la catastrofe*, Milan, 1948 (p. 274).
[6] German Archives, X, 209.

I think it is my duty to make one further appeal to the reason and good sense of Great Britain. Moreover, I launch this appeal not as one conquered, but as a reasonable conqueror. I can see no further purpose in prolonging the war".

None the less, in making his appeal Hitler gave vent to his ill-temper, and censured Churchill; and Great Britain rejected the offer at once.

To Hitler Britain's rejection was quite incomprehensible. The German military leaders were running round in circles. As the navy was incapable of conveying the Wehrmacht to the site, they discussed the possibility of crushing Britain by making landings elsewhere — in India, Africa or Gibraltar. Jodl said: "The only object of a landing in England would be to give the coup de grace".

Thus the O.K.W. set about getting the invasion forces in position, without quite believing that the operation would materialize. Thirteen divisions (90,000 men) left for the Channel coast; they constituted the first wave, and set off on the 19th July under the command of von Rundstedt. Six divisions were to be shipped from Boulogne and Calais under General Busch; four from Le Havre under General Strauss, and three from Cherbourg under Marshal von Reichenau. These were to be followed by six armoured divisions, and they in turn by a third wave together with reinforcements, amounting to twenty divisions. The mustering of these forces in position was expected to be completed by about the 20th August 1940.

The troops were to disembark along a three hundred kilometre front, from Lyme Bay to Ramsgate; but on the 21st July Admiral Raeder again visited the Führer to repeat that the navy was incapable of handling the transportation of such an army. Apparently this discordant note did not bother Hitler who continued to nurse his dream of breaking down British resistance.

Halder noted in his diary on the 22nd July: "The war is won. The situation in England is desperate".

On the 31st another conference took place at the Berghof. All members of the General Staff were present — Raeder, Keitel, Jodl, Halder and Brauchitsch. Both Raeder and Halder left accounts of the talks. At his conference the admiral again enlarged on the obstacles: "If the first wave crosses the Channel under favourable weather conditions, that is no guarantee that the second and third waves will do likewise".[7] He said that the landing front would have to be reduced to

---

[7] See *Führer Conferences on Naval Affairs*, British Admiralty, 1947, and Halder, Diary, 31st July 1940 (The Hoover Library).

one hundred kilometres, and that it would be preferable to invade in
May 1941. The generals were powerless; they suggested diversionary
operations, such as in Gibraltar or Africa.

But Hitler refused to allow himself to be lured away from his dream:
Operation Sea Lion had to be ready by the 15th September; they must
try to meet that date. No decision was, however, reached, and the
invasion remained subject to conditions. No Luftwaffe leaders were
present at the conference, but everyone was convinced that southern
England should first be pounded by the air force. If the Luftwaffe
succeeded, then Sea Lion would be put into operation in September.

Directive No. 17 was therefore issued on the 1st August:

> With a view to creating conditions necessary for the final conquest of England I
> intend to continue and intensify the war at sea, and in the air against the English,
> capital. To this end I give the following orders:
> 1 — The German air force must destroy the English air force with all the
> means at its disposal;
> 2 — After achieving air superiority, locally or temporarily, the war in the air
> must be directed against the ports, and especially against those establishments
> concerned with the supply of food... Attacks against ports on the southern
> coast must be undertaken on the most restricted scale possible in view of the opera-
> tions that we envisage...
> 3 — The Luftwaffe must remain at full strength for Operation Sea Lion;
> 4 — I reserve to myself the decision to make terrorist attacks as reprisals;
> 5 — Intensified aerial warfare may begin on the 6th August or later... The
> navy is authorized to commence intensified naval warfare on the same date.

From that date a minor war began between the army and navy
leaders. On the 1st August Keitel wrote to his subordinates that despite
objections by the navy preparations must be continued on the basis of
a three hundred kilometre landing front. On the 7th Halder noted in
his diary that the difference between the ideas of the army and those of
the navy constituted an impassable barrier.

On the 10th Brauchitsch notified Keitel that he could not accept
the reduced front of 100 kilometres proposed by the navy. On the 13th
Jodl laid down the conditions he considered necessary for the success
of Operation Sea Lion. On the same day Raeder insisted that Keitel
should select a shortened front. On the 14th Hitler, no doubt briefed by
Raeder, decided in favour of a shortened front.

On the 16th August Keitel issued a new directive, from which it was
clear that he accepted the reduced front, and gave up the three divisions
under von Reichenau which were to embark at Cherbourg. From then
onwards the generals no longer took Operation Sea Lion seriously. On

the 20th Brauchitsch announced that the execution of the plan would depend on the political situation; and on the 3rd September, when the landing craft were proceeding towards the ports from Ostend to Le Havre to take on the troops, Keitel stated definitely that the landing would not take place until the 21st September.

Raeder saw Hitler again on the 6th. Hitler was then thinking about Gibraltar and Suez, and hardly at all about Sea Lion. Raeder came to the conclusion that Hitler's decision was not by any means firm, for he considered that he could inflict defeat even without making a landing. Everyone awaited the outcome of the air offensive by the Luftwaffe, which had begun on the 12th August and was intensified from the 7th September. It ended on the 15th with a serious defeat for Germany — the first great military turning point in the history of the war.

The date for Operation Sea Lion was postponed several times. The meeting of Commanders-in-Chief which took place in Berlin on the 14th September demonstrated the extent to which the Führer was still torn between conflicting projects. After his defeat in the air the Führer again postponed Sea Lion on the 17th, when the British Royal Air Force began to carry out a severe pounding of the fleet grouped in the Channel ports. By the 21st September twelve per cent of the invasion fleet had been destroyed by the R.A.F. On the 19th Hitler deferred the operation *sine die*, and decided to cancel the assembling of further landing craft. On the 12th October in his final directive the Führer put off Sea Lion until the spring of 1941.

This examination of the facts and of the testimony of German military leaders who were continually with Hitler at this period shows, therefore, that, although Operation Sea Lion was planned in great detail and with precision for the purpose of invading England, the Führer, in agreement with his associates, had stipulated that its execution was subject to certain preliminaries that were never realized. The first of these was victory in the air by the Luftwaffe.

Operation Sea Lion was abandoned because Germany was defeated in the air. Stories of the failure of attempted landings are entirely without foundation.[8]

---

[8] See, for example, G. W. Feuchter, *Geschichte des Luftkriegs*, Athenäum Verlag, Bonn, 1954, p. 441. It is, however, certain that several German departments had prepared in detail "the occupation of England". For instance, the Hoover Library contains the original of the Sonderfahndungsliste G.B. (list of personages to be arrested immediately) prepared by the Gestapo.

2. *The Wooing of Franco*

The Battle of Britain which the Luftwaffe lost on the 15th September 1940 was obviously the first great military turning point of the war. The Grand Admiral Raeder pointed out to the Führer[9] on the 26th September 1940 that the Mediterranean question would have to be solved during the winter, and that success in this sphere would to a large extent cut Great Britain off from her Empire. The Admiral also considered that it would eliminate all possibility of Britain's using North Africa later on as a base for an attack against the Axis.

Hitler yielded to Raeder's reasoning, just as he had followed Goering's advice at the time of Operation Sea Lion. He determined to proceed to a preliminary study of the project with Pétain, Franco and Mussolini.

On the 23rd October the Führer was in Hendaye awaiting the arrival of Franco. Dr Schmidt, Hitler's interpreter, and a very reliable witness, has left an account of the meeting.

Franco's special train was due to arrive on a side-track with wide rails, as used in Spain. The train was over an hour late; but the sun shone beautifully, and everyone was in good spirits. Hitler and Ribbentrop stood chatting on the platform.

'We cannot give the Spaniards any written pledge to assign to them any of the French colonies,' Hitler was saying to Ribbentrop. 'If they received the tiniest piece of paper on this delicate subject, the French would certainly learn of it eventually: the indiscretion of the Latin races is notorious.'

Then he mentioned an interesting point. 'During my interview with Pétain I wish to try to thrust the French into active war against England. I cannot therefore demand that they surrender territory; quite apart from the fact that, if such an understanding with Spain became known, the French Empire would probably pass over to de Gaulle *en bloc*.'

Those few sentences spoken on the platform at Hendaye showed more clearly than any long statement might have done the extent of the problems involved in this meeting between the two dictators. That conversation also disclosed to me the real causes of the subsequent failure of the talks.

At about three in the afternoon the Spanish train appeared on the international bridge over the Bidassoa. There was military music, an inspection of the guard of honour, and the usual brief ceremony surrounding a meeting between dictators. There began at once those talks, pregnant with possibilities, which were to put an end to the fellow-feeling between Franco and Hitler. Franco was short and plump, and his skin was dark. As he sat down in the German saloon car I noticed his black, lively eyes. In the pictures I had seen of him he had always appeared taller, and not so fat. I began to think that if he wore an Arab cloak he might quite easily have been taken for an Arab . . .

[9] See Raeder's account in *Führer Conferences on Naval Affairs*, Admiralty, London, 1947.

I was also struck by his hesitant manner and his diffident way of conversing.
I very soon appreciated that he was a prudent negotiator, and did not intend to
allow himself to be tied up.

Hitler began by describing the position of Germany in the most glowing
colours. After speaking of Germany's chances of victory he said, 'England is quite
definitely beaten already. It just happens that she is not yet prepared to admit it.'

Then he referred to Gibraltar: if the English could only be driven from Gibraltar, they would be deprived of access to the Mediterranean and Africa.

Then Hitler laid his cards on the table. He proposed that he and Franco should
conclude an immediate alliance, and he asked Franco to come into the war in 1941.
Gibraltar would be taken on the 10th January by the use of those specially developed
methods that were used to capture the fort Eben Emael, near Liège, in such a
surprisingly short time. The new German methods of attack which were employed
on that occasion had since been technically perfected to such a degree as to eliminate
any possibility of failure. I understood him to say that German detachments were
already undergoing training in southern France for this purpose, using a model
that was a perfect reproduction of Gibraltar. Then, without beating about the bush
Hitler offered Gibraltar to Spain, and followed this by a rather vague offer of
some colonial territory in Africa.

At first Franco remained silent. He sat humped up. I could not gather from
his inscrutable features whether Hitler's proposal had taken his breath away, or
whether he was just quietly preparing his reply. Then he put up a sort of smoke
screen, as his Italian counterpart had done at the beginning of the war: the food
situation in Spain was very bad; the country badly needed corn — more than
100,000 tons. Was Germany in a position to provide it? He asked with the air of
one who was keenly on the alert. Spain also needed modern armaments. Heavy
artillery would be required against Gibraltar, and Franco stated a very high figure
for guns that Germany would have to supply. Moreover, Spain would have to
defend her long coast line against British naval attacks. Franco also lacked anti-
aircraft guns to repel planes. How could Spain prevent the capture of the Canary
Islands, for this was always a possibility. Besides, the pride of Spain could not
permit her to accept Gibraltar as a gift after its conquest by foreign troops. The
fortress must be taken by the Spanish army.

As an outsider I was extremely interested in Franco's reply to a statement
by Hitler that, from the position occupied by Gibraltar, Africa could be cleared
of the British by the use of armoured forces. 'This would be quite possible,' said
Franco, 'as far as the fringe of the open desert, but central Africa would remain
protected by the desert belt against all large scale land attacks, just as an island
would be by the sea. I have fought a great deal in Africa, and I am quite certain
of that.'

But Hitler's inordinate optimism which caused him to contemplate the conquest
of England as a certainty was subdued by Franco's words to a glimmer of hope.
Franco thought that it might, of course, be possible to conquer the British Isles;
but even if that happened, the government and the fleet would continue the
struggle from Canada with the support of America.

Franco continued to talk in a calm, subdued tone of voice, a melodious mono-
tone, like the drone of a muezzin; and Hitler gradually became more and more
restless. The conversation was obviously getting on his nerves. Once he even rose,

declaring that it was useless to continue the discussions further. But he sat down immediately, and returned to his attempt to make Franco change his mind. Franco declared himself ready to conclude a treaty, but he brought up so many conditions relating to provisioning, the supply of arms, and the precise time of his active intervention, that his willingness was nothing but a façade behind which there was no substance.[10]

The talks were then suspended. Schmidt's evidence is the only one we have of the conversation, but it is corroborated by evidence of another kind. Hitler retained a very bad impression of his meeting with Franco at Hendaye. On the 7th July 1942 Keitel and his associates, Jodl and Hewel, were dining with Hitler. Good courtier that he was, Keitel reminded Hitler that, "At the time of the meeting the detachment of soldiers forming the guard of honour created a lamentable impression. Their rifles were so rusty as to be unserviceable."[11]

But Franco's conduct on this occasion was extremely shrewd, and it is difficult to appraise him without taking into account a number of factors often overlooked twenty years after the events:

The defeat of France, which had been rapid, brutal and unexpected, had brought the German army to the Spanish frontier. Had Spain openly opposed Nazi Germany she might have had to suffer immediate invasion.

The destruction resulting from civil war had not yet been repaired. Spain had no desire whatever to participate in a new war while she was still licking her own wounds.

The Spanish army was not equipped for war, nor was it in a position to put up a serious defence of its own soil.

Spain's supplies of corn and petrol depended largely on foreign imports. *The chances of a British victory* were slender and very widely discussed, especially in the United States.

All these facts were known to foreign ambassadors in Madrid; it was their business to actuate the Spanish government in the interests of their respective countries.

As for Spain,

War was repugnant to her. Nobody in Spain wanted war because the price to be paid was always too high and the advantages uncertain. But since war had broken out, contrary to her interests and her wishes, it was expedient for her to adopt *vis-à-vis* Germany an attitude of friendly expectation. This offered Spain the immediate advantage of sparing her an invasion and perhaps a favourable position later on.

[10] Schmidt, *Statist auf diplomatischer Bühne*, Bonn, 1950, p. 502.
[11] This conversation was taken down in shorthand under Bormann's instructions.

Whether one cares to admit it or not, from the point of view of a Spanish patriot this attitude was the most sound.[12]

The adoption of this shrewd policy demanded a great deal of flexibility of approach, and General Franco discussed it at length with his brother-in-law, Serrano Suner.

Minister Suner came from the north of Spain. Trained as a lawyer at the Bologna Institute, he turned towards Italian Fascism. He was a zealous man who made his mark in the party under Robles; he opted for the Phalanx, and introduced to it the concept of totalitarianism. He and his family had suffered from the anguish of the Revolution: his two brothers had been killed by the Reds, and he himself had been imprisoned. During the difficult period of the Spanish dictatorship he displayed courageous energy and resolution. With his white hair, a chronic cough and occasional nervous twitchings, his manner stood in contrast with the calm and prudent demeanour of Franco.

Franco sent Suner to Berlin to probe the intentions of Germany. On the 15th September 1940 he saw Ribbentrop whom he described in his reminiscences:[13]

I did not find him a very likeable person, and I am inclined to think that that was the impression he made on all politicians who had dealings with him.

Although he cut a good figure he was neither well-dressed nor distinguished in appearance. One reason, I think, for my not finding him either clever or amiable is that he was puffed up with affectation. He had a certain clumsiness, a starchiness of manner. His stolid manner and tight-lipped appearance made me think he was deliberately trying to compose his features. It was difficult to hit upon any quality in him that might serve as the basis of sincere relations.

In any case, I personally did not succeed in getting to the bottom of him, despite his consistent courtesy towards me, because he manifested a sort of stiff vanity against which one inevitably came into collision. It was not that Prussian stiffness which, though perhaps not very pleasant, is at least quite spontaneous; his kind of stiffness seemed studied and intentional. I never could account for that man's political success.[14]

Suner also met Hitler; he even paid a visit to Belgium and France, where he learned that Sea Lion was likely to be put into effect in the near future. This knowledge made him all the more convinced of the importance of Spain's neutrality. As soon as he returned to Madrid he was invited by Franco to take over the post of Foreign Minister. He

[12] Serrano Suner, *Entre Hendaya y Gibraltar*, Madrid, 1947, p. 131.
[13] Serrano Suner, *ibid.*, p. 150.
[14] Suner, *op. cit.*, p. 150.

was present at the meeting in Hendaye, and he reiterated in his talks with Ribbentrop what Franco had told Hitler: Spain would not join in the war at present.

On the 18th November 1940 Suner was invited by Hitler to visit him at Berchtesgaden, an invitation which he could not possibly refuse to accept. He did not know that on the 4th November Hitler had had pre-pared operation "Felix and Isabella" (Directive No. 18), a scheme which envisaged the capture of Gibraltar and the consequent locking-up of the Mediterranean. The Führer calmly informed his generals that Franco was in agreement — a statement that he was anxious to hear corroborated from the lips of Serrano Suner.

Suner relates that Hitler told him,[14]

'The complete closing of the Mediterranean is indispensable. To the west of Gibraltar we can — indeed, we must — effect this lock-out, smoothly and speedily. And at the same time we shall make a thrust to the east by attacking the Suez Canal.'

'The honour of blocking the western strait,' he went on, 'must fall to Spain, as it also falls to her to defend the Canary Islands and safeguard their integrity; for we must anticipate that the English will attempt a landing there to establish bases, the consequences of which would be extremely dangerous.'

'After a pause the Führer continued: 'With regard to the economic worries which you put forward as demanding the postponement of Spain's entry into the war, I must say that the situation of Spain is such that she has nothing to gain by continually deferring action. On the contrary, her position would at once be improved by a speedy termination of the conflict.' And he added, 'Moreover, of the 230 divisions which the German army has at present at its disposal,' — his voice emphasized the figures as he spoke — '186 are inactive, and in a position to proceed forthwith wherever they are required . . .'

If these words did not constitute a threat, they might at least have been regarded as a warning. In any case, that is how I understood them; and, however I looked at the problem, I found this enforced idleness of German troops very disturbing.

'As far as war material is concerned,' Hitler continued, 'you have nothing to bother about, for Germany is able to face up to any eventuality, whether it is a matter of guns or planes. The only opposition our aircraft meets is in the weather conditions; and, despite that, flights over England have not stopped for a single day. We are only waiting for a settled lull in the weather to put into execution our project for a mass attack against England with a total of four thousand planes . . . But for the moment,' he observed, 'this mass attack is unfortunately impossible. Somehow we must turn the waiting period to our advantage, and the best way to do this is to oppose England resolutely in the Mediterranean. I have, therefore, decided to attack Gibraltar, and my operation has been meticulously planned. All that remains is to put it into effect; it must be done . . .'[16]

[15] From the shorthand notes taken by Suner's secretarial staff.
[16] Serrano Suner, op. cit., p. 206.

Suner endeavoured to gain time by saying that Spain needed two months to accumulate the essential food supplies that Spain must have. On his return to Madrid Suner was able to inform the Caudillo that his mission "Not to agree in any way to take part in the war" had been a success.[17]

But no one knew anything of the purpose behind Suner's journey to Berchtesgaden, or of its consequences. Spanish diplomacy remained absolutely discreet, an attitude consistent with national interest.

About a month later, on the 7th January 1941, a new figure made his appearance at the palace — Admiral Canaris, head of the Abwehr.

At that time Canaris was 53. He was a Westphalian, the son of a manufacturer whose remote ancestry had its origins in Lombardy, and eventually established itself within the Holy Empire. His naval career began with the destruction of commercial shipping in the Pacific and South Atlantic during 1914 and 1915. It ended on the day the cruiser *Dresden*, in which he was serving as Intelligence officer, was forced to take refuge in a creek along the Chilean coast.

Lieutenat Canaris then disguised himself as a Chilean, and entered Spain aboard an English boat in 1915. He lived in Madrid, and served the naval attaché, von Kron, in espionage missions and Intelligence work. He retained some happy memories of his stay in Spain and learned to love the country. When he returned to Germany in 1920 he became naval aide-de-camp to Noske, and later controlled various fleet Intelligence services in Kiel (1921) and Berlin (1926). The post of commandant on the battleship *Schlesien* in 1932 was his last active employment with the navy, and he was subsequently placed in control of counterespionage — the Abwehr.

Generally speaking his activities are shrouded in mystery. There were occasions when he served Hitler loyally; on others he campaigned against him, and ended by falling a victim to the purge that followed the 20th July conspiracy. It cannot be said with certainty that he plotted against Hitler with the desire to put an end to the excesses of Nazizm, or that he played a double game because of some kind of distorted attitude inherent in his profession of secret agent. Even his closest collaborators were reduced to guessing.

He was a brilliant man, extremely talkative, and as unlike the military type as one could imagine. He was sensitive to the cold of the north,

---

[17] This directive was given to Suner on the 16th December 1940 by General Franco, Generals Vigon and Varela, and Admiral Moreno.

where he was always muffled up in his naval greatcoat; he was never really happy anywhere except in southern countries, where it was not unusual to see him in a soft hat and a light suit. He was short, head-strong, exceptionally intelligent, rather fastidious about his hair, and despite his inordinate tendency to talkativeness, he assumed an air of indifference even towards the most serious matters. Hitler entrusted him with the task of conveying to Franco his desire to enter Spain on the 10th January 1941.[18] General Franco replied that "for reasons already stated it was impossible for Spain to enter the war at the present time". Apparently as a result of this reply Hitler decided on the 11th December to cancel Operation Felix and Isabella, because "the political situation had changed".

On the 6th February 1941 Hitler, who was always reluctant to abandon an objective, wrote a long letter to Franco reminding him that the war was the common struggle of the Axis and Spain, and that all their fortunes were bound up in the war.

Franco replied on the 26th to the effect that the situation had changed, and did not require his immediate intervention. Hence Hitler's conclusion to Mussolini on the 28th February: "The sum total of all this blabbering with Spain, together with her written explanation, is that she has no desire to join the conflict, and is determined not to do so."[19]

From this examination of the facts it seems that Franco never really changed his attitude. With the aid of Minister Suner he strove consistently to keep his country out of the war for the reasons already stated.

Many documents, however, claim that in 1940 Franco did wish to intervene. The first document of capital importance is a report by von Stohrer, the German ambassador. He sounded Franco shortly after the fall of France, and on the 10th August 1940 he sent Ribbentrop a secret report summing up an interview with Franco. According to von Stohrer the Spanish government was ready under certain conditions to abandon its position as a non-belligerent State, and enter the war on the side of Germany and Italy. Firstly, Spain wished to be satisfied that certain demands would be met with regard to territories over which she had a claim: Gibraltar, French Morocco, the regions of Algeria

---

[18] General Vigon, the Air Minister, the only witness of that meeting, has left no account of it.

[19] Hitler and Mussolini — *Lettere e documenti*, Milano, 1946.

inhabited by Spaniards, Rio de Oro and Guinea. Secondly, Spain asked for military and economic assistance.[20]

What is one to think of this "offer to intervene" which some writers have read into these demands? It is certain that Stohrer, like most German diplomats, was eager to anticipate the Führer's desire. Did he ask Spain to state the conditions under which she would join issue, or did the Caudillo pass them to him spontaneously? There exists nothing to suggests that Franco might have anticipated the Führer's wishes. His whole attitude from September 1940 to February 1941 suggests that he sought only to temporise. Moreover, the list of conditions is such that Germany could only surmize a possible intervention, but not an early one.

Stohrer was under no delusion. He believed that Suner was entirely won over to the ideas of entering the war, and said so in Berlin.[21] With this tendentious report before them Ribbentrop and Hitler would naturally be surprised at the attitude of the Spanish Minister, and would accuse him strongly of adopting a dishonest policy towards the Axis powers.[22]

The foreign ambassadors did not understand the shrewd, discreet policy of the Spanish government. Pietri, the French ambassador, and Hayes, the American ambassador, were satisfied with what they were told without trying to explain it or understand it for themselves.

The British ambassador, Samuel Hoare, clever at boasting to Churchill of the "diplomatic victories" that he imagined he was always winning, did not grasp the fine shades of Spain's diplomatic evolution. He believed that Suner never ceased to steer towards intervention; he worried Churchill at every opportunity, especially at the time of Canaris's visit to ask for immediate intervention.

Samuel Hoare was sixty-one; a rather eccentric Quaker, but a sportsman, an intellectual, a student of philosophy and a sceptic — his favourite author was Montaigne. He was courageous and straightforward, but anxious at any cost to make a success of his mission to Spain. In 1935 he had to resign as Foreign Secretary owing to the failure of the Hoare–Laval Pact; he joined the War Cabinet only in 1939 as Chamberlain's man-of-all-work, and was forced to resign with Chamberlain on the

[20] See also *The Spanish Government and the Axis*, Washington, Department of State, 1946.
[21] Stohrer, in German Archives, III, 81.
[22] *Ibid.*

10th May 1940. But thanks to the support of Lord Beaverbrook he had succeeded in joining the Cabinet again through a narrow door — as Secretary to the Minister of Aircraft Production. In May 1940 he was delighted to accept the new post offered him by Lord Halifax — the ambassadorship in Madrid. He waxed enthusiastic about the post, even to the point of taking his hopes for realities. His reminiscences show that he schematized too much, and sinned on the side of oversimplification.

The best informed of all were undoubtedly the Italians. Ciano had established cordial relations with Suner. They shared a common distrust of the excesses of Germanism. Their relationship with their master and their political ambitions bound these two "napoleonides" together for several years. The Duce and Ciano, as well as Anfuso, Ciano's colleague, followed Franco's difficult manoeuvres with interest and understanding.[23]

It is certain that Mussolini gave but weak support to Hitler's demands from Franco. He made no proposals and presented no demands; and on the 12th February 1941, the occasion of his meeting with Bordighera, he told the Caudillo:

> I appreciate your grave responsibility in having to decide whether your country will enter into war. In any case, you must make your decision only when it is both the least inconvenient to Spain and the most useful to the common cause.[24]

It is not generally known that Canaris played a part in influencing Franco. The head of German counter-espionage had a great affection for Spain, and, according to some of Canaris's colleagues (for instance, Colonel Jenk),[25] the Admiral strongly advised Generals Vigon and Martinez Campos, Chief of General Staff, to remain neutral. Outside conjecture no reliable evidence has been brought forward to support Canaris's statements. What is certain is that, while the Allies never had the slightest suspicion of the private politics of the Admiral, he frequently

[23] See the Duce's letter to Suner, dated the 11th June 1944, in Serrano Suner, *Entre Hendaya y Gibraltar*, p. 277.

[24] According to Suner, *op. cit.*, p. 229. See also Ciano, *L'Europa versa la catastrofe*, Milan, 1948, p. 586, and Anfuso (French edition), *Du Palais de Venise au Lac de Garde*, Paris, 1949, p. 139. Anfuso believed that Franco acted mainly on his own initiative. We have not used Ciano's diary because he made numerous alterations to the text before his trial.

[25] Colvin (in *Chief of Intelligence*, Gollancz, London, 1951, p. 125) also mentions other evidence. This is confirmed by Abohagen, another of Canaris's biographers, but he does not go into details.

visited Spain where he maintained excellent personal relations with his pberal and monarchist friends. Canaris's attachment to Spain and his lioposition to Hitler are both indisputable facts.

Nor is it easy to establish whether Canaris's approaches to Franco were indeed influenced by his personal attitude. Suner speaks of this strange, "disconcerting individual" who "opened talks and made contacts in Spain outside the sphere of the Ministry for Foreign Affairs".

In answer to the questions we put to Suner he told us:

> I do not remember the conversation you mention. It is true that we received advice from Mussolini to the effect that Spain should not join the war. In principle, during the days of the spectacular victory of the armies of the Third Reich against the West, neither Germany nor Italy attached the slightest interest to any intervention by Spain. When things began to change, Mussolini, unlike Hitler, displayed no impatience towards us. He always showed an understanding of our many difficulties, and maintained a calm and friendly attitude towards us. His expressed opinion was that Spain should not intervene until it was the least inconvenient for Spain and most useful to the common cause".[26]

In any case, Suner was not present at the meeting of the 7th December, or at any of the succeeding ones. His assistant, Doussinague, was unaware of all these activities. Nor did Suner refer to another event which played an important part in the Caudillo's decision — the visit by Colonel Donovan on the 17th February 1941. Donovan was President Roosevelt's special envoy, and formerly commanded the 69th Regiment which won glory on the French front in 1917. He was a lively and energetic man; short, thick-set, tenacious, determined and of Irish descent, with cold, blue eyes, a man unaccustomed to mincing words. He told us in the quiet of his New York office in 1952[27] that he knew nothing of the comings and goings of Canaris; but he made it clear to Franco that America would support the British and assist Spain economically.

Donovan did not, as Samuel Hoare said, treat Suner as a "prisoner at the bar"; but his firmness and resolution impressed his hearers. No doubt Italy's friendship, the firmness of America, and possibly the advice of a friendly German, all contributed to keep Spain out of the war. But the ultimate decision on the 26th February 1941 lay with Franco alone. That decision favoured the cause of the Allies, but above all it served Spain and the Spanish people.

[26] This statement was obtained by the writer on the 1st August 1961. See also J. de Launay: *Secrets diplomatiques 1939–1945*, p. 126.

[27] Evidence collected by the author on the 8th December 1952.

3. The Barbarossa Plan

When did Hitler make the irrevocable decision to attack Russia? Many writers date this attack to coincide with the Barbarossa Plan of the 18th December 1940 (Directive No. 21).

We must first take into consideration the deep-rooted purpose of Hitler who had for nearly twenty years regarded Russia and eastern Europe as zones of expansion for Germany. Many indications of this attitude of mind are to be found in *Mein Kampf* and *Hitler's Secret Book*.[28] The Führer firmly believed in an Anglo-German entente. He also imagined he could buy off France's interest in German expansion by abandoning all claims to Alsace-Lorraine, and stirring up conflict between France and Italy in the Mediterranean. Such were the broad themes of his foreign policy.

Ribbentrop's journey to Paris in December 1938 and Hess's proposal to Britain in the spring of 1941 prove clearly that these ideas remained the overriding postulates of Hitler's diplomacy, and of which he constantly reminded his colleagues.

The Russo German entente of 1939 — the non-aggression pact — was purely tactical, even if we accept that economic relations between the two countries continued right up to the last, especially at the insistence of the Russians who were anxious to retard as far as possible the prospect of war.

One must then consider the question of the plans prepared by the O.K.W.[29] Hitler's military associates held in reserve a number of operational plans covering almost every eventuality. According to Gigli, who does not mention the sources of his information, by the end of December 1940 there existed about forty plans in the O.K:W. files. These were not, as some writers allege, operational orders. We know, for instance, that from the 30th October 1940 an "Ostfall" plan had been designed against a possible attack by Russia. Later, on the 31st July 1941, Hitler summoned the chiefs of the O.K.W. and O K.H[30] to the Berghof. He expressed his concern at the sight of England clinging to the forlorn hope of Russian support. If Russia were crushed, England would be crushed at the same time.[31]

[28] Grove Press, New York, 1961. The book is annotated by G. Weinberg.
[29] O.K.W. — Oberkommando der Wehrmacht: High Command of the Armed Forces.
[30] O.K.H. — Oberkommando des Heeres: High Command of the Land Army.
[31] Entry in Halder's diary on the 31st July 1940.

Thus, in the spring of 1941 Hitler had thought of destroying Russia. The leaders of the O.K.W. welcomed the idea with joy,[32] and by the 1st August plans were drawn up for the invasion of the U.S.S.R. and the destruction of the Red Army. After several months of inaction Hitler's military chiefs were happy to seize this outlet following the failure of Operation Sea Lion. From the 26th August divisions were gradually brought up from the West to the East, and Halder hastily prepared his "Otto" Plan.

In the meantime the Führer passed to the O.K.W. details of his ideas as and when they occurred to him, and with the help of Ribbentrop he continued to allay the suspicions of the Russians. On the 12th November Molotov arrived in Berlin hoping to tone down the atmosphere. The diplomatic situation was bad in the Balkans, and tension was likely to increase; the Russians therefore wished to dispel as far as possible any grounds for German aggression, which they had begun to regard as inevitable. The Germans, on the other hand, sought to extend their influence as far as the Soviet frontier. The tension reached its climax when Yugoslavia joined the Tripartite Pact. Molotov's mission was thus bound to be a failure, despite Ribbentrop's anxiety to avoid rousing Soviet fears.

Also on the 12th November Hitler told his generals that the talks with Molotov meant nothing.

"The decisions arrived at verbally with regard to the plans for Russia will be put into effect, I await the operational details from the O.K.H.[33]

On the 5th December Halder and Brauchitsch submitted their plans, which Hitler took four hours to study and approve. On the 18th he issued Directive No. 21 — the Barbarossa Plan — to become effective on the 18th May.

The armed forces of the German Reich must make ready to crush Soviet Russia in a short campaign before the conclusion of hostilities against Britain. To achieve this end the army will allocate to operation Barbarossa all available troops, subject to the maintenance on the western front of forces adequate to ensure the safety of occupied territory against any possible sudden attack ... The preliminaries of the operation will be completed by the 15th May 1941 ... It is essential to observe the greatest circumspection so that the purpose of these preliminaries may not become apparent.[34]

---

[32] In contrast with what they pretended later to a number of credulous writers.
[33] Nazi Conspiracy and Aggression, III, 406.
[34] The complete text may be found in The Nuremberg Documents, XXVI, PS 446.

The plan, which was based on the ideas of the O.K.W. and O.K.H. had not yet reached the stage of an operational order. It was favourably received by the leaders of both organizations, who exercised the utmost caution concerning it. We may conclude that even if Hitler had not taken the irrevocable decision to attack the U.S.S.R., he had none the less returned to his basic idea of looking to the east for German expansion.

His statement as to motives also implies that the Führer believed that through Operation Barbarossa he would impose on the world *his* foreign policy which he had so often stated: an Anglo-German entente, the neutralization of France and Italy, and German expansion to the east.

The *coup d'état* in Belgrade on the 27th March 1941 upset the Barbarossa timetable. Hitler therefore determined to dispose of Yugoslavia in a lightning campaign, and postpone the execution of Barbarossa by four weeks. We know that this delay did considerable harm to the efficient carrying out of his scheme for the invasion of Russia.

It was only after his victory over Yugoslavia on the 30th April 1941 that Hitler gave the order for the operation against Russia to begin on the 22nd June.[35] A chronological study of the facts reveals that although Hitler had wavered with regard to Operation Sea Lion, he was speedily convinced of the necessity to undertake an aggression against Russia. Even though the irrevocable decision was not taken until the 30th April 1941, his resolve went back at least as far as the 18th December 1940.

Hitler wrote to the Duce on the 31st December: "Present relations with the U.S.S.R. are very good." But the words no doubt implied nothing more than diplomatic caution.[36]

Although Goering advised against the invasion of Russia his purpose in so doing was to avoid a war on two fronts. He suggested to the Führer that he *postpone* the execution of the Barbarossa Plan, not that he should cancel it.[37] The Russian campaign developed until Stalingrad (February 1943) — the second great military turning point in the war's history.

---

[35] *Nazi Conspiracy and Aggression*, III, 633.
[36] Hitler used to say, "Whatever Ciano knows London also knows".
[37] Nuremberg Documents, IX, p. 370.

4. The Russo-Japanese Pact

Yosuki Matsuoka, the Japanese Foreign Minister, undertook a long voyage to the west in the spring of 1941. On his arrival in Berlin on the 26th March he was unable to see the Führer at once because Hitler was busy with his instructions concerning the military operations in Yugoslavia. Matsuoka was therefore forced to endure the wearisome chatter of Ribbentrop.

The Führer's idea, Ribbentrop told Matsuoka, was that Germany and Japan should be linked together for centuries to come, and Japan's sudden entry into the war would have the effect of forestalling America's entry. Japan would attack British possessions, in particular Singapore. That would prevent American intervention, which must not occur as it did in 1917; moreover, Japan's entry would certainly help to pull down Britain.[38]

On the 27th March Hitler himself saw the Japanese Minister, and had a long conversation with him. According to Hitler the war was virtually won. The collapse of England was expected from one day to another: an attack on Singapore would precipitate her defeat. But Matsuoka remained as cold as marble.

The talks were continued on the 29th March with Ribbentrop, on the 4th April with Hitler, and again with Ribbentrop on the 5th April.

Little by little the German statesmen revealed what they were prepared to give in exchange for Japanese intervention; they wanted an attack on Singapore, but if America entered the war Germany would declare war on her at once. Interpreter Schmidt in his account of the proceedings refers to the conclusion drawn by Matsuoka:

Matsuoka continued, saying that it seemed incumbent upon him to give the Führer an absolutely clear picture of Japan's views. He regretted to inform the Führer that he, Matsuoka, in his capacity of Japanese Foreign Minister, could not utter a single word in Japan of what he had expressed to the Führer and to the Reich Foreign Minister concerning these plans. That would do him considerable harm in political and financial circles. On a previous occasion, before he became Foreign Minister, he had made the mistake of discussing his intentions with a friend, who repeated what he had said. This gave rise to all kinds of rumours which he, when he became Foreign Minister, had to deny strongly, although he was in the habit of speaking the truth. In such circumstances he could not now say when he would discuss these matters with the Japanese Prime Minister or the Emperor.

[38] *Nazi Conspiracy and Aggression,* VI, 906.

It was first necessary to study carefully the development of the problem of Japan, to be able to make the right decision at the right moment, and declare his own plans to Prince Konoye and the Emperor. Afterwards they would have to reach a decision within a few days, otherwise the plans might miscarry as a result of indiscretions. If he — Matsuoka — could not put his intentions into effect, his failure would prove that he lacked the required influence, conviction and skill. Nevertheless, if he succeeded, it would prove that he had a great deal of influence in Japan — and he himself was confident of success.

When he was questioned on his return he would inform the Emperor, the Prime Minister, and the Navy and War Ministers that Singapore had been discussed. He would say, however, that everything had been considered on a purely hypothetical basis.[39]

Ribbentrop was unbelievably indiscreet. Although the Führer had told Matsuoka that he did not believe there would be a Russo-German war, the Minister declared,

The greater part of the German army was disposed along the eastern frontier of the Reich, ready to launch an attack at any moment whatever . . . The situation was such that one had to consider that a conflict was possible if not probable.[40]

Hitler said not a word about the Barbarossa Plan, which was ready. Matsuoka, however, was shrewd enough to penetrate the stupidity of Ribbentrop. As Matsuoka was leaving he referred, as though incidentally, to Russo-Japanese relations: he wondered whether it might not be a good thing on his return journey to negotiate a non-aggression pact with Russia. Ribbentrop was surprised: it would be better, he said, not to discuss that question at the moment.

Matsuoka's return journey allowed for an important stop in Moscow. On the 7th April 1941 Molotov told him that Russia hoped to sign a non-aggression pact with Japan. Matsuoka was quite eager to do so, but was surprised at Stalin's unexpected offer. He wondered what he would be expected to give in exchange.

The diplomatic discussions between Matsuoka, Stalin and Molotov proceeded in a strained, though extremely courteous, atmosphere.

Stalin was uneasy about German military preparations along their frontier; every traveller arriving in Moscow mentioned these preparations. Stalin was anxious to avoid the risk of having to fight on two fronts — against Germany in Europe and against Japan in Asia — and Matsuoka's round of visits had hardly reassured him.

---

[39] Nuremberg Documents PS 1881.
[40] *Ibid.*, PS 1877.

The German aggression against Yugoslavia, Russia's traditional sphere of influence in Europe, was a source of grievous annoyance to the Soviet rulers, who now desired above all to safeguard their country without having to be preoccupied with eastern problems. For all these reasons Stalin wanted peace, and the neutrality of Japan seemed to constitute a highly desirable protection in the east.

Matsuoka left Moscow by train between the 22nd and 24th March, and

left behind him the impression of a man of ambition, with an active, alert mind. He expressed himself easily in English, and was very much in touch with European affairs. The Japanese Minister sang the praises of the Axis powers, and dined in the evening in the intimacy of the United States Embassy. He was credited with vast plans for world peace; he considered himself obliged, in order to reassure his allies, to parade his optimism and a "tripartite" zeal. He was none the less regarded as one who felt generally well-disposed towards agreements and compromise.[41]

In point of fact, Prince Konoye's government, of which Matsuoka was a member, was holding on to power by a mere thread. Matsuoka's mission and the results expected from it could decide the fate of the government; the Minister did not, therefore, wish to return to Tokyo empty-handed. Stalin was aware of this, and made Matsuoka dance to his tune. The U. S. S. R. was willing to sign, but the points in dispute between Russia and Japan had to be settled at the same time; for instance, the return to Russia of mining concessions in the island of Sakhalin which had been granted to Japan under the Treaty of Portsmouth. Gregorio Gafencu, at that time Romanian ambassador in Moscow, writes:

But the essential point, was to ensure the neutrality of Japan in case of a German attack. That condition was indispensable: without it the agreement with Japan had no value. For if it became necessary to exclude from the agreement the possibility of a war with the Reich, the neutrality of Japan meant nothing. As things stood, the U.S.S.R. could make pacts with whomsoever she wished; but she could make war only with Germany. In view of the close relations existing between Japan and Germany, an absolute guarantee from Japan, without reservations and provisos, would tend to limit the chances of German aggression.

Stalin himself presided at the negotiations, and he endeavoured to make his guest appreciate the circumstances. Matsuoka was in no hurry to understand. Perhaps he was embarrassed by the warm support explicit in German diplomacy; but the purpose of that support was to fashion future events on the principles and in the interests of the Tripartite Pact. The curious and significant thing was that Japanese resistance seemed to centre around mine concessions. On Saturday, the 12th April, the Japanese spokesmen abandoned all hope of an agreement, and left

[41] Gafencu, *Preliminaires de la guerre de l'Est*, Paris, 1944, p. 188.

the Kremlin at midnight. Apparently Matsuoka was resigned to an agreement 'without exception and without reservation', but he did not wish to surrender the mines at Sakhalin. Stalin had proved intractable, and had not agreed to any compromise.

The departure of the Japanese Minister was announced for Sunday at three in the afternoon; upon which the Germans spread rumours that the negotiations had been a complete failure.[42]

Stalin then received the staggering news that the Wehrmacht had entered Belgrade on the 13th April. The day of German aggression against Russia was drawing closer.

Gafencu continues:

Moreover a sensational turn of events occurred during the morning of Sunday, the 13th April. Tokyo telephoned Matsuoka authorizing him to promise in writing that he would settle the question of concessions on the terms desired by the Soviet. The Japanese negotiators were therefore summoned to the Kremlin to sign the agreement. The ceremony took place in an atmosphere of great cordiality. The extraordinary relaxation of tension, the mild and kindly atmosphere, contrasted strangely with the early stormy negotiations.

Matsuoka was received by Stalin in the most friendly manner. The departure of the Trans-Siberian express had to be delayed by an hour.

When the Japanese Minister, surrounded by the members of his mission, eventually arrived at the station, he was met by diplomats, economists and military attachés of the Axis powers. Then occurred a further sensation. The bustling police, the soldiers of the guard of honour and the crowd of bystanders were amazed to see Stalin appear at the end of the platform, and advance towards the group of Japanese. His appearance created the greatest surprise among the diplomats: never had the master of Russia, whose public appearances were so rare, paid such an honour to a foreign guest.

None the less, Stalin's step was unsure, as though the very air, the direct contact with the crowd, and perhaps his own courage might have gone to his head. He recognized a brother in every passer-by; he shook hands with those who were travelling and with the employees on the platform. Then, after having saluted his Japanese guest who came up to him with a grave and solemn air, he turned towards the group of bedecked military attachés, and embraced all the officers who were presented to him. Stalin stopped before von Krebbs, the German Staff Colonel, who stood stiffly to attention; putting his arm around the Colonel's neck, Stalin said to him with a wink: 'We shall always remain friends, your people and mine, won't we?'

Within half-an-hour those famous words, which did not escape any of the journalists lined up behind the diplomats, had reached every corner of the earth.

---

[42] Gafencu, *op. cit.* p. 191. In fact, Molotov received Matsuoka on the 7th, 9th and 11th April, and Stalin did not see the Minister until the 12th April. Soviet historians did not make it clear whether Stalin was, or was not, present at the previous meetings.

The departure of the train taking Matsuoka away passed unnoticed; all eyes were directed towards Stalin, and the master's return to his car was a veritable triumphal march. The crowd, having recognized him, cheered; the members of the Japanese Embassy, excited by the honour done to their country, were enthusiastic and grateful, and escorted Stalin back to his car. The little ambassador, Tatekawa, standing on a seat on a platform, waved his handkerchief and shouted in a shrill voice, 'Spasibo, spasibo' (Thanks, thanks).[43]

In the evening von der Schulenburg, the German ambassador, took the train to Berlin in order to make his report. The significance of the Russo-Japanese Pact was considerable. For the Japanese the guarantee of Soviet neutrality allowed them to pursue their expansionist aims in the direction of south east Asia. As for the Germans, the pact would facilitate the attack on Singapore; and, since Hitler considered — at least until the 28th June[44] — that he did not need Japanese assistance to crush the Soviet, it was not a diplomatic defeat. For the Americans it very soon became apparent that the pact would increase tension in south east Asia,[45] and they reduced their pressure on the Germans.[46] The Russians felt certain that the pact would minimize the risk of German aggression, while it guaranteed their rear should conflict with Germany become inevitable.

At least such were Soviet intentions. As for the consequences, the facts at present available do not permit us to believe that by this pact Stalin really wished to provoke a conflict in the Far East. The pact was, moreover, a victory for the Konoye government, and not for the Japanese military clique. However, apart from the Russo-German Pact of 1939, the Russo-Japanese Pact proved to be the second great diplomatic milestone in the Second World War.

5. Pearl Harbour

The Japanese flag-ship *Akagi*, belonging to the striking force destined to attack Pearl Harbour, left Japan on the 17th November. By the 21st thirty-two vessels had gathered in the Bay of Tankan. On the 25th Admiral Yamamoto gave the order to get under way.

---

[43] Gafenco, *op. cit.*

[44] From that date onwards the Germans redoubled their efforts in Tokyo to induce Japan to attack Russia.

[45] United Press despatch dated the 14th April 1941.

[46] Sherwood, *Roosevelt and Hopkins*, New York. 1948, p. 291.

On the 2nd December the Admiral telegraphed the agreed code words for the attack — "Scale Mount Nutaka". This message, together with the date of the attack — 7th December — was received by the squadron during its passage towards Pearl Harbour.

The plan was a very unusual one, and Admiral Onishi had been preparing it since the end of the previous February. The undertaking was momentous, for it entailed risking the fate of the élite of the Japanese navy in a single action. Admiral Yamamoto favoured the plan, but having been a naval attaché in Washington he had a high regard for the American navy. He therefore wished to leave nothing to chance. Before Admiral Kusaka could secure Yamamoto's approval of the operation he had to guarantee its secrecy, ensure the provisioning of the vessels on the high seas, and arrange for 350 planes and six aircraft carriers to cover the action of the navy.[47]

In Washington Admiral Nomura, the Japanese ambassador, continued his talks with Secretary of State Cordell Hull. Since the 15th November he had been accompained by ambassador Kurusu who had brought further instructions from Tokyo. The Japanese were striving to obtain a free hand in south east Asia, where the Americans were anxious to safeguard the "open door" policy. The talks seemed to be making no headway, but General Tojo, head of the Japanese government, had already fixed upon the 25th November as the last possible date for the signing of a treaty between the United States and Japan . . . After that date, war!

Since 1940 the American counter-espionage division had succeeded in deciphering the code used by the Japanese, and secret messages from Tokyo to the Japanese embassy in Washington very soon found their way to the desk of the Secretary of State. On the 5th November Cordell Hull learned that Tojo had settled with Nomura on the latest date for the terminating of negotiations.[48] The arrival of the second Japanese diplomat, Kurusu, coincided with the receipt of new instructions which, contrary to what Hull and Roosevelt had at first hoped, were no more favourable than the previous ones. Kurusu had orders to try to reach a conclusion by the 29th November at the latest; and, in the event of failure, to drag the negotiations on in order to facilitate the

[47] Cf. W. Lord: *Pearl Harbour*, 1958, p. 28, and M. Giuglaris, *Le Japon perd la guerre du Pacifique*, Paris, 1961. Both these works have made use of Japanese reports.
[48] Cf. Cordell Hull, *Memoirs*, pp. 1056–1074. See also Duroselle, *De Wilson à Roosevelt*, Colin, Paris, 1960, p. 291 et seq.

planned aero-naval operations, of which the main ingredient was surprise.

It is easier to understand now why Tojo gave his diplomats a time limit. In the event of disagreement, the order to set sail could be given on the 25th November. The 29th was more or less the latest date on which the order to attack could be cancelled. It seems clear that the decoded Japanese messages constituted a warning to Roosevelt that Japan's entry into the war was imminent. At nine o'clock in the evening of Saturday, the 6th December, Roosevelt addressed an appeal to the Emperor of Japan[49] with the object of avoiding recourse to war. On the same day he learned that Nomura had received orders to destroy all codes and secret documents.

At 9.30, while he was in the oval room of the White House with his friend Hopkins, Roosevelt received a visit from Commander L. R. Schultz, assistant naval aide-de-camp to the President. This officer brought him a copy of a new secret message from Tojo to Nomura. Commander Schultz gave an account of the facts before the Congress court of inquiry:[50]

Mr. Richardson. Now, what happened when you delivered these papers to the President? You remained there?

Commander Schultz. Yes, sir, I remained in the room.

Mr. Richardson. What happened?

Commander Schultz. The President read the papers, which took perhaps ten minutes. Then he handed them to Mr. Hopkins.

Mr. Richardson. How far away from the President was Mr. Hopkins sitting?

Commander Schultz. He was standing up pacing back and forth slowly, not more than ten feet away.

Mr. Richardson. Did the President read out loud when he was reading the papers?

Commander Schultz. I do not recall that he did.

Mr. Richardson. All right. Now go ahead and give us in detail just what occurred there, if you please, Commander.

Commander Schultz. Mr. Hopkins then read the papers and handed them back to the President. The President then turned towards Mr. Hopkins and said in substance — I am not sure of the exact words, but in substance, 'This means war.' Mr. Hopkins agreed and they discussed then for perhaps five minutes the situation of the Japanese forces, that is, their deployment, and —

Mr. Richardson. Can you recall what either of them said?

Commander Schultz. In substance I can. There are only a few words that I can definitely say I am sure of, but the substance of it was that — I believe Mr. Hopkins mentioned it first, that since war was imminent, the Japanese intended to strike when they were ready, at a moment when all was most opportune for them.

[49] Through Grew, United States ambassador to Japan.
[50] Sherwood, *Roosevelt and Hopkins*, p. 426 *et seq.*

The Chairman. When all was what?

Commander Schultz. When all was most opportune for that. That is, when their forces were most properly deployed for their advantage. Indo-China in particular was mentioned, because the Japanese forces had already landed there and there were implications of where they should move next.

The President mentioned a message that he had sent to the Japanese Emperor concerning the presence of Japanese troops in Indo-China, in effect requesting their withdrawal.

Mr. Hopkins then expressed a view that since war was undoubtedly going to come at the convenience of the Japanese it was too bad that we could not strike the first blow and prevent any sort of surprise. The President nodded and then said, in effect, 'No, we can't do that. We are a democracy and a peaceful people.' Then he raised his voice, and this much I remember definitely. He said, 'But we have a good record.'

The impression that I got was that we would have to stand on that record, we could not make the first overt move. We would have to wait until it came.

During this discussion there was no mention of Pearl Harbor. The only geographic name I recall was Indo-China. The time at which war might begin was not discussed, but from the manner of the discussion there was no indication that tomorrow was necessarily the day. I carried that impression away because it contributed to my personal surprise when the news did come.

Mr. Richardson. Was there anything said, Commander, with reference to the subject of notice or notification as a result of the papers that were being read?

Commander Schultz. There was no mention made of sending any further warning or alert. However, having concluded this discussion about war going to begin at the Japanese convenience, then the President said that he believed he would talk to Admiral Stark. He started to get Admiral Stark on the telephone. It was then determined, — I do not recall exactly, but I believe the White House operator told the President that Admiral Stark could be reached at the National Theater.

Mr. Richardson. Now, it was from what was said there that you draw the conclusion that that was what the White House operator reported?

Commander Schultz. Yes, sir. I did not hear what the operator said, but the National Theater was mentioned in my presence and the President went on to state, in substance, that he would reach the Admiral later, that he did not want to cause public alarm by having the Admiral paged or otherwise when in the theater where, I believe, the fact that he had a box reserved was mentioned and that if he had left suddenly he would surely have been seen because of the position which he held and undue alarm might be caused and the President did not wish that to happen because he could get him within perhaps another half an hour in any case.

Why did Hopkins not take some action at once? The President's close adviser was not by any means a man to postpone an important decision. He had never failed to support the President in his most daring undertakings, including lease-lend, assistance to Russia, and so on. Everything tends to suggest that he would have advised, had he guessed at the operation being prepared, immediate action to forestall Japan.

When Schultz left the President's office the conversation between Roosevelt and Hopkins continued, but no record was kept of it. We have therefore to depend upon the indirect testimony of Robert Sherwood, a close friend of Hopkins; Sherwood's objectiveness and integrity are beyond question. We have also to consider the information available to the President at that time.

On the 6th December the British had advised Roosevelt, through Winant, American ambassador in London, that a Japanese fleet was steering west in the direction of Indo-China and Siam — not Hawaii.[51] Furthermore, on the morning of the 7th December the American navy had a complete list of all shipping in the Pacific; according to this list the greater part of the Japanese fleet should still have been in Japanese waters.

It was known in London as well as in Washington that a conflict was imminent; but there was nothing to suggest that it would take place on the 7th December (the 8th for the Japanese). As far back as the 27th November Admiral Stark had put out a warning alerting all commanders in the Pacific. There was no indication whatever that Pearl Harbour was to be the objective.

Several witnesses are of the opinion that Roosevelt had a foreboding that an attack would take place within three days. It is not therefore surprising that he took the precaution of warning Admiral Stark. In contrast, Admiral Stark's reaction was slow and undecided. While the Admiral was at the theatre in Washington, Rear-Admiral R. A. Theobald, commanding the First Destroyer Flotilla, was dancing until midnight at the Pearl Harbour Pacific Club. He was never able to understand how it happened that he and his colleagues became the victims of that extraordinary surprise attack a few hours later.

When he did seek to understand he discovered, with some bitterness, that Admiral Stark did not warn General Marshall until nine o'clock in the morning. It happened that the General was taking a ride on his horse, and was not told of the imminence of the attack until 11.25 a.m.; only two hours before the Japanese attack. Marshall alerted Pearl Harbour at 12.01 hours by RCA cable, instead of using the telephone, or the wireless, or even the police; in other words, he used the slowest method of communication. General Marshall did not state that the fleet and air force should "clear the decks for action", but only that at 13.00 hours (7.30 a.m. Hawaiian time) an ultimatum would expire, after

[51] See Sherwood, *op. cit.*

which something indefinite would happen.[52] Marshall's message, received at the Pearl Harbour post office twenty-two minutes before the attack, did not, however, reach Admiral Kimmel — through a cyclist — until two hours after the departure of the last Japanese plane.

A much more serious fact was that when the court of inquiry tried to obtain the copy of Tojo's message — the one which Schultz had brought to the President — that message, the actual ultimatum to which Marshall referred, could not be traced. Admiral Theobald quickly came to the conclusion — and Roosevelt's political opponents echoed the same sentiments without insisting too much on details — that the President deliberately concealed the imminence of attack.

But was Tojo's ultimatum really that clear? And what was the purport of the conversation between Roosevelt and Stark when the Admiral returned from the theatre? If the President believed an attack would take place within three days, did he tell Stark to give the alarm immediately? If Stark had one or two days in which to take action, should he have roused everybody concerned on that Sunday morning? Did he really appreciate the significance of a further warning when the whole of the Pacific fleet was threatened?

Indeed, a surprise attack on Pearl Harbour would have suited the President's policy admirably. The Japanese raid transformed the American people into a single-minded nation; it put an end to the criticism of the Isolationists, and provided Roosevelt with a magnificent *casus belli*, because he had believed for many months that the United States was bound to come into the war.

But if we are to accept Admiral Theobald's theory we should have to reproach the President with Machiavellianism. Roosevelt was indeed a very shrewd and intelligent President who, a few weeks after Pearl Harbour, made the momentous decision to give priority to the European theatre of operations, despite the Japanese attack; but he was also the leader of land, sea and air forces, and it would have been detrimental to his interests to allow his fleet to be destroyed or reduced to inactivity for many months.[53]

Revisionists have endeavoured to accumulate evidence to establish a so-called "plot" by Roosevelt and his friends to provoke Japan, and

[52] Marshall said that he did not know the time the ultimatum was presented, but he ordered everybody to be on their guard. He meant also to imply, apparently, that he did not know exactly what the Japanese were preparing to do.

[53] Six ships were sunk, 2897 men were killed, 879 were wounded and 26 men were unaccounted for.

therefore to break into the war despite American public opinion. These accounts are prejudiced, and constitute no proof of any plot.[54] They reached the very depths of wrangling when they descended to unfounded suppositions. The historian has to be satisfied with the evidence of documents or, if necessary, prove that they are unsatisfactory. He cannot invent the missing links. The Pearl Harbour dossier, such as it is, does not allow us to draw any conclusion which might suggest that Roosevelt did not act in good faith.

[54] Duroselle, *De Wilson à Roosevelt: Politique extérieure des Etats-Unis (1912–1945),* 1960, contains a bibliography covering these events (pp. 478 and 479).

CHAPTER III

UNCONDITIONAL SURRENDER

1. Did any secret contact exist between Algiers and Vichy in November 1942?

2. Was the term "Unconditional Surrender" coined at Casablanca?

3. Did Mihailović offer resistance to the Germans?

4. Did Badoglio endeavour to surrender from the 3rd August 1943 onwards?

5. Did the French Resistance movement hold up the arrival of German reinforcements in June 1944?

6. Did the action of General von Choltitz facilitate the liberation of Paris?

7. Was the liberation of the Port of Antwerp made possible by the activities of Belgian Resistance?

8. Did Italian Resistance hamper the progress of the German army during the winter of 1944?

9. Did the U.S.S.R. deliberately bring about the failure of the Warsaw uprising?

10. Did the U.S.S.R. put any obstacle in the way of Japanese surrender?

1. The Secret Orders of Admiral Darlan (10th–13th November 1942)

On the 10th November 1942 Commander Jouannin informed Admiral Auphan, French Secretary of State for the Navy, that Admiral Darlan had retained, despite the specific terms of the armistice agreement of June 1940, a secret code which he was using for his own purposes. This code was known only to Jouannin and Admiral Battet, Darlan's permanent assistants.

Auphan was a staunch friend of Darlan's whom, moreover, he represented in Laval's cabinet. Auphan was delighted to learn this news, and immediately informed Marshal Pétain. This heaven-sent code was to enable Pétain and Darlan to maintain a secret liaison at a time when communication between them became almost impossible.

When the British and Americans made a landing in North Africa on the 8th November 1942 Admiral Darlan, who happened to be in

Algiers at that time,[1] was faced with an entirely new politico–military situation. His first reaction when he learned of the landing from Murphy during the night, just a few hours before the event, was a categorical refusal to give an order not to resist the landing. General Juin,Weygand's successor in North Africa, knew nothing about the landing either; he, however, gave his backing to Murphy's request. After a long discussion Darlan agreed at the very most to telegraph Pétain for new instructions.

At 8.45 a.m. a reply was received from Pétain:

You may take action and inform me accordingly. You know that I have every confidence in you.

Shortly afterwards Krug von Nidda, Germany's Consul General in Vichy, called on Laval, and proposed that he should declare war on England and the United States, and sign a sworn alliance with Germany. Laval, after consulting Pétain, refused categorically; to comply would have meant destroying his dream of some day effecting a compromise between the belligerents. Krug von Nidda then asked Laval to be in Munich on the 9th November at 11 p.m., where Hitler would be waiting to receive him.

Meanwhile, in Algiers, Darlan, armed with the blank cheque received from Pétain and urged on by Juin, signed the surrender of Algiers at 5.40 p.m., which eventually led to the naval battles of Casablanca and Oran.

On the 9th November Laval journeyed to Munich and, while he was crossing the Black Forest, Hitler ordered the occupation of the free zone and Corsica, and the despatch of a hundred bombers of the Luftwaffe to Tunisia. In Algiers on the same day Darlan continued his manoeuvring, very much aware that, if he did not order a cease-fire, he was threatened with harsh armistice terms at the hands of the American General Ryder.[2]

A continual exchange of telegrams went on all day long between Vichy and Algiers. Pétain neither approved nor disapproved the surrender of Algiers; he adhered to the orders already given, and did not contemplate any negotiation in the absence of Laval. One is inclined to feel that to the end Pétain preferred to avoid the occupation of the free zone, and was confident that Laval would appease the Führer.

---

[1] He had been to see his son who was sick. There is no evidence whatever to suggest that Darlan's presence in Algiers was anything but a coincidence.

[2] Aron, *Histoire de Vichy*, Paris, 1954, p. 553.

Darlan did not really know what to do, and he tried to gain time. At the end of the day he transmitted to Pétain the terms laid down by the Americans, and asked for instructions.

The 10th November was the day of decision. According to some of Pétain's loyal supporters (Trochu, Gibrat, Bouthillier, Lehideux, etc.) he was due to join Darlan in Algiers; but the Marshal refused to go — "A pilot must remain at the helm during a storm", he said. He was determined to hold out against the Germans. At ten o'clock General Clark made an urgent appeal to Juin and Darlan; he demanded a general armistice for the whole of North Africa.

The difference in character between these two men was emphasized by the events. Darlan was a true Gascon. He was sixty-one years of age, the son of a former minister, and he had spent a great deal of his life in a political atmosphere. His hour struck in 1940 when, at the head of a State within a State, "his" navy began to occupy a leading role in the political game. Blending technique with politics, he schemed ceaselessly, assisting Pétain to thrust Laval aside; not hesitating for all that to be guilty of serious faults of collaboration. He considered that he had the future mapped out; he imagined that with the support of a band of efficient and loyal naval officers he could play several games at once. Thus, on the 10th November, in Algiers, he continued his political game, confident of the future despite the obvious.

Juin, on the other hand, clearly appreciated the position of the A.F.N., and knew that it must swing to the side of the Allies. Juin was fifty-four. His father had been a policeman in Bône, Algeria. Juin sensed the reactions of North Africa, and did not believe that those in authority should go against the sentiments of the people. Politically he was also a realist. In May 1940 he had manifested his qualities of military leadership at the battle of Lille. Having been taken prisoner and sent to Germany, he was repatriated at the request of Marshal Pétain; the Marshal appointed this valued leader to replace Weygand, who was dismissed under pressure by Germany. After being summoned to Berlin by Goering on the 15th December 1941, Juin simply transmitted to Vichy the demands that had been put to him, and thus avoided committing himself. On the 10th November 1942 he felt convinced that the British and Americans had the upper hand in Africa, and he urged Darlan to yield.

Clark was not interested in what Marshal Pétain was thinking; he insisted on the order to cease fire, and if Darlan would not sign it he would have it signed by Giraud who had just arrived. Juin made it clear to Darlan that Pétain could not possibly give him a clear reply, and that in a few hours he — Darlan — would be out of the game. The Admiral yielded to Juin's reasoning, and signed a military document which Juin at once despatched to all the A.F.N. It was an order to cease fire and to resist the Germans.

Pétain's reaction was to send another telegram: "I gave instructions to defend Africa. I stand by those instructions. Pétain".

Darlan was dumbfounded. He replied to Vichy: "Your message received. I am cancelling my order, and am giving myself up as prisoner. Darlan".

Juin did not, in fact, countermand the order, and it was then that the secret code was used for the first time. At 3.15 p.m. Auphan sent Darlan a secret telegram after consulting Pétain, Jardel, principal private secretary, and Ménétrel, who was a doctor and the Marshal's secretary: "You must understand that this order was necessary to the negotiations under way. Auphan".[3] Auphan was trying to explain away Pétain's telegram, thereby diminishing its effect. The original of this telegram, as well as two others that followed, were destroyed; we have, therefore, followed the version given by the principal witness, Commander Archambaud, who personally coded the telegrams.

According to Jardel[4] the telegram ran: "You have all my confidence. Act for the best. I leave the interests of the Empire in your hands".

This text was, of course, false, but it was none the less accepted by Aron.[5] According to Ménétrel, who did not remember the exact words, the sense was: "Take no account of my messages and official instructions despatched under duress. Am in full agreement with you".[6] The Ménétrel text, published by Kammerer, is also false, but these inaccurate texts have formed the basis of several historical works.[7]

[3] Deposition by Commander Archambaud on the 9th August 1945. J. O., p. 280. The same wording is in Auphan, Histoire de mes trahisons, p. 281.

[4] At his trial on the 14th March 1947 — five years after the events.

[5] Aron, Histoire de Vichy, Paris, 1954, p. 560. This author bases his account above all on the files of the Haute Cour de Justica.

[6] See Dr Ménétrel's notes in Nougères, Le véritable procès du Maréchal Pétain Paris, 1955. See especially Kammerer, La passion de la flotte française, Paris, 1951, p. 408.

[7] In particular by Admiral Docteur, in La grande énigme de la guerre, Darlan, Paris, 1949; L. D. Girard-Montoire, Verdun Diplomatique, Paris, 1948; General Hering, in Révision, Paris; Chamine, in La querelle des généraux, Paris, 1952. The text was also sustained by General Bergeret during his trial on the 25th November 1948.

Indeed, the depositions by Archambaud and Auphant prove that the free hand given to Darlan on the 8th November 1942 was never confirmed; but he did receive a message softening down Pétain's order to resist. The 10th November was a dramatic day in Vichy, where Pétain learned that Laval had given in to Hitler too quickly, especially with regard to Tunisia. Laval telephoned from Munich requesting that no decision be reached in his absence." But Pétain was furious, and whilst at lunch with Auphan he talked of having Laval arrested on his return.

During the morning of the 11th November the Wehrmacht invaded the French free zone, and Weygand and Auphan asked Pétain to protest. Rochat, Laval's assistant, told the Marshal that reprisals would be taken against the civil population if the government gave its support to the slightest reluctance to comply, and he suggested they should await the return of Laval.

It was then that Pétain, apparently offended by Darlan's action, nominated General Noguès as his "sole representative in North Africa".

Auphan returned to the use of the secret code, and at 11.50 a.m. telegraphed to Darlan:

"It is only because we assume that you are held prisoner that you have not been appointed as the Marshal's representative in Africa. Auphan.[8]

Once again the tension was reduced; the telegram was a further attempt at an explanation, but it certainly did not cancel the appointment of Noguès. The wording of this telegram has also been the subject of many variations, either inaccurate or entirely false. In any case, it settled nothing, and only added to the confusion as to who really was in authority in Algiers. In Morocco Noguès himself signed an armistice with the Americans on the 11th November; and when, on the 12th, he learned the contents of the secret telegram, he was quite at a loss. During the evening of that day he telegraphed Pétain informing him that the armistice he had signed safeguarded the existing political and administrative structure, and he suggested that Darlan be again nominated to supreme direction of affairs.

According to Auphan, Pétain favoured the appointment of Darlan; but he wanted Laval to agree, and Laval on his side was anxious to secure the consent of the German authorities, which was obviously out of the question. The Marshal was unable to extricate himself from

[8] Archambaud's deposition.

this impasse, and Auphan took it upon himself to send a final secret telegram to Darlan:

"Close agreement exists between the Marshal and President Laval; but before a reply is sent to you the occupation authorities are being consulted".[9]

The wording of this telegram also has been presented under numerous versions in the works already referred to. Most of the variations are merely interpretations.

Such is the history of the secret contacts between Vichy and Algeria in November 1942. We have seen that, although the historical fact of the secret telegrams is not in dispute, there exists no trace of the actual documents. The originals were destroyed, and de Gaulle has enjoyed himself bantering about these telegrams which no one has ever seen.

Everything has depended upon the evidence of Archambaud and Auphan. The revisionists made quite a good story out of the events, and have even claimed that the return of North Africa into the war was decided by Marshal Pétain; this in itself would suffice to prove the continuity of the national policy of the Vichy government. We have seen that no such thing occurred,[10] and General Schmitt has shown this decisively in a remarkable critical study. We are forced to rely upon the only two direct witnesses — those who despatched the telegrams. During the course of a discussion on the 2nd June 1957 Admiral Auphan stated:

The American chargé d'affaires in Vichy, ambassador Tuck, who succeeded Admiral Leahy, assured us that they would not intervene in Africa without warning us in advance. We expected something to happen in the spring of 1943.

The 1942 landing was a complete surprise. The French had not been warned; they could only obey the orders they had received, so that the Americans ran on to our bayonets. Despite German pressure I endeavoured to bring the hostilities to an end in order that some policy might be formulated. Such was the object of my telegrams. It has been alleged that the telegrams were too brief to be understandable, but they have to be viewed as a whole, and in relation to other exchanges, such as the mission of Commander Bataille. Further, I never found time to write stylishly; and the messages were transmitted by telegraph centres in Lyons or Marseilles which, from the 11th November onwards, were occupied by the Germans. If the French Admiralty can find no trace of them it is because I gave instructions to destroy everything on account of the complete occupation of France by the Germans. There were not three telegrams but four,[11] as well as the replies from

[9] Archambaud's deposition. Auphan resigned after despatching this telegram.
[10] Schmitt, *Les accords secrets franco-britanniques de Novembre–Décembre 1940 : Histoire ou mystification?*, Paris, 1957.
[11] The fourth announced Auphan's resignation.

Darlan; these are never quoted, but they are none the less important. The telegrams were coded in my office by an officer who was later arrested by the police. He is at present living in retirement in Nevers, and is available to give evidence.[11]

Once these telegrams were decoded they were the means of rallying the A. O. F. to the support of Darlan, and so continuing the war. The fact that the wording differs from one witness to another is due to our having considered it prudent to destroy the originals; the persons concerned quoted from memory, and merely retained the general sense. I succeeded in finding the exact text only because I took the precaution to write it out immediately after my resignation, and bury it in a box which my family saved after the investigations they had to endure.[13]

It thus becomes clear that the revisionists are trying to read too much into the wording of the telegrams. We must, however, take account of the written deposition of Juin at Pétain's trial:

I can state that the two telegrams sent by Admiral Auphan were a great help to us. They enabled us to soothe many consciences tormented by their oath of allegiance and still uncertain as to what action they should take.

The secret telegrams do not, therefore, prove that the Marshal agreed to the secession of the A.F.N in November 1942. In fact, the telegrams had only an indirect influence on the political and military activities of the A.F.N. The very existence of the secret telegrams, that is to say, of the secret contact with the Marshal, allowed Darlan and Juin to avail themselves of the fact, without the necessity to show the documents in order to rally to themselves and the Allies many influential people, including members of the administration, who remained loyal to Marshal Pétain.

2. Unconditional Surrender

On the 24th January 1943, on the termination of the Casablanca Conference, Roosevelt summoned the Press, and told them that he and Churchill had decided to accept from Germany, Japan and Italy nothing short of unconditional surrender.

According to Roosevelt[14] it was on the 18th January 1943, while he was lunching with Harry Hopkins and Prime Minister Churchill, that the term "unconditional surrender" was born. His father was also there, and it was he apparently who first used the words. Churchill considered them as he was eating; he frowned, thought again, and then

[12] Archambaud.
[13] Taken at the meeting of the Société d'Histoire Moderne.
[14] E. Roosevelt, *As he saw it*. New York, 1946.

smiled. "Perfect", he said at length. He added that he could almost hear the howls of Goebbels and all the pack.

On his return to London Churchill was criticized for using the term, because it was considered dangerous and contrary to the traditional principles of Anglo-German relations; but he said that Roosevelt was the author of the expression.[15] We may naturally wonder whether Roosevelt's formula was an improvisation, a kind of slogan chosen lightheartedly. It would also be interesting to know whether the term "unconditional surrender" prolonged the war. On the first point Robert Sherwood, an intimate friend of Hopkins, has shed some light:

I wrote Winston Churchill asking him if he had discussed the unconditional surrender statement with Roosevelt before the press conference at Casablanca, and his reply was as follows:

'I heard the words "unconditional surrender" for the first time from the President's lips at the Conference. It must be remembered that at that moment no one had a right to proclaim that Victory was assured. Therefore Defiance was the note. I would not myself have used these words, but I immediately stood by the President and have frequently defended the decision. It is false to suggest that it prolonged the war. Negotiation with Hitler was impossible. He was a maniac with supreme power to play his hand out to the end, which he did; and so did we.'

Roosevelt himself absolved Churchill from all responsibility for the statement. Indeed, he suggested that it was an unpremeditated one on his own part. He said, 'We had so much trouble getting those two French generals together that I thought to myself that this was as difficult as arranging the meeting of Grant and Lee — and then suddenly the press conference was on, and Winston and I had no time to prepare for it, and the thought popped into my head that they had called Grant "Old Unconditional Surrender" and the next thing I knew, I had said it.'

Although Roosevelt implied that he went into the press conference at Casablanca unprepared, Hopkins wrote in his description of the conference that Roosevelt consulted notes as he talked. The photographs of the conference show him holding several pages which had been carefully prepared in advance. Those pages contained the following paragraph:

'The President and the Prime Minister, after a complete survey of the world war situation, are more than ever determined that peace can come to the world only by a total elimination of German and Japanese war power. This involves the simple formula of placing the objective of this war in terms of an unconditional surrender by Germany, Italy and Japan. Unconditional surrender by them means a reasonable assurance of world peace, for generations. Unconditional surrender means not the destruction of the German populace, nor of the Italian or Japanese populace, but does mean the destruction of a philosophy in Germany, Italy and Japan which is based on the conquest and subjugation of other peoples.'

[15] It should be added that on the 19th January Churchill telegraphed the War Cabinet for approval of the term "unconditional surrender". He wished to exclude Italy, but the British War Cabinet was unanimous in approving its application to Germany, Italy and Japan.

What Roosevelt was saying was that there would be no negotiated peace, no compromise with Naziism and Fascism, no "escape clauses" provided by another Fourteen Points which could lead to another Hitler. (The ghost of Woodrow Wilson was again at his shoulder.) Roosevelt wanted this uncompromising purpose to be brought home to the American people and the Russians and the Chinese, and to the people of France and other occupied nations, and he wanted it brought home to the Germans — that neither by continuance of force nor by contrivance of a new spirit of sweet reasonableness could their present leaders gain for them a soft peace. He wanted to ensure that when the war was won it would stay won.

Undoubtedly his timing of the statement at Casablanca was attributable to the uproar over Darlan and Peyrouton and the liberal fears that this might indicate a willingness to make similar deals with a Goering in Germany or a Matsuoka in Japan.

It is a matter of record that the Italians and the Japanese were ready to accept unconditional surrender as soon as effective force was applied to their homelands. Whether they might have done so sooner, or whether the Germans might ever have done so, under any circumstances whatsoever, are matters for eternal speculation. One thing about Roosevelt's famous statement is certain, however — he had his eyes wide open when he made it.[16]

With regard to the second point — whether the use of the expression actually prolonged the war — it seems that the Germans were unaware of the origin of the statement "unconditional surrender". For the Germans, as for the Allied military leaders, the only thing that really mattered was the statement itself and what it implied. Since the end of the war authors have tried to show that the formula did prolong the war, because it stood in the way of national resistance, especially within Germany, from manifesting itself. Weizsäcker[17] was quick to say that the formula prolonged the war, but he made no attempt to prove it.

In fact, although Goebbels made use of the formula for propaganda purposes, he did not think of advising the Führer in 1943, after Casablanca, to negotiate with the west.[18] It was also after 1943 that the conspiracies against Hitler gradually developed until they reached their peak in 1944.

And although Roosevelt's colleagues criticized the statement, it was above all because the President adopted it without having consulted them beforehand; nor did they think at the time of the reactions of the

[16] Sherwood, *Roosevelt and Hopkins*, 1948, p. 695 *et seq.* After Casablanca the Allies professed their adherence to the formula. Churchill did so on the 30th June 1943, and Roosevelt on three occasions in 1943 — 12th February, 25th August and 24th December.

[17] Secretary of State for Foreign Affairs.

[18] Marwell and Fraenkel, *Goebbels*, London, 1960, and *The Goebbels Diaries*. London, 1948, pp. 298, 299, 302, 386, 387.

German opposition. There is, therefore, no evidence at present available to allow anyone to conclude that the statement "unconditional surrender" had the effect of prolonging the war, or that any American statesman advised the President to follow a different course.

The most significant factor immediately following the Casablanca statement was the position taken up by Stalin, who, on the 13th July 1943, created the Committee of Free Germany. The U.S.S.R. thus made a distinction between the Nazis and the Germans, a distinction which Soviet propaganda emphasized more plainly day after day.[19]

While Roosevelt was hardening American opinion towards Germany, Stalin was opening the door to reconciliation with a view to the post-war era. But the generous attitude of the Soviet Union by no means shortened the war in the east; and this is an additiona largument in favour of the assumption that the Casablanca statement, while clarifying the relations between the Allies and the Axis, did not have any proven effect on the duration of the war.

3. The Treachery of Mihailović

The Yugoslav campaign lasted twelve days. The German forces overwhelmed the small Yugoslav army, and King Peter, with his government under the leadership of Simović, had to flee to Cairo and then to London.

The Germans set up a docile government in Yugoslavia, and made General Nedić president. But the wooded and mountainous regions of the country lent themselves admirably to ambush, camouflage and guerilla warfare. A Serbian officer named Colonel Mihailović determined, in accordance with Serbian army traditions, to resist the dominion of the occupying power. In May 1941, instead of throwing down his arms and surrendering to captivity, he sought refuge in the mountains of Ravna Gora. There he established the Chetnik movement, and was very quickly joined by a number of officers and non-commissioned officers,[20] who supported him in his aim to align Yugoslavia on the side of the Allies.

Mihailović's idea was to create a cadre of officers who, on the eventual day of insurrection, would be able to draw a great part of the

---

[19] *European Resistance Movements 1939–45,* Pergamon Press, Oxford, 1960 and 1964.

[20] Twenty-six, according to thε historians of the Yugoslav partisan war.

population into a general uprising against the occupying power. He was a professional officer and loyal to his king; military matters were his sole interest. He aspired only to the re-establishing of the Yugoslav régime, represented by the Karageorges dynasty, which implied the political ascendancy of the Serbs. There exists no proof that Mihailović intended to set up a Serbian Fascist régime, or that he intended to fight the Croats. In conformity with the conservative spirit of the Yugoslav army of 1940 he wished simply to re-establish the political régime in Yugoslavia just as it had existed on the departure of King Peter.

Mihailović had no desire to operate a perpetual guerilla warfare which he knew would entail cruel reprisals, out of all proportion to the results achieved. He intended to train his army, to conserve his resources with the object of a general uprising, without undue speed or running the risk of premature operations. Josip Brož, known as Tito, was Secretary General of the Yugoslav Communist Party. Like Mihailović he was inspired with the impulse to resist the German occupation. With a handful of comrades who had formerly served with him in the international brigade in Spain, he decided in the early days of the German occupation (May 1941) to set up a partisan movement.[21] It has not been proved that the U.S.S.R. fostered this movement in its early days.

It is none the less true that Tito had political and military ambitions; political in the sense that he was anxious to turn the war of liberation into a rising of the proletariat against the middle classes, and military in his determination to conduct a continual guerilla warfare with all the means in his power. Tito also wished to change the political basis of the Yugoslav government by giving it a federative form. His partisan movement, despite its origin and its Communist tendencies, appealed to all the political and moral forces of the nation.

From July 1941 violence began to break out in the towns, resulting in reprisals and localized revolt; but they were serious. These activities enabled the partisans to set up immediate new political régimes in the regions which were provisionally "liberated".

One historically important event hastened the launching of the insurrection contemplated by the Yugoslav Communist Party (PCY): that was the German invasion of the U.S.S.R. on the 22nd June 1941. On the 27th a military committee was formed, and Tito was nominated Com-

---

[21] Cf. *European Resistance Movements*, p. 303. Lieutenant-Colonel Brajusković describes the origin of the partisan movement.

mander-in-Chief. On the 4th July the PCY central committee decided to launch the uprising, undoubtedly to bring immediate aid to the Red Army, although this purpose was never admitted. These conflicting aims were bound to lead to a quarrel between the Chetniks and the Partisans; but the PCY, whose aim was to group together all the national forces, wished to reach an understanding with Mihailović. The first contact had been made by the Partisan leaders in central Serbia during August 1941, but the meeting achieved no result, because Mihailovć expressed his disapproval of the premature measures being taken by the Partisans.

At these talks Ranković represented the Partisans. According to his account Mihailović had no desire to take any action until the Allies had regained the initiative in military operations, and were able to contribute direct aid to Yugoslav resistance.[22]

On the 19th September 1941 a delegation from Tito's Partisan Committee of National Liberation, led by him personally, met Mihailović at Struganika.[23] They reached an understanding on a *modus operandi*, under which the spoils of war would be divided equally between the two movements, and the free choice of the liberated populations in favour of Chetniks or Partisans would be respected.

This understanding was not really deep-rooted, and as early as October an event occurred which endangered relations. On the 2nd August Tito had telegraphed the Komintern, in Moscow, to announce the first successes of the rebellion. But the Soviet government, preoccupied with the German advance towards Moscow, was ill-informed concerning events in Yugoslavia.[24] Mihailović on the other hand had succeeded in establishing a radio link with London and the Simović government.[25] On the 26th June and the 2nd July 1941 Churchill and Eden had already received the Yugoslav President and Foreign Minister, and promised them that Yugoslavia would be reconstituted after victory had been won. Encouraged by this support the Yugoslav government broadcast on the London radio on the 22nd July an appeal to the Yugoslav people, urging them to avoid premature encounters and to await a call from London. This attitude was in perfect harmony with the views of the Chetniks.

---

[22] See D. Plenca, in *European Resistance Movements*, 1939–45, Milan Conference, 1961 Pergamon Press, Oxford, 1963, p. 497.

[23] B. Lazitch, *La tragédie du Général D. Mihaïlovitch*, Yverdon, Haut Pays, 1946, p. 35.

[24] It was not until the 23rd August 1941 that *Pravda* announced the setting up of the Partisan movement.

[25] Via Malta, in September 1941, through the Peterson system.

The information received in London[26] influenced the Simović government to invest Mihailović with great authority to act in its name. Within a few days the Chetnik leader was promoted General, Commander-in-Chief in Yugoslavia, and later Minister for War. At the same time Simović sent him from London very precise intructions: "Await the signal for co-ordinated action. Meanwhile do not provoke the enemy unless absolutely necessary".

At the beginning of October a military mission commanded by an Englishman, Captain Bill Hudson, was landed at Ravna Gora with the object of establishing permanent liaison. The Partisans had taken possession of Uzice, in western Serbia, and there they ran a Bank, a printing office and an armaments factory. This was a source of anxiety to the Chetniks, because the town happened to be in the centre of their sphere of activities. The Germans were determined to crush the revolt, and despatched strong forces to the regions liberated by the Partisans.

It is a fact that several Chetnik groups, taking advantage of the difficulties of the Partisans, attempted to retake Uzice. Whether this action was or was not decided upon by Mihailović has never been proved.

General Simović then paid a visit to Maiski, Soviet ambassador in London. He saw Maiski on the 28th October and the 4th November, and requested that the U.S.S.R. approach the Partisans with a view to bringing them under the jurisdiction of Mihailović. Simović subsequently saw Anthony Eden, and asked him to make similar approaches to Moscow.[27] On the 17th November the Yugoslav ambassador in Moscow paid a visit to Vyshinsky for the same purpose. On the 18th Simović repeated his request to Maiski; and Stafford Cripps, the British ambassador in Moscow, brought the matter up again with the Soviet Defence Minister.

The precise reaction of the Soviet government to these approaches is not known. According to certain sources Stalin deprecated the excessive Communist tendencies of the partisan movement. Whether he censured Tito and advised him to throw in his lot with Mihailović, we do not know.

Whatever the case may be, on the 25th October 1941 when the Partisan forces surrounded the G.H.Q. at Ravna Gora, after the events at

---

[79] In his messages Mihailović probably drew attention to the Communist menace.
[80] From the unpublished reminiscences of Simović.

Uzice, Tito met Mihailović once more, and they endeavoured to reach an understanding. Historians of the Chetnik movement speak of this meeting at Bragići as an outburst of mutual castigation;[28] but historians of the Partisan movement claim that the two leaders reached a partial understanding.[29]

> The meeting took place in a spacious country house. In the centre of the room stood a large table, on one side of which sat Tito and his companions, while Draže and his adherents, including his political adviser, Dragisha Vasić, and his second in command, Lieutenant-Colonel Pavlović, sat on the other side. Our eight bodyguards, holding their machine guns, stood behind us, and those of Draže Mihailović stood along the wall behind him. Our boys were young and beardless, though some wore moustaches; all the others had long beards.[30]

The Partisans suggested to Mihailović the signing of a twelve-point covenant, to cover combined operations against the Germans and traitors, a single command, the sharing of the spoils of war, and so on. The negotiations proceeded laboriously. Mihailović showed Tito the Chetnik positions on a map, and gave details of the numerical strength of his forces. During the meeting a young lieutenant arrived from Valjevo, and he was called in to give information about the forces situated in the village.

> A young man in uniform entered, and saluted in faultless style. Mihailović asked him 'How many men have we in Valjevo, Lieutenant?'
> 'Two, Colonel,' he replied.
> Draže gave him a withering look. 'Please do not joke'.
> 'There are exactly two, Colonel.'
> 'Get out at once,' roared Mihailović.
> On the 2nd November Mihailović telegraphed London:
> 'I have become reconciled with the Communists. Peace cannot last very long because they do not wish to give us Cacak and Uzice. The munitions factory at Uzice is of the greatest importance to our followers. I fear, therefore, that we shall be compelled to occupy the town by force. We must impede the strengthening of the Communist movement'.[31]

The split between the Chetniks and the Partisans thus became complete. From December 1941 the British maintained a constant flow of

[28] B. Lazitch, *La tragédie du Général D. Mihaïlovitch*, Yverdon, Haut Pays, 1946 p. 35.

[29] Dedijer, *With Tito Through The War : Partisan's Diary*, London, 1951, p. 40. MacLean (*Eastern Approaches*, London, 1949) also gives an account of the meeting; but he was not present.

[30] Dedijer, *ibid*.

[31] Cf. Plenca in *European Resistance Movements* Oxford 1964, p. 497.

supplies to the Chetnik forces; arms and money were sent regularly, and propaganda was undertaken on their behalf.

The Partisans on their side tried to obtain similar aid from Moscow. They made repeated appeals to the Komintern; but the Soviet government, absorbed in its great national war, was ill-informed concerning the conflict in Yugoslavia, and it was not until April 1942 that it began to give support to the Partisans. The Komintern had no desire to take sides, and it sent two replies to the Partisans.

The first merely stated that the policy of the U.S.S.R. towards the Yugoslav resistance movement was dependent upon the Soviet relations with London and Washington. Moscow was not inclined to believe the collaborationist accusations alleged against the Chetniks. The second stated that the policy of the PCY included certain sectarian deviations from Communist principles. This policy must be modified.

The Yugoslav government in London continued its efforts with the Soviet to bring Tito to the side of Mihailović. Russia, however, did not make her position really clear; but the Soviet government offered to send a liaison mission to Mihailović, a proposal which was not accepted. The truth is that Moscow knew well that the Chetniks were not very active at a time when any diversion in the Balkans might alleviate German pressure on the Russian front.

Mihailović was above all anxious to develop his contacts with the western Allies;[32] Tito, on the other hand, paid scarcely any heed to the warnings from Moscow, and so organized his forces as to enable him to pass from a war of ambush to a war of movement.

In April 1942 four brigades of Partisans crossed Yugoslavia, going from Montenegro to Serbia, back to Montenegro, and then in the direction of Bosnia. The guerilla tactics of these brigades inflicted very severe losses on the Germans and Italians. Just when they were on the point of being surrounded, they broke off the battle, vanished, and renewed their attacks in a neighbouring province.

It was a costly struggle. Of a force of 20,000 Partisans nearly half were either killed or wounded by the Germans in the operations.[33]

The Chetniks also increased the number of their forces, but, in accordance with their leader's instructions, they avoided a head-on clash.

[32] Wilson, in *Eight Years Overseas (1939-1947)* has told the story of British liaison missions.
[33] *Ibid.* See Brajusković regarding operations carried out by the Partisans.

The end of 1942 marked the decisive period. After the German army had been stopped at Stalingrad the U.S.S.R. prepared to throw the Germans back. Once more the Soviet government began to show a lively interest in territory that had traditional links with Russia.

Hitler grew uneasy about the Yugoslav uprising; he feared an Allied attempt to land in Yugoslavia. At the end of November he received in Winitsa Generals Ler and Pavelić, the leading statesmen in Croatia, and ordered them to crush Yugoslav resistance. On the 18th and 19th December, while in Rastenburg with Ribbentrop and Ciano, Hitler gave his instructions to the German and Italian Chiefs of Staff. On the 16th February 1943 he wrote to the Duce:

If an Allied landing occurs anywhere in the Balkans, Duce, the Communists and the forces under Mihailović, as well as all other Comitadji bands, will at once unite to support our enemies by attacking German and Italian troops.

I regard it as very unfortunate, Duce, that, after our arms have conquered all this territory, local political factions should now raise up organized formations, armed and prepared to turn against us when the opportunity arises. In support of this I could show you documents whose authenticity I can personally guarantets and whose meaning cannot be suppressed by statements from unofficial sources. The documents contain ample proof of the wiles of these people; they reveal an undying hatred of Germany, but perhaps an even greater hatred of Italy.

The extent of the rebel organizations under Tito is a source of anxiety and amazement. We have little time at our disposal to suppress a revolt if we wish to avoid the danger of an attack in our rear by an Anglo-Saxon landing in the Balkans.

I must insist most strongly, Duce, that you give the necessary instructions for prompt and flexible co-operation to be established between our local commanders on the spot, as well as co-ordination in using all the means at our disposal.

Apart from the operations at present being conducted against the Communists, h regard the long term plans which Mihailović's partisans are formulating to anni-Iilate or disarm your own forces in Herzegovina and Montenegro as especially dangerous, together with the progress of the Anglo-Saxons in their scheme to establish a controlled link between the Communists and Mihailovitć's partisans to our disadvantage.

In any case, the liquidation of the Mihailović movement is no longer an easy task in view of the forces at present at his command, and the number of Chetniks who possess arms. To begin with we must put a stop to the delivery of arms and material. Formations outside the territory under Mihailovitć's control must be disarmed unit by unit. Areas under the control of armed bands must then be encircled cautiously, so as to weaken their resistance by lack of food, arms and munitions. Ultimately the remainder of their forces may then be annihilated by concentrated attacks.

If, Duce, it proves impossible to disarm both the Communists and the Chetniks and really to pacify the country, a revolt will again break out in the event of an Allied landing; lines of communication with the Peloponnesus will be cut, and our few German divisions will be forced to fight against the Communists and the,

Chetniks. The Italian forces alone cannot prevent a landing in the Peloponnesus or in the Adriatic.

It is my opinion, Duce, that there are certain tasks there cannot possibly be brought to a successful issue purely by political skill. Force must be used, whatever the cost in human lives. The pacification of the Balkan regions is one of those tasks.

It seems that Hitler dreaded Mihailović as much as he did Tito. There is no doubt, however, that some of the Chetnik leaders established contact with the Germans. Hagen[34] mentions that Kosta Pecianac, whose attitude was extremely anti-Communist, was backed by the Germans, and it appears that a certain amount of bargaining went on between them. He points out that Dr Mirko Kosić, a director of the Serbian National Bank, had a meeting with General Nedić with the object of studying how the Chetnik movement might be financed; but Hagen adds that nothing came of the discussion. Leverkuhn,[35] a colleague of Canaris in south-east Europe, produces reasons for the German contacts with the Chetniks, but puts forward no definite proofs.[36]

In contrast, the attitude of the British towards the Chetniks was somewhat ambiguous. Their liaison mission under Colonel Bailey kept them well informed, and the Yugoslav army of liberation occupied a place within the scheme of their European strategy. While Churchill refused to give Stalin his second front, he expressed dissatisfaction with the activities of the Chetniks. Later on he contemplated an Allied landing in the Balkans, which Stalin and Roosevelt did not want; and on the 11th and 21st January 1943 Eden and Jovanovitć, the new Yugoslav President, discussed the Yugoslav military problem in this light.

Did Eden, with a view to future negotiations, really ask Mihailović to cease all attacks against the German occupying forces?[37] And, while all this was going on, how could Commander Peter Boy, the British military adviser, have expressed the desire that Mihailović's forces be immediately made effective to attack the Germans? And again, did the British intend to associate Mihailović with the Allies at the moment of their landing?

[34] Hagen, *Die Geheime Front Organisation : Personen und Aktionen des deutschen Geheimdienstes*, Zurich, 1950, p. 247. English translation — *The Secret Front*, New York, 1954.

[35] Leverkuhn, *German Military Intelligence*, New York, 1954, p. 151.

[36] During Nedić's trial (from documents quoted at Nuremberg, VII, 249) he stated that early in September 1941 a delegation from Mihailovic contacted him with a view to opening up negotiations. Money was advanced with German approval.

[37] Cf. Plencain, *European Resistance Movements*, p. 447.

It is impossible to provide definite answers to these questions because evidence is lacking. In the spring of 1944 a new British mission arrived in Yugoslavia; it was commanded by Brigadier MacLean, and attached to Tito's general staff. The British were just as eager as the Russians to follow closely the development of the Communist Partisan movement. On the 27th May another military mission arrived under the command of Captain Deakin.

The accounts furnished by MacLean and Deakin, which were welcomed in London, demonstrated the efficiency of Partisan activities. According to MacLean the Partisans numbered approximately 150,000 in 1943 — a very considerable force. There is no evidence to suggest — and this has been confirmed by Deakin[38] — that the British had any intention of charging Mihailović with the task of "liquidating" the Communist resistance movement. On the other hand, a letter from the Duce to the Führer, dated the 9th March, 1943, indicates the General attitude of the Germans and Italians:

Your minister, von Ribbentrop, has probably informed you, Führer, of the conversation we had on the subject of the Partisans and the Chetniks. We agreed absolutely that both the Partisans and the Chetniks are enemies of the Axis; and that they would be prepared, particularly in the event of an Allied landing, to make common cause with our adversaries. If this happened we should be placed in a very difficult position.

In various localities several thousand Chetniks have been provided with arms by leaders of Italian units, and they are able to conduct a guerilla type of warfare for which, like all Balkan races, they are especially suited. Up to the present the Chetniks have energetically opposed the Partisans. In the circumstances, I called Generals Roatta and Brizio-Piroli to Rome, and I gave them the following instructions:

(a) No further distribution of arms is to be made to the Chetniks.

(b) They are to be disarmed when the Partisans, as an armed movement, cease to be dangerous — allowing for the fact that brigandage, of a more or less political nature, will always remain an inherent disease in these parts.

(c) General Brizio-Piroli has been instructed to make contact with the O.K.W., so that we may arrive at some common arrangement as to our attitude towards General Mihailović's movement.

Although the Partisan radio refers to Mihalović as a traitor, he is none the less our enemy since he is War Minister of the Yugoslav government in London. I am very well aware of this individual's plans for territorial revision at Italy's expense.

I have just now received a report alleging that German forces who have made contact with the Chetniks in the upper valley of the Narenta have agreed to

---

[38] Based on an interview between F. Deakin and J. de Launay in Milan on the 27th March 1961.

collaborate with them, and have provided the Chetniks with cartridges and hand grenades.[39]

There seems to be no doubt whatever that at this period the Axis and Chetnik forces were in contact. On the 23rd January 1943 Tito sent a note to London, Washington and Moscow protesting against the collaboration existing between the Chetniks and the Axis.

It was the reports from MacLean and Deakin that gradually led Churchill to adopt a definite attitude with regard to the Partisans. He considered that the military strength of the Partisan forces was such that they should be given the utmost support, and that politics should be subordinated to military requirements.[40]

From June to December 1943 London continued to send arms to the Chetniks as well as to the Partisans; but events were precipitated by the landing of the Allies in Italy and the surrender of the Italians. It was not the Chetniks but the Partisans who disarmed four Italian divisions; and London began to lose patience with the inaction of Mihailović's forces. As a result of Eden's enquiries the Yugoslavs made changes in their émigré cabinet. Jovanović hoped that Mihailović would take advantage of the Italian capitulation to regain mastery of the situation. But nothing of the sort happened.

On the 28th November 1943, at Teheran, the Allies unanimously decided to give their backing to the Partisans. On Churchill's return journey he stopped at Cairo on the 10th December, and told King Peter that Great Britain had decided to recall her mission to Mihailović, and terminate the aid accorded to him. From that date Mihailović was utterly abandoned by the Allies, and with the despatch of a Soviet military mission to Tito in February 1944, the recognition of the Partisan movement became official.[41]

An important naval aviation base was set up by the Allies at Vis for the sole purpose of aiding the Partisans. King Peter himself parted company with the most reactionary of the émigrés, and on the 25th August 1944 he relieved Mihailović of his functions. On the 12th September he ordered the Chetniks to join forces with the Partisans.[42]

[39] This letter explains General Roatta's attitude towards Hitler.
[40] See Churchill, *Memoirs*, Vol. V, p. 414.
[41] The Americans were ill-informed, and continued to give token aid to the Chetniks. The last supplies dropped by parachute were sent in September 1944.
[42] At Praniane in September 1944 negotiations were entered into between Mihailović and Ačimović, security chief in the Nedić government, with a view to inducing the Germans to surrender to Mihailović. This meeting took place in the presence of the American Colonel MacDawn. Nothing came of the meeting.

Thus, Mihailović was lost, and he eventually attempted a rapprochement with the Croat Ustashis. Arrested in March 1945, he was tried, condemned to death and shot on the 17th July 1946.

Is it true to say that Mihailović was a traitor? In the light of the facts that we have recorded one may conclude that from March 1941 to December 1942 Mihailović's attitude was in strict conformity with the directives of his government and of the Allies, even though some of his lieutenants did for various reasons act against the Partisans.

One must consider, however, that Mihailović's original idea of keeping to military action only was a mistaken one. In a total war of ideologies a resistance movement could evolve only in the search for a better future. Mihailović would not, could not, understand that the peoples of Yugoslavia were not prepared to fight for a return to the situation that obtained in 1941. The federal statute, the democratization desired by Tito, were not Communist objectives, but those of all Yugoslavs.

Mihailović remained a prisoner of his own principle that action should be postponed until the end of the war: he was condemned to a policy of temporizing, and was therefore bound to be led into a policy of compromise with the occupying power. After January 1943 he was inevitably dragged down the incline which caused him to betray the interests of the Yugoslav nation. Tito, whose attitude was clear from the beginning to the end of the conflict, was determined to give expression to the hopes of the nation in war and in peace. This determination took precedence over the aims of the Communist party.

Our conclusion is that of Henri Michel:

> In short, the victory of Tito and his Partisans was the most complete of all those won by national resistance movements; a new Yugoslavia was born, having been conceived in fire and blood. It is quite true that they received an enormous amount of aid from the British; but this aid was not given to them until the Partisans had already demonstrated their strength, and proved that the aid would be profitable. They imposed their views on all the Allies, and were capable of moulding their own destiny.[43]

One has to weigh the results accomplished against the losses suffered — 1,705,000 of the population, 820,000 houses, two-thirds of the livestock, ninety per cent of the railways; but in 1944 fifteen German divisions were locked up in Yugoslavia in the struggle against the Partisans.

[43] Michel, *Les mouvements clandestins en Europe*, Paris, 1961, p. 105.

4. Badoglio Surrenders

The Allied landing in Sicily on the 10th July 1943 precipitated the evolution of political events in Italy. Within a few hours Fascism collapsed, and on the 24th and 25th July Mussolini was overthrown.[44] The King of Italy took over control, and placed the direction of affairs in the hands of Marshal Badoglio.

On the 26th July the Marshal declared:

> The war continues. In the spirit of her centuries-old tradition Italy remains loyal to her word.

But he entered into negotiations with the Allies for the signing of an armistice, which took place on the 3rd September, although the armistice was not made public until the 8th.[45]

Badoglio's capitulation was regarded by the Germans as a betrayal, but the real intentions of the Marshal were not made clear. To begin with, the accusation was based upon Badoglio's published statement of the 26th July — "The war continues". Later Badoglio wrote:

> It was agreed (between the King and Badoglio) that in view of our precarious position it was not possible to state that Italy was retiring from the war. Such a declaration would at once have provoked violent reaction by Germany, which the newly-formed government was not in a position to counter. His Majesty showed me two recently printed proclamations which the King and I, as head of the government, should address to the people.
>
> Both these texts, in the preparation of which — as I subsequently learned — V. E. Orlando had participated, declared that the war would continue.[46]

General Castellano, who was at that time very close to the Marshal, affirms that Badoglio's proclamation was passed to him already drawn up. He does not say who was its author.[47]

E. Dollmann, who usually acted as interpreter between Hitler and Mussolini, was generally well informed; he wrote that the incriminating words "appeared to have been introduced at the wish of King Victor Emanuel".[48] It seems, therefore, that Badoglio himself neither conceived nor desired the declaration with which he has been reproached. We must

---

[44] See J. de Launay in *Le Monde en Guerre*, p. 274.

[45] See J. de Launay, *Secrets diplomatiques 1939—45*, p. 92.

[46] Badoglio, *L'Italia nella seconda guerra mondiale*, Verona, 1946. p. 73.

[47] Castellano, *Come firmai l'armistizio di Cassibile*, Milan 1945.

[48] E. Dollmann, *Du Capitole à la Roche tarpéienne*, Paris, 1957, p. 225.

also consider the situation in which the King, the Marshal and the
Italian government found themselves at this period. Rome was in the
zone of German operations, and any mistake could provoke an extremely brutal German reaction.

Between the 25th July and the 3rd September the Marshal had to
play a very shrewd game to foil German observation.

By the end of the first world war Marshal Badoglio had become
deputy chief of staff. After being ambassador in Rumania, in the United
States and then in Brazil, he had been promoted marshal in 1925.
Governor of Libya (1928–1933), conqueror then Viceroy of Ethiopia,
he put up a feeble opposition to Italy's entry into the war, and resigned
his post of Major-General Chief of Staff on the 6th December 1940.
He had always evinced a marked antipathy towards the Germans, and
was a severe critic of German military leaders. One may assume that
this attitude of opposition was blended with some apprehension, and is
perhaps explained by his fear of precipitating German reaction.

Badoglio's declaration did not by any means inspire Hitler with
confidence, and he decided to carry out a Roman version of the St.
Bartholomew's Massacre.

On the 27th Dollmann was invited by Marshal Kesselring to dinner
in Frascati. At table he met the celebrated conqueror of Crete, General
Student, commander of the Parachute Division, and Skorzeny, an SS
officer as yet unknown. Under the bond of secrecy Skorzeny informed
him that Student's paratroopers, supported by eighty SS men, were
going to take possession by night of the Italian government ministries
and the royal family. Everything was ready to be put into operation in
two days' time.[49]

At that moment SS General Sepp Dietrich, leader of the "Leibstan-
darte Adolf Hitler", arrived in Rome to take up command of his division
in southern Italy. He came to Frascati to present his respects to Kesselring
who had been Commander-in-Chief since the 25th July. Dollmann has
since related:

> I had known him for many years, and I met him again near a petrol station
> in a suburb of Munich; he never imagined that the Fuhrer would one day make
> him a general, and even the general of his Praetorians! There was nothing of the
> "gentleman" about Dietrich; but that was not important. His main qualities
> were a natural shrewdness, and the characteristic *joie de vivre* of the Bavarians.

[49] Despite the bond of secrecy Dollmann warned the royal princesses, and took
them away to hide them. Skorzeny's second mission was to free Mussolini. Kesselring was not in sympathy with these activities.

Over and above all this he had always maintained great freedom of speech with his Adolf; he used and abused this privilege without bothering over much about the demands of etiquette.

On arriving in Rome he expressed a desire to see me. We met in a street near the Piazza del Popolo, in the house where Togliatti now lives. Dietrich confided to me that the Marshal was very worried. He had an easy, familiar way of speaking to everybody, and he said to me, 'You see, he's anxious about that stupid thing Adolf wants to do in Rome. But you are an experienced diplomat; what d'you think about it?'

I seized the opportunity to tell him in the strongest terms in the Bavarian vocabulary exactly what I thought. I described the dreadful atrocities which this stupid action would let loose if it were not prevented. In reply he said that if he could take a dozen of the Liebstandarte boys, it would give him real pleasure to lay hold of the "nut-cracker king" with his own hands. But that was merely a detail; he regarded the whole entreprise as sheer foolishness — another of Adolf's bluffs, or perhaps the result of his insomnia. However, he said that he would fly to Hitler at once to try to get him to change his mind. He added that he and Hitler were both from Munich, and that I could rely on him to succeed — as sure as his name was Sepp Dietrich.

He repeated this promise on the spur of the moment during the course of a party arranged one evening by Scarpone, outside the Porto San Pancrazio. If the "St Bartholomew's Massacre" was to be foiled there was no one more capable of achieving this than Sepp, with his good humour and a few bottles of excellent Frascati wine. Sepp was really more powerful than all the ambassadors and all the marshals. He did succeed in getting Hitler to abandon his mad project; and he told me later that in his talk with Hitler he had spoken very frankly.[50]

After the failure of this operation Skorzeny undertook his second mission — the freeing of the Duce.[51]

On the 29th July Colonel Dollmann paid a visit to General Castellano, Badoglio's associate, at the Ambassadors Hotel, and asked him if "the downfall of Fascism was the prelude to the collapse of the Axis". Castellano reassured him, and tried to persuade him to regard the event as a matter of Italian internal policy, and not to allow the Germans to be in any way alarmed.

The Germans meanwhile had gained time. They moved eight divisions to the Po valley, and concentrated a parachute division around Rome, ready to meet any eventuality. By the 30th July the abrupt capitulation which Badoglio might have risked on the 25th — as Grandi had suggested — had become impossible. These troop concentrations made the Italians uneasy, and Castellano and Dollmann agreed

[50] E. Dollmann, *Du Capitole à la Roche tarpéienne*, Paris, 1957, p. 162.
[51] Skorzeny, *Missions Secrètes*, Paris, 1950. Hitler also intended to carry out two other projects: the capture or destruction of the Italian fleet and the military occupation of Italy.

on the urgent need to ease the tension. Such was the purpose of the conference at Tarvis, which took place on the 7th August only, for it had been necessary to await the arrival of Guariglia who had returned from Turkey to take up the post of Foreign Minister.

To quote Dollmann again:

"The morning session opened in the saloon car of the special Italian train Ribbentrop in his lordly manner gave an account of German-Italian relations since the 25th July. Nobody could expect Germany to have the same unlimited confidence in the Badoglio government that she had had under the Fascist régime; it was up to Badoglio and Guariglia to furnish proof that their aims had not changed. Hitler noted with satisfaction that "the war continued", but this declaration did not by itself dispel Germany's doubts. Ribbentrop then drew attention to the enormous dangers to which, according to him, Italy would be exposed as a result of the preparations then under way for a Communist uprising, as well as from Socialist propaganda in general; in fact, various internal political measures taken by Badoglio had already given rise to some astonishment. Hitler and the entire German people naturally had the Duce's fate very much at heart; Hitler believed that it was his duty and his right to demand definite guarantees of the safety of his best friend. Finally, the Führer was prepared to render military aid to Italy 'to the limit of what was possible in present circumstances'.

Ribbentrop's tone of voice and attitude were cold and aggressive. Every one of his words and gestures manifested his scorn for the new Italian government. Guariglia replied that he held within his grasp, safely and firmly, the helm of foreign politics, and that his main desire was to collaborate closely with his colleague Ribbentrop. Rome's diplomacy in the past was a guarantee that her sole aim was to bring the war to a speedy and victorious conclusion; she remained a loyal ally at Germany's side, and this was made abundantly clear in Badoglio's proclamation published at the expressed wish of the sovereign. Guariglia assured Ribbentrop that his fears with regard to Italy's internal politics were without foundation; it had been indispensable to make certain concessions, but neither the King nor Badoglio would ever link up with the Leftists, as the composition of the new government clearly showed.

Badoglio had instructed Guariglia to go to this conference prepared to "win back confidence", and he was in a position to give absolute assurance that the life and safety of the Duce were not in the least threatened; Badoglio himself had stated this to him before his departure. Only in exceptional cases would other Fascist leaders be pursued and brought to justice, and any possible German wishes in this respect would be taken into account. Up to the present the Duce had made no protest or complaint; he had spent his birthday quietly reading the works of Nietzsche — a present from Goering which Badoglio had hastened to send him. Guariglia was firmly of the opinion that the new government, unhampered as it now was, constituted a definite advantage to the Axis: it would enable the war to be brought to a victorious conclusion. It was in that sense that Guariglia interpreted the purpose of his mission.[52]

[52] E. Dollmann, *Du Capitole à la Roche tarpéienne*, Paris, 1957, p. 167.

On the 10th August Badoglio and Guariglia decided to send an emissary to sound the Allies. This incredible project was entrusted to General Castellano.[53] The talks took place in Lisbon from the 16th to the 19th August. On the 27th Rome accepted by radio the Allied conditions. On the 31st Italian and Allied plenipotentiaries met again in Sicily, and the surrender document was signed on the 3rd September. Three hours later Badoglio received Rahn, the German ambassador, and said to him:

I am Marshal Badoglio, one of the three senior marshals in Europe — Mackensen, Pétain and I are the oldest. It is impossible to understand why the Reich is so suspicious of me. I have given my word and I intend to keep it. Please have confidence in me".[54]

The surrender was made public on the 8th September at six in the evening. During that night the King and the government left Rome in the greatest secrecy.

Why this last minute double-dealing, this wealth of emphasis in Badoglio's statement to Rahn? Was it to facilitate the nocturnal flight of the government and the royal family, or to thwart Hitler's plans? During the afternoon of the 8th September Hitler flew from Zaporozh'ye to the Ukrainian front, and "a strange foreboding urged him to proceed to his G.H.Q. at once. As soon as he arrived he learned the bad news from Italy, and set to work at once".[55]

Hitler was now faced with the problem of trying to smooth out a catastrophic situation. He began to study a number of projects which had been ready since the 27th July — Operation Eiche (the freeing of Mussolini), Operation Schwarz (the military occupation of Italy) and Operation Axe (the capture and destruction of the Italian fleet). We have seen that the fourth project — Operation Student, or the Roman "St Bartholomew's Massacre" — was abandoned on the advice of Sepp Dietrich.

The Führer called Kesselring to the telephone, and gave him instructions to carry out these operations. But the headquarters at Frascati had been destroyed on the morning of the 8th as the result of Allied bombing, and Hitler had great difficulty in transmitting his instructions relating to the three operations.

---

[53] J. de Launay, *Secrets diplomatiques, 1939–45*, p. 91.
[54] Rahn, *Ruheloses Leben*, Düsseldorf, 1949, p. 288.
[55] *The Goebbels Diaries*, London, 1948. Goebbels also referred to a letter from Badoglio to Hitler in which the Marshal explained away his defection "with wily and hypocritical reasoning". The letter has never been found.

In fact, Badoglio's trick made it possible to frustrate the German plans, with the exception of "Oak" (Operation Fiche), which Skorzeny carried out a few days later. It allowed the royal family and the government to escape captivity; it enabled the fleet to sail from Spezia to Malta during the evening of the 8th September, so that the German submarines which set out to destroy it arrived too late.

It is also known that Castellano tried to persuade Eisenhower to land sufficient Allied forces in Italy to ensure the safety of the King and the government in Rome. General Taylor betook himself secretly to Rome on the 7th September to organize the occupation of aerodromes in the neighbourhood of the capital during the night of the 9th. But he found that the Germans had strong forces at their disposal, and that the Italian army was dispirited. The scheme was therefore abandoneed.[56] It is quite possible that Badoglio's attempt to "reassure" the Germans was due to the failure of Taylor's mission.

As a matter of fact, Kesselring thought, as Hitler had done on the 8th, that the Allies would exploit the situation immediately, make a landing to the north of Rome, capture the city, and throw the Germans back north.[57]

Although this ambitious scheme was realizable the Allies rejected it, and were content to welcome Badoglio's government in Brindisi, leaving Kesselring time to collect his wits and put Operation Schwartz into action. Badoglio's dealings with Germany, undoubtedly influenced by his fear of the Germans, has been the subject of various interpretations. It may certainly have facilitated the Allied advance and shortened the war. Above all Badoglio made it possible for the Italian fleet to escape and re-enter the war on the side of the Allies.

5. The Importance of French Resistance

There never has been any doubt whatever about the historic fact of French Resistance, although most works dealing with military history seem to ignore it. Its importance and efficacy have, however, been disputed, as well as the opportunity given to military leaders to take the Resistance movement into account in their operational plans.

---

[56] Cf. Churchill, *Memoirs.*

[57] For full details see Kesselring, *Soldat bis zum letzten Tag*, Bonn, 1953. Kesselring expected the worst, and was surprised at the dilatoriness of the Allied reaction.

With regard to opportunity, Liddel Hart,[58] a widely read military critic, writing after the war, expressed the opinion that the Resistance movement's contribution to victory was offset by a series of disorders. He considers that those who encouraged insurrection within the framework of war policy neglected the lessons of history.

In expressing this view it seems that Liddell Hart has overlooked one factor that became apparent for the first time in history during the second world war: Total war implies the participation of the people in all aspects of the war. Had the Resistance movement not been favourable to the Allies it would have been unfavourable, and on that depended the result of the conflict. It was impossible to exclude the population factor from the balance of forces.

Another eminent military critic, Chester Wilmot,[59] expresses an opinion diametrically opposed to that of Liddell Hart. He draws attention to the fact that the landing in Normandy in June 1944 would certainly have been repelled if the Germans had not been forced to fight the Russians in their rear. Wilmot's conclusion springs from an elaborate analysis of the battle of Normandy; he also shows how the German army, in its attempts to throw back the invaders, was hampered by French Resistance forces. Wilmot does not say that without the French Resistance and the Red Army the Allies would have been compelled to retreat, but clearly demonstrates that the forces of the Resistance played an essential role in the issue.

As to the efficacy of the Resistance, such military leaders as Eisenhower, Bradley, Montgomery, de Lattre de Tassigny, and the German General Tippelskirch, are very circumspect; they say little, or nothing at all, of the role of the French Resistance. Generals Marshall and Arnold, however, and Admiral King, the American commanders of the three arms of the Service, did recognize in their accounts that military operations were substantially assisted by the activities of French Resistance.[60] But their statements are not very precise.

Other witnesses regard the military role of the Resistance as an established fact, and they quote a number of details which are not in themselves absolutely convincing. Buckmaster, a British officer who was in command of an important network, mentions numerous cases of sabo-

[58] *In Defence of the West*, London, 1951.
[59] Wilmot, *The Struggle for Europe*, London, 1951.
[60] Marshall, Arnold and King, in *The War Reports*, Philadelphia, U.S.A., p. 189.

tage; Ryan and Robichon, who questioned many witnesses, refer to numerous instances of Intelligence work. General Giraud, who directed operations in Corsica, relates that Resistance obstructed the roads on the island. General de Gaulle writes of the role of the Resistance at the time of the Normandy operations, but he does not go into details. Jacques Soustelle refers to secret radio transmissions which guided the Allied bombers to German columns on the march, but fails to give a systematic account of these activities. Churchill stresses that the armed members of the Resistance numbered 25,000 in southern France, but he makes no attempt to prove it.

Bernard talks of the important part played by the FFI. Shirer mentions incidentally "French Resistance Groups". Forrest C. Pogue mentions the sabotage of railways in southern Normandy, the valley of the Rhône, and in the regions of Toulouse and Orleans. He estimates that by the end of July 1944 the Resistance movement totalled 70,000 men, and he adds that they protected the ports of Toulon, Sète and Marseilles.

The real importance of French Resistance is nowhere stated. Indeed, Eisenhower admits that the FFI played an important role, and assisted the invasion forces in a thousand ways; he recognizes that without their aid the liberation of France and the defeat of the enemy in western Europe would have taken much longer, and would have been more costly in lives. But he brings forward no proof to support this assertion; any more than Churchill, who mentions 25,000 men, or Pogue, who quotes 70,000. It is understandable that these fragmentary details leave historians puzzled.

It will perhaps always remain a very difficult task to describe precisely the extent of the importance and efficacy of French Resistance in the second world war. We are faced with an indisputable historical fact in the existence of the Resistance; we are also confronted with an almost complete absence of traces of the fact. It is this lack of detail which is at the root of the stories, legends and exaggerations, all of which quite rightly disturb historians. A characteristic of the Resistance movement was its secrecy, and the participants themselves destroyed all traces of their activities for security reasons. All that remains to the historian, therefore, is to tread very warily in this particularly uncertain field.

An attempt has first to be made to trace documents, to supplement them frequently by verbal enquiry; everything has to be filed, clasified, listed; and only when this has been done may a really critical analysis begin.

Such was the task assigned to the *Comité d'Histoire de la Deuxième Guerre Mondiale*, of Paris.[61] The *Comité* questioned 2500 witnesses, and checked all their evidence. Printed documents in code and packed with assumed names were collected and indexed. This valuable collection will serve at some future date to describe precisely what the French Resistance was during the years 1940 to 1944.

At the present time any publication on the French Resistance movement would be premature, and historians must await the result of the researches undertaken by the *Comité d'Histoire*, so that they may have at their disposal documents which have been prepared on a scientific basis.

Nevertheless, two essays of a rather different type have been published. The first is a summary: *Histoire de la résistance*, by the French historian Henri Michel.[62] It provides a bold outline of the development of French Resistance — the creation of the movement, the role played by political parties, networks, liaison, the underground Press and the Maquis. The work describes the organization of the French Forces of the Interior (FFI). But this short study does not aspire to be anything but a rough outline, requiring additions and alterations. One senses in Michel's work an earnest desire to avoid the publication of documents before adequate analysis has been carried out.

The second essay springs from the pen of another French writer named Aron. Under the title *Histoire de la libération de la France*[63] the author endeavours to synthesize documents in his possession. He collected the verbal testimony of 287 prominent Frenchmen who took part in the events from June 1944 to May 1945. He made use of unpublished official documents and private documents with a definite interest.

The book brings to light the abundance of documents available on certain matters, although Aron gives them perhaps too much importance. In brief, the work confirms that it is more or less impossible to proceed to a synthetic study until the *Comité d'Histoire de la Deuxième Guerre Mondiale* has published its systematic chronology of the Resistance movement — monographs of networks, regions, etc.[64] There is, however, one point debated by most non-French historians — the

---

[61] Its President is Maurice Baumont, a member of the Institute; its General Secretary is Henri Michel, 22 Rue d'Athènes, Paris 9e.

[62] Paris, POF, 1950.

[63] See the detailed study of Aron's work in the *Revue d'Histoire de la Deuxième Guerre Mondiale*, No. 29, p. 45, published in Paris in July 1960.

[64] Aron, *Histoire de la Libération de la France, Juin 1944 – Mai 1945*, Paris, Foyard, 1955.

participation of French Resistance in the gigantic Allied operation in
Normandy — on which it appears especially useful to throw some
light even now.

Was French Resistance as valuable and efficacious an aid to the Allies
in June 1944, as Eisenhower stated within a few lines in his 582 page
work? The following account from Michel's work is all that may be
quoted from the facts at present available:

> In April 1944 a scheme was devised in conjunction with the Allies to make
> the best possible use of the FFI on D-Day and during the period that followed.
> In the battle zone the Allies were to depend upon the Resistance for the supply of
> information. But in the zone behind the lines, subject to continual change connected
> with the Allied progress, sabotage had to be organized. The regions most suitable
> for the operations of the Maquis were, therefore, "non-operational" areas, which
> extended across terrain difficult to reach, or beyond into areas that could not pos-
> sibly be penetrated.
>
> To carry out these broad directives several plans had been prepared. The
> "Green" Plan aimed at paralysing transportation by French railways for about
> a fortnight, to allow a bridgehead to be established and thus concentrate the forces
> landed. The destruction of navigability by river and canal, and the blocking of the
> highways, constituted subsidiary elements of the plan. Another project, known as
> the "Blue" Plan, included the sabotage of electrical systems; while the "Tortoise"
> Plan was devised to delay enemy troop concentrations through guerilla tactics.
> Attacks on petrol dumps and munition depots completed the general scheme of
> operations.[65]

To realize these plans the FFI would have to be supplied with the
necessary arms — about sixty tons a day; but, even on their most successful days, the Allies never succeeded in parachuting more than one or
two tons a day. The Allies also had doubts about the military value of
these non-military volunteers, and were afraid that their use might
involve political repercussions.[66]

They scarcely knew what use to make of this military potential
which could prove either the best or the worst of weapons. And the
cruel and costly failures of the Maquis of Vercors and Auvergne (Mont–
Mouchet) were to demonstrate how erroneous it was to employ bodies
of Resistance men to hold strong enemy forces.[67]

Undoubtedly that explains why the Allies preferred to use Resistance
units for Intelligence work, in which they were engaged most of the time

[65] Michel, *Histoire de la Résistance française*, Paris, 1950, p. 107.

[66] On this point see Baudot, *La Résistance en France et les Alliés*, in *European
Resistance Movements*, Milan Conference, 1961, Pergamon Press, p. 369.

[67] See Aron and Michel, *op. cit.*

under the orders of armed Allies, or for sabotage and guerilla activiites, forms of warfare to which the Resistance was particularly adapted.

The British and Americans parachuted ninety teams of three officers — the Jedburgh teams — to train the men and organize their activities for Intelligence and especially sabotage. One day the history of these operations will be written, but broad lines may already be traced in the fighting of June 1944.

On the 6th June, when the Allies landed in Normandy, the Germans had seventeen divisions on the spot (about 250,000 men). By the 13th the Allies had disembarked sixteen divisions, which balanced the forces. But the Allies had landed a million and a half men by the 29th July. While the Germans were bringing up ten divisions of reinforcements to Normandy, the Allies brought[68] thirty-six across the Channel with arms, material and provisions. These figures show clearly the extraordinary effect which the early or late arrival of German reinforcements could have on the battle front in Normandy. This was especially evident in the battle for Caen.

Aron[69] and Michel quote different figures for the Breton FFI who took part in the battle (19,500 and 5000 respectively in June 1944); but it is a fact that one German division was immobilized, and eventually compelled to take refuge in Brest.

During the month of July the FFI along the coast of the Nord province carried out by themselves two hundred sabotage operations against railways; they organized forty derailments, cut three hundred telephone lines, planned fifty ambushes, and carried out thirty attacks against enemy observation posts, besides capturing a large petrol dump.[70]

The "Green" Plan (i.e. the sabotage of railways) was extremely successful. Systematic sabotage was carried out on the south–west lines and in central France; it considerably hampered the progress of a dozen German divisions, including the "Das Reich" division which was proceeding towards Normandy.[71] All these divisions arrived on the Normandy front two weeks late — too late to enable them to throw the Allied forces back into the sea. If these divisions had reached Caen in

[68] Wilmot had access to the records of the 6th German Army telephone communications, as well as to the papers of Colonel Tempelhoff, head of Operations under Rommel. Wilmot, *The Struggle for Europe*, London, 1951 (p. 504).

[69] Aron, *op. cit.*

[70] Michel, *op. cit.*, p. 111.

[71] Aron and Michel, *op. cit.*

time, it is quite possible that the Allies might not have been able to maintain their bridgehead.

We shall end this section with Michel's conclusion:

> If the Allies had not arrived, the Resistance would have been eventually exterminated. Without the material provided by the Allies the Resistance would have been powerless. On the other hand, without the aid of the Resistance the task of the Allies would have been incomparably more difficult, and their success much less speedy.[72]

6. The Liberation of Paris

By the end of July 1944 the Battle of Normandy had taken a decisive turn, and the population of Paris prepared feverishly for the liberation of their capital. On the 10th August the railway employees went on strike; on the 15th the police and the underground railways followed suit, and on the 18th post office employees did likewise.

The Allies were faced with two opposing ideas. General Koenig, Chief of Staff of the French Army of the Interior (FFI), whose business it was to co-ordinate plans under Allied instructions, hoped for an uprising in Paris "to avoid an Allied administration, to assert the sovereignty of the French people, and to prove that the Resistance was not a myth". But Koenig did not wish to start the uprising without a definite order and then only when the Allies were at the gates of the city.[73] General Bradley, on the other hand, wished to avoid Paris, which he considered easier to take by encirclement, for it presented serious problems of provisioning the civil population. His colleagues were in complete agreement.

Bradley wrote:[74]

Yet tactically the city had become meaningless. For all of its past glories, Paris represented nothing more than an inkspot on our maps to be by-passed as we headed toward the Rhine. Logistically it could cause untold trouble, for behind its handsome façades there lived 4,000,000 hungry Frenchmen: The diversion of so much tonnage to Paris would only strain further our already taut lines of supply. Food for the people of Paris meant less gasolene for the front.

General von Choltitz, commanding the German 84th Army Corps had just been appointed commandant of greater Paris, replacing General Heinrich von Stulpnagel who had been involved in the conspiracy of the 20th July.

[72] Michel, p. 118).
[73] Michel, ibid p. 112.
[74] Bradley, A Soldier's Story, New York, 1951, p. 384.

Choltitz had taken part in the Normandy battles. He was a general of the old school, and in his youth he had served as a page to the Queen of Saxony. There had been nothing outstanding in his progress; he had climbed all the rungs of the military ladder, attaining the rank of general at the age of fifty. Hitler insisted on seeing him on the 7th August when he was appointed to his new mission of trust.[75] It was the first time that Choltitz had met the Führer, and he left the interview somewhat stunned. His mission was to destroy Paris, both the buildings and the population: he was to turn Paris into a "scorched earth" zone. Hitler asked him, rather than ordered him, to undertake measures that were so extreme, so extraordinary, that Choltitz came away horrified. He was expected to ignore the traditions of the German army and use SS methods. His orders were to be given to him by that bully Marshal Model, Rommel's successor, who was in charge of operations on the western front. After his meeting with Hitler, Choltitz contacted General Speidel, Chief of Staff of Army Group B, who had recently served with Rommel in that capacity.

We do not know what Speidel told Choltitz, for no trace of their conversation exists. It seems that this friend of Rommel's, on the eve of his arrest for having taken part in the 20th July plot, must have urged Choltitz not to take Hitler's mad visions too literally.

On the eve of the liberation of Paris the Allied commanders immediately concerned were perplexed and undecided. Koenig favoured an uprising, but he wanted to await an opportune moment. Bradley, who had made no decision, so planned his operation that he would by-pass Paris. Choltitz, who had been ordered to destroy Paris, was battling with his conscience. Events were precipitated in Paris in an atmosphere of revolt. On the 17th August Pierre Taittinger, President of the Paris Municipal Council, and a member of the Right in the Paris "parliament", decided to pay a visit to General von Choltitz at the Hôtel Meurice. Taittinger, a conservative and a democratic leader who stuck at nothing, has left an account of the interview:

General von Choltitz was sitting at his desk in the middle of the room. Standing on his right was Councillor Eckelmann, and on his left his chief of staff. Behind them stood a few officers representing the various branches of the Service, and among them Major von Gunther.

General von Choltitz was a plump man with a florid complexion and a powerful chest. He wore a monocle, as did many officers of the old German school.

[75] Hitler had recently escaped from the July attempt on his life.

His manner was rather stiff, but he endeavoured to soften it by mildness of language. He was wearing the field-service uniform of the Wehrmacht, and his trousers bore the regulation red stripes. The German governor of Paris began by reiterating the warning that he had addressed to the people of Paris through the Press. His speech was curt, his voice sharp and incisive, his manner deliberate and resolute. His officers stood motionless around him. Their faces were grave, and I could not read in them the slightest indication of compromise.

'I am instructed', said the General, 'to enforce respect for the Wehrmacht by taking possession of Paris. I must tell you that I have decided to apply collective sanctions in retaliation for any act that might be committed against members of the German forces. If a shot is fired disciplinary measures will be taken immediately. You may judge for yourself; my plans are simple. Imagine, for instance, that one of our soldiers has been shot at from some premises in the Avenue de l'Opéra, between the Rue Gomboust and the Rue des Pyramides. In such a case I shall set fire to the buildings in that block, and have their occupants shot. I have at my disposal 22,000 men, most of whom are SS Storm Troopers; I also have a hundred "Tiger" tanks and ninety bombers. I hope you understand me.'

The General changed his position, and his eyes kindled. He replaced his monocle and leaned gently back in his armchair. Then he picked up a pencil, and waved it rapidly across the map opened up before him. Returning to the question of repressive measures he said:

'If the matter is more serious than an isolated rifle shot I shall extend the area of punishment. In the event of a riot or an uprising I shall use the air force, and destroy the whole area with incendiary bombs. As you see, it is quite simple.'

"This preamble sounded dreadful. General von Choltitz got up, walked a few steps, and stopped in front of me.

'You represent the capital,' he said; 'and you have authority. Use it then. If the population makes no move, I shall not; and you and I together shall see if everything can be brought to a happy conclusion without much trouble. But if not, beware!'

The General then returned to his desk, examined the map once more, and passed his pencil rapidly along the course of the river Seine.

"You are an officer, Monsieur Taittinger, and you cannot be unaware of the security measures I am compelled to take to safeguard the forces for which I am responsible. I am speaking to you now as a soldier. Do I make my meaning clear?'

I was afraid to understand.

'Yes, of course,' the General continued; 'the bridges, the electricity works, the railway stations . . .'

I felt utterly crushed. The man standing before me had the appalling power to destroy Paris, and he planned to use it! He had already contemplated this destruction. Perhaps while we were talking at this very moment, his sappers were cramming dynamite beneath the stones.

With unexpected mildness, a touch of weariness perhaps, he added, 'It is my duty to hold up the advance of the Allies'.

I managed to control my feelings. Above all I had to prevent this conversation from ending abruptly. I told General von Choltitz that I recognized his preoccupations, and I broached the question of law and order. I first gave him details of the situation in Paris; then I pointed out what would be, in my opinion, the consequences of a policy of brutal repression of the extent he contemplated. I ran the risk of hurting him; I might even annoy him. Anyhow, we should see; it was now or never.

'At this moment,' I said, 'we have in the Paris zone five hundred thousand people; they are excited and in a state of alarm. In the suburbs we have 350,000, and 150,000 in the city alone. They only await an opportunity to rise up. If a quarter of Paris is burnt down tomorrow, or if there are any mass shootings, the German army must expect a "Parisian Vespers", which would be very much like the famous *Sicilian Vespers* massacre. This is not merely a possibility, General; it is a certainty. Every German soldier will become a target, and will be struck down when the moment is opportune by the patriots of Paris in revolt. Do you wish to run this enormous risk, a risk so easily avoided?'

The General remained silent. He stared at me impassively through his monocle, but I noticed a tremor in the hand resting on the table.[76]

The member for Paris was able to continue the conversation in a less strained atmosphere. He relates that he told General von Choltitz that he — the General — had a choice between going down in history as the destroyer of Paris or as the man who saved Paris from destruction.

Choltitz eventually agreed to "close his eyes to isolated acts, but he appealed to the discretion of the Parisians". He stated that he would hold on grimly to the key points in the German command — the Hôtel Meurice, the Avenue Foch, the Place de l'Opéra, the Palais du Luxembourg and the barracks on the Place de la République.

After the interview Taittinger considered the battle won: Choltitz would not destroy Paris. The talk did not, however, greatly affect the course of events, for Taittinger was arrested by the Resistance on the 20th August.

The various branches of the Resistance acted without taking into account an interview of which they knew nothing. The Paris Committee of Liberation, which was composed of three Communists and three non-Communists, decided on the 18th to launch the insurrection without awaiting the anticipated signal from General Koenig. It is important to note that with the meagre details at present at our disposal, there seems to be nothing to suggest that the decision taken was altogether of Communist origin; and still less can it be proved that the position adopted by the Communist members was based upon Soviet instructions.

Colonel Rol, the regional leader of the FFI, was put in charge of the military operations.[77]

[76] Taittinger, *Et Paris ne fut pas détruit*. Paris, 1948, pp. 160–164.
[77] A copy of the most important relevant documents is contained in Massiet, *La préparation de l'insurrection et la bataille de Paris*. Paris, 1945.

Posters calling on the people to rise were put up all over Paris. The first reaction came from General Koenig's representatives. While the insurrection burst on the 19th August, and Colonel Rol was issuing his instructions for the safeguarding of water, gas and electricity, and the conduct of street fighting, an order was sent out by representatives of the de Gaulle government:[78]

Paris, 19th August 1944.
In view of the assurances given by the German commander to refrain from attacking public buildings occupied by French forces, and to treat all French prisoners in accordance with the laws of war, the provisional government of the French Republic and the National Resistance Council ask you to withhold fire against the occupying power until the promised evacuation of Paris.[79]

No one is quite certain what these German assurances were. They had nothing to do with the Choltitz-Taittinger conversation; but it has since been ascertained that two officers of the entourage of General von Choltitz — Bender and Poch-Pastor — were won over by the Allies, or at least were anxious to save the capital.

Von Poch-Pastor was an Austrian baron[80] who had married the Duchesse de Talleyrand on the 25th March 1944, having already joined the Allies in August 1942. He persuaded Commander Bender, deputy chief of the SD, to join him.[81] They informed Eisenhower that the Germans would not put up any serious resistance. There exists no documentary evidence of these details, but they no doubt have some bearing on the "assurances" referred to in the order issued by the GPRF on the 19th August.

But the CPL and Colonel Rol were sceptical. Parodi was undecided; he agreed with Colonel Rol, and made no attempt to hold up the promulgation of the order to rise up. Chaban-Delmas protested strongly, and reproached Parodi for having exceeded Koenig's instructions.

At that juncture a new personage came into the picture — Raoul Nordling, the Swedish consul-general. For several days he had been in touch with the Germans in an attempt to secure on humanitarian grounds the freedom of political prisoners whom certain German authorities wished to massacre before their departure. During the course

[78] The order was despatched by Parodi, delegate of the GPRF. He had received it from Chaban-Delmas, the national military delegate, who informed him that the Allies were not expected to reach Paris before the 1st September.
[79] Massiet, *op. cit*, p. 135.
[80] His father was the last Austrian ambassador to the Vatican.
[81] After the departure of General Oberg Bender was made chief of the SD.

of a visit to Choltitz he learned that the commandant of Paris had received orders to destroy the city, and he considered the possibility of an armistice.

On the 20th August, when street fighting began to break out more or less everywhere, the Resistance National Council met[82] to hear Chaban-Delmas state his reasons for wishing to check the insurrection. He pointed out that the Germans had vastly superior forces and arms at their disposal, and that the Allies would not arrive for at least a week. The Committee of Military Action (COMAC) of the CNR, composed of Ginsburger–Villon, Kriegel–Valrimont and de Vogue–Vaillant (the last two being Communists), was strongly opposed to the idea of an armistice. Only Villon was present at the CNR meeting, and by five votes to one it was agreed to send a delegation to Nordling composed of three men — Chaban-Delmas, Roland-Pré and Léon Hamon — to negotiate an armistice which would enable them to gain time and delay the general uprising until the arrival of the Allies.

Nordling did not lose a moment. He drafted the armistice terms, and summoned the Germans. At noon the armistice was concluded: the Germans would evacuate Paris by way of the outer boulevards; they would refrain from attacking points already held by the FFI, but would keep their own key points; that is to say, the Hôtel Meurice and the immediately surrounding district. The text of the armistice was promulgated in Paris, but at 4.15 p.m. Rol let it be known that he intended to ignore it and to stand by the order to fight. The COMAC, summoned in the night, adopted a similar attitude.

The armistice was not, in fact, put into effect. What could Choltitz do when he received from Marshal Model on the 20th August a per-emptory order to "Resist in order to allow the components of the western army to cross the Paris bridges"? On 22nd August he received another order: "You must continue to resist up to a thirty per cent loss in man-power". And on the 23rd August he received an order from the Führer himself: "Effect the widest possible destruction; in particular blow up all bridges. Carry out reprisals. Do not evacuate Paris until this destruction has been completed, and until you have lost up to thirty per cent of your personnel."

Choltitz was in a particularly difficult and complex situation: his wife and children were in Nuremberg, and they would serve as a guarantee

[82] At 41 Rue de Bellechasse. It was a meeting of the governing body of the CNR, and not a plenary session, as Aron states at p. 404 of his *Histoire de la Libéra-tion de la France, Juin 1941–Mai 1945*, Paris, 1955.

of his loyalty. His associates advised moderation; it was his duty to protect his men. But he had also received orders to destroy Paris, and he was afraid the SS would outflank him.

On the 22nd August a special mission composed of five men (among them Rolf Nordling, brother of the Swedish consul who had been compelled to take to his bed with a heart attack, de Saint-Phalle, representing Parodi, and von Poch-Pastor,) went to Trappes. Commander Bender escorted them through the German lines to ask the Allies to hasten their advance towards Paris. On the same day Colonel Rol sent Commandant Gallois, one of his staff officers, to General Bradley, to inform him that the Paris Resistance required immediate support if they were to avoid being overwhelmed.

All the Resistance leaders, whether they were or were not in favour of the armistice, apparently knew that Choltitz could wipe out the Resistance and destroy Paris. And Choltitz himself was still in a dilemma. He telephoned Speidel at his headquarters in Cambrai, and the conversation went as follows:

Choltitz. I am phoning to thank you for that marvellous order you sent me.
Speidel. What order, Herr General?
Choltitz. The order to reduce Paris to a pile of rubble. *(His voice was quite calm.)* Perhaps you will allow me to acquaint you with the arrangements I have made. Three tons of explosives have been placed in the Cathedral of Notre-Dame; two tons in the Invalides, and a ton in the Chamber of Deputies. I am preparing to blow up the Arc de Triomphe to clear the range of fire. Well, I suppose you agree with all this, my dear Speidel?
Speidel. Yes . . . Yes, of course, Herr General.
Choltitz. After all, it was you who gave orders for this to be done, wasn't it?
Speidel. No, no; we did not order it. The order came from the Führer.
Choltitz. I beg your pardon; it was you who transmitted the order, and you will bear the responsibility before history.

I can also tell you what other arrangements I have made. We shall blow up the Madeleine and the Opera House at a single charge. Similarly the Eiffel Tower, because the iron girders will obstruct access to the bridges which I shall also destroy later.
Speidel. Herr General, we are certainly very fortunate in having you in Paris.[83]

This conversation, charged with undertones, confirms the existence of a tacit understanding between the two generals who had protested against the Führer's excesses. What happened subsequently is well known. Bradley and Eisenhower, urged by de Gaulle and Koenig, authorized Leclerc's division to march on Paris with the object of

[83] Speidel, *Invasion 44*, Stuttgart, 1949.

liberating the city. This became a fact when Choltitz signed the surrender document on the 26th August.

We also know that Choltitz was tried *in absentia* and condemned for high treason in April 1945. His friends succeeded in dragging out the trial, so that it became impossible to carry out the sentence.

From the examination of all this evidence it appears clear that Choltitz received both the order and the means to destroy Paris. It is equally true that he could have crushed the insurrectionary forces. His humanity and courageous action in the story of the liberation of Paris deserves a special tribute.

7. The Liberation of Antwerp

Antwerp was an objective of primary importance. The artificial Channel ports could not suffice to route all the necessary supplies and material towards the front to keep up with the advance of the Allied armies.

On the 10th June a "pipe-line under the Ocean" (Pluto) was put into service from the Isle of Wight, and supplied the Allied armies with fuel as they advanced. By the end of the war Pluto was 2400 kilometres long. But that was not enough. Food, ammunition, motor transport and other materials were needed. All these essentials were required at an ever increasing rate.

From the beginning Cherbourg was unserviceable, and remained so a long time after the liberation (27th June). Furthermore, as the German forces withdrew they shut themselves up in the ports of Saint-Malo, Brest, Lorient and Saint-Nazaire. In fact, Brest resisted until it was completely destroyed on the 18th September. Later on La Rochelle, Calais, Boulogne and Dunkirk suffered the same fate.

Taking all these facts into account, the importance of the port of Antwerp increased day after day. Eisenhower said so quite definitely;[84] Churchill maintained that the Allies attached great importance to the capture of Antwerp and keeping it intact. Then, suddenly, Montgomery's forces entered Antwerp on the 4th September, and found the port installations intact. How could such a thing have happened?

Montgomery[85] did not explain this when describing the battle for the mouth of the Escaut, which he erroneously calls the Battle of

[84] Eisenhower, *Crusade in Europe*, London, 1948, p. 291.
[85] Montgomery, *The Montgomery Memoirs*, London, 1958, p. 196.

Antwerp. W. Bedell-Smith[86] Eisenhower's Chief of staff, Confirms
that the Allies found Antwerp intact, but offers no explanation. Admiral
Ruge, a staff officer of Rommel's Army Group B,[87] said that Antwerp
remained practically undamaged, he but did not enter into details.

Military historians are no more precise. Commander Kenneth
Edwards, the biographer of Admiral Ramsay who commanded the
inter-Allied forces, mentioned all the ports damaged by the enemy
before surrender, and expressed astonishment on finding that Antwerp,
the largest of them all, fell almost intact into their hands.[88] He gives no
details, but says that the condition of Antwerp was not due to the fact
that the Germans did not attempt to destroy the port, but that their
efforts were frustrated by the Belgian Resistance forces.

Pogue,[89] the official historian of the Pentagon, writes only of the
battle for Antwerp, without mentioning the part played by the Belgian
Resistance, except in so far as the Ardennes was concerned.

Chester Wilmot, who had access to British documents, and refers
briefly to the Belgian Resistance forces, writes:

> On September 4th, however, the 11th Armoured Division, having skirted
> Brussels to the west, moved into Antwerp so boldly and swiftly that the leading
> tanks reached the docks by early afternoon and found them unguarded and almost
> unscathed. This was a tremendous stroke of fortune, for the sluice gates and the
> dockside equipment, all electrically operated, could so easily have been put out
> of action.[90]

The truth is that it was not altogether a tremendous stroke of fortune
that the 11th Armoured Division was able to enter "so boldly and
swiftly", but rather the result of a plan carefully prepared and elaborated
to the last detail early in 1944. It was extremely fortunate, as General
Bouhon has shown in a very detailed study, that "we were able to
make it possible for the Belgian Resistance to play a vital part in the
liberation of the port of Antwerp".

Bouhon's work provides a most valuable account of the history of
this period. According to him the Germans fortified Antwerp at the
beginning of 1944; and in consequence the Belgian Resistance forces

[86] Bedell-Smith, *Eisenhower's Six Great Decisions : Europe 1941-45*, New York,
1956, p. 83.

[87] Ruge, *Der Seekrieg, 1939-45*, Stuttgart, 1954, p. 314.

[88] K. Edwards, *Operation Neptune*, London, 1946, p. 301.

[89] Pogue, *The European Theater of Operations : The Supreme Command*, Government Printing Office, Washington, 1954, p. 300.

[90] Wilmot, *The Struggle for Europe*, London, 1951, p. 474.

prepared an important scheme to protect the port. The various branches of the Resistance, such as the Secret Army, the Independence Front, the National Royalist Movement and the Witte Brigade created a co-ordinating committee whose aim was to save the port from destruction. The control of military operations was placed in the hands of a lieutenant of Engineers named Urbain Reniers. This self-contained military unit prepared a plan of action as follows:

> On the 19th May 1944 precise orders were issued for the carrying out of the 'operational' phase, and this included three missions:
> *First mission* — Steps to be taken with a view to dislocating rail traffic; action against bridges and roads to be undertaken secretly and by zones. The agreed code message to be used: 'Solomon has put on his big clogs'.
> *Second mission* — Harassing tactics, to include sabotage of the enemy telecommunications network. The agreed code message to be used: 'The yellow jonquil is in flower'.
> *Third mission* — Open fighting to be conducted by organized units. Warning message to be: 'The foliage of the trees hides the old mill from your sight'.[91]

The preservation of the port of Antwerp is an undisputed historical fact, and it was the achievement of the Belgian Resistance forces. From the 28th November to the 8th May, 1140 Allied ships docked at Antwerp. They unloaded five million tons of material of all kinds and more than seventy thousand vehicles. Antwerp thus became the Allies' principal port, and for several months their only port; and it played a decisive part in the final battle of the western front. Its importance was demonstrated when the Germans made their last attempt to recapture the initiative: the Ardennes offensive, which had selected Antwerp as its objective.[92]

From the 25th to the 31st August essential destruction was carried out, and from the 1st to the 4th September steps were taken to forestall destruction by the enemy. "It will be appreciated," wrote Bernard, "that these missions necessitated a single command combined with excellent liaison."[93]

It then remained to open up Antwerp to the Allied forces and make the port available — an extremely delicate operation. Major Lovinfosse,

[91] Bouhon, in *European Resistance Movements*, p. 269.
[92] Research in this connexion has been undertaken by the *Centre National des Deux Guerres Mondiales*, of which V. van Straelen is President and J. Willequet is the General Secretary.
[93] Bernard, *La guerre et son évolution à travers les siècles*, Tome II: *de 1939 à aujourd'hui*. Brussels, 1957.

charged with the task of co-ordinating the activities of the British 2nd Army and the Belgian Resistance, proceeded to Laeken to make contact with General Horrocks, commander of the 2nd Army. The General's tent was in the grounds of the royal castle. He welcomed the Major warmly, and said that his army had just advanced seventy kilometres, a feat probably without precedent in history. He thanked Lovinfosse for the support of the Belgian Resistance, without which his progress would have been impossible. He was not sure, however, whether he could continue to advance at his present pace, in view of the strength of enemy forces that lay between Brussels and Antwerp.

General Horrocks consulted General Pire, commanding the Belgian Secret Army. Pire was installed at a farm called La Renardière, in Malaise, Brabant. After the talks, and while the Belgian Queen Mother, Queen Elizabeth, was entertaining the three officers at the royal castle, the 2nd Army continued to roll in the direction of Antwerp.

In the port itself Lieutenant Vekemans, an Engineer of the Resistance, inspected the approaches to the port during the afternoon of the 3rd September, and found that all the bridges had been mined.

At 8.15 in the morning Vekemans sat at a table in a café near the cross-roads of the Brussels–Antwerp motorway. While he was having breakfast his eyes remained fixed on the road in the direction of Brussels, waiting for the first Allied tanks to appear.

At about nine o'clock he perceived a mass of tanks which he at first thought were German tanks in retreat. But when he heard the joyful shouts of the people — 'The English are coming! The English are here!' — he rushed out into the road. Standing in the middle of the cross-roads, Lieutenant Vekemans made frantic signs in an attempt to stop the first tank; but it paid no attention to his appeals, and went on its way over the cross-roads in the direction of Antwerp. He managed to stop the second tank, and the officer in command told him that any information should be addressed to Major Dunlop who was in the fourth tank.

It seemed impossible that one man in a raincoat, standing in the middle of the highway, could hold up this mass of armour sweeping at speed towards the Rupel bridges under orders to make for Antwerp with the minimum delay. How could this stranger influence a column of tanks whose mission it was to open up a way for the army of liberation?

Yet the miracle happened, and what seemed quite impossible occurred. Major Dunlop stopped his tank, and after a few moments of suspicion during which, revolver in hand, he held Vekemans at a safe distance, he listened to his story, ascertained his identity and qualifications, and was made acquainted with the Lieutenant's plan.[94]

[94] De Villers, *La résistance belge dans la libération du port d'Anvers* (Thése).

Vekemans managed to persuade Major Dunlop to call the leading tanks back to the cross-roads, and direct them to a point where they could not be spotted by the Germans who were waiting to blow up the bridges at Boom. Major Dunlop followed the advice of Vekemans, and directed the first two tanks towards the bridge at Entschodt, where the brave lieutenant was able to disconnect the fuse from the mine.

Owing to the speed of the advance the German defence was taken by surprise from the rear. This success was quickly exploited by the British under the guidance of the Resistance forces, with the result that the principal port installations were captured within a few hours.

Then followed the battle for the "mouth of the Escaut", and once again the Resistance rendered valuable service to the Allies. But the capture of the port of Antwerp intact remains their greatest feat of arms.

8. The Italian Resistance Movement

The historical fact of Italian Resistance has never been disputed, but little attention has been paid to the question of its efficacy. The researches carried out by various Italian organizations, in particular by the *Istituto Nazionale per la Storia del Movimento di Liberazione*,[95] have made it possible to assess the importance of the Italian Resistance movement.

It is known that the movement lost 72,000 killed (including civilians massacred) and 39,167 wounded and disabled. It is also well known that the Italian Resistance was the first of the European movements, and that it started in 1924. Anti-Fascists were few and divided among themselves. They developed their activities with determination, and tended to unite, especially at the time of the Spanish civil war to which they sent five thousand volunteers.

Despite Franco's victory, followed by the defeat of France, the Italian anti-Fascist movement continued to spread. Even in Italy propaganda and an underground Press developed considerably. The overthrow of Mussolini by the Fascists themselves created a revolutionary atmosphere which allowed the Resistance movement to assert itself more freely, despite the fact that the Badoglio goverment imprisoned the anti-Fascists. It was only on the 9th September 1943, after the departure of the King and Badoglio, that the Resistance became sufficiently firmly established to be able to set up a Committee of

---

[95] Its President is Senator Parri, and its Secretary General is Professor Vaccarino.

National Liberation to take an active part against the German occupation army.

Italy was not yet liberated, and the members of the Italian Resistance at first stood alone against Marshal Kesselring's forces. They were later joined in the north by the forces of Mussolini's neo-Fascist republic; but the Allied advance had the effect of cutting northern Italy off from the south. The Resistance in the south then linked up with the Italian liberation army which by the end of 1943 numbered 14,000 men, and in October 1944, 54,000. The Committee of National Liberation was at first hostile to the Badoglio government, but supported it in April 1944.

The movement in the north formed a Committee of National Liberation of Northern Italy (the CLN), as well as a unit of Freedom Volunteers (the CVL), which was placed under the command of General Cadorna.[96] When the Allies were halted in the summer of 1944 the Resistance forces in the north were more or less free to take the initiative. Their activities developed in two directions: preparing for an armed uprising, and safeguarding conquered territory.

This state of affairs continued from the summer of 1944 to April 1945. The armed insurrection began with skirmishes, and sometimes took the form of guerilla warfare; but eventually their activities were systematized and carried out in co-ordination with the Allied armies.

It is impossible to recount in detail the skirmishes, the guerilla fighting that went on all over Italy.[97] It must suffice to say that Marshal Kesselring has written of the great difficulties he encountered as a result of the action of Italian Resistance. The Marshal has also shown how the partisans' methods of warfare upset the plans of the Wehrmacht on numerous occasions. The Alpine valleys, the Friuli and the high plateaux of Venetia were in the hands of the partisans, and any German force that ventured in those regions was subjected to harassing attacks. In August 1944 nearly 100,000 armed men held these regions, and they obliged the Germans and the Fascists to hurl several divisions against them. For instance, the district of Montefiorino, near Modena, was attacked by two divisions, and the partisan troops were destroyed. The same thing happened at Monte Grappa. All these guerilla activities provoked the most cruel reprisals. The most bitter battles took place during August and September 1944.

[96] Son of the 1918 Commander-in-Chief.

[97] See Battaglia, *Storia della Resistenza italiana*, Turin, 1953; Longo, *Sulla via dell'insurrezzione nazionale*, Rome, 1954.

It is also noteworthy that on 30th May 1944 Juvenal, representing the FFI, and Bianco, representing the CLN in the Piemonte district, met at Saretto, in the valley of Maira, and perfected a plan of sabotage to be carried out in the Alpine hills; this resulted in closing the Alps at the time of the landing in Provence, and rendered impassable several retreat roads.[98]

These activities culminated in a meeting in Rome on the 7th December 1944 between General Wilson, Allied Commander-in-Chief, and Pizzoni and Parri, representatives of the CLN in northern Italy. This meeting resulted in the recognition of the CLN of northern Italy, which received a delegation from the Bonomi government and was regarded by the Allies as exercising governmental functions in the occupied zone until the arrival of the liberation armies. The CVL also fought within the framework of the Allied strategical and tactical command. President Parri gave us the following account of the results of the Rome meeting:

Our talks with General Wilson took place in a room of the Grand Hotel. We already had regular contacts with the Allies through the intermediary of an information centre of the OSS and the Intelligence Branch installed in Lugano, under the direction of MacCaffery and Allen Dulles. In the second half of 1944 a more regular and permanent contact was considered necessary, and the object of our mission to Rome was to establish this contact.

General Wilson had the majestic bearing of a pro-consul; he greeted my friends and myself with an air of great condescension, and his aloof and distant manner left us puzzled.

The talks were particularly difficult, and subject to frequent disagreements. Several meetings were necessary between the 23rd November and the 7th December, when we managed to reach agreement. The Allies were divided between their desire to control the Resistance in northern Italy and an inclination to give it moderate support.

We do not want men who are politicians', said General Wilson; 'we want administrators, men who are honest, competent and impartial, and who will not encourage one trend or another.'

'But we want legal recognition of our existence and our authority,' we replied.

'The Commander-in-Chief's first reaction was to refuse us this recognition, but he eventually yielded to our reasoning. The Rome agreement influenced the Italian government to regard us as its representatives in northern Italy as from 26th December. On 13th December a new delegation of the CLN, to which I also belonged, went to Lyons to take the necessary steps in conjunction with the committee of Italian émigrés in France to repatriate Italian partisans who had taken

[98] Agreements were reached between the French and Italian Resistance in the region of the Maritime Alps. For other instances of French and Italian co-operation see *European Resistance Movements 1939–45*, Milan, March 1961 Conference Pergamon Press, 1964.

refuge in France, and to ensure a permanent liaison between Milan, Turin and Rome, via France. In any case, the Rome agreements entirely changed the conditions of the war in northern Italy.

The partisans helped the Allies to advance more rapidly. They liberated Florence, Belluno, Padua, Genoa, Turin and Milan, and in Venetia alone they took more than 100,000 prisoners.

It was at this moment that the second aspect of the efficacy of Italian Resistance — the protection of territory — really came into its own. In the industrial towns widespread strikes, hampering economic production in the rear of the German army, took place in September 1944 and in April 1945. The partisans set themselves as objective the protection of port installations and the industrial organizations of Milan and Turin, and to a great extent they succeeded. In this sphere alone the value of Italian Resistance is proved.

If the views expressed by the Allies are not entirely convincing, those expressed by Marshal Kesselring show that the Germans certainly recognized the efficacy and military value of the Italian Resistance movement. According to the British there were 90,000 partisans to the north of the Apennines in April 1945. Kesselring puts the figure at 200,000 to 300,000 during the same period who hampered his operations. It was the moral value of the Resistance that lay behind the new Italian democracy, and has preserved the territorial unity of the Italian peninsula.

9. The Battle of Warsaw

More often than not the liberation of occupied capitals, such as Paris, Prague, Sofia, Budapest and Bucharest, was the occasion of serious uprisings. The Warsaw insurrection was typical of the uprisings in the east, just as Paris remained the model of those in the west of Europe. In any case, the battle for Warsaw was conducted on an exceptional scale, and merits close study because of the controversies to which it has given rise.

The essential facts are well known. An army of the interior (Armija Krajowa — AK) had been created in 1940 to organize underground warfare. This army obeyed the émigré Polish government in London after the fall of France. Polish patriots, those belonging to the AK and those based in London, strove for the restoration of Polish independence, which for Britain and France had been the original objective of the second world war.

The AK was a very well-disciplined organization, and obtained surprising results in the sphere of Intelligence work and sabotage (25,000 cases of alleged sabotage). This army of Resistance fought as strongly against the Germans as it did against the Red Army, Their activities made Russo-Polish co-operation extremely difficult, though this co-operation was very necessary to the Allies following the German invasion of Russia in 1941.

When the Russians set their Polish prisoners of war free innumerable fresh problems were created, which complicated the renewal of normal diplomatic relations between Poland and Russia. The Soviets were anxious to see a friendly Poland on their frontiers after the war, and to this end they sanctioned the activities in the U.S.S.R. of a Polish émigré organization known as the Union of Polish Patriots. In Poland itself the Polish Workers' Party, set up at the beginning of 1942, formed a secret army — the People's Army (Armya Ludowa — A. L.) — which played a part in the struggle against the German occupation forces. On the 31st December 1943 a national council (Krajowa Rada Narodowa), a kind of underground parliament, was created in Warsaw; it was from this council that the Polish Committee of National Liberation (Polski Komitet Wyzwolenia Narodowego) — subsequently called the Lublin Committee — was formed on the 21st July 1944. This Committee raised an army composed of the First Polish Army, formed in Russia, the A. L., and a few military units of the Resistance.

After the German propaganda machine had announced the discovery by the Germans in April 1943 of the Katyn charnel-house, the Polish government in London asked the Red Cross organization to institute an enquiry. The request offended the Russians, and Moscow replied on the 25th April by breaking off diplomatic relations.

The antagonism between the government in London and the Lublin Committee became complete and irreparable during the summer of 1944; and Mikolajczyk, President of the Council, who had ideas of hiss own concerning the revision of the Polish frontiers, was rejected by his colleagues.

It was in this gloomy political atmosphere that the Red Army approached the Vistula. On the 1st August the Warsaw insurrection flared up. By the 28th September 1944 twenty thousand had taken part in the uprising. According to the Polish émigrés this revolt was crushed by the Germans, while the Red Army remained almost inactive on the right bank of the Vistula. The casualties were 10,000 killed and 7000 wounded; nearly 200,000 killed among the civil population, and Warsaw destroyed. Such were the consequences of the uprising.

Since then propagandist writers in both east and west have not
ceased to pour down reproaches on both the AK. Poles and the Russians.
The question at issue has always been: Did the Russians intend that the
Warsaw uprising should fail in its purpose? To seek the reply it is
necessary to consider two aspects of the question: the order to rise up,
and the part played by the Russians in the development of the battle.

1. Who gave the order for the insurrection, and why?

The decision was naturally political rather than military, and it came
from London. The plan of the uprising — the Puzak Plan — had been
prepared in great detail since the end of 1943.

Warsaw, as the Polish capital, had been extremely active throughout the war.
At a time when the fate of the nation was at stake, when the city itself had become
the front line, the people of Warsaw impatiently awaited the call to take up the
struggle against the hated occupying power. The longing to revenge all the atrocities committed by the Germans was reaching its peak.

Clearly the very fact that our capital would be liberated by our own soldiers
accentuated the determination of the nation to safeguard the sovereignty of the
Polish State. We saw in this final struggle against the occupying power the surest
means of preserving the national rights of Poland.[99]

But the decision to launch the uprising had been entrusted to a committee of three members: Engineer officer Jan Jankowski, the representative of the government in London, General Bor-Komorowski,
leader of the AK, and Kazimierz Puzak, a former director of the military
school and president of the co-ordination committee of Resistance
organizations. The decision was taken in Warsaw on the 31st July
because several circumstances appeared favourable:

1 — The German communiqué issued by the O.K.W. on the 31st
July announced that the Russians had launched a general attack
against Warsaw;

2 — The German army reckoned on being able to organize the
defence of Warsaw;

3 — The Soviet radio called on the people of Warsaw to rise up;[100]

[99] Bor–Komorowski in *European Resistance Movements 1939-45*, Vol, I p. 289.
[100] According to Mikolajczyk, in *The Rape of Poland*, p. 66, New York, 1948,
this reason was decisive. He says that the Koscivsko Radio Station (Soviet transmission to Poland) broadcast the following message: "Poles, the moment of liberation is approaching! To arms! Let every Polish house become a citadel in the
struggle against the invader! There is not a moment to lose." (29th July.) He
concluded that it was a definite appeal to Warsaw to rise up. This conclusion appears
to us, however, to be exaggerated. Similar appeals had been made by London to
the French patriots, well before the 6th June 1944. But for all that the population
of Paris did not rise up.

4 — The Soviet air force had air mastery over Warsaw.

General Tadeusz Komorowski (known as Bor) was then 46 years of age, and therefore in the prime of life. Short, energetic, a beloved and much respected leader, he was a splendid example of the chivalrous tradition and gallantry of the Polish army. We met him several times, and he reiterated to us the statement he had often made in 1952 and 1958. This testimony, although published eight years after the events, and in exile following captivity (he was a prisoner of the Germans from October 1944 to April 1945) corroborates the chronological facts already known. It shows clearly that he regarded the battle of Warsaw as a military operation, and that the internationally political aspect, with which he was not very well acquainted, was not his problem; even though he may have been aware of the political and ideological issues behind the uprising.

On the 31st July General Bor judged that the moment was opportune; and Jankowski, the government delegate who had plenary powers to make a decision in the event of the Russian advance being more rapid than anticipated, gave his approval. General Bor issued the order for action on the 1st August at seventeen hours. The decision was premature; and, in any case, the Poles in London were divided on the matter.

General Anders, who followed the operations from his headquarters in Ancona, Italy, has since related:

When General Sosnkowski, relying upon a previous understanding between the Polish authorities in London and those in Poland, told me that an early armed uprising in Poland was contemplated, I thought the matter over carefully during the little leisure that remained to me outside my existing duties, and I arrived at the conclusion that the success of the uprising depended upon three things:

1 — The degree of disintegration of the German army;
2 — The aid which the Polish armed forces and the western Allies could furnish;
3 — Russian aid, and the attitude that Soviet Russia might adopt.

We were especially uneasy about the third condition. The German army was falling back along the whole length of the eastern front; some of its divisions had been wiped out, but in general it showed no signs of demoralization or disintegration. The German retreat was being carried out in good order and in compact units, fighting bitterly against a Soviet army which was vastly superior numerically. It was not the kind of retreat that might portend the success of an uprising carried out exclusively by underground forces without outside aid.

The only aid that might be expected from the Polish troops and the western Allies was air support. General Sosnkowski gave his estimate of the value of this assistance in the following telegram dated the 20th October 1943, addressed to the Commander of the Army of the Interior:

'... The fulfilment of the above-mentioned conditions will enable us to support the uprising from our own resources, but certainly not earlier than the beginning of 1945 ... Any independent and premature use of the Polish air force — which could not reach the fighting zone in Poland without excessive consumption of fuel — would be nothing but an act of despair. This kind of use of air resources would result in the destruction of our air power at a single blow and on the first occasion, and would not exert the slightest influence on the course of operations ...'

Owing to the distance from the bases, and the radius of action of the planes then in use, western aid could not be efficacious at that time.[101]

If such were the existing conditions how could the decision to rise up have been precipitated? On the 7th July 1944 General Sosnkowski, the army commander, telegraphed to Bor an order to launch against the Germans a gradually expanding series of actions in order to create diversions, but not a general uprising. The Council of Ministers, however, meeting in London on the 25th July, agreed to authorize Jankowski, their delegate in Poland, to make all necessary decisions regarding the insurrection, even without reference to London.

On the 26th July Mikolajczyk, on his departure for Moscow, drafted a telegram for Jankowski which ran: "The Council of Ministers has unanimously agreed to authorize you to order the uprising at a time to be chosen by you. If possible advise us in advance".[102]

On the 28th July the Council of Ministers met again, and were informed of Mikolajczyk's telegram in the latter's absence. Raczkiewicz, President of the Republic, forbade the despatch of the telegram, and ordered Sosnkowski to return urgently to London. Sosnkowski did not do so until the 6th August!

It is therefore clear that the decision taken by Bor, in conjunction with Jankowski, to launch the insurrection was founded upon prior instructions from London. The decision was absolutely premature. Anders telegraphed Kopanski on the 3rd August: "I personally regard the decision taken by the Commander of the Army of the Interior as a calamity".

Anders's military unit was in Ancona, and Sosnkowski discussed the problem of the Warsaw uprising with him. Anders asked Sosnkowski to forbid categorically any revolt in the existing circumstances. Sosnkowski yielded to his arguments, and sent a new telegram to Bor on the 28th July: "In view of the unilateral action taken by the Soviet and their

[101] Anders, *Mémoires (1939–1946)*, Paris, 1948, p. 293.
[102] Anders, *ibid.*

policy which involves violation of agreements, an armed uprising would be devoid of all political sense, and could only result in useless slaughter."[103]

Mikolajczyk, President of the Council, was at that time proceeding to Moscow in an attempt to reach some sort of understanding with the Soviet. Roosevelt and Churchill had both asked Stalin to receive Mikolajczyk, who left London by air for Moscow, via Cairo.[104]

On the 29th July Sosnkowski sent a further telegram to Bor: "In view of the existing political situation I am absolutely opposed to a general uprising . . ." And on the 30th to General Kopanski, the Chief of Staff: "I am definitely opposed under present conditions to a general uprising . . . The Council of Ministers should not consider the matter without first knowing the result of the Moscow talks".[105]

Bor's decision was, however, conformable in every respect with the intentions of the Council of Ministers when it met on the 25th July. The evidence of Anders was written four years after the events, but it is based on indisputable documents. The subsequent statements by Mikolajczyk in 1948 do not invalidate the account given by Anders.

Thus, the only documents of the Polish émigrés extant show that the decision in favour of the uprising was unbelievably reckless. The three Warsaw statemen acted in pursuance of their personal appreciation of the facts, which was very inadequate; and the Polish authorities in London acted with extraordinary ignorance of the facts. Even if we allow that their purpose was to impose legal recognition of their government by using their army to liberate the capital, nothing can excuse the absence of the President of the Council and that of General Sosnkowski at this decisive moment. The most important fact of all was that Mikolajczyk had gone to Moscow at that precise moment to seek a basis of agreement with the Russians, an agreement which would certainly have had some bearing upon the liberation of Warsaw.

Moreover, the British and American governments had not been forewarned, and from the outset the uprising was completely isolated, without hope of support from the western or eastern Allies.[106]

---

[103] Anders, *op. cit.*
[104] Mikolajczyk, *The Rape of Poland*, New York, 1948, p. 66.
[105] Anders, *op. cit.*
[106] Marshal Rokosovsky subsequently stated that he had warned General Bor by telegram that "any initiative on his part would be premature, so long as it was not possible to concentrate sufficient troops to fight a decisive action". Bor told us that he never received the telegram.

2. Why was the uprising crushed?

When the rebellion broke out the Polish government in London did everything it could to support General Bor's forces which, as Mikolajczyk himself admitted, had sufficient supplies of food and munitions for seven days only — although Bor actually held out for sixty-three days, until his forces were completely annihilated.

Many authors have given accounts of the battle for Warsaw, which marks one of the heroic pages in the history of the second world war. But the root of the matter lies in a statement made by Mikolajczyk in 1948, that, following the intrigues of Stalin and the Party, the Red Army deliberately allowed the Polish patriots to be massacred in order to get rid of an élite which would never have submitted to the enslavement of their country.[107]

In 1944 President Mikolajczyk was forty-three years of age, and the leader of the Peasant Party. He introduced a new leaven into the direction of the Polish government, which up to then had been controlled by more conservative elements, men who were in closer contact with the army. He very quickly showed his desire to take over supreme control of the army, but General Sosnkowski, the Commander-in-Chief, refused to allow himself to be manipulated. The astute peasant leader was a realist, and he yielded. He was prepared to bring the question up again at the first opportune moment, but the relationship existing between himself and the army remained one of distrust and suspicion.

It was this same quality of political realism that subsequently led him to seek a rapprochement with Russia; but his efforts were opposed by his colleagues. After the battle for Warsaw he resigned dramatically. In 1945 he returned to Poland to join the Polish government that had sprung from the Lublin Committee. In 1947, when he was about to be arrested, he fled from Poland and found refuge in the United States.

His testimony, written in exile, dates from 1948, four years after the events. He expressed strong resentment against the Russians with whom he had ceased to be on good terms in 1944. We met Mikolajczyk in Warsaw in 1946, and at the time of our talks with him he had not yet come to adopt that strong anti-Soviet attitude that he evinced in 1948. This unique evidence must therefore be used with caution, and we must keep closely to the established facts.

We know that on the 2nd August General Bor asked the western Allies and Russia for aid. Raczkiewicz, President of the government

[107] Cf. Mikolajczyk, *The Rape of Poland*, New York, 1948.

in London, asked Churchill, and then Roosevelt, for immediate aid; but it was not until the 12th August that the British general staff decided to approach General Wilson and ask him to consider aid to Warsaw. The British suggested that they and the American general staff might co-operate in organizing aerial support from Great Britain or Italy, and ask the Soviet authorities to grant speedy aid to Warsaw by bombing and parachute landings.

On the 17th August Churchill replied to Rankiewicz that everything possible would be done to assist Warsaw, but that technical and geographical conditions were such that aerial operations would entail great losses. On the 23rd Marshal Brooke promised General Anders his support, and on the 26th Churchill told Anders that they were not prepared to undertake air action above Warsaw, although everything in their power was being done to give air support.

Anders pointed out that for three years the Soviet had been urging Warsaw to rise up. As the Russians advanced further into Poland they increased their propaganda to this effect, until they finally announced that they were in the outskirts of Warsaw. However, from the moment the insurrection broke out, that is, from the 1st August, they remained quite silent, and did not raise a finger to afford the slightest aid to the Army of the Interior. Churchill told Anders that he was aware of this. The Americans went so far as to say that they were prepared to undertake flights over Warsaw from England: a shuttle service of fifty flights, with landings at Poltava in Soviet territory. When Stalin was approached he refused to agree even to that.

Prime Minister Churchill said that the Russians would have no difficulty in providing aid, as they were scarcely thirty kilometres from Warsaw; whereas the British would have to fly 780 miles from their bases in Italy. Churchill also told Anders that Great Britain's treaty with Poland did not guarantee her frontiers; she regarded her engagements as relating to Poland's existence as a free, independent, powerful and sovereign State, whose citizens should live there happily, and enjoy freedom in their country without being threatened by any foreign influence. He added that the Poles should not be set on maintaining their eastern frontiers.[108]

---

[108] Anders, in *Mémoires (1939–1946)*, p. 307, mentions the report by Brigadier Frith, British liaison officer with the 2nd Polish Army Corps. The losses sustained by the First Polish Army between the 16th and 23rd August were 3764 killed (J. Margules, *Przycky Warszawie*, p. 241, MON, Warsaw, 1962).

In any case, the Poles had not given the western Allies any prior warning; their reaction was therefore at first unfavourable, and the British even forbade the Poles to address Warsaw through the BBC. Despite that the Allies attempted the impossible to come to the help of the insurgents: from the 1st to the 27th August 160 flights were carried out, involving the loss of 27 planes. Of 71 parachute drops made, 58 were successful in landing supplies to the insurgents. Between the 28th August and the 1st September 12 planes flew from Italy; two returned without having reached their objective, and the others were lost. On the 18th September 110 American Flying Fortresses set off from London, and made 107 parachute drops over Warsaw from a very high altitude; 15 containers reached their destinations.

From the beginning of September the battles were merely defensive, and the Germans offered a truce which was rejected. As for the Russians, their attitude was at first one of surprise: there had been no prior contact between the AK and the Red Army.

When the Red Army reached the Vistula it had accomplished an almost uninterrupted march of 500 kilometres, and had attained its objective. Should Marshal Rokosvsky have gone beyond his operational orders and attacked Warsaw, while his forward troops were experiencing a serious shortage of munitions, and when their supply services were not keeping up with them?[109] Could he have done this while his front line presented a gigantic salient exposed to the German attacks,[110] and in the knowledge that the Germans would obviously defend Warsaw vigorously?[111]

It seems likely that the halting of the Red Army at the Vistula was based entirely on military requirements. Any other decision would have had to be taken on a political level. Stalin was concerned with future policy in relation to Poland; the question whether Russia remained on friendly terms with Poland was bound up with traditional Russian policy.

On the 3rd August Stalin received Mikolajczyk, who said to him, "Above all I am here to ask you to give immediate assistance to our men engaged in an unequal and dreadful struggle against the Germans", To which Stalin replied, "I cannot rely upon the Poles. They suspect

[109] It is important to note that the Russians had to rebuild the railway tracks.
[110] E. Boltine in *European Resistance Movements* (L'Union Soviétique et la Résistance en Europe), Pergamon Press, 1962.
[111] The Germans had withdrawn the Hermann Goering Division from Italy for this purpose. See Bor-Komorowski, *Histoire d'une armée secrète*, Paris, 1952.

me of wishing to occupy Poland again, and they create many problems for me".[112]

Stalin told Mikolajczyk that he should first come to an agreement with the Lublin Committee. Mikolajczyk met the Committee's leaders, but did not succeed in reaching an understanding. Moreover, Stalin depended on the Lublin Committee whose members would ensure that the two countries remained on friendly terms; he could therefore afford to treat the representative of the Poles in London in a lackadaisical manner. He had certainly not been informed by London of the Warsaw uprising.

Churchill wrote to Stalin urging him to take action. In his acknowledgement of the 5th August Stalin told Churchill that he thought the information given to Churchill had been grossly exaggerated; it did not, therefore, inspire him with confidence. The Polish nationalist army consisted merely of a few detachments, wrongly referred to as divisions. They had no guns, no air force and no armour. Stalin said that he could not understand how such small forces hoped to take Warsaw, while the Germans had four armoured divisions to defend it, including the Hermann Goering Division.

When Stalin had examined the position he changed his attitude, and wrote to Churchill to the effect that he had had a talk with Mikolajczyk, and had afterwards given orders to the Red Army to carry out an intensive parachute drop of arms in the area of Warsaw. A liaison officer was also parachuted into Warsaw, but, according to the garrison commander, the officer was killed by the Germans before he was able to reach his destination. Later on, when Stalin was better informed about Warsaw, he told Churchill that he was convinced the Warsaw operation would be a mad and dreadful adventure, resulting in a large number of victims among the civil population. Such a thing could not happen had the Soviet commander been informed beforehand, and had the Poles maintained contact with him. Stalin added that the Soviet commander had decided from the situation thus created that he had no alternative but to break his ties with the Warsaw adventure, and that he bore no responsibility, direct or indirect, in the operation.[113]

In point of fact, the attitude of the Red Army followed a logical development. We have seen that when Rokosovsky attained his ob-

[112] Mikolajczyk, *The Rape of Poland*, New York, 1948.
[113] See *Correspondence between the Chairman of the Council of the U.S.S.R. and the President of the U.S.A. and the Prime Minister of Great Britain during the Great Patriotic War 1941–45*, in two volumes, Moscow, 1957.

jective he halted his summer offensive on the Vistula, before Warsaw.[114] On the 10th September, having re-established his lines of communication, he proceeded to attack Praga with the 47th Army from the Byelorussia front; and on the 4th he succeeded in entering the city. The A.L. was charged with the task of establishing bridgeheads across the Vistula. It succeeded, but failed to hold its position and had to retire on the 23rd September. On the other hand the Soviet air force dropped arms and ammunition by parachute between the 14th and 29th September — 2243 sorties, according to the Russians. Bor stated that twelve drops were successful.

On the 30th September Bor sent a message to Marshal Rokosovsky "advising him that it was impossible to continue the combat more than three days longer without immediate assistance". On the 2nd October he brought the fighting to an end.

The heroism of the combatants in Warsaw has never been questioned. The Soviet attitude must be seen from two points of view, the military and the political. The Soviet military leaders apparently acted strictly in accordance with pre-arranged plans. Had they at that time laid siege to Warsaw, they would have jeopardized the success of their offensive in Rumania.[115]

From the political point of view it has never been established that Stalin and his associates deliberately decided to allow the Warsaw uprising to be crushed, although they certainly wished to encourage the Lublin Committee to the detriment of the Polish government in London. Indeed, several facts suggest that the Russians wanted the rebellion to succeed. For example, on the 4th August the Warsaw Communists joined up with the AK; and the forces attacking Praga clearly anticipated the plans of the Red Army. From a military point of view the AK had ammunition for seven days only, and expected to have to hold out for two or three days before linking up with the Soviet army.

Further, it is quite wrong to compare the Warsaw uprising with the liberation of Paris. Even though the uprising in Paris was premature,

[114] Zhukov told General Stirling afterwards that, when they arrived near Warsaw, the German forces facing them were so formidable that they thought they would not be able to cross the Vistula unless those forces were considerably reduced. (Cf. Wilmot, *The Struggle for Europe*, p. 814.) Moreover, the Russians were afraid that Hitler might withdraw his divisions from the west and bring them up to the east to defend the road to Berlin. The Russians were completely re-assured when they had news of the Ardennes offensive.

[115] Wilmot, *op. cit.*, p. 564.

the Germans did not expect to undergo a siege; the Parisians were in communication with the Allies, and the German commander abandoned his intention to destroy the city. In any case, the Allied offensive began in the west, and their armies intended to encircle Paris, while the Russian offensive near Warsaw came to an end before their forces reached the city.

It is also interesting to note that strong German forces were held down in Warsaw in the action against the insurgents. This concentration of German troops enabled the Red Army to reorganize and pursue more confidently its offensive against Yugoslavia. The Germans, who always imagined that they could provoke distrust and division among the Allies, made a grave political error in not allowing Warsaw to be liberated by the AK, for that would have aggravated the disagreements with regard to Poland, and allowed the German divisions to be used more profitably in south east Europe. But Hitler did not think of that, and the military, wholly taken up with the battle, were too busy defending themselves to bother about politics.

The Battle of Warsaw really emphasized the difference of concept as between soldiers and politicians, both Allied and German.

10. The Potsdam Conference

On the 8th May 1945 the Germans accepted the Allies' terms — "unconditional surrender" — and the war in Europe was at an end. On the 17th July the Big Three met again in Berlin, or more precisely at Potsdam, in order to draw up new plans.

Roosevelt was no longer with them; he had died on the 12th April, and Truman had replaced him. Churchill was present, but his spirit was in London where the first post-war General Election was taking place, an election in which he was defeated, and replaced[116] at the Potsdam Conference by his opponent Clement Attlee. Stalin acted as host at the Conference, surrounded by a numerous suite, on territory that his armies had conquered.

The Conference lasted two weeks. The agenda included the drafting of the peace treaty, the occupation of Germany, the question of reparations and the political organization of liberated Europe. As is well known, the discussions ended in compromise.

[116] On the 25th July 1945.

The statesmen broached the problem of the war with Japan almost by accident. This subject, with which in different circumstances Roosevelt and Churchill would have dealt in detail, was scamped almost by common agreement; by Truman and Attlee because they were unfamiliar with the ways of Stalin and scarcely knew how to deal with the Marshal of the U.S.S.R.; and by Stalin because he had no desire to return to the subject of his previous talks with Roosevelt.

At Yalta President Roosevelt was anxious to be able to count upon the participation of Russia in the war against Japan, and had promised Stalin in exchange for his intervention the return to Russia of the Kurile Islands and the northern part of the island of Sakhalin, the internationalization of the port of Dairen, and the lease of Port Arthur.[117] Stalin had therefore promised that the Soviet would join the war against Japan ninety days after Germany's capitulation. Stalin regarded this agreement as fundamental.

On the 24th July Stimson, the American Minister for War, received from Los Alamos a detailed report on the atomic bomb tests that had been carried out since the 16th July in New Mexico;[118] the experiment was a success. Stimson arrived in Potsdam by plane to inform Truman, who had been made aware of the existence of the bomb on the 25th April 1945 by Stimson.[119] Until that day the "Manhattan Project" (the name given to the construction of the bomb) had remained a secret. Since the 15th June 1940 two milliard dollars had been allocated to the scheme, and the number of people employed on it amounted to 100,000. None the less the scheme had been kept completely secret, and Admiral Leahy, who was President Truman's Chief of Staff, knew nothing of it up to the at time. Hmade it clear that he was sceptical of the "absurd" project which, in his opinion, could end only in disaster

Stimson had faith in the project and supported it, but Leahy did not fail to acquaint the President of his scepticism. As for Churchill, his mind was more concerned with his departure for London; and Stalin paid little attention to this news which Truman could no longer hide from him.

[117] Cf. Byrnes, *Speaking Frankly*, New York, 1947. This secret text, signed on the 11th February 1944, was locked up by Roosevelt in his safe at the White House, and was discovered only after his death.

[118] At Dr Oppenheimer's ranch.

[119] The Minister of War suggested to Truman that he should leave it to a committee of experts to decide on the use of the bomb, a suggestion which Truman accepted with relief.

On July 24th I casually mentioned to Stalin that we had a new weapon of special destructive force. The Russian Premier showed no unusual interest. All he said was that he was glad to hear it and hoped we would make 'good use of it against the Japanese'.[120]

There is no evidence to show that Stalin was really aware of the importance of this extraordinary weapon, the construction of which had been carefully hidden from him up to that time.

Japan faced a dilemma. The Battle of Guadalcanal, fought on the 15th November 1942, was the third military milestone in the history of the second world war,[121] for it marked the extreme limit of the Japanese progress. After February 1943 the Japanese were in retreat before the advancing forces of MacArthur and Admiral Nimitz who drove them from island to island.

In July 1945 the American troops under MacArthur, the supreme commander, prepared to invade Japan. On the 4th July 100,000 tons of bombs were dropped on Japan. The capital was defended by 2,000,000 men and 9000 planes; but the Japanese had 2,000,000 men in China, 650,000 in Malaysia, Indo-China and the Dutch East Indies, while 200,000 more were scattered around the islands. In Okinawa and the Philippines the Allies made ready for the final assault.

But the ultimate decision lay with Truman. He summoned his colleagues — Byrnes, the Secretary of State, Admiral Leahy, Generals Marshall and Arnold, and Admiral King.

We reviewed our military strategy in the light of this revolutionary development. We were not ready to make use of this weapon against the Japanese, although we did not know as yet what effect the new weapon might have, physically or psychologically, when used against the enemy. For that reason the military advised that we go ahead with the existing military plans for the invasion of the Japanese home islands.[122]

General Willoughby,[123] head of MacArthur's Intelligence service, has since stated that the Commander-in-Chief of the Pacific forces was advised by the United States government that Japan was at the end of

[120] Truman, Year of Decisions, 1945, New York, 1949, p. 346. This interesting detail is not to be found elsewhere. There is no mention of it in American documents or in any of the unpublished Soviet records.

[121] After the Battle of Britain and the battle of Stalingrad.

[122] Truman, Year of Decisions, 1945, p. 345.

[123] Willoughby and Chamberlain, MacArthur, 1941–1951, New York, 1956.

her tether, and that within a few weeks the final blow might be dealt with conventional weapons.

Apparently MacArthur's reports did not convince the American leaders of the three arms of the services, who advised Truman at Potsdam to make no changes to the pre-arranged plan; that is to say, concerning the intervention of Russia and the use of the atom bomb. They appear to have been influenced by two factors: firstly it was at that time impossible to foresee the effects of the atom bomb, and secondly, the victory over Japan by conventional weapons alone (based upon Mac-Arthur's reports) would cost the lives of a million men.

MacArthur's advice was not therefore followed, and Truman went off to spend a quiet week-end in Stuttgart. On the return of Attlee and Bevin (who had succeeded Churchill and Eden) a meeting took place -at 10.15 on the night of the 26th July.

Stalin said he wished to make an announcement before we went into the business of the meeting. He stated that the Russian delegation had received a proposal from Japan and that although the Soviet delegation had not been officially informed when the Anglo-American ultimatum was drawn up against Japan, nevertheless he wished to keep the Allies informed of an overture on the part of Japan.

The Russian interpreter then read for Stalin a communication from the Japanese ambassador to Moscow, Sato, which was, in substance, as follows:

On July 13 the Ambassador had had the honour to submit a proposal of the Japanese Government to send Prince Konoye to Moscow. He had received the reply of the Soviet Government which did not see the possibility of giving a definite reply to the approach because no definite proposal had been made. In order to make the matter more precise, he was communicating the following: The mission of Prince Konoye was to ask the Soviet Government to take part in mediation to end the present war and to transmit the complete Japanese case in this respect. He would also be empowered to negotiate with respect to Soviet-Japanese relations during the war and after the war . . .'

Stalin had told me, shortly after our arrival in Potsdam, that the Japanese had asked the Kremlin if it would be possible for Prince Konoye to come to Moscow. The Russians, so Stalin had informed me, had replied that they could not answer such a request until they knew what he wanted to talk about. It now appeared that the Japanese had sent another message, advising the Soviet Government that Prince Konoye would request Russian mediation and that he was acting on behalf of the Emperor who wanted to prevent further bloodshed in the war.

After the interpreter finished reading the Japanese message to Russia, Stalin declared that there was nothing new in it except that it was more definite than the previous approach and that it would receive a more definite answer than was the case the last time. The answer would be in the negative, he said.[124]

[124] Truman, *Year of Decisions, 1945*, p. 325. Truman's evidence is dated ten years after the events — 21st October 1955.

Thus, on the 26th July two of the Big Three were in agreement that Japan should be sent an ultimatum demanding unconditional surrender.[125]

We have dealt with the mystery of these negotiations with Japan by setting the established facts out in their chronological order. It is important to know whether Russia deliberately held up the Japanese peace offers to enable her to join in the war and thus make the most of her rights at the share out:

14th February 1945 : Hirohito, the Japanese Emperor, regarded the war as lost, and told Prince Konoye that he had no desire to be dragged on to catastrophe by the military clique. Despite Prince Konoye's promise to help, the Emperor remained none the less uneasy about his dynasty.

20th February 1945 : Hirohito informed his government that he had instructed Hirota, his Foreign Minister, to open up unofficial talks with Viktor Malik, Soviet ambassador to Japan. At the same time Sato, the Japanese ambassador in Moscow, sounded Molotov, who referred once more to Russia's traditional claims: the Kuriles, Sakhalin, Dairen and Port Arthur.

Stalin informed Harry Hopkins concerning these soundings; for they were indeed soundings, and not a firm offer to surrender.

5th April 1945 : Hirohito summoned Admiral Suzuki to power, thus sweeping away the opposition of the militarists.

Herbert Hoover, one-time President of the United States, wrote President Roosevelt drawing his attention to the importance of the evolution of Japanese policy.

2nd July 1945 : J. Grew, former American ambassador in Japan, and at that time acting Secretary of State, suggested to President Truman, before the latter's departure for Potsdam, that a solemn warning to Japan could bring about surrender without having to resort to invasion of the Japanese mainland.

7th July 1945 : Hirohito instructed Suzuki to seek Stalin's approval to send Konoye to Moscow to negotiate. He intended that Prince Konoye should make contact in Moscow with Harriman, the American

---

[125] The text of the ultimatum is in Butow, *Japan's Decission to Surrender*, Stanford, California, 1954, p. 243. The document was not submitted to the Soviet for approval, but it was approved by China.

ambassador, with a view to capitulation, while safeguarding the dynasty.[126]

10th July 1945 : The despatch of the note to Moscow.

We have already referred to subsequent events. R. J. C. Butow has made[127] a detailed study of these negotiations; his research included interviews with Japanese representatives concerned in the events.

The Japanese rejection of the Potsdam ultimatum (by radio on the 26th July) and military intervention by Russia on the 9th August brought all these negotiations to an end. The Japanese officially rejected the ultimatum on the 28th July; the atom bombs were dropped on the 6th and 9th August, and on the 10th Washington received their unconditional surrender.

From the examination of the facts in their chronological order we may conclude that, although Russia persisted in her traditional claims against Japan, we have no reason to state that the U.S.S.R. really delayed the Japanese surrender. The negotiations were long drawn out, and, despite the wishes of the Emperor, no formal decision to put an end to hostilities could have been reached before the 9th August. It is even possible that without Russian intervention the Americans might have resorted to the costly landing that was causing them so much apprehension.

Two facts deserve special attention. On the morning of the 9th August three of the six members of the Japanese Supreme Defence Council were in favour of continuing the war; secondly, during the months of May and June air raids over Japan, and Tokyo in particular, had caused dreadful carnage, but they did not compel the military leaders to yield. In fact, one of the last big raids on the Japanese capital resulted in 185,000 killed and wounded.

In the light of these two factors we cannot be sure that the first two atom bombs alone were decisive in bringing the war to an end. It is difficult to judge whether Soviet intervention or the bombing of Hiroshima was the more effective in influencing the Emperor to make his final decision.

---

[126] The Americans had been decoding Japanese messages since July, and they were perfectly acquainted with the text of the messages from Suzuki to Sato. If Stalin wished to minimize the importance of the Japanese offers — and this has never been substantiated — his intentions were frustrated, and Washington could not pretend to be ignorant of the goings-on between Tokyo and Moscow.

[127] Butow, *op. cit.*

OTHER SOURCES OF INFORMATION IN PART THREE

The following is a list of the principal works consulted in addition to those named in the bibliography.

Operation Himmler

There is no Polish account of these events, and the German version was given world-wide publicity. An account was published in the *New York Times* of the 1st September 1939. A German journalist named Günter Peis has stated that he met Naujocks in 1959, and he has published a biography of this strange man. The account of the Gleiwitz incident (pp. 135-155) is given in more detail than in the deposition made by Naujocks at the Nuremberg trials; but it furnishes no new facts of any importance. Some of the details differ, but the verbal testimony was not given until twenty years after the events.
Naujocks, by Günter Peis, London, Odhams Press, 1960.
    A number of short comments are also to be found in:
The SS, Alibi of a Nation, by G. Reitlinger, London, 1956.

Exercise Weser

Führer Conferences on Naval Affairs, British Admiralty, London, 1947.

Lord Gort's Retreat

We interviewed General François d'Astier de la Vigerie.

Operation 'Sea Lion'

Most of the documents are contained in:
Dokumente zum Unternehmen "Seelöwe", by K. Klee, Musterschmidt, Göttingen, 1959 (460 p.).

The Wooing of Franco

We questioned Serrano Suner and General Donovan.

The Barbarossa Plan

Soviet historians also are of the opinion that Stalingrad was a turning point in the war. It is not, however, the opinion of Marshal von Manstein, who considers

325

that the Battle of Kursk was the turning point and that Stalingrad was a mere episode. This view is strongly contested by Marshal Eremenko in *Protiv falsifikatsiyi istoriyi mirovoi voiny*, Moscow, 1959. German military historians, such as Tippelskirch and Doerr, do not share Manstein's point of view. They consider that the advance of the German army was decisively halted at Stalingrad; undoubtedly through Hitler's fault, since he stubbornly persisted in a siege which had no real strategic importance.

The Russo-Japanese Pact

We also interviewed Foreign Minister Gafencu.
We consulted L. V. Kutakov's indispensable work, *Istoriya sovetsko-yaponskikh diplomatitcheskikh otnoshenii*, Institute of International Relations, Moscow, 1962 (113 p.).
This work demonstrates that the Soviet proposals to Japan for a non-aggression pact had formed the basis of Russian policy since 1931.

Pearl Harbour

We also consulted the thirty-nine volumes of the American Congressional Commission of Inquiry, and Walter Lord's work, *Pearl Harbour* (1958). Lord follows a new technique in his presentation of the events which took place on the 7th December 1941. *Pearl Harbour* is a remarkable work and is gaining adherents; it does not, however, answer the questions we have posed.
Admiral Theobald's papers are retained at the Hoover Institute.

The Secret Orders of Admiral Darlan

We have also consulted:
Revue d'Histoire moderne, Paris, No. 4, 1957 (supplement).

Unconditional Surrender

We also consulted the following:
As He Saw It, by Elliott Roosevelt, Duell, Sloan and Pierce, New York, 1946 (230 p.).
Goebbels, by Roger Manvell and Heinrich Fraenkel, London, 1960.
Memoirs, by Cordell Hull, MacMillan, New York, 1948.
On Active Service in Peace and War, by Henry Stimson, Harper, New York, 1948.
European Resistance Movements, Milan, 1961, Pergamon Press, Oxford, 1963.
See the studies by Dr Krausnick and W. Bartel on pp. 507 to 566.
Unconditional Surrender, by Anne Armstrong, Rutgers University Press, New Brunswick, 1963.

The Treachery of Mihailović

We also interviewed F. Deakin and Colonel V. Piletić.

Badoglio Surrenders

We also consulted the following:
Missions secrètes, by Otto Skorzeny, Flammarion, Paris, 1950 (253 p.).
Come firmai, l'armistizio di Cassibile, by Giuseppe Castellano, Mondadori, Milan, 1945 (226 p.).

The Liberation of Paris

We also consulted the following:
Et Paris ne fut pas détruit, by Pierre Taittinger, L'Elan, Paris, 1948 (315 p.).
La Préparation de l'Insurrection et la Bataille de Paris, by Raymond Massiet, Payot, Paris, 1945 (260 p.).
See also the Dansette-Taittinger controversy in *Le Monde*, Paris, 3rd February to 1st March 1949, and von Choltitz, "Je n'ai pas détruit Paris," in *Le Figaro*, Paris, 3rd October 1949, *et seq.* General von Choltitz stated:
'If I did not carry out the instructions which required me to destroy Paris, it was not because the idea of obeying orders was repugnant to me, but because I was forced to recognize, in the most grave circumstances, that the orders I had received sprung from a mind that had become a prey to madness; a sick man whose decisions were utterly stupid. In the interests of my country and my people I was compelled to assume the responsibility of disobeying the dictator.'
The collection of COMAC directives may be found in the Hoover Institute.
We questioned General von Choltitz in 1959.

The Liberation of the Port of Antwerp

We questioned General Horrocks (through Colonel Lovinfosse) and Colonel Lovinfosse himself.
In addition we consulted the following:
La Résistance belge dans la Libération du Port d'Anvers, by Michel Devillers, Ecole Royale Militaire, Brussels, 1959 (not published).
L'Exploit du Lieutenant R. Vekemans, by P. Eygenraam, in *L'Armée et la Nation*, Brussels, No. 9, 1947.

The Italian Resistance Movement

European Resistance Movements, Liege, 1958, Pergamon Press, Oxford, 1959.
European Resistance Movements, Milan, 1961, Pergamon Press, Oxford, 1961, and *La Résistance Italienne*, CVL, Milan, 1947.
We also interviewed Senator Parri.
The principal documents dealing with the CLN mission to Rome are to be found in:
Il movimento di liberazione e gli Alleati, by Maurizio Parri, July, 1949.
La missione dei CLNAI al Sud, by Franco Catalano, May, 1955.
I rapporti con gli Alleati e la missione al Sud, by Giorgio Vaccarino, July, 1958.
All the above studies are to be found in *Movimento di liberazione in Italia*, Milan.
An account of the operations undertaken by the Italian volunteers engaged at the side of the Allied armies during the period 1944–1945 appears in the publications of the Ufficio Storico, Stato Maggiore dell' Esercito: *Il Corpo italiano di Liberazione* and *I gruppi di Combattimento*, Rome, 1950 and 1951.

The Battle of Warsaw

To obtain the Soviet point of view we consulted the following works:
La Résistance polonaise et les Alliés, by S. Okecki, in *European Resistance Movements*, Milan Conference, 1961, Pergamon Press, London, 1962. This study provides a very important bibliography (Institute of Military History, Warsaw, 1961).

We interviewed General Bor-Komorowski, and we have seen the Okecki-Bor-Komorowski controversy, published in *Cahiers internationaux de la Résistance*, Vienna, Castellezgasse 35, Nos. 5 and 7, 1961.

L'Union soviétique et la Résistance en Europe, by E. Boltine, in *European Resistance Movements*, Milan Conference, 1961, Pergamon Press, Oxford, 1962. This study quotes the main Soviet sources.

We also took the following into account:

Der Warschauer Aufstand, 1944, by H. von Krannhals, Bernard und Graefe, Frankfurt on Main, 1962 (445 p.).

Strange Alliance, by J. R. Deane, New York, 1946. This work emphasizes the technical difficulties underlying inter-Allied co-ordination in relation to air operations. Concerning the question of bridgeheads and the dropping of supplies by parachute we consulted:

Przycky Warszawie, by Josef Margules, MON, Warsaw, 1962 (430 p.), and the unpublished accounts of General Kopanski and Professor Willetts given at Oxford in December 1962.

Concerning the People's Army see:

Armia Ludowa w Powstaniu Warszavskim, by Jozef S. Malecki, Ed. Ishry, Warsaw, 1962 (225 p.).

No direct liaison was established between the Red Army and the A.K during the insurrection. Kalugin, a former officer of the Vlasov forces, claimed to have acted as liaison officer; but he was an imposter.

On the other hand, three Soviet officers were parachuted into the interior of the town. Their sole mission was to correct the range of artillery fire. One of them — Captain Kolos — published his reminiscences.

A complete text of the instructions sent out from Kosciusko has been collected in Warsaw, and it does not agree in any respect with the fictitious versions which have been circulated from time to time.

Among the most interesting discussions that have been published are the following:

Powstanie Warszawskie w swietle analizy polozenia operacyjnego na froncie radziecko — niemieckim, by S. Okecki, in *Mysl. wojak*, Warsaw, 1954, pp. 75–103, and T. Petczinski, in

O powstaniu Warszawskim, in *Bellona III*, 1955, Inst. Sikorski, London.

In conjunction with the works by Bor, Anders and Mikolajczyk we must consider the important contributions by Kirchmayer, Borkiewicz and Skarzynski (the as yet unpublished thesis for the doctor's degree of the last named).

Kirchmayer is of the opinion that the Red Army's advance on Warsaw was too rapid, and therefore provoked a German counter-attack from the direction of East Prussia. We have taken no account of the supposition as it seems rather unconvincing.

1939–1945 PERIOD — WORKS CONSULTED: 312

	Number of works dealing with the question	Number of works containing worth-while facts	Number of works containing secondary matter	Original testimony contained in the works mentioned in the bibliography	New evidence collected by J. de Launay
Controversial Questions					
45. Operation Himmler	19	4	4	I	—
46. Retreat from the Warndt . . .	II	2	7	2	I
47. Plan of the Western offensive .	22	10	6	6	I
48. Exercise Weser: reply to Allied plan	39	17	19	3	—
49. "Flight" of the B.E.F.	32	12	10	10	I
50. Operation "Sea Lion"	27	10	10	7	—
51. The Canaris approach to Franco	28	12	12	4	2
52. The Barbarossa Plan	33	8	19	6	—
53. The Russo-Japanese Pact . . .	15	3	8	4	I
54. The secret of Pearl Harbour . .	20	I	12	6	—
55. The Algiers-Vichy secret contacts	25	9	12	4	—
56. Badoglio's intentions	39	10	13	16	—
57. The real importance of French Resistance	30	9	10	11	2
58. The role of Italian Resistance . .	20	5	10	5	I
59. Liberation of Antwerp	25	6	19	I	2
60. The resistance of Mihailović . .	19	5	5	9	2
61. Choltitz and the Liberation of Paris	21	6	12	4	I
62. The Battle of Warsaw	19	3	II	5	2
63. Unconditional Surrender . . .	30	—	20	10	—
64. The Potsdam Conference . . .	16	6	5	5	—
				119	16

UNPUBLISHED SOURCES OF INFORMATION

Evidence collected
by the author

General François d'Astier de la Vigerie
Georges Bonnet
General Bor-Komorowski
Prince Xavier of Bourbon-Parma
General Corap
Edouard Daladier
Francis Deakin
General Donovan
General Doumenc
Gregorio Gafencu
General a. D. Friedrich Hossbach
Juvenal
John Knittel
Colonel George Lovinfosse
Dr Ludwig
Stanislas Mikolajczyk
Dr Josef Mueller
Baron Pierre Nothomb
His Imperial Highness the Archduke Otto of Hapsburg
Senator Ferruccio Parri
Gabriel Perreux
Colonel Velimir Piletic
Colonel Georges Rebattet
Oreste Rosenfeld
Tarbe de Saint-Hardouin
Walter Schevenels
Dr Paul Schmidt
Serrano Suner
General Warlimont

The author thanks all these distinguished persons who were kind enough to spare the time to answer his questions. He is also grateful to them for having perused their own private papers on his behalf.

PUBLISHED SOURCES OF INFORMATION

The writer has found particularly useful the outstanding works of the following authors:

The 1914–1918 period

P. Renouvin: The European crisis and the First World War
Sydney Fay, Jules Isaac, Bernadotte Schmitt: The origins of the war
Gerhard Ritter: The Schlieffen Plan

The 1919–1939 period

M. Beaumont: The failure of the Peace of Versailles
J.-B. Duroselle: Diplomatic history
E. Weill–Raynal: Reparations
W. Shirer: The Third Reich
P. Renouvin: International relations
M. Vaussard: Italian questions

The 1939–1945 period

J.-B. Duroselle: The United States of America
General Schmitt: Algiers–Vichy relations
Henri Michel: The French Resistance
M. Beaumont: The German Resistance
General Bouhon: The liberation of Antwerp
R. J. C. Butow: The Japanese surrender
General E. Boltine: Soviet questions

The writer wishes to take this opportunity of expressing his indebtedness to the above authors.